SGI President Ikeda greets young people, Miami, February 3, 1993.

SGI President Ikeda meets members of the future division outside the San Francisco Culture Center, March 14, 1993.

# DISCUSSIONS

## *on*

# *Youth*

Published by WORLD TRIBUNE PRESS
606 Wilshire Boulevard
Santa Monica, CA  90401

© 2010 Soka Gakkai

Printed in the United States of America.
Interior photos and back cover photo courtesy of Seikyo Press.
© Seikyo Press

Interior and cover design by *the*BookDesigners

ISBN 978-1-932911-93-0

10  9  8  7  6

FOR THE LEADERS OF THE FUTURE

# DISCUSSIONS

## *on*
## *Youth*

## DAISAKU IKEDA

NEW EDITION

World Tribune
*Press*

# Contents

INTRODUCTION......................................................................................ix
PREFACE by SGI President Ikeda ...........................................x
EDITOR'S NOTE .................................................................................xii

## PART ONE  The Hopes of Youth

**1** The Worries and Hopes of Youth .....................................3
**2** Youth: A Time of Challenge .......................................... 19
**3** Friendship and Perspectives on Life ........................... 37

## PART TWO  The Heartbeat of Youth

**4** What Is Love? ....................................................................... 59
**5** Finding Happiness in Your Work .............................. 71
**6** What Is a Global Citizen? ............................................ 83
**7** Bringing Out Your Best ................................................ 95
**8** What Is Kindness? ........................................................ 107
**9** The Essence of Human Rights ................................ 121

## PART THREE  Youth and Self-Improvement

**10** The Joy of Reading .................................................... 137
**11** Knowing History Is Knowing Yourself ............ 149
**12** Appreciating Art and Culture .............................. 161
**13** Dialogue With Nature ............................................ 183
**14** Discovering Great Literature .............................. 195

# PART FOUR  Youth and Faith

**15** Why Do We Chant Every Day? ....................211
**16** Why Do We Have an Organization? ..............237
**17** Weaving the Fabric of Peace ....................253

# PART FIVE  The Questions of Youth

**18** What Is Freedom? ....................269
**19** What Is Individuality? ....................283
**20** What Is the Power of Prayer? ..............297

# PART SIX  Youth and the Future

**21** What Is a Good Friend? ....................315
**22** It Takes Courage ....................327
**23** Why Are the Good Despised? ..............341
**24** Why Go to College? ....................357

# PART SEVEN  The Energy of Youth

**25** Life and Death Are One ....................375


POSTSCRIPT ....................402

APPENDICES:
**A** You Are the Hope of the World ..............404
**B** Youth Are Struggling Between Problems and Hopes....419

GLOSSARY ....................427
INDEX ....................437

# Introduction

THE DISCUSSIONS in this book took place among Soka Gakkai youth leaders and SGI President Daisaku Ikeda during the course of several years. They were published in serialized form in the Soka Gakkai's high school division semimonthly newspaper, *Koko Shimpo*. Part one appeared from August 28, 1996, through August 27, 1997, and part two ran from November 26, 1997, through February 10, 1999.

SGI-USA previously published part one as two volumes in English. This new edition of *Discussions on Youth* includes both part one and part two, the latter appearing here in book form for the first time in English. This book also includes as appendices a discussion with youth from the United States, and a summary of a question-and-answer session President Ikeda held with students from the Kansai region in Japan, which were not part of the *Discussions on Youth* series.

The voices of the youth are set in italic type and President Ikeda's responses are set in roman type.

# Preface

## Each of You Is Hope Itself

DR. MARTIN LUTHER KING JR. said, "I have a dream!"

What dreams do you have in your heart now? What hopes? A life filled with hope is strong. Hope is the greatest weapon in the world.

I receive many letters from young friends throughout the world. I sometimes receive pictures, too. And from these, I can see that all of you are bursting with the vibrant energy of youth seeking ever to grow and develop.

Youth is the time of great change, and so it is equally a time of great confusion. Society offers little comfort, and you may feel as though you are standing alone in a wasteland or on a battlefield. At times, you may feel that you cannot believe in anyone, that no one loves you or that you have no reason to live. But do not judge yourselves. You must never give up on yourselves. There is no one who does not have a mission in this world. You would not have been born if you did not have a mission to fulfill. It doesn't rain or snow all year long. And remember, the sun is always shining above the clouds.

Charlie Chaplin, one of the world's greatest comedians, was born four days before Adolf Hitler. As a youth, Chaplin was very poor and could not afford to go to school. In addition, his mother suffered from mental illness. Despite all these trials, he lived with great optimism. Whereas Hitler went on to take millions of lives and covered the earth with blood and grief, Chaplin gave hope to people throughout the world. The final chapter of Chaplin's life was victorious and adorned with the applause and cheers of the people. Life is defined by how it concludes, not by how it begins. There are no irredeemable mistakes in youth.

I cannot forget the words my mentor, second Soka Gakkai president Josei Toda, said to me about sixty years ago when I was going through hardships. He said, "Daisaku, you must go through struggles in life. Only by struggling can you understand this faith. That's how you become a great person."

My mentor taught me everything. He tutored me each morning, even on Sundays, covering every subject. Because of this, I can say that I studied at "Toda University." As Mr. Toda once shared his knowledge with me, I am now speaking to all of you. That's how this *Discussions on Youth* series began.

Since Japanese society is often a point of reference in these discussions, some things we say may not apply in other countries. But I believe the fundamental principles we touch upon are universal.

I trust all of you. I live for your happiness, for your future. You are the hope of humanity. Each of you is hope itself. Each possesses a precious treasure.

Please accept this book as a companion on the journey called life, and live courageously in the twenty-first century—the most important century for humankind.

I am praying from the bottom of my heart for your good health, growth and successful endeavors.

*—Daisaku Ikeda*

# Editor's Note

THE CITATIONS most commonly used in this book have been abbreviated as follows:

- LSOC refers to *The Lotus Sutra and Its Opening and Closing Sutras*, translated by Burton Watson (Tokyo: Soka Gakkai, 2009).

- OTT refers to *The Record of the Orally Transmitted Teachings*, translated by Burton Watson (Tokyo, Soka Gakkai, 2004).

- WND refers to *The Writings of Nichiren Daishonin*, vol. 1 (WND-1) (Tokyo, Soka Gakkai, 1999) and vol. 2 (WND-2) (Tokyo: Soka Gakkai, 2006).

# PART ONE

---

# THE HOPES
## *of Youth*

# 1

## The Worries and Hopes of Youth

*Thank you so much, President Ikeda, for making this discussion series for youth possible. I believe it will become a lifelong treasure for the high school division members. We look forward to learning from your rich wisdom and experience.*

It is I who must thank you. I am determined to give my all to these discussions. I wish to speak honestly, to leave the truth as my legacy to all of you. Why? It is because my sole desire now is to raise genuine leaders for the twenty-first century. The cultivation of truly humanistic leaders is imperative—for the sake of the world, humanity, kosen-rufu and peace. The whole world cries out for this.

Raising young leaders is also my greatest joy. The second Soka Gakkai president, Josei Toda, once said, "Nothing is more enjoyable than meeting young people who are pure-hearted and searching for the correct path in life." I feel exactly the same way.

The members of the Soka Gakkai's future division—collectively comprising the elementary, junior high and high school divisions— are very important. I have the greatest expectations for each of you, as people who will take on active roles in the twenty-first century, a critical time for all humanity. I am praying for your success and victory in life. Your growth and activities, after all, are in themselves kosen-rufu. I have no intention of treating the members of the high school division

3

like children. I hold you in the highest esteem and think of you as adults of fine character; I regard you as ladies and gentlemen.

As such, I will speak with you frankly and unreservedly. You may not understand everything I have to say to you right now. And you may not agree with everything I have to say. That's perfectly all right. I would be happy if, however, from this discussion, you could glean something, however small, that might help you and be of benefit to your growth. That is all I seek.

Please know that my most fervent wish is that each of you, whom I hold close to my heart, spends your youth without regrets. It is especially important not to leave behind regrets about your teens, the time to establish the all-important foundation for the rest of your lives.

I would like all of you to experience the satisfaction of having accomplished something—it doesn't matter what—in your own way and capacity, even if it's something as simple as cleaning, participating in club activities, doing volunteer work or whatever. The main thing is to be satisfied knowing that you've contributed something, that you've done your best. Please become individuals of whom others can say with admiration: "There is something different about him that sets him apart" or "She is someone I can really respect."

*We are looking forward to learning much from these discussions.*

*Many high school students today want to take on a challenge, but they don't know exactly what to challenge. Others don't seem to be interested in anything, or if they do show an interest, they don't have the courage to pursue it. They become angry at themselves and at their indecision and weakness, which gives way to despair. I think many youth feel this way.*

*One high school student said to me recently, "In schools these days, students who have trouble learning are treated as less than human." These words struck me deeply. Many students are extremely discouraged because grades seem to be the basis of everything, ultimately determining their overall evaluation and ranking in school. They feel like failures when they cannot gain admission to a school with a high academic reputation.*

*Even among those who excel in their studies, many are so drained and exhausted that they have no room to form big dreams or aspirations. So the important question is how to live in a way true to ourselves.*

## Press Forward in the Midst of Problems

What you are describing are the harmful effects of society's overemphasis on academics. In Japan, students are not taught the all-essential whys and wherefores of things and events, nor are they taught the path they should follow as human beings. This negligence causes them needless suffering. Japan has truly become a lamentable country.

So what do you do in such a situation? Hold a grudge against society, your schools, your parents or yourselves? Will you feel happy then? I don't think so.

You are each precious and irreplaceable. Please do not allow yourselves to succumb to negativity and cynicism. Suffering is to be found in any era. Youth is a time of problems, pain and confusion.

And grades are probably not the only source of worry or anguish you face. You may have problems at home, with your health, with how you feel about your looks, with members of the opposite sex or with friends. Feelings of pain, insecurity, frustration and sadness may assail you. Youth means grappling with all kinds of problems. It means resolving them, in spite of all difficulties, pushing aside the dark clouds of despair and advancing toward the sun, toward hope. This strength is the hallmark of youth.

Having problems, making mistakes or feeling regrets is only natural. What's important is to be undefeated by them. In the midst of worries and struggles, always look forward and advance.

Suppose you are lost in the jungle. You want to find your way out and reach the ocean but don't know which way to go. What do you do? The answer is to keep moving ahead, taking a course that leads to a river. If you follow the river downstream, you will eventually reach the ocean.

The important thing is to keep pressing forward. While struggling with various problems, it is vital that you chant Nam-myoho-renge-kyo and advance somehow—even if it's only one or two inches. If you do so, when you look back, you'll see that you have actually made your way through the jungle in no time.

Your lives will be enriched and deepened in proportion to the pain and grief you suffer, the degree to which you struggle and how much you chant Nam-myoho-renge-kyo. The hardships you face now will all serve to nourish your growth into leaders of the twenty-first century.

For example, if your life is made miserable by the present overemphasis on school performance and educational background, you might well decide to bring about truly humanistic education in the future that, instead of demoralizing students, will leave them with hope. One who undertakes such an endeavor would certainly be considered a leader of the twenty-first century.

# A Great Leader Is a Friend
## to the Suffering

Your studies are of course important. But the grades you get in high school will not determine the course of your entire life. Your future depends on the efforts you make and whether you are walking the correct path. It's not important how you compare yourself to others but how you compare yourself to whom you were yesterday. If you see that you've advanced even one step, then you've achieved a victory.

A famous person once told his son, "Your grades can be mediocre, but please become a person of outstanding character." Greatness as a human being is not determined by educational background or social position. Even people who graduate from top universities may engage in criminal activities. And there are some among the so-called elite who are overbearing and arrogant. I want to foster leaders, not elitists.

A truly great person is a friend to those in suffering, pain and misery. Such a person can be called a leader of the new century.

More often than not in today's society, the suffering and disadvantaged are ostracized, despised and pushed to the margins. Many of our current leaders are guilty of doing this. This is a deplorable mistake.

Study should be for the purpose of finding a way to help those who are suffering. Many leaders today, however, look down on them and only add to their misery. There is no society as cruel, arrogant, cold or cowardly as ours. I want to change this at all costs. And it is toward this end that I have devoted all my energies. I pray that you will understand my sentiments and carry on this work with the same spirit in the future.

*What about students who are discouraged because the school they are attending was not their first choice?*

Not attending the school of your choice may certainly be disappointing. But viewed in the long term and from the essential point of study, it doesn't really matter that you graduate from a well-known school.

I studied at night school. Like many others in those turbulent years following World War II, I had no money, so I had to work during the day to put myself through school in the evening. It was a painful struggle, but an experience of which I will always be proud.

Later, President Toda tutored me privately. He taught me everything he had learned. He once told me, "Become an inspiration for those who cannot attend good schools." Those who start out under difficult circumstances and go on to become first-rate individuals can be sources of hope and inspiration for many. Please remember always that academic background isn't everything.

At any rate, since you have been accepted to a school—even if it is not your first choice and regardless of how society judges it—it's important to decide that the place where you are is the very best, that it is the perfect place for you to learn all you want. This way of thinking is far more constructive and beneficial in the long run.

It's foolish to allow your confidence to be undermined by the opinions of others. You are all in your teens; limitless possibilities are open to all of you.

*Is going on to university the best thing?*

I'm all for it. In many cases, a university can provide an environment conducive to fostering students' abilities, to equipping them with certain qualifications that may enable them one day to contribute to more people in society.

## Realizing Your Inherent Potential

Nevertheless, you are free to choose your path. If you feel the road you must follow to fulfill your mission lies somewhere other than in a university classroom, then that's perfectly OK.

The important thing is not to cause your parents to worry. I hope each of you will cherish a dream of what you would like to do—something that is just right for you—and continue to challenge yourselves to achieve it.

The purpose of study is not just to get into a university. Study contributes to your growth and self-enrichment. There is a saying "Not to learn is to debase yourself." What makes human beings human is their art of learning.

We are now living in an advanced age of information. If you do not continue to study throughout your lives, you will soon be left behind. To develop a lifelong study ethic is an important requisite for future leaders. The deadlocks society faces today are in fact the deadlocks of its leaders. And the reason for this is usually that they do not study. They lack the spirit and broad-mindedness to listen to the ideas and opinions of the younger generation and to incorporate and implement those that have value.

Especially during your teens, I'd like to see you develop a passion and enthusiasm for learning that will endure throughout your lives. Consider this time as training for your brain in order to develop such a foundation.

I cannot say this too strongly: Do not compare yourselves to others. Be true to who you are, and continue to learn with all your might. Even if you are ridiculed, even if you suffer disappointments and setbacks, continue to advance and do not be defeated. If you have such a strong determination in your heart, you are already halfway to victory.

When you hold fast to your beliefs and live true to yourself, your true value as a human being shines through. Buddhism teaches the concept of manifesting one's true nature. This means to reveal your genuine innate self, your true inherent potential, and bring it to shine, illuminating all around you. It refers to your most refined individuality and uniqueness.

*It's like the story of the hare and the tortoise. I think some people are hares and others tortoises. But those who make their way forward steadily and continuously until they reach the finish line win in the end. Completing the race is itself a victory. It's all a question of staying focused on your goal and never giving up on yourself, isn't it?*

*One runner in the men's marathon at the 1996 Atlanta Olympics was the twenty-year-old Abdul Baser Wasiqi from Afghanistan. Because of an interruption in his education by the protracted war in his country, he was still a high school student. Mr. Wasiqi finished the marathon in last place, a full two hours behind the winner. He was the slowest Olympic marathon runner in history. But he crossed the finish line, undaunted.*

*His goal, Mr. Wasiqi said, was not to come in first or second place; it was to go to Atlanta and run. "It is very important to finish," he said in halting English. "I run for Afghanistan. I represent my country to the world, to show that Afghanistan is living, that they have not died during sixteen years of civil war."[1]*

*I was very moved to see this young man run for the sake of the people of his war-torn country.*

## A MISSION ONLY YOU CAN FULFILL

The important thing is to be patient, to have the confidence and determination that you will achieve something meaningful in the future. Youth is not a time for impatience. Your true substance as human beings will be determined ten, twenty or thirty years from now. What matters is the kind of people you become and whether you are fulfilling your mission then. Each of you has a mission that only you can fulfill. If you did not have such a mission, you would not have been born.

There are many kinds of mountains in this world. There are high ones and low ones. And there are a great many different kinds of rivers. There are long and short rivers. Despite their differences, however, we cannot dispute the fact that all mountains are mountains and that all rivers are rivers.

There are serene mountains like the ones in the ancient Japanese capital of Nara, and there are active volcanoes like Mount Aso.[2] Then there are the grand snowcapped peaks of the Himalayas. All of these mountains are beautiful and impressive in their own way.

The same is so with rivers. There is Japan's Ishikari River, home to magnificent salmon, as well as our poetic Chikuma River.[3] There is the Yellow River in China, and there is the Amazon in South America, rivers so wide that in some places, the opposite shore cannot be seen. Each of them has its own special beauty.

The same is true of people. Each of you has a unique mission in life. Moreover, you have encountered the Mystic Law while still young. You have a mission that is yours and yours alone. That is an indisputable fact, one in which I would like you to have conviction and pride.

*How do we become aware of our own unique missions in life?*

You won't find them by standing still. You must challenge yourselves in something, it doesn't matter what. Then, by your making consistent effort, the direction you should take will open up before you quite naturally. It's important, therefore, to have the courage to ask yourselves what you should be doing now, this very moment.

The key, in other words, is to climb the mountain before you. As you ascend its slopes, you will develop your muscles, increasing your strength and endurance. Such training will enable you to challenge still higher mountains. It is vital that you continue making such efforts. Chanting Nam-myoho-renge-kyo will enable you to bring forth the life force necessary to succeed.

Chant Nam-myoho-renge-kyo and climb the mountain in front of you. When you reach the summit, wide new horizons will stretch out before you. Little by little, you will understand your own mission.

Those who remember they have a unique mission are strong. Whatever problems they have, they will not be defeated. They can transform all their problems into catalysts for growth toward a hope-filled future.

*Be confident we have a mission, and climb the mountain before us. That seems very clear, but challenging.*

Yes. Life is about scaling one mountain, then facing the next one, and the one after that. Those who persevere and finally succeed in conquering the highest mountain are victors in life. On the other hand, those who avoid such challenges and take the easy route, descending into the valleys, will end in defeat. To put it simply, we have two choices: We can either climb the mountain before us, or descend into the valley.

Of course, there are also those who just go round in circles as they try to make their ascent.

## Become a Person of Depth and Substance

I know some of you may come from poor families and have difficulty paying your monthly school fees. Others among you may feel frustrated because you cannot buy the things you want. But you must realize that these are not uncommon situations. Many people have had similar experiences. Poverty is nothing to be ashamed of. What is disgraceful is to have an impoverished heart or to live dishonestly. Being born in a stately mansion is no guarantee of happiness, any more than being born in a shack dooms one to misery.

Many people today think that money equals happiness. They are making a grave mistake. Whether one is happy or unhappy depends not on how many material possessions one has. Even an affluent and seemingly enviable family can be struggling with some serious problem that may not be apparent.

I once spoke with a world-renowned businessman who said: "Even though I have achieved fame and fortune, I felt a greater sense of purpose and fulfillment when I was poor. I had goals, and life was filled with challenge." He went on, "I've recently come to understand that to regain that sense of fulfillment, I now have to contribute to the well-being and happiness of others."

His words are truly profound.

You mustn't think you're unfortunate just because your parents are poor or lack education or are constantly quarreling with each other. Instead, you should adopt the view that this is a most human state of affairs, one that will allow you to develop into a truly humane person.

11

You may think it far more ideal to have been born into a distinguished family. But too often those who live in such a world act like well-behaved automatons, bound by formality, tradition and appearances, lacking genuine warmth, emotion and spontaneity.

So even if you see your parents quarreling, even if you are scolded, and even if others make fun of you, keep on smiling. View it all as something that will enable you to develop a big heart and become individuals of depth and substance.

Only by experiencing such difficulties can you become the kind of people who understand others' feelings. Those who cannot empathize with others will never become true leaders. One great misfortune of our world today is the presence of too many leaders who do not understand people's hearts. Pain and sorrow cultivate the vast earth of your inner being. And from there, you can bring forth the beautiful flower of a desire to work for people's happiness.

## UNDERSTANDING YOUR PARENTS' CONCERNS

*I have heard many students say they're having a hard time at home.*

*Also, some admit that they get angry with their mothers for telling them what to do and end up not speaking to them at all. There are some who fight with their mothers about the path they should take in life and how they choose to go about their daily affairs. They may think: "Leave me alone! Let me do my own thing!"*

*Of course, there are also those who have good, open communication with their mothers.*

Mothers are always giving their children a hard time. That's what makes them mothers. From the beginning of time, mothers have been saying things like: "Do your homework!" "Turn off the television!" and "Wake up or you'll be late!" It's not something we can change. But you'll understand how your parents feel when you become parents yourselves.

So, it is important that you be big-hearted and, if your mother yells at you, please think: "A loud voice means she is healthy; that's great" or "Oh, she is expressing her love for me. I'm so appreciative." Until you can accept your parents in this way, you risk being labeled immature.

Most animals learn to hunt, how to eat and the wisdom needed to live from their parents. This is even truer in the case of human beings. Our parents teach us so many things that launch us in the right direction. This is something we appreciate when we become adults ourselves.

Once I heard a story about a youth who was sitting forlorn and dejected by the road after quarreling with his father. A man he knew came along and, guessing the cause of his sadness, said: "Back when I was around eighteen, my father told me nothing but dull, boring things. I got really sick of hearing them. But ten years later, I started feeling that everything my father was saying made a lot of sense. I wondered, 'When did my father develop so much wisdom?'"

Of course, the father's words had not changed; rather, he, the son, had changed. He had grown up. By relating this story in such a light-hearted way, the man encouraged the youth.

If you cannot even understand the feelings of your own parents, you certainly cannot help others become happy.

I would like you to be good sons and daughters. I hope you will have the determination to become great successes in your chosen fields in the future and that you will always cherish your mothers and make them the happiest people in the world. I'm certainly not suggesting that you neglect your fathers. Rather, I ask you to please take special care of your mothers.

I also think it's important that you use your wisdom to avoid quarreling with your parents. And when they quarrel between themselves, as most parents are wont to do from time to time, the wisest thing is for you to stay out of it—otherwise, it could turn into a three-way tug-of-war.

## BECOME LIKE THE SUN

*Those who have lost one or both parents might well wish that they could have a chance to complain about both parents being constantly on their back.*

That's right. Some young people have lost a mother or father or even both parents. I can imagine their sadness. And they may envy those who have both parents. But a hundred years from now, with very few exceptions, none of us alive today will still be here on this planet. That being the case, everyone must part with their parents at some point.

Some may have a parent who is suffering from a serious illness. Some may be experiencing difficult times because of a parent's failed business. Some may have to endure the pain of seeing a parent criticized and attacked, even though he or she has done nothing wrong. All of these seemingly adverse situations, however, are exactly the right nourishment you need to grow even stronger. You must courageously spur yourselves on, reminding yourselves that the deeper the pain and grief, the greater the happiness that awaits you. Have the determination to become pillars of support for your family. Buddhism teaches this way of life.

Many great people, during their youth, have suffered the loss of one or both parents or have had a parent who suffered from a serious illness. Does having both parents alive and well necessarily guarantee happiness in and of itself? I don't think so. We've all heard about parents who have murdered their own children and children who have murdered their parents. Happiness is not determined by outward appearances.

What's important, therefore, is that you resolve to become the "sun" within your family. If you do so, all darkness will be dispelled. Since you can light the way to happiness for a deceased parent through chanting Nam-myoho-renge-kyo, you can surely help your parents become happy while they are still living. It is your responsibility, not your parents' responsibility. No matter what happens, live confidently with the conviction that you are the sun.

Of course, in life there are sunny days and there are cloudy days. But even on cloudy days, the sun is still the sun. The same is true for people. Even if we are suffering, it is vital that we strive to keep the sun shining brightly in our hearts.

*One high school division member has no father, his mother is incapacitated by serious health problems, and his older sister is in the hospital. On top of that, his relatives live far away. But he's been vigorously chanting Nam-myoho-renge-kyo with the support and encouragement of his local young men's leader and striving to help out at home and care for his sister while keeping up with his studies.*

How admirable! Those who endure many hardships in youth have already scaled a high mountain in life, well ahead of others. Such people will be the leaders of the twenty-first century.

My deepest praise and admiration go to the youth of the Mission for the Twenty-first Century Group, those who serve as the leaders of the Soka Gakkai's future division—collectively comprising the elementary, junior high and high school divisions. Those who support future division members behind the scenes are nobler than any person of celebrity or renown.

I hope that all of you will grow to be people who respect the dedicated efforts of such seniors in faith.

The Soka Gakkai and the SGI have been built by just such sincere individuals, including your leaders from the youth division and your parents. You might think them monotonously single-minded, but because of their tenacious efforts over the past several decades—for people's happiness, for a better society and for the realization of world peace—the SGI has become a large and respected international organization. Nichiren Daishonin praises such nameless heroes as bodhisattvas.

Certainly, there is nothing wrong with being successful in society and enjoying a degree of fame. But ultimately those dedicated to the welfare and happiness of others, even if unrecognized, are the ones truly worthy of respect. Great victors in life are those who have developed a strong sense of self that allows them to say, "I may receive no praise, but I am satisfied." I hope all of you will become the kind of people who can clearly distinguish the true essence of things.

*Some young people feel hurt because their parents have divorced or separated, and some even complain that their parents don't love them and ignore them, looking out only for themselves.*

Every family has its own set of circumstances and problems that only its members can fully understand. One thing I can say, however, is that, no matter what kind of people your parents are, they are your parents. If you did not have those parents, you would not be alive. It is important that you understand the deep significance of this point.

You may wonder why you were born into your family, or why your parents aren't as kind as others, or why you are not blessed with a more beautiful home and a better family. You may even want to run away from home. But the fact is, you were born to this particular family in this particular place on this planet Earth. You were not born into any other family. This fact encompasses the meaning of everything.

In Buddhism, nothing happens by chance. Everything has meaning. Please be convinced that you already possess every treasure. It's vital to recognize that, no matter how difficult your situation may be, you are alive now. There is no treasure more precious than life itself. Furthermore, you are still young and blessed with a youthful spirit, the greatest treasure of the universe. Please do not destroy or harm that treasure by giving way to feelings of despair.

*How do we become like the sun?*

There is no special secret. Just continue chanting Nam-myoho-renge-kyo every day, at your own pace. Even just a little at a time is fine. If you chant Nam-myoho-renge-kyo, the "sun" will begin to rise in your lives quite naturally.

Just as the sun rises each day, just as your mother prepares meals for you each day, you must have the spirit to keep striving, to study hard and to go to school each day. From this, we can learn something important. If you abandon what you have to do, you're the one who loses out. Therefore, you must never give up.

The sun rises every day. On cloudy days, stormy days, winter or summer, the sun is always shining. This is a law of the universe. No one can deny that truth. We, too, must live each day of our lives to the fullest. It makes sense that we do so. Victory belongs to those who persevere tenaciously in such efforts.

No matter what your present situation, the final outcome of all your endeavors will be determined at your life's end. For instance, in baseball, the winning team isn't decided until the last out of the final inning. In any endeavor, the outcome is never certain till the very end. It's not decided at the beginning. As the English saying goes, "He who laughs last, laughs best."

## Don't Depend on or Leave Things to Others

Therefore, it's important that we keep pressing forward amid the various sufferings we may encounter.

Please allow me to share something from my personal experience, from when I was writing my book *My Perspective on Life*. This was around 1970, when the Soka Gakkai was facing a particularly stormy period in Japan. I was suffering from pneumonia and running a temperature of 100 to 102 degrees. Nevertheless, I continued writing without fail. With an ice pack wrapped around my head, I laboriously wrote one page after another.

At one point, someone asked me, "Why are you writing when you are so sick?"

"If I struggle to write one page, then I have written one page," I replied. "And if I write two pages, I have accomplished two pages. If I don't write anything, nothing will be gained. I have to challenge myself and progress, even if just a little bit. Each day I want to accomplish something."

I kept a record of how many pages I had written by making a tally mark on a piece of paper after I finished each page. I will never forget completing that manuscript. I gave the piece of paper with the tally marks to my eldest son as a family treasure.

It is important to become strong and to not be defeated. Don't become the kind of people who are always depending or leaning on others, or who weakly and timidly leave all the hard work and responsibility to others. If you allow yourselves to be sad and negative people who envy and despise others, the sun of your inner lives cannot shine through the heavy cover of clouds that blankets it.

Whatever obstacles you may encounter, please use them as launching pads for your growth and keep advancing, bravely enduring all hardships, telling yourselves, "I'll show them what I'm made of!" Please continue patiently and tenaciously along your own paths.

Resolve to be the sun. This is the first thing you must do. As long as you are the sun, no matter what problems you may be facing now, the dawn will always break, fine weather will always return, and spring will never fail to arrive.

1. "Pride Drives Afghan to Complete Race," *The Ottawa Citizen*, August 6, 1996, "Sports Section," p. D4.

2. Mount Aso, in Kumamoto Prefecture of Kyushu, Japan's southernmost major island, is the largest active volcano in Japan.

3. The Chikuma River is the name of the headwaters of the Shinano River, the longest river in Japan, where it flows through Nagano Prefecture. The Shinano River empties into the Sea of Japan in Niigata Prefecture on Japan's northwest coast.

# 2

## YOUTH: A TIME OF CHALLENGE

*It gives us great pleasure to inform you that the response to this series has been tremendous. We've not only heard from high school division members, but from their parents and members of the Mission for the Twenty-first Century Group, who, as you know, are leaders of the Soka Gakkai's future division—collectively comprising the elementary, junior high and high school divisions. They all express their great joy.*

I am happy to hear that. There are still a great many things I want to share with you, as it is my earnest wish to leave a legacy with all the high school division members. I will speak clearly and frankly about the true nature of things. It is my deepest hope that my true successors will emerge from among you. I seek to foster people who will devote their lives selflessly to working for the happiness of humankind, helping those who are suffering.

In the past, there have been members whom I sincerely encouraged to become politicians or lawyers dedicated to working on the side of the people but who later became unprincipled and corrupt in their privileged positions. Some of these people have even tried to destroy our organization. They abused the pure world of faith to advance their own base ambitions, to obtain fame and status in society.

They chose the course of betrayal and brought about their own downfall; they betrayed the Soka Gakkai, to which they owe a great debt of gratitude; they betrayed me; they betrayed all the people whose happiness they should have been working for; and, ultimately, they betrayed themselves. They tried to seize control of the Soka Gakkai for their own selfish ends so that they could exploit this great organization and the sincere commitment of its members.

Of course, such people existed even during Shakyamuni's and Nichiren Daishonin's lifetimes. Nor is such a phenomenon limited to the world of Buddhism. President Toda once said that we must advance, "stepping over the 'bodies' of those who have abandoned their faith."

You may come across unscrupulous seniors in faith or people whom you cannot trust. When you do, speak out courageously to correct them. Strive to surpass them in integrity and ability.

Please live as true friends of those in misery and never betray the people. To do so, you must train yourselves now. Youth is the time to lay the foundation for living life to its fullest.

There is a time for everything. Youth, for example, is a time of construction. It largely determines the whole course of life; that's why it's so important.

## The Starting Point Is One's Teens

Many of your seniors in faith, who are active in a whole range of fields today, can trace their starting point back to their teens. There are countless examples of such people.

One who comes to mind in particular now lives in Mexico. I recently received a letter from him, and he kindly gave me permission to share its contents with you.

He writes: "I was a member of the high school division when you [President Ikeda] first established it [on June 7, 1964]. Immediately after graduating from university, I came to Mexico, where I have been living for the past twenty-five years. Right before I left Japan, my parents and I were fortunate to receive encouragement from you directly.

"At that time, you gave me three guidelines: You urged me to be a person who has guts, who makes tenacious efforts and who does not drift aimlessly through life. These three points became the eternal guiding principles of my life."

The man I am speaking of was born in Kanagawa Prefecture [adjacent to Metropolitan Tokyo]. He was one of the first leaders of the high school division to whom I presented a divisional corps flag. While still a member of this division, he resolved to play an active role on the world stage in the future. After he entered college, he earnestly applied himself to learning Spanish.

Inspired by the experience of interpreting for SGI-Mexico members when they visited Japan, he moved to Mexico in 1971 to continue his studies. When he arrived, he discovered that he was unable to communicate very well with the Spanish he had learned in Japan, so he joined an evening Spanish class at a local elementary school. He attended class from six in the evening after working during the day loading cargo onto trucks to support himself.

In 1974, he enrolled at the National Autonomous University of Mexico in Mexico City. He had to work his way through school, and the pressures of work and study became so great that he considered dropping out. But he persevered, reminding himself to become "a person who has guts, who makes tenacious efforts."

Scaling one daunting mountain after another, he finally became the first Japanese to qualify as a certified public accountant in Mexico. Now he is working in an international accounting firm and is also active as an ambassador of friendship between Mexico and Japan. He was even invited to attend an exchange sponsored by the Mexican president. I am truly pleased by his achievements.

The prime motivation for his endeavors was formed in his high school years. His example underscores that the determinations made during this period are truly important.

## The Gap Between Dreams and Reality

*Many say, "I have big dreams, but there is a huge gap between my dreams and my actual situation."*

That's fine. President Toda declared: "It's perfectly all right for youth to cherish dreams that may seem almost too big. What we can achieve in a single lifetime is always but a fraction of what we would like to achieve. So if you start out with expectations that are too low, you'll end up not accomplishing anything at all."

Of course, if you make no efforts, your dreams will amount to nothing but sheer fantasy. Effort and hard work construct the bridge that connects your dreams to reality. Those who make steady efforts are filled with hope. And hope, in turn, arises from steady efforts. Embrace your dreams and advance as far as they can carry you. That is the hallmark of youth.

*Far from cherishing big dreams, however, I find many high school students saying: "I just want to get married like everyone else and have a happy family" or "I don't know what I want to do in the future, but whatever it is, I want to be a kind person."*

Well, it's entirely up to each person to decide what he or she wants to do. No one else can make that decision.

At the beginning of Japan's Meiji period (1868–1912), an American educator, William S. Clark, taught at Sapporo Agricultural College [now part of Hokkaido University]. He gave his students the now-famous words, "Boys, be ambitious!"

I don't think he meant merely to strive to be successful or gain prominence in society. Instead, I think he was calling to his students to live in a free, unfettered way. You don't have to do something just because other people do. What matters is the extent to which you realize your potential and how much you contribute to others' happiness. What's important is whether you leave behind a meaningful legacy for those who come after. In that respect, I think Professor Clark's call urges youth to live to be truly satisfied with their lives. To do this, you have to forge a solid self. You have to become strong. In other words, you need to build a foundation.

For instance, you may say you want a happy family, but happiness is not something that can be handed to you. You will become happy only to the extent that you develop a strong inner core. You may say that you want to be a kind person, but you must be strong to exhibit true kindness.

22

Whatever happens, please don't be superficial and judge others by outward appearances. Please become individuals of depth and substance, who are broad-minded and tolerant. You mustn't allow yourselves to be caught up solely with immediate concerns and desires—whether it be focusing obsessively on grades on the one hand, or playing video games all the time and wanting only to have fun on the other.

I want you to savor the joy that comes from living with ever-fresh aspirations as you strive to realize the dreams and goals for the future you have personally resolved to pursue.

## NOTHING CAN BE BUILT WITHOUT A FOUNDATION

*Many young people say: "I don't know what my hopes are for the future" or "I don't have any goals."*

It's still crucial to *try* to accomplish something—anything. The winner of the men's marathon at the 1952 Olympic Games was the famous track star Emil Zátopek of Czechoslovakia. He trained relentlessly, even on his way to work. For instance, he challenged himself to run as far as he could while holding his breath. On a street lined with telephone poles, he sometimes would tell himself, for example, "Today, I'll try to make it to the fourth pole." Then, when he reached it, he would say to himself again, "OK, next time, I'll make it to the fifth." In this way, he increased his endurance. Sometimes he would feel as if he would faint, but these persistent efforts to keep challenging himself ultimately led him to victory.

Do something, start something. As you make consistent efforts, you will begin to see your goals come into focus. You will discover your mission—the one only you can fulfill.

For example, it is important to develop skills in a field that you like or that interests you. The key is to have something you can take pride in, something you can challenge. It might be something like excelling in math, in a foreign language, in a sport, in an extracurricular activity, in making friends or in doing volunteer work. The people around you may know you better in some areas than you do yourselves, so if you summon up the courage to ask them for advice, you might find the doors to new possibilities opening unexpectedly.

A person who has firm goals is way ahead of a person who has none. Setting goals is the starting point from which our lives' construction begins. Youth is a struggle to develop and shape oneself—an ongoing challenge to train oneself spiritually, intellectually and physically.

A solid foundation is essential in all things. No building or house can stand without a foundation. The same is true in life. And the time to construct that foundation is now, during your youth. As the French writer Romain Rolland (1866–1944) noted, a pyramid cannot be built from the top down.

In the Buddhist sutras, there is a story of a wealthy man. Envious on seeing the beautiful, towering three-story home of another, he hires a carpenter to build him a mansion of equal grandeur. The carpenter agrees and naturally begins building from the foundation up, but the foolish rich man is impatient and says: "I don't want a foundation. And I don't want a first or second floor. I just want a mansion that is three stories high. Hurry up and build the third floor!" This may seem like a silly story, but there are many people who behave this way.

*Some people make determinations but have a difficult time following through with them.*

That's all right. Most people have this problem. Still, resolving to do something in the first place is proof that you are progressing. Even if you have the tendency to make a determination but only stick to it for two or three days, it is OK as long as you keep refreshing that determination. Those who can keep renewing their resolution have great patience.

It's also important to get in the habit of pushing yourselves an extra five minutes. When you think, "I cannot do anymore; I want to go out and have some fun," that is the time to challenge yourselves to keep at it another five minutes. Those who persevere for an extra five minutes are truly admirable. Victory is theirs. This is one of life's truths.

# Never Give Up on Yourself

*I have met some people who are convinced that they are not smart and that their future is therefore limited.*

I once asked President Toda the difference between someone who is bright and someone who isn't. He took his writing brush and drew a horizontal line across the center of a piece of paper and then said: "This fine line is all that stands between the two. The difference is inconsequential." He believed that we all have much the same kind of brain but that everything is determined by the amount of effort we make. I clearly remember his words to this day.

It has been said that at most we use only about half our brain cells during our lifetime. Some scholars even maintain that we use less than 10 percent. In other words, hardly anyone is using their brain to its fullest potential.

I also have heard that the brain continues to grow until our early twenties. In that respect, how much we can develop our intellect before the age of twenty or so will greatly affect the rest of our lives—which again underscores the importance of the teenage years. Of course, your entire future does not hinge on your grades at school, nor do good grades automatically guarantee happiness or poor grades unhappiness.

Still, it might be a good idea to try to get grades that won't incur the wrath of your parents, the pity of your friends—or the possible future threat of divorce from a spouse who might one day come across your old report cards!

Joking aside, you mustn't put yourselves down or sell yourselves short. Human potential is a funny thing. If you tell yourselves that you're not smart, your brain really will grow sluggish. Instead, tell yourselves with conviction: "My brain is asleep because I'm hardly using it. So if I just make some effort, I can do anything." This is, in fact, the truth. The more you use your brain, the brighter you will become. Especially for those who chant Nam-myoho-renge-kyo and continue to make efforts, nothing is impossible.

*Some young people I've spoken to have lost all confidence and self-esteem. They admit to feeling hopeless and pessimistic. There are others who no one even suspects have any problems, yet who are secretly suffering, worried that they've committed what seems to them some dreadful, irredeemable mistake.*

Nothing is irredeemable in youth. Rather, the worst mistake you can make when young is to give up and not challenge yourselves for fear of failure. The past is the past and the future is the future. Keep moving forward with a steady eye on the future, telling yourselves: "I'll start from today!" "I'll start fresh from now, from this moment!" This is the essence of Nichiren Buddhism, the Buddhism of true cause, the spirit to start from the present moment. This is the heart of chanting Nam-myoho-renge-kyo.

True success or failure in life is not apparent until one reaches one's forties or fifties. My experience after nearly seventy years of life has taught me how to clearly recognize the human patterns that determine victory and defeat.

Do not despair or grow impatient over transient phenomena. Life is long. Even if you have problems, even if you have done things you regret or have made mistakes, your whole future still lies ahead of you. Don't become spiritless people who fret or plunge into despair over every little thing.

Many of history's most famous people seemed far from outstanding in their youth. Winston Churchill was known for always failing at school. Mahatma Gandhi wasn't a remarkable student either; he was shy, timid and a poor speaker. Albert Einstein, also, was a mediocre student, but luckily he excelled in math. And Wilhelm Roentgen, the discoverer of X-rays, was expelled from his polytechnic school when classmates falsely accused him of causing an accident. So what did these four young men have in common? Their refusal to give up on themselves.

One who has had poor grades, or who has been bullied or betrayed by others, or who has suffered from illness or financial difficulties is more likely to understand others' feelings and have deep insight into life.

Therefore, don't let yourselves be defeated. Then whatever suffering you've had to endure will definitely be transformed into your good fortune in the future.

## CONTINUE WITH A FIGHTING SPIRIT

You must respect your life. You will be unhappy if you allow yourselves to be swayed by society's prejudices, passing trends and contradictions. Never forget to live true to your convictions.

President Toda emphatically stated, "The true evaluation of our lives is determined by how happy we are in our final years."

Happiness in life does not depend on how well things go in your youth. And no matter how many mistakes you make, you always have a second chance. "Be ambitious" and keep striving toward the future. If you don't do well in elementary school, try harder in junior high. If you don't do well in junior high school, do your best in high school. And if you're not happy with your achievements in high school, give it your all in university. If that's not to your satisfaction, there's still hope after graduation, as you challenge yourselves as active members of society. If you experience setbacks along the way, continue with a fighting spirit into your forties, fifties, sixties and seventies.

Moreover, from the profound viewpoint of Nichiren Buddhism, if you don't accomplish everything you set out to in this lifetime, you can continue to fight in the next lifetime and so on throughout eternity. There is no more lofty aspiration than the Buddhist Law.

Even if you think you're hopeless and incapable, I know you're not. I have not the slightest doubt that each of you has a mission. Though others may disparage you, please know that I respect you, I believe in you. No matter what circumstances you now face, I have absolute confidence that a wonderful future awaits you.

Each time you fall down, just get back up. If you can pick yourself up, you can move forward. You are young. Now is the time for challenge and construction. Now is the time to begin some endeavor.

During one of my meetings with the noted American scientist Dr. Linus Pauling (1901–94),[1] I asked him in jest if there was any medicine that could make us smarter. For a moment, the renowned professor looked puzzled, as if searching for an answer.

*Having won two Nobel prizes, and being renowned for advocating the efficacy of vitamin C in preventing various diseases, I'm sure his answer was a good one.*

Yes. That's why I asked him this question: "Since your research on vitamin C has been so successful, couldn't you invent a medicine that would make people smarter?" After a moment's thought, he admitted that it would be a difficult task.

When I jokingly expressed my disappointment, he replied that we can develop our minds only through effort. If we really use our brain, he said, forcing it to work, squeezing out every ounce of its potential, we can develop a truly great mind. I agreed fully.

If someone were to invent a "brain-improving medicine," it would probably have the effect of a narcotic. People would cease to make efforts, which would lead no doubt to the downfall of humankind.

Without difficulty, you cannot hope to build great character. Our character is determined by how we challenge ourselves, how hard we try and how we go about grappling with the problems that confront us, while staying true to ourselves. In this way, our character is polished like a diamond. This comes about only when we forge and strengthen ourselves to the best of our abilities, and persevere through whatever difficulties we encounter.

## GREAT PEOPLE POSSESS HUMILITY

Dr. Pauling was a person of outstanding character. Though famous throughout the world, he always wore a warm smile and was never the least bit arrogant.

*I remember hearing that he flew from San Francisco to meet with you at the Los Angeles campus of Soka University, which opened in Calabasas, California, as a branch campus of Soka University in Japan. That was in February 1987.*

*With the spirit that he would go anywhere for a heart-to-heart talk with someone about peace, Dr. Pauling traveled hundreds of miles to meet you. That's very impressive, obviously a sign of the tremendous regard he had for you.*

One thing all great people have in common is their modesty. Arrogance is a sign one lacks true ability.

I have met hundreds of world leaders, many of whom are truly excellent and very capable people. Those who stand out in my mind are leaders not driven by ego, but those whose lives shine with an invincible spirit to devote themselves to humanity.

In the midst of the Cold War, Dr. Pauling boldly called on the United States to forge closer ties and develop a relationship of cooperation with the Soviet Union. When he openly declared his opposition to all forms of nuclear weapons, some Americans viewed him as a Soviet sympathizer, while the Soviets regarded him as clearly anti-Soviet. He was harshly censured by U.S. authorities.[2]

Nevertheless, in his famous "No More War" speech given in Tokyo in August 1959 after a visit to Hiroshima,[3] Dr. Pauling earnestly spoke out against nuclear weapons, saying that the enemy was neither the Soviet Union nor America, but war itself.

*What he said was perfectly correct, yet it must have taken tremendous courage for him to speak out like that, especially given the times.*

Yes, doing the right thing is very important. But it is precisely because most people don't that our world faces so many problems.

Someone once observed that countless statues are erected in honor of war's victors, but why so few honoring those killed or imprisoned for their resolute opposition to war? Here we can see the distorted values of human society and one of history's grave errors. Deploring such contradictions, someone else observed that if you kill one person, you will be called a murderer; but kill millions, and you will be revered as a hero.

## Don't Be Fooled by Outward Appearances

*It's hard to tell who the truly great people are, isn't it?*

Human beings may sometimes seem very intelligent, but they can often be extremely foolish.

For example, many automatically think that one who boasts of high status in society is fortunate; that one who enjoys fame is admirable; and that one who has a great deal of money and property is respectable. These perceptions are misguided illusions.

Who, then, is fortunate? Who is respectable? Who is genuinely a person of truth and integrity? Granted, these are difficult questions, but be assured that the answers have nothing to do with outward appearances .

*In a survey conducted by* Nihon Keizai Shimbun *(Japan Economic Journal) asking high school students who their idols were, athletes ranked first, cartoon and comic book heroes second, and television personalities and musicians third. One can see the powerful effect the media has on young people.*

That survey certainly reflects the times we live in—and not necessarily negatively. In Japan and many other countries, people have fought with their lives to obtain freedom of speech—which includes freedom of the press and broadcast media. However, that such freedom exists today is all the more reason each of you must develop the ability to keenly discern what is true.

Something isn't true simply because it appears in print. The media easily can present corrupt people as upstanding citizens, just as it can depict respectable people in a negative light. History can also be written so that a truly deplorable era appears as a most commendable one. It's difficult to know the truth merely from reading an article or hearing a radio or television report. It is a great tragedy for society if people take media-manufactured images at face value and base their opinions on them.

Buddhism has a different perspective. It teaches us to look at a person through the eyes of the Law and the eyes of the Buddha—in other words, to focus on a person's life, state of being and what is inside, just as it is, free of external embellishments.

Happiness is not determined by whether one has status in society or enjoys media recognition. Truly respectable are those who base their lives on the truth—on the reality of things.

Each of you knows yourself best. The opinions or evaluations of others may be based on emotion or ill intention. You can never tell.

That's why it's important to view yourselves continually through the eyes of Buddhism, pondering from time to time, "Am I living a respectable life?"

You may see someone and think: "He's so cool!" or "There's a celebrity!" But you mustn't become shallow, superficial people who are dazzled by such illusions and lose sight of your true selves.

President Toda once said to me: "The strength of youth is like the strength demonstrated by participants in a beach sumo wrestling match, who are armed only with their own ability. Competing armed with honors or titles is no true test of strength. It all comes down to how strong one is as an individual human being, to whether one has the strength and determination to contribute to people's happiness."

*In Japan, there seems to be an obsession with getting into a good school and, subsequently, a good company. Hardly any thought seems to be given to human development.*

*People overseas have dubbed us "economic animals." They tend to view Japan as a country preoccupied with money.*

Yes, and for that reason, Japan is not respected by the rest of the world; rather, it is looked on with disdain.

That reminds me of a humorous story that I'd like to share with you. A Japanese businessman went to an island in the South Pacific, where he found some of the local children lying around relaxing on the beach. He said to them: "Stop idling away your time. Get yourselves to school immediately and start studying!"

They replied, "Why should we go to school?"

"If you go to school and study hard," the man said, "you can get good grades."

"Why do we need good grades?" the children asked.

"Ah," said the man. "If you get good grades in school, you can get into a good university."

"And what will happen if we get into a good university?" they asked.

"If you graduate from a prestigious university, you can work for a big company or serve in a prominent public office. You can also earn a high salary and maybe create a good marriage."

"Then what?"

"You can live in a beautiful home and enjoy life."

"And then?"

"You then can work really hard until your retirement and send your children to a good school."

"And?" the children queried.

"Then you can go to a nice warm place and spend every day relaxing."

"If that's the goal," the children responded, "then we don't have to wait. We've already achieved it!"

In other words, if life's ultimate goal were simply "to relax and have a good time," then, as far as the children were concerned, there wasn't any point in going to all the trouble of getting an education and expending a great deal of time or energy studying.

Why, then, do we study? For what purpose do we live our lives? What is money for?

Even if you chase after good schools and good jobs, there is no guarantee you'll be happy if you get them. If our sole reason for living is to have an easy existence, then perhaps there's no need to make such arduous efforts to get into a good school or good company.

Actually, when all is said and done, the purpose of study is not to be accepted into a prestigious university. It is to cultivate your minds and hearts so that you can become well-rounded individuals and leave some proof of your existence in this world.

Fulfill the mission that is yours and yours alone. And do your best to help those who are suffering. To do so, you will need strength and character. That is why I stress constantly how much there is to gain by working hard and challenging yourselves now.

## THE VALUE OF HARD WORK

*Some young people ask: "What's wrong with having a good time when we're young?" and "What's the point of working hard?"*

Granted there is no need to take on unnecessary hardship. Nevertheless, those who shun hard work are missing out on the satisfaction of knowing they have accomplished something.

When I was a young man, I had a friend who excelled in everything and whom everyone admired. So you can imagine my surprise when I received a letter the other day from another friend from those days telling me that this person had ended up leading "a sorrowful life that could only be described as hellish, filled with illness and family problems."

How could this happen to someone who had shown such promise in his youth, you may ask. Most likely it was because, having been pampered and fussed over from an early age, he never learned what hard work was, or what it meant to struggle to accomplish something, or what a life of genuine depth and substance was. Thinking that everything he desired would just fall in his lap, he may have forgotten to challenge himself, perhaps even going out of his way to avoid making strenuous efforts.

*What kind of advice might you give to students who don't go to school— either because they feel out of place or because they suffer from illness? There are also, of course, those who have quit school altogether.*

There are many reasons why people may be unable to attend school, including illness. However, when viewed from the long perspective of a person's whole life, such hardships are never wasted. Each of you is your own person; you don't need to compare yourself to others. Just keep advancing, even if only by one or two steps, in a way that is true to you.

Those who live their lives to the fullest, unperturbed by the noisy clamor around them, are victors in life. Never give up. If you persevere, someone will definitely support and protect you. Never lose hope. In the long run, being unable to go to school for two or three years is not such a grave concern. Some people, for various reasons, even drop out of school.

But I personally hope that you will attend high school and, if possible, college. You also have the option of correspondence courses or professional schools, as well as high school equivalency exams.[4] I am, of course, aware that some people may not wish to pursue such paths or that their situations may prevent them from doing so. And that is fine.

One student I know became fed up with high school and found a job that he liked. He is such an excellent worker that he has become invaluable to his employers. Like him, many people are living their lives with a great deal of satisfaction about the choices they've made. I think that is perfectly all right.

There are already signs in Japanese society of a gradual shift in emphasis from academic background to actual ability and from there toward more humanistic values.

President Toda said: "A favorable environment does not guarantee that one can study. The classroom exists wherever you are, on a train or even in the bathroom." The important thing is to develop your ability and cultivate a commitment in your heart to work for the happiness of others.

## POLISH YOUR "INNER SWORD"

Those who are determined to win in the end, no matter what, are strong.

In the depths of our lives, we each possess a precious "jeweled sword" that is uniquely our own. This mighty sword of the spirit pierces negative forces and defends justice. As long as we realize we possess this inner sword and polish it continuously for the sake of good, we will never be defeated. We will win without fail. Such is the wondrous sword we possess within.

This jeweled sword is your own heart, your determination. Having strong faith and conviction in the Mystic Law is what's known as the world of Buddhahood. If the sword of faith remains sheathed, it is useless in battling obstacles; if it is not polished, it will grow dull and weak. Those who neither unsheathe nor polish their inner sword lead fearful and timid lives. This magnificent sword is your own heart; it is your character. Thus, to polish the sword within means to study, develop friendships and build a solid self.

This sword I speak of is not a cruel and evil sword that harms others but a spiritual sword committed to good and to benefiting others. As such, it is an infinitely precious treasure.

I have met with Nelson Mandela, president of South Africa, on two occasions. President Mandela endured twenty-seven-and-a-half years— nearly ten thousand days—in prison for his anti-apartheid activities. He is an indomitable champion of human rights who brought an end to the inhuman policy of apartheid, or racial segregation, in his country.

South Africa maintained a state of harsh discrimination for a long time. Under apartheid, it was a crime for native Africans to ride a "Whites Only" bus, to use a "Whites Only" drinking fountain, to walk on a "Whites Only" beach, to be on the streets past eleven at night, to be unemployed or to live in certain places. In short, black South Africans were not treated as human beings.

Mr. Mandela witnessed and experienced countless incidents of degradation and contempt under apartheid. Filled with outrage at the unforgivable discrimination he saw all around him, he resolved to do something about it. Such passion for justice was the "jeweled sword" wielded by Nelson Mandela. He stood up, determined to completely reform this inhumane society. He never yielded, even under the hellish conditions he suffered in prison, and he succeeded in defeating a tradition of discrimination in South Africa that had lasted since the seventeenth century.

Those who have suffered persecution for the sake of justice are truly noble. Mr. Mandela, who was mocked and humiliated at one time, is now respected all around the world.

## YOUR GROWTH AND SUCCESS ARE MY VICTORY

*We, the members of the high school division, will also continue to stand up to injustice without being defeated. We will do our utmost to change Japan, a country where still today people's rights are all too casually ignored or trampled on.*

It is not people's words but their actions that convince me.

Regarding a comment made earlier about young people idolizing athletes, I'll share with you a story about the famous American heavyweight boxing champion Jack Dempsey.[5]

*Didn't he become a legend for his knockouts?*

That's right. It is said that Jack Dempsey decided to become a boxer because his mother had been ill-treated by a train conductor. When he was eight years old, he was riding on a train with his mother, who was very sick. She only had enough money to buy one adult ticket, and the conductor threatened that if she didn't pay her son's fare, he would throw him off the train. Even though his mother told the conductor she was terribly ill and had no money, he just shouted at her that rules were rules. At that point, a kind-hearted passenger who couldn't stand to sit by and watch this scene any longer offered to help them out.

This incident with the conductor was the catalyst that led the young Jack to vow that, when he grew up, his mother would never face such humiliation again. Based on this resolve, and after long years of rigorous training, he became a world champion.

This determination was Jack Dempsey's inner sword, which he polished with all his might.

Those who possess the "jeweled sword" of justice in their hearts will be protected by the Buddhist gods throughout their lives. On the other hand, those who hold cruelty and malice in their hearts will end up bound in chains in the world of hell without fail.

I have vowed to myself that my victory in life will be represented by your endeavors in society. My happiness lies in all of you becoming outstanding human beings, in all of you succeeding to your hearts' content in your communities, in society and on the world stage and leading lives that shine with vibrant brilliance. Until then, I don't care how much criticism I have to face.

From the depths of my heart, I call to all of you: "Polish the 'jeweled sword' within you! Stand up with unwavering determination to win!"

1. SGI President Ikeda and Dr. Linus Pauling (1901–94) published a dialogue together under the title *A Lifelong Quest for Peace*.

2. Dr. Linus Pauling was castigated by U.S. Senator Joseph McCarthy and his communist witch hunt during the 1950s.

3. On August 6, 1945, the world's first atomic bomb was dropped on the Japanese city of Hiroshima, destroying 90 percent of the city and killing about two hundred thousand people.

4. In Japan, students must take an equivalency exam to enter high school.

5. Jack Dempsey held the world heavyweight title from 1919 to 1926.

# *3*

## FRIENDSHIP AND PERSPECTIVES ON LIFE

Today's theme is friendship, a very important topic. Someone once said, "A man with friends is rich, so I am rich." Of course, this applies to women, too.

Having just one good friend doubles one's happiness in life. This is genuine wealth. The German poet Johann Friedrich von Schiller said that friendship doubles one's happiness and halves one's sadness. And as true as those words still are today, the question is, how does one acquire such friendship?

You cannot choose your parents, but since you can choose your friends, it's an important choice to think about.

*Yes, I think worries about friends are a big concern for youth. I have heard some say that school is fun because they have friends there. And others say that while they have friends, they don't have any close enough for a heart-to-heart talk. Still others, I think, are so competitive they panic when they see their friends studying and then pressure themselves to exceed them.*

*I have also heard people express such worries as "My friend and I used to be close, but then out of the blue, she began giving me the cold shoulder," "My so-called friend let me down" or "My friend's been ignoring me, and it hurts."*

A young person's heart is as sensitive as a thermometer. One minute you feel everything is great, and the next, you feel so down on yourself that you're convinced you must be the most inadequate and worthless person in the world. But that is one of the many characteristics of youth, so don't worry. What's important is to keep living life, never being defeated whatever painful things may sometimes happen.

You may encounter situations or events that bring great sadness and despair—such as problems with friends, heartache over love, being involved in a car accident or having a parent fall ill. But when you look back on such hardships later, they will all seem like a dream.

After World War II, I was in a state of despair. I literally didn't know if I would survive, and the future looked very bleak. But I pushed on and here I am today. Even those difficult times now seem as unreal as if they had never happened.

No matter what hardships we face, if we keep moving forward without giving up, they will all eventually vanish like a mirage. This is an important premise on which to base our lives. So we must live optimistically.

With this point in mind, today let's talk about friendship.

## HARDSHIPS STRENGTHEN FRIENDSHIPS

*The Great Hanshin Earthquake that struck Kobe and surrounding areas in January 1995 plunged thousands into the dark abyss of despair. Many lost loved ones and relatives. But one thing I think we all learned from this disaster is that, in times of pain and suffering, there is nothing one appreciates more than a friend. Many earthquake survivors are striving earnestly to rebuild their lives—not only for themselves but for their friends whose lives were so tragically cut short.*

*A teacher from the Kansai Soka Junior High School and Kansai Soka High School remarked that the bonds of friendship among the students had been strengthened as a result of surmounting the tragedy of this earthquake together.*

*A student from Kobe's Suma Ward, who graduated from Kansai Soka High School in March 1996, had his house completely destroyed by the earthquake. He said, "When things were at their worst, President Ikeda and my schoolmates were my greatest source of encouragement." He also said: "I really felt how wonderful it was to have warm, caring friends with whom I could struggle through hard times. The earthquake brought us all much closer together."*

*A first-year high school student from Kobe's Chuo Ward said she realized for the first time how much we depend on others. She said: "I felt gratitude from the depths of my heart for my friends. Like the air we cannot see but which sustains our lives, I promise wholeheartedly to support all the friends I encounter throughout my life."*

That's very beautiful. And just like air, the heart is also invisible to the naked eye. But that heart holds all of people's happiness and sadness, their beauty and their luminance, as well as their dark and unattractive side.

The intangible tie that links the heart of one person to another is friendship. It is not about personal gain or status, nor is it about strategy or superficial interactions. It is a relationship built on the genuine sincerity of those involved.

Friendship is the most beautiful, most powerful and most valuable treasure in life. It is your true wealth. No matter how much status people may gain or how rich they may become, a life without friends is sad and lonely. It also leads to an unbalanced, self-centered existence.

There is nothing more wonderful or precious than the friendships of one's youth. In adulthood, self-interest or personal gain often comes into play in human relationships, or fleeting friendships are formed as a result of some temporary circumstance, but the friendships made in one's school days are generally free of such artifice.

You were born in this vast universe on the tiny planet Earth and in the same era as the people around you. Yet, it is extremely rare to find, among the some 5.8 billion[1] people on this planet, genuine, unconditional friends with whom you can be totally yourselves and who will intuitively understand your thoughts and feelings without need for words. From this perspective, because you and your schoolmates are learning together, a strong bond exists among you. I'm sure you regard one or two among them as true friends—please treasure them.

But if some of you feel that you don't have any close friends right now, please don't worry. Just decide that the reason you don't have any now is so that you can have wonderful friends in the future. Concentrate your energies now on becoming fine people.

I'm also sure that in the future, some of you will have friends all around the world.

In any event, it's important to understand that friendship depends on you, not on the other person. It all comes down to your attitude and contribution. I hope you will not be fair-weather friends, only helping others when circumstances are good and leaving them high and dry when some problem occurs. Instead, please become people who stick by your friends with unchanging loyalty through thick and thin.

And when you graduate from school, I hope you will have grown to be generous, warmhearted people who can say to their friends with all honesty: "I will never forget you. If you ever have a problem or something you want to talk about, don't hesitate to come to me. And I hope I can go to you, too."

## OPEN THE CHANNELS OF COMMUNICATION

*Sometimes it's hard to stand by your friends no matter what. What advice would you give those who feel they have been treated coldly by a friend out of the blue but have no idea why?*

I think the best thing is to have the courage to ask that person directly. In many cases, you will find that the last thing that person wanted to do was treat you coldly, and that in reality, while you neglected to find out what was wrong for fear of being hurt, that person, too, was feeling rejected and lonely.

Our human relationships are like a mirror. So if you're thinking, "If only so-and-so were a little nicer to me, I could talk to her about anything," then that person is probably thinking, "If only so-and-so would open up to me, I would be nicer to her."

You should make the first move to open the channels of communication. If, despite these efforts, you are still rebuffed, then the person you should feel sorry for is your friend.

The human heart is truly complex; we cannot read what's in another person's heart. People change. What do *you* do? My advice is that you hold fast to your identity with the spirit that "others may change, but

I will stay who I am." If you should be snubbed or let down by others, have the strength of character to vow that you will never do the same to anyone. Those who betray others' trust are truly pitiable; they are only hurting themselves, as if driving a spike through their own hearts. And, sadly, they don't even realize it.

*So people who have the courage to strike up a conversation with others can make friends. But sometimes when we do approach someone in the spirit of friendship, we may be slighted or ignored.*

Even if that happens, I don't think it's necessary to be overly worried about it.

The Buddhist scriptures clearly reveal that Shakyamuni Buddha was a person who initiated dialogue with others. You need to be strong to initiate a dialogue. You must remember that experiencing rejection and disappointment is an inevitable part of life.

Even Nichiren Daishonin was abandoned by many of his followers. I, too, have been betrayed by people whom I trusted and sincerely tried to encourage. But that didn't surprise me at all; it is something I have learned to expect.

It's crucial that you be courageous and live proudly, believing in yourselves. Those who betray or bully others are the ones making bad causes; they are truly to be pitied.

If you feel hurt or betrayed by someone, isn't it better to make a new friend, rather than stop trusting people altogether? If you don't trust anyone, yes, certainly, you might avoid being hurt or let down, but you'll only end up leading a lonely, barren existence locked up in your shell. The fact is that only someone who has experienced pain and hardships can empathize with others and treat them with kindness. It's essential, therefore, that you become strong.

Be like the sun, for the sun shines on serenely even though not all of the planets will reflect back its light and even though some of its brilliance seems to radiate only into empty space. You may find that those who reject the radiant light of your friendship will naturally fade out of your lives. But the more you shine your light, the more brilliant your lives will become.

No matter how other people are or what they do, it is important that you walk your own paths, believing in yourselves. If you remain constant and stay true to yourselves, others will definitely one day come to understand your sincere intent.

More important, you have the power of chanting Nam-myoho-renge-kyo behind you. I have heard many people recount that they were victims of bullying, but after sincerely chanting Nam-myoho-renge-kyo, they suddenly found one day that the bullying had ceased. By chanting about your problems, you will find yourselves quite naturally overcoming all your hardships and sufferings, almost without your even being aware of it. When you look back later, you will appreciate this fact.

It is also important that you chant for your friends. This is a sign of true friendship.

*One student sent a postcard to the* Koko Shimpo *[the Soka Gakkai's high school division newspaper], in which she wrote: "I am so fortunate to have someone I can call a close friend. This friend has experienced a life crueler than I could ever possibly endure. Sometimes she closes her eyes and says, 'I wish I could just fall asleep and never wake up.' Whenever she says that, I shout: 'You mustn't think of dying! Your suffering will not end in death. You will only become unhappier.'*

*"One day I told my friend that I was a Soka Gakkai member and gave her a note saying that I am praying for her to become truly happy. She thanked me and said that when she read the note, tears came to her eyes."*

*I think that chanting for the happiness of our friends is of prime importance.*

That's right. You may have friends who are sick, who cannot attend school or who are struggling to cope with problems at home. Whatever the case may be, the best thing you can do is to chant for them. Your prayers, like radio waves, though invisible, will definitely reach them.

And when you chant, you should do so sincerely and honestly, following the feelings in your heart without restraint, just as an infant instinctively seeks its mother's milk. There is no need to be stoically formal when you chant; there is no need for pretense. If you are suffering, then take that suffering to the Gohonzon; if you feel sad, then take your sadness to the Gohonzon.

It is also best to chant with a clear determination, having a concrete goal in mind about how you want to grow or change or what it is that you want to accomplish.

It's also important to chant for those people whom you may not like or find hard to deal with or feel resentful toward. It may be difficult and perhaps even impossible for you at first, but if you challenge yourselves and chant for them, the wheels of change will definitely be set in motion.

Either you will change or the other person will. Either way, you can open a path leading in a positive direction. Many people have experienced this firsthand. Most important is that you transform yourselves, that you become people who can pray even for those you do not like. This will be your greatest fortune.

## MAKE GOOD FRIENDS

*Some students have been told by teachers at school to avoid associating with people who aren't as smart as they are because it would be detrimental. Consequently, they no longer even try to make friends.*

It is difficult to define what it means to be "smart." We cannot determine whether people are intelligent solely by their grades in high school. When viewed from a broader perspective, labels put on people in high school, such as "smart" or "not very bright," are not of great importance. Rather, staying power and the energy to take action toward completing something you have set out to accomplish are the strengths that tend to be great assets in life.

Therefore, I hope you can be open-minded enough to learn from all your friends, irrespective of their academic abilities. If you judge people based on grades alone, you will limit the richness and diversity in your own lives. Of course, the teachers who gave that advice probably thought they were being helpful.

Associating with self-destructive people, however, can certainly have harmful consequences, dragging you down with them. You must have the courage not to succumb to such negative influences.

Sometimes your friends can have a stronger influence over you than your parents or anyone else. So if you make good friends—friends who are interested in improving and developing themselves—you will move in a positive direction as well.

Andrew Carnegie (1835–1919), the American industrialist and philanthropist, modestly attributed his success to having gathered around him people who were far more talented and capable than he.

Ultimately, the only way to make good friends is for you to become a good friend yourself. Good people gather around other good people.

President Toda would become enraged when he saw young people obsessed with playing mah-jongg, reading frivolous magazines or staggering around babbling in a drunken stupor. He would quickly lose his temper with them, shouting, "What spiritless youth you are!" He would say that young people ought to be talking about their future by the lakeside or shaping their hopes and dreams while gazing up at the stars. It was his wish that they discuss, with a healthy mind and attitude, their plans for a sound and happy future.

You probably have many different kinds of friends—friends who live in the same neighborhood and with whom you walk to school every day; friends who are in the same class; friends with whom you participate in extracurricular activities; friends with whom you just spend time. But the best friends are those with whom you can advance together toward a shared goal.

And we can surely have no more wonderful friends than those we find in our fellow SGI members who share with us the same beliefs, lofty purpose and ideals. As SGI members, we are all friends devoting our lives to kosen-rufu, that is, the eternal happiness of all humankind.

Nothing is more beautiful than friendships developed among people challenging themselves and encouraging one another as they work toward the realization of a common goal. Such relationships are even more beautiful than those between parent and child, husband and wife, and sweethearts. This kind of profound friendship is the highest mark and the very flame of humanity.

*That reminds me of Japanese writer Osamu Dazai's novel* Hashire Merosu *(Run, Melos!), in which the protagonist keeps running in order to fulfill his promise to never betray his friend.*

Yes, what others do doesn't matter. The important thing is that you fulfill the promises you make.

I have made many friends all around the world. One that I will always remember is Dr. Aurelio Peccei (1908–84), cofounder of the Club of Rome.[2]

The first time I met Dr. Peccei, he shared his experience of being imprisoned during World War II. Tears filled his eyes as he spoke. Dr. Peccei fought in the Resistance against the Fascist regime in Italy.

In waging their courageous underground struggle, the members of the Resistance had to stay constantly on the move to evade capture. Each day was an intense life-and-death struggle. As many as seventy thousand people were murdered by Fascist forces. People were executed, tortured or shot to death by the roadside. Along with many of his friends, Dr. Peccei was imprisoned and sentenced to death.

In prison, Dr. Peccei came to notice that arrogant, critical people folded easily when reproached and were quick to disclose secret information. Though they were skillful at putting on a display of confidence and leadership to win popularity or incite a crowd, they were weak at the crucial moment. On the other hand, those who were humble and seemed quiet and meek remained courageously calm even under the most hellish circumstances. They never yielded, their noble spirit shining through.

I have been jailed, too, and it's not a place for the fainthearted. It is a place that reveals what a person is really made of. You cannot tell a person's true nature by outward appearance or behavior when everything is going well.

I think that those who have suffered truly devastating blows or lived through great tragedy can deeply appreciate the profundity of life and the beauty of genuine friendship.

People of conviction, who stand alone, who pursue their chosen path are not only good and trustworthy friends themselves, but can make genuine friends of others.

The bamboo groves of autumn are gorgeous. Each bamboo tree stands independently, growing straight and tall toward the sky. Yet in the ground, out of sight, the roots of each tree are interconnected.

In the same way, true friendship is not a relationship of dependence but of independence. It is the enduring bond that connects self-reliant individuals, comrades who share the same commitment, on a spiritual dimension.

Friendship is also determined by the way we live our lives.

## BE SINCERE IN CULTIVATING FRIENDSHIPS

*I think everyone feels that friendship is important. Many, however, discover that friendships with schoolmates last only as long as they attend the same school, are in the same class or involved in the same extracurricular activities. Once they move on, such friendships tend to fizzle out. As a result, some complain how difficult it is to find a lifelong friend.*

There are many kinds of friendship. Some friendships last a lifetime. But there are also friendships that only endure for a certain time—it might be twenty years, five years or one year. Sometimes your feelings may not change, but the other person's do. You don't have to be obsessed with the idea that friendship must last a lifetime. A friendship still has meaning even if it only lasts a short while. The main thing is that you respond with sincerity to each encounter.

Your classmates are your peers; they are the people with whom you will graduate, so I hope you can truly enjoy the time you spend with them, without worrying how long your friendship will last. Deep friendships are a rare thing. Cultivating them is like growing a mighty tree—a process that involves a different method of cultivation than that required for growing many small shrubs and plants.

If you remain sincere in your interactions with others, you will one day naturally come to find yourselves surrounded by good friends. And from among those people, I'm sure you'll forge lifelong friendships that are as strong and unshakable as towering trees. Don't be impatient. Please work first on developing yourselves. Rest assured that an infinite number of wonderful encounters await you in the future.

*Is there some secret to making friendships last?*

You may think friendships just happen spontaneously and develop by themselves, but they must be infused with and supported by the eternally youthful spirit to grow and advance. They involve an unflagging commitment to always be there to encourage and help one another as you work toward your respective aims and goals in life. It is important to have some ambition—such as graduating from university or making a meaningful contribution to society. Friendships among people who lack a clear positive purpose or direction in life tend to be complacent and dependent in nature. Friendships among people who cheerfully encourage one another while striving to realize their dreams are the kind that deepen and endure.

What is friendship? It is not simply a matter of being favorably disposed toward someone because he or she spends a lot of time with you, or lends you money, or is nice to you, or because you get along well and have a lot in common. True friendship implies a relationship where you empathize with your friends when they're suffering and encourage them not to lose heart, and where they, in turn, empathize with you when you're in the same boat and try to cheer you up. A friendship with those qualities flows as beautifully as a pure, fresh stream.

The purest and most beautiful stream that can be found in human existence is friendship. When the pure streams of friendship flowing from each person converge, they give rise to an even broader, deeper and purer river of friendship, which will inspire all who see it to proclaim its beauty and clarity and want to drink from its waters.

*It would be truly wonderful if we could all develop that kind of friendship. Ultimately, it is all up to the individual, isn't it?*

Yes. The key lies in creating a beautiful stream of friendship in your own life as you strive together with your friends toward your respective dreams—struggling and growing together, sharing one another's problems and hardships and always encouraging and supporting one another.

If your friends share the same feelings about the friendship as you do, then it is likely to last a long time; but if they decide to opt out, then it will be short. You yourself may unintentionally let a friend down, causing a rift in your relationship.

In any event, should a friendship end, there's no need to grow despondent. You don't have to beat yourself up, thinking friendship should last forever. The important thing is that you never forget the true meaning of friendship, and that you make it the basis for your interactions with others.

Nichiren Daishonin writes of a "friend in the orchid room" (WND-1, 23). This expression means that, just as orchids in a room impart their exquisite fragrance to all who enter, we should strive to be the kind of friend who has a positive and uplifting effect on others.

All you have to do is become like the orchid. In the East, the orchid is symbolic of a person of lofty character. Therefore, please develop your character so that it exudes a beautiful orchidlike fragrance.

*Colombia, as I recall, is famous for orchids, which are its national flower. It produces 10 percent of all orchids in the world and is home to about three thousand different varieties.*

*I remember hearing a story about your friendship with Colombia. You visited that South American country in early 1993 at a time when it was facing a major national security crisis. You went because you were determined to keep your promise to your friends in Colombia,.*

Yes. Colombia's President César Gaviria Trujillo and First Lady Ana Milena Muñoz de Gaviria also value trust and friendship most highly. In 1990, the people of Colombia generously allowed us to hold the "Colombian Gold Exhibition" at the Tokyo Fuji Art Museum. We displayed for the first time outside of Colombia one of the world's largest uncut emeralds (weighing seventeen hundred carats, or twelve ounces), as well as some five hundred treasured cultural objects. I will never forget this warm gesture of friendship expressed in the form of cultural exchange.

Actually, a short time before my departure, I received a message from President Gaviria's office asking whether I was really planning to visit Colombia as scheduled.

# Take Sincere Action
# When a Friend Is in Trouble

The drug cartels had been stepping up their terrorist activities, and a huge bomb explosion had just claimed the lives of many innocent people in the Colombian capital. An important international conference slated to be held in Colombia had already been canceled due to concerns about security. Even foreign reporters were fleeing the country. Many people advised me to postpone my visit. But I didn't. I told the staff of President Gaviria's office to rest assured that I would indeed travel to their country as planned.

I will always remember the conversation I shared on that visit with President and First Lady Gaviria, who warmly welcomed me to their country.

The Fuji Art Museum's "Treasures of Japanese Art" exhibition, incidentally, which opened at the Colombian National Museum at that time, was also a great success.

*So the bottom line is that when our friends are facing difficulties, we should take sincere and heartfelt action on their behalf.*

*There are all too many fair-weather friends in the world—friends who stay with us in good times but quickly disappear when some problem or setback assails us. That isn't true friendship. To be a good and reliable friend to others, we need strong conviction.*

As the saying goes, "A friend in need is a friend indeed."

I have noticed that other countries, particularly Western ones, take a much deeper perspective toward friendship than Japan. In the West, there is a tradition of viewing friendship as something profoundly noble and eternal. I find evidence of this in the novels of many Western writers, as well as in real-life examples. In Japan, friendship, on the whole, seems to lack such depth and noble purpose, being formed solely on the shallow criterion of "we get along well together."

I have a friend who was once an ambassador to Japan. He served in this post for many years and played a leading role in the foreign diplomatic community here. He was also an important and influential political figure in his own country. I met with him on three different occasions and each time found him to be a truly outstanding individual of great humanity and profound insight. Several times he invited me to visit his country. He even wrote an essay about my activities, which he sent to people in various fields. To this day, I regret that circumstances prevented me from traveling there at that time. Later, in the wake of political turmoil that saw a new regime seize control of the country, the ambassador was forced to flee for his life. He lived in exile in the United Kingdom until his death.

Before this turn of events, I was invited to a dinner party hosted by the ambassador at the embassy. This was shortly before his departure from Japan. There, he showed me to a room in which the walls were decorated with portraits of influential leaders of countries around the world. And there was one of me. I will never forget the ambassador telling me that my picture hung there because he regarded me as his lifelong friend and comrade in the cause of peace. He turned to the other photos and said, "These are all wonderful friends and comrades of mine," and he shared with me something of the background and history of each person.

Pointing to one photo of a friend from abroad, the ambassador explained as tears filled his eyes: "He is still in jail as a political prisoner. He is a person of conviction, but he may never again see the outside world." I asked the ambassador if he thought dying in prison for one's beliefs was a tragedy. Fighting back tears, the ambassador said unhesitatingly: "People such as my friend have given their lives to truth and justice. They may die in prison, but to die a martyr for the sake of one's beliefs is truly noble. Such a life is one of absolute victory." His words moved me deeply.

These prisoners of conscience could easily gain their freedom if they would but turn their backs on their convictions or hand their comrades over to the authorities. But they stand firm, never giving in, even though they may be betrayed by others and may face death alone in prison. Such strength is the hallmark of true human greatness and genuine friendship.

## TRUE FRIENDSHIP CREATES VALUE

*That reminds me of the undying friendship between David Rossi and Rocco Bruno, the protagonists of Hall Caine's novel,* The Eternal City.[3]

Yes. It's so important to keep the promises made to friends. This is the true meaning of friendship. To become people who can do so, however, we must first learn to keep our resolutions—the promises we have made to ourselves.

True friendship contributes to our growth as people and the creation of positive value in our lives. We cannot say the same of associating with bad influences, where the only result is stagnation and negativity; this is just hanging out together, not friendship. As a well-known saying goes, "You can judge a person by the company he keeps." People are greatly influenced by the kind of friends with whom they mix. And like another old proverb says, "He that toucheth pitch shall be defiled." I hope you will not associate with negative and destructive individuals.

*President Ikeda, you have made friends all around the world. Just communicating with people in one's own immediate circle of acquaintances is a challenge, so I think it absolutely amazing that you've made friends transcending bounds of country, language, religion and culture.*

I am very proud to have so many friends of outstanding character and ability throughout the world. Almost all of them speak frankly in our dialogues and never manipulate or exploit the discussions for selfish ends.

In one respect, nothing is nobler or stronger than heart-to-heart bonds among people who share their hopes and dreams and are committed to working for society. Many years of experience have led me to this conclusion. Such people have deep-rooted conviction and their own solid philosophy. They strive to lead a worthwhile existence and have a humble spirit to contribute something. Unity and cooperation among people of such altruistic aspiration is the highest ideal of friendship. If such lofty friendship ceases to exist, the world will be plunged into eternal darkness. In the same way, because of our friendships with people around the globe, the Soka Gakkai and the SGI have always found fresh hope to break through the darkness into light.

*Expanding ties of friendship is the way toward peace, isn't it?*

Yes, just as an exquisite tapestry is woven from many varied threads, if countless beautiful friendships are woven around the world, forming bridges that span the oceans to connect all countries, they will lead to the creation of a happy and peaceful world. Treasuring friendship is deeply meaningful in that it embodies the spirit of humanism and peace. It is the first step toward realizing an ideal society where people can live together in harmony.

Many have long noted the truth of the observation: "Evil people flock together, but the good remain aloof." So it goes without saying that when people of sincere intent *do* come together in pursuit of a lofty goal, something really beautiful and worthy of respect takes place. This is the essence of true humanity.

*Yes. Morally corrupt people are easily drawn together by self-serving motives. People of integrity, in contrast, tend not to be motivated by self-interest, and are therefore independent.*

*Many Japanese seem to lack a spirit of generosity toward others. They find it difficult to be happy for others' success. Jealousy seems to be the uppermost emotion, and anyone who dares to excel or stand out from the rest is likely to be the target of criticism and attack.*

*How we love conformity! But such disregard for a person's individuality isn't what friendship is about, is it?*

That's right. Generosity of spirit to respect those whose character and personality are different from yours is the very foundation of friendship. With a big heart, you can form many wonderful friendships. But a small, stingy heart cultivates nothing but a narrow, barren, lonely life bereft of genuine friendship.

*I see what you're saying. But what do we do about the people we just don't like?*

Just as there are some foods that you find unpalatable, having people in your environment that you dislike is an unavoidable part of life. While there's nothing wrong with not particularly liking some people, it is wrong to put them down or be mean to them. They have every right to exist, just as you do—and to have their own opinions and way of doing things. It's important to cultivate a broad-minded outlook.

*One student came to me with the problem that she had a hard time making friends because she was very shy, unable to come out of her shell.*

Admittedly, our basic nature doesn't change easily.

There's nothing wrong with being a little sensitive or timid, although it's preferable to be strong and confident. Things like personality, and even sometimes our circumstances, are difficult to change. That's why the way to victory lies in continuous efforts to develop and strengthen ourselves.

Those who realize their own shortcomings and then chant Nam-myoho-renge-kyo while striving to improve themselves will definitely see their lives change. Someone who is quiet and introverted, for instance, may come to shine as someone who is thoughtful and discreet. In the long term, such people tend to develop closer, deeper friendships than their louder, extroverted peers, who sometimes tend to act before they think.

*One student asked me how to encourage a classmate he didn't know very well, but who had stopped coming to school.*

To be concerned about others' welfare is truly admirable. If you want to help people, the best thing to do is chant Nam-myoho-renge-kyo for them. And then, in terms of concrete encouragement, you could, depending on the situation, let them know that you're worried about them or that you're looking forward to seeing them at school again. You might pay them a visit, write them a letter or give them a call.

There are many ways to express your concern. The situation probably won't change immediately. But simple words like "I'm looking forward to seeing you back at school. It's not the same without you" can make it easier for them to return when they feel ready. In other words, smooth the way for them and make them feel welcome. Developing a warm spirit of mutual concern among your classmates shouldn't be overlooked.

*Some students are envied and resented by others because of their good grades.*

They should be proud of themselves. Outstanding people are bound to meet with envy and resentment. That is life. A famous ancient philosopher once observed that we live in a world where even if one has impeccable character, one will inevitably be slandered and criticized.

Of course, I am not suggesting that you go around boasting about your good grades, either.

When I was in elementary school, one student from an affluent family was always well dressed and seemed so happy. I remember harboring feelings of jealousy toward him, and I wasn't alone. Today, such envy would surely make him the object of bullying at the hands of his classmates. But to succumb to such feelings is to be driven by the life-condition of animality. The brilliance of true humanity, on the other hand, lies in surmounting feelings of envy with the resolute attitude, "I'll create an even more wonderful life for myself." If you are jealous of others, you will not advance; you will only become miserable. Please do not be defeated or consumed by such emotions.

Isn't it far better to be envied by others than to be one who envies? I hope you can embrace others with warmth and understanding. I want to see all of you become people with hearts as broad as a great river, as wide as the ocean and as vast as the blue sky. From such a big heart will unfold a grand and beautiful drama of friendship.

1. 5.8 billion people on earth in 1996, today 6.8 billion people.

2. The Club of Rome is a "think tank for humanity" of renowned scholars, including several Nobel Prize winners. A dialogue between SGI President Ikeda and Dr. Peccei has been published under the title *Before It Is Too Late*.

3. Hall Caine, *The Eternal City* (London: William Heinemann, 1901).

PART TWO

THE HEARTBEAT

*of Youth*

# *4*

---

# WHAT IS LOVE?

*Along with having questions about friendship, many students are asking about love and relationships.*

*The other day, the following inquiry came from one member of the young women's high school division: "My mother forbids me to date anyone. Is it really best to avoid relationships while I'm in high school?"*

Your high school years coincide with adolescence. It's as natural to feel attracted to, be interested in and fall in love with members of the opposite sex during your youth as it is for flowers to bloom in the spring or snow to fall in winter. This is just one of many phases you'll go through. Like a brilliant sun rising at dawn, adolescence marks your entry into a new stage of life.

The agonies of love, too, are many and varied. Each person has a unique character and personality, background and circumstances. No set rule applies equally to everyone. In addition, everyone is perfectly free to fall in love or be attracted to someone. Whom a person dates is also a matter of personal choice. Essentially, no one has any right to meddle in your private affairs.

As one who has many years of experience, however, I want to stress at the outset how important it is not to lose sight of pursuing your personal development.

The true purpose of your studies and participation in club or team activities is to build a foundation for a strong self. Your problems, too—be they a lack of self-confidence or a strained relationship with a friend—enable you to construct a solid core.

The same can be said about love. It should be a force that helps you expand your lives and bring forth your innate potential with fresh and dynamic vitality. That is the ideal, but, as the saying "love is blind" illustrates, people often lose all objectivity when they fall in love.

If the relationship you're in is causing your parents to worry or making you neglect your studies or engage in destructive behavior, then you and the person you're seeing are only being a negative influence and hindrance to each other. Neither of you will be happy if you both end up hurting each other.

I'm sure the mother of the student you mentioned earlier had such concerns. They are the expressions of a parent's heart—all the more so when it comes to parents of daughters.

*The bottom line, then, is not to lose sight of the fundamental goal of developing lives that are truly valuable and meaningful.*

*A student told me: "Having someone you really like makes each day so much more exciting. I think liking someone is wonderful, and if that person inspires you to grow, it's even better."*

The question is: Does the person you like inspire you to work harder at your studies or distract you from them? Does her presence make you more determined to devote greater energies to school activities, be a better friend, a more thoughtful son or daughter? Does he inspire you to realize your future goals and work to achieve them? Or is that person your central focus, overshadowing all else—your school activities, your friends and family and even your goals?

If you are neglecting the things you should be doing, forgetting your purpose in life because of the relationship you're in, then you're on the wrong path. A healthy relationship is one in which two people encourage each other to reach their respective goals while sharing each other's hopes and dreams. A relationship should be a source of inspiration, invigoration and hope.

## DANTE'S UNREQUITED LOVE

Dante Alighieri (1265–1321), one of the greatest Western poets, had as his source of inspiration a young woman named Beatrice, whom he loved from afar since childhood. One day, after years spent apart, the eighteen-year-old Dante ran into her on the street. He later composed a poetic work about his joy at that encounter, titled "La Vita Nuova" (The New Life). In his struggle to convey his feelings for the young woman, he created a new poetic form. Without a doubt, Beatrice unlocked Dante's artistic potential.

She would remain, however, an unrequited love, for she married another man and then died at an early age. But Dante never ceased loving her. Ultimately, that love enabled him to strengthen, elevate and deepen the capacity of his heart into something truly noble and sublime. In his masterpiece, *The Divine Comedy*, Dante depicts Beatrice as a gentle, benevolent being who guides him to heaven.

Of course, Dante lived in a different age and a different country from us. But I think many things are to be learned from this great poet who stayed true to his feelings, whether they were reciprocated or not, and transformed them into his guiding inspiration in life. I truly believe that love must be a positive impetus for our lives, the driving force that rouses us to live courageously.

*One high school student sent a letter to the* Koko Shimpo *[the Soka Gakkai's high school division newspaper in Japan], in which she wrote: "There's an older student in a class above me that I like and respect very much. One of my girlfriends told me I should stick to respect and forget about love. I'm not completely satisfied with her answer, but I don't know what I should do."*

There is no set answer. There are as many views on love as there are people. So I don't think we can find a blanket policy on love that will win everyone's consensus. Love is a complex matter that reflects each person's attitude and philosophy toward life. That is why I believe people shouldn't get involved in relationships lightly. It is like the saying, "Love is not a game."

Nevertheless, I understand how this student feels, not being satisfied with merely respecting the young man on whom she has a crush. If love could be explained logically, all the agonizing it causes would vanish from the world. Nonetheless, the bottom line is that, without respect, no relationship will last for very long, nor can two people bring out the best in each other.

The late Chinese premier Zhou Enlai and his wife, Madame Deng Yingchao, were admired far and wide as a model couple. Though sadly both have died, they always treated my wife and me warmly.

## LOOKING AHEAD TOGETHER

When her husband died, Madame Deng placed the words *Zhou Enlai, comrade-in-arms* next to his coffin. "Comrade in arms"—what profound feelings that contains. It speaks volumes about their mutual commitment, the respect they had for each other as comrades and their side-by-side struggle for the realization of a great goal. Perhaps their example will offer those of you who are contemplating love something to think about.

Rather than becoming so lovestruck that you create a world where only the two of you exist, it is much healthier to learn from those aspects of your partner that you respect and admire and continue to make efforts to improve and develop yourself. Antoine de Saint-Exupéry, the author of *The Little Prince*, once wrote, "Love is not two people gazing at each other, but two people looking ahead together in the same direction."[1] It follows then that relationships last longer when both partners share similar values and beliefs.

Men, too, must respect women as individuals. Doing so is a sign of maturity.

I once heard that a female student from a neighboring Asian country remarked: "Japanese men don't take women seriously. They lack the maturity to respect women as human beings."

*On television and in magazines, love is frequently depicted as the ultimate goal in life or, to the other extreme, as some kind of game or casual diversion.*

*The media treats women as sex objects—products to be packaged and sold. And they single out the most extreme stories to sensationalize. For example, there are never articles on such topics as "High School Girls Study Hard," but the media goes crazy for a story like "High School Girls Patronize Telephone-Dating Clubs!"*

*Swayed by the media and peer pressure, many young people seem to be in a hurry to start dating. They may feel they are missing out if they don't have a boyfriend or girlfriend when everyone else around them does.*

There's no need to be influenced by such superficial trends. Please don't get caught up in doing something just because everyone else is.

The behavior of some of the media and other negative influences that prey on youth reflects a warped adult society that exploits young people for profit without a thought for their happiness.

It is so important that you see these things for what they are and not be deceived by them. Your youth is precious. Each of you is valuable beyond measure. It is foolish to become a puppet of media manipulation. I hope you will resolutely follow your own path in life.

Furthermore, please don't succumb to the view that love is the be-all and end-all, deluding yourselves that, as long as you are in love, nothing else matters. Nor, I hope, will you buy into the misguided notion that sinking ever deeper into a painful relationship is somehow romantic.

When asked what was most important in this world, a well-known philosopher responded that it is "normality, common sense and reason."

There is a time for everything in life—a time to be young, a time to enter the adult world, a time to get married and so on. Moving forward step by step into each different phase accords with reason.

All too often, when a relationship ends, the great passion it once inspired seems nothing more than an illusion. The things you learn through studying, on the other hand, are much more permanent. It is important, therefore, that you never extinguish the flame of your intellectual curiosity.

Please don't live without direction but, rather, pursue lives of meaning and purpose. Just as a house will be uninhabitable if its foundations are laid carelessly, or as certain types of rice won't cook properly if they haven't been washed, it's clear what kind of results you can expect if you take shortcuts or neglect to make proper efforts. In that respect, it is certainly not wise to try to act like adults before you can properly look after yourselves.

The important thing is for you to do your very best in the endeavors you have to concentrate on now. Through such efforts, you will grow into individuals who have truly wonderful futures ahead of you. I hope you will not sell yourselves short and stifle your vast and limitless potential before it even has a chance to bloom. Far too many people nip their brilliant promise in the bud because of their blind pursuit of love.

*Some people start out with a clear idea of what they want to do in the future, the kind of work they want to pursue, but then get swept away by the excitement of love. Finally, when they come to their senses, they realize they've missed their chance to achieve their goal and are totally lost as to what to do.*

Much of daily life tends to be ordinary and unexciting. Making steady efforts day to day can be trying. It's not always going to be fun. But, when you fall in love, life seems filled with drama and excitement; you feel like the leading character in a novel.

If you get lost in love just because you're bored, though, and consequently veer from the path you should be following, then love is nothing more than escapism. What you are doing is retreating into a dream world, believing that what is only an illusion is actually real.

If you try to use love as an escape, the euphoria is unlikely to last long. If anything, you may only find yourselves with even more problems—along with a great deal of pain and sadness. However much we may try, we can never run away from ourselves. If we remain weak, suffering will follow us wherever we go. We will never find happiness if we don't change ourselves from within.

Happiness is not something that someone else, like a lover, can give to us. We have to achieve it for ourselves. And the only way to do so is by developing our character and capacity as human beings—by fully maximizing our potential. If we sacrifice our growth and talent for love, we absolutely will not find happiness. True happiness is obtained through fully realizing our potential.

While in your teens, your scope of experience is still quite limited, and you may not yet have found the area in which your talents are best suited. It's easy to fall into the trap of thinking that nothing could be more desirable than love. But there is more to life than love. Particularly in the case of women, I feel, real happiness is determined after they enter their forties and onward.

Let me also add here that to embark on a relationship simply as an escape is extremely disrespectful to both your partner and yourself.

In any event, the point is not to be in a hurry. You are young. What's important now is to work hard at developing into truly wonderful human beings.

## Work on Polishing Yourself First

Each of you has a precious mission that only you can fulfill. Suffering people around the world are waiting for your brave endeavors. To neglect your mission and seek only personal pleasure is a sign of selfishness. It is impossible for an egotistic, self-centered individual to truly love another person.

On the other hand, if you genuinely love someone, then through your relationship with him or her, you can develop into a person whose love extends to all humanity. Such a relationship serves to strengthen, elevate and enrich your inner realm of life. Ultimately, the relationships you form are a reflection of your own state of life.

The same is true of friendship. Only to the extent that you polish yourselves now can you hope to develop wonderful bonds of the heart in the future.

*Some members are concerned about friends who are only hurting themselves by living for momentary thrills. There is a growing attitude among young people that as long as two people like each other, anything goes.*

*One student told me she thinks boys are selfish and deceitful. The fact is, some boys are only out to use girls. So girls have to be on their guard and cultivate their powers of wisdom and judgment in order to see through such people.*

*Although this doesn't apply to all cases, some people worry when they see female high school students dating older men, like college students; they are concerned that such relationships are not in the young women's best interests. And indeed, all too often such relationships do end up with the young women being hurt emotionally and, perhaps, even physically.*

Some young women prove extremely vulnerable to the insistent advances of the opposite sex. They act as though stunned and lose their ability to make calm, rational decisions. It is precisely for this reason that young women must develop inner strength and self-respect. Since they are the ones who most often get hurt, they have every right to assert their dignity and look after their welfare. And if the young man in question does not respect this right, then he isn't worth being with.

With some people, however, once they have gotten into a relationship, they have a hard time saying "no" to the other person for fear it will be taken as a lack of commitment. In such cases, love becomes like riding in a car with no brakes. Sometimes, even if you want to get out, you cannot; even if you regret having gotten in, the car won't stop. People often get involved in relationships thinking they are free and independent but at some point find they have become captive to the relationship.

Each of you is infinitely precious. Therefore, I hope you will treat yourselves with utmost respect. Please do not follow a path that will cause you suffering; rather, take the road that is best for your well-being.

The truth is, ideal love is fostered only between two sincere, mature and independent people. It is essential, therefore, that each of you work on polishing yourself first.

*Sometimes, in a relationship, one person tries to become or do whatever the other wants in order to avoid losing him or her.*

It is demeaning to constantly seek your partner's approval. Such relationships are bereft of real caring, depth or even love. For those of you who find yourselves in relationships where you are not treated the way your heart says you should be, I hope you will have the courage and dignity to decide that you are better off risking the scorn of your partner than enduring unhappiness with him or her.

Real love is not two people clinging to each other; it can only be fostered between two strong people secure in their individuality. A shallow person will have only shallow relationships. If you want to experience real love, it is important to first sincerely develop a strong self-identity.

True love is not about doing whatever the other person wants you to do or pretending you are something you're not. If someone genuinely loves you, that person will not force you to do anything against your will or embroil you in some dangerous activity.

Furthermore, I personally want to see men be extremely courteous and caring toward women. Men should always remember to respect women, doing their utmost to support them. Rather than depending on women like children, men should become strong enough, compassionate enough and adult enough to care about the lifelong happiness of their partners as their top priority. This is the quality men must strive to cultivate; it is also an expression of true love.

To the young men, I say: Please think when the time comes for you to become a parent and have a daughter of your own. If she were to fall in love, how would you like to see her treated? If you cannot imagine this kind of scenario, then you are not yet qualified for love.

As for those who are concerned about their friends' well-being, the best thing is to chant Nam-myoho-renge-kyo and be there for them. I think it's important for everyone to have at least one person with whom they can talk about anything. In matters concerning love, it is to your benefit to accept that you are not necessarily the best judge of your situation and have the wisdom to turn to others for their objective opinions and advice.

It's fine to keep some things to yourselves, but please remember that sometimes secrets may hurt you. I am especially concerned about those who have closed themselves off from their friends.

No matter how much you may appear to be enjoying yourselves now, or how serious you think you are about your relationship, if you allow your love life to consume all your time and energy to the detriment of your growth, then you're just playing a game. And if you're always playing games, then your life will be just that, a game.

Regardless of how large a number is, if multiplied by zero, it will inevitably come to zero. To have a relationship that wipes out the value in your life is truly sad.

# Never Allow Yourself To Be Blinded, Injured or Defeated by Love

*Some people are plunged into deep despair and lose all meaning in life when a relationship ends or their hearts are broken. Some take the rejection as a personal negation of everything they stand for and feel as if they have no value or worth left as human beings.*

Many people can probably relate to such feelings. But you are only letting yourselves down if you succumb to unhealthy obsessions in your youth or are so blinded by love that you cannot see anything else. No matter what, you must always do your best to live courageously. You mustn't be weak-hearted. Youth is a time for advancing bravely into the future. You must not veer off course, fall behind or hide in the shadows.

Youth is not a time for pessimism, self-pity or sadness. Such a mind-set is for losers. Please have the confidence and fortitude to think to yourselves when you face rejection, "It's their loss if they cannot appreciate how wonderful I am!" This is the kind of resilient spirit you must strive to cultivate.

John D. Rockefeller (1839–1937), the American industrialist and philanthropist who built an unprecedented fortune, was such a person. In his younger days, when he was poor, he proposed marriage to his first love, but she turned him down. The reason, in retrospect, is most amusing: The young woman's mother wouldn't allow her daughter to marry someone whose prospects did not seem very bright. This is another case in point of how difficult it is to correctly evaluate others' potential. But rather than feeling depressed, this rejection seems to have been just the thing to inspire young Rockefeller. Please don't let a broken heart discourage you. Tell yourselves that you're not so weak or fragile as to let such a minor thing bring you down. You may think no one could possibly compare to the one you are interested in, but how will he or she compare to the next hundred, the next thousand, the next ten thousand people you will meet? You cannot declare with certainty that there won't be others who far surpass him or her. As you grow, the way you look at people will change as well.

I'm sure quite a few among you have had your hearts broken or been badly hurt and perhaps felt unable to go on, your self-esteem in tatters. But you must never believe that you are worthless. There is no substitute for you, who are more precious than all the treasures in the universe. No matter what your present circumstances, I think of all of you as my irreplaceable sons and daughters, and I have the greatest expectation that you will overcome all obstacles and rise out of any suffering and despair.

It is crucial that you become strong. If you are strong, even your sadness will become a source of nourishment, and the things that make you suffer will purify your lives.

Only when we experience the crushing, painful depths of suffering can we begin to understand the true meaning of life. Precisely because we have experienced great suffering, it is imperative that we go on living.

The important thing is to keep moving forward. If each of you uses your sadness as a source of growth, you will become a person of greater depth and breadth—an even more wonderful you. This is the harvest of your pain and suffering.

Hold your head high. Because you have lived with all your might, you are victors. You must not sink into depression or take a path that leads to self-destruction.

*I have heard the saying: "If you are sad, cry. Cry until your tears have washed away all the pain." It's like crossing a river of suffering. Those who have done so have a depth and radiance unknown to those who are strangers to such experience. The thing is not to drown in the river.*

Whether we are happy, sad or suffering, if we chant honestly to the Gohonzon with the feelings in our hearts, our lives will naturally proceed in the best direction.

*One member told me she was worried about a friend who is so desperately afraid of being on her own that when she breaks up with one boyfriend, she immediately goes out and finds a new one.*

People have the freedom to live as they chose, and each person's character is different. Nevertheless, I think it's a shame to spend your youth constantly chasing the opposite sex.

If you're going to fall in love, wouldn't it be wonderful to have one great love that lasts a lifetime? And how much more wonderful would it be if that love led to marriage? Of course, this won't always happen. Nevertheless, it is unfair to both you and the other person if you enter a relationship having already decided that it is just for fun, putting casual relationships in one box and serious relationships or even marriage in a completely separate one.

I'm sure you still have many questions, but the fact is that a future of unlimited possibilities lies before you. There is no need to rush into anything; you don't need to be in a hurry to grow up. If there is someone you like, what's wrong with holding on to that feeling inside your heart for a while and resolving to polish yourself so that you can become the kind of person he or she, or anyone, would be proud to be with? Such a spirit of self-development is most admirable, I feel.

Whether or not that person ever learns how you feel in your heart, with time those feelings will grow and mature like a fine wine. When you become an adult, the memories of your youth will envelop you like a beautiful fragrance.

I truly feel that these experiences are the means by which you will all become people of great depth and character.

1. Antoine de Saint-Exupéry, *Wind, Sand and Stars*, trans. Lewis Galantiére (San Diego: Harcourt, Brace & Company, 1939), p. 215.

# 5

## FINDING HAPPINESS IN YOUR WORK

*Today, we'd like to ask about employment and careers. Everyone has hopes for the future. Some want to become diplomats and others, kindergarten teachers. Some dream of becoming computer programmers, singers, journalists fighting for a just cause, welfare workers, refugee relief workers, makeup artists, cartoonists or educators able to awaken great hopes and aspirations in their students.*

*And among those who say they know what they want to do in the future, I'm sure some are working hard to realize their dreams, while others aren't taking any concrete steps toward attaining them.*

*Some students aren't sure if they want to do the kind of work their parents want them to do, or if they have what it takes to do what they want to do. I've also heard comments like, "I'm not interested in anything in particular, but I'd like to be famous in some area and be in the spotlight" or "My dreams keep changing with every new person I meet." Some have also said to me, "I get scared sometimes because I have no idea what I want to do in the future."*

Life is long. The real result of your daily efforts will be revealed in your forties, fifties and sixties. So it is important that each of you find something—it doesn't matter what—with which to challenge yourself while young. Regard youth as the time to study and train yourself.

We each have a unique mission that only we can fulfill. But that doesn't mean you should simply wait for someone to tell you what yours is, doing nothing until then. It is fundamental that you discover your mission on your own.

Precious gems start out buried underground. If no one mines them, they'll stay buried. And if they aren't polished once they've been dug out, they will remain in the rough.

All of you, high school division members, have a rare jewel in your lives. You are each like a mountain concealing a precious gem. What a shame it would be to end your lives without having uncovered this inner jewel. So when parents or teachers tell you to study hard, they are saying in effect, "Unearth the jewel in your life and polish it!"

Of course, studying is but one means by which to reveal your inner gem. So please don't evaluate yourselves based solely on the grades you get. Human potential is not so limited that it can be measured merely by one's aptitude for rote learning.

It has been said recently that one's emotional intelligence quotient (EQ) can be more important than one's IQ (intelligence quotient).[1] This attests to the importance of such broad-ranging human qualities as empathy and a fighting spirit, which no IQ test can gauge. For this reason, it is foolish to think that your grades at sixteen or eighteen will determine the rest of your lives. There's much more to human potential than that.

The problem is when you fall into the trap of thinking that grades are the be-all and end-all and decide that your present grades doom you to a less-than-bright future. If you think this way, you will keep yourselves from nurturing those abilities you have. If you give up on trying to mine the gem in your lives, your development will cease. This is something to avoid at all costs.

Some get accepted at universities but fail to work hard once there. Others stop striving for personal growth after entering a big company or becoming bureaucrats, doctors or lawyers. Many people, achieving the careers they aimed for, forget the spirit to work for others. Such people give thought only to what they want to become—not to what they can contribute to society. Actually, achieving such goals is just the beginning, not the final destination.

*Some students believe they are incapable because their grades are poor. Others think they no longer need to make efforts once they've landed a great job. You're saying that both of these attitudes are wrong.*

Exactly. People should constantly strive to unearth the jewel in their lives and polish it. There are countless examples of people who did not stand out in high school but who struck a rich deposit of hidden potential when they entered society and gained life experience. Therefore, getting a job is just the starting point in uncovering your true ability; it is absolutely not the final goal. There is no need to be impatient. It is important that you make your way up the mountain of life steadily, without rushing or giving up.

For those of you who have already decided what you want to do in the future, I would like for you to forge ahead purposefully. You mustn't be halfhearted. When you pursue something with a strong determination, you will have no regrets, even should you fail. And if you succeed, you can achieve truly great things. Whether you fail or succeed in achieving a specific goal, your steady efforts will lead you to your next path.

For those of you not yet decided on your future course, please concentrate your energies on what you need to accomplish right now. You will discover your path as you keep searching, chanting earnestly to find your direction and seeking advice and guidance from those around you.

## Make a Habit of Exerting Your Utmost

*Some people tell me they have no special talents.*

That just isn't true. The problem lies in people limiting themselves. A saying goes that everyone has some kind of gift. Being talented doesn't mean just being a good musician, writer or athlete—there are many kinds of talent. For instance, you may be a great conversationalist or make friends easily or put others at ease. Or you may have a gift for nursing, a knack for telling jokes, selling things or economizing. You may be always punctual, patient, reliable, kind or optimistic. Or you may love new challenges, be strongly committed to peace or bring joy to others.

Each of us is as unique as a cherry, plum, peach or damson blossom (see OTT, 200), as Nichiren Daishonin explains. Cherry blossoms and plum blossoms possess their own distinct wonder; accordingly, you must bloom in the way that only you can.

Without a doubt, you each have your own jewel, your own innate talent within you. How can you discover that talent? The only way is to exert yourselves to the limit of your ability. Your true potential will emerge when you give everything you've got to your studies, sports or whatever you take on.

The important thing is that you get into the habit of challenging yourselves to the utmost. In a sense, the results you get are not so important. The actual grades you receive in high school, for instance, won't decide the rest of your lives. But the habit of pushing yourselves to the limit will in time bear fruit. It will distinguish you from others without fail. It will bring your unique talent to shine.

There is a saying that people will not exceed their dreams. That is why you should have big dreams. But you must recognize that dreams are dreams and reality is reality. It's natural, therefore, that to achieve big dreams, you must view your situation realistically and work with your entire being to see that they come true.

Second Soka Gakkai president Josei Toda once said, "It is vital for youth to have the tenacity to become the very best at something." Tenacity is crucial. You cannot make the gem inside your life shine with easygoing efforts.

*High school students in Japan seem to have a very narrow view of what work is all about. Television portrays a good job as one where you wear nice suits, carry a cellular phone and use computers. And many students want to become television celebrities or musicians. It's difficult to know what a good profession really is.*

For those who just cannot decide what kind of work you'd like to do, why not start out with a job you can get easily, something you are familiar with? That way you can gain practical experience and find out what you're good at.

Many young people may be under the impression that it is better to work for a large corporation or a government agency than for a small, unexciting business. But often this is not the case. There are so many things you just won't understand until you actually start working. Plus, there are as many kinds of companies as there are people.

Therefore, it is important to have the inner strength and common sense to learn everything you can where you are, to develop the means by which to support yourselves, to pursue substance rather than the ephemeral, and to explore the depths of your potential. It is vital that you become irreplaceable wherever you are.

I once heard the following story: In the nineteenth century, the president of France was invited to a banquet sponsored by a wealthy countryman. Strangely enough, the French leader found himself seated not as the guest of honor but sixteenth from the head of the table. A railroad engineer occupied the first seat; a literary scholar, the second; and a science professor sat in the third.

A guest, puzzled by the seating order, asked the host why. The response was: "The guests have been seated according to their true importance. By people of true importance, I mean those who possess an outstanding ability and cannot be replaced by anyone else." In other words, because the guest of honor was the world's foremost authority on trains, he was irreplaceable. The guests occupying the second and third seats were also leading experts in their fields. The president, however, could be replaced: Someone else could take over his job.

Whether this story is true or not, it takes a truly mature society to openly spread such frank, candid ideas.

I want you, the high school division members, to become people who support society not in name but in substance. I also hope you will create a society that cherishes such people.

At any rate, we have to make a living to survive. That's why jobs exist. Such is the way of society; it is the way life goes.

You have the right to decide what type of job you want to do; the choices are open. Having said that, however, many jobs do require a certain level of academic qualification and experience.

Some people start working right out of high school, either by choice or because of their family situation. Others join the work force after graduating from college, while others become homemakers. Some people aim to become public servants, and still others strive to gain technical proficiency in some field. The bottom line is that there are many different options, all of which you are at liberty to choose from.

# A JOB OF VALUE

*What criteria should we go by when looking for a job?*

The Japanese poet Takuboku Ishikawa (1886–1912) once penned this verse, which I recorded in my notes when I was young: "Would that I had a vocation / To carry out with joy / Once I have fulfilled it / I wish to die." He is talking about his mission, the work he was born for.

However, few people are fortunate to find their ideal job at the outset. Sometimes the career you wish to pursue may differ from the ideas your parents or others in your life have for you. In such a situation, what are you to do?

President Toda once said the criteria for selecting a job could be found in *The Philosophy of Value*, a philosophical treatise by his mentor, the founding Soka Gakkai president, Tsunesaburo Makiguchi. Mr. Toda upheld the path of mentor and disciple throughout his life.

Mr. Makiguchi taught that there are three kinds of value: beauty, benefit and good. In the working world, the value of beauty means to find a job you like; the value of benefit is to get a job that earns you a salary that can support your daily life; the value of good means to find a job that helps others and contributes to society.

Mr. Toda once said, "Everyone's ideal is to get a job they like (beauty), that offers financial security (benefit), where they can contribute to society (good)."

*I couldn't agree more.*

But not many can find the perfect job from the start. Some may have a job they like, but it isn't putting food on the table; or their job pays well, but they hate it. That's the way things go sometimes. Also, some discover that they're just not cut out for the career they dreamed of and aspired to.

President Toda said that the most important thing is to first become indispensable wherever you are. Instead of moaning that a job differs from what you'd like to be doing, he said, become a first-class individual at that job. This will open the path leading to your next phase in life, during which you should also continue doing your best. Such continuous efforts are guaranteed to land you a job that you like, that supports your life and that allows you to contribute to society.

Then, when you look back later, you will see how all your past efforts have become precious assets in your ideal field. You will realize that none of your efforts and hardships have been wasted. Mr. Toda taught that this is the great benefit of the Mystic Law.

## Excel at Something!

*What about those who set out to achieve one dream, then have a change of heart and pursue a different path?*

That's perfectly all right. Few people started out with the ambition of doing what they're doing.

My experience was that I wanted to be a newspaper reporter, but my poor health prevented me. Today, however, I have become a writer who can hold his own in the literary world.

At one point, I worked for a small publishing company. Because of its limited personnel, I had to work very hard—but to the extent that I did, I gained practical experience.

After the war, I worked for the Kamata Industries Association [established in 1946 for the promotion of small- to medium-sized businesses in Kamata, Ota Ward, Tokyo]. It, too, was a small operation, but what I went through on that job gave me a chance to really look at myself. Everything I learned back then is of value to my life now. The important thing is to develop yourselves in your present situations, to take control of your growth.

Once you have decided on a job, I hope you will not be the kind of people who quit at the drop of a hat and are always insecure and complaining. Nevertheless, if after you've given it your all you decide that your job isn't right for you and you move on, that's perfectly all right, too. My concern is that you don't forget you are responsible for your environment when you make your decision.

Taking your place as a member of society is a challenge; it is a struggle to survive. But wherever you are is exactly where you need to be, so you must strive there to the best of your ability.

A tree doesn't grow strong and tall within one or two days. In the same way, successful people didn't get to where they are in only one or two years. This applies to everything.

There is a saying that urges us, "Excel at something!" It is important to become trusted by others wherever you are, to shine with excellence. Sometimes people may dislike their job at first but grow to love it once they become serious about doing their best. "What one likes, one will do well," goes another saying. Growing to like your job can also enable you to develop your talent. Once you have decided to work at a certain place, it is important that you pursue the path you have chosen without being discouraged or defeated, so that you will have no regrets over making that choice.

*Some students say, "I just want to get into a big-name company."*

Each of us is free to select where we'd like to work. I hope those students will work very hard to achieve their goals. Japan, however, is in the midst of an economic recession; the outlook isn't good. What's more, Japan has one of the largest budget deficits in the world, and its system of lifetime employment is breaking down. Companies once considered prestigious no longer guarantee security, while educational background alone no longer assures a good job. These days even large companies go under. People won't be protected just because they work for a company with a big name. That's the reality today.

So what, then, is important? The answer is true capability. It is vital to develop all kinds of strengths and abilities, such as an inquisitive mind, specialist skills, mental strength and flexibility.

Study is a lifelong endeavor; just graduating from university isn't enough. Someone once said that we learn only about 10 percent of what we need in life from college, no matter how prestigious the school.

There are also some people who never go to college and others who go back to school later in life. You can also participate in a correspondence program like the one at Soka University.

All of you face the challenge of triumphing in a society that stresses real ability more than ever.

*Some have friends who, given the choice, wouldn't work at all, or who only want easy jobs and won't take on work if it's strenuous or requires getting dirty, or who go to college because they don't want to look for a job right away.*

*Some view work as an unpleasant chore they must do to earn money to support their leisure activities.*

I'm not going to criticize this line of thinking. However, I will share with you words of the Russian novelist Maxim Gorky (1868–1936) from his play *The Lower Depths*, in which one of his characters says: "When work is a pleasure, life is a joy! When work is a duty, life is slavery."[2] Your attitude toward work, which takes up the better part of your day, decisively determines your quality of life.

Dr. David Norton, the late professor of philosophy at the University of Delaware, once observed that many students are caught up in the notion that the only purpose of employment is to earn money, that happiness means having money to gratify their desires. But since there is no limit to those desires, they can never truly be satisfied. Real happiness is found in working. Through work, one can develop and fulfill oneself and bring forth the unique value that lies within—and share that value with society. Work exists for the joy of creating value.

It is just as Dr. Norton says. Someone else has pointed out that a person's work should bring happiness to others. Life is truly wonderful when you're needed somewhere. How boring and empty life would be if, for instance, just because we had the means, all we did every day was pursue idle diversions.

*I think people can gain something much more valuable than money from working.*

Yes. It's natural to work if you earn a salary; work is essentially a contract between employer and employee. But to slack off at work just because the salary isn't high is foolish.

Moreover, all of you are young. It might even be a good idea to have the spirit to do more than you are paid to do. This is how you can train yourselves.

To receive a salary—compensation earned through honest labor—is precious, regardless of the amount. Of course, there's nothing better than receiving a good salary, but one hundred dollars earned through hard work is a golden treasure. That same one hundred dollars, though, if stolen or acquired through other illicit means, has no more value than dung or rubble. Stolen or extorted money is dirty. It will not bring happiness. As the saying goes, "Ill gotten, ill spent."

There are some who once enjoyed great prestige as influential government officials but who accepted bribes and consequently must live the rest of their lives labeled as criminals.

Depending on one's state of life, money can be used toward either ill-intentioned or noble ends. The state of one's heart can change everything.

Ultimately, the greatest happiness is found in applying yourselves with confidence and wisdom in your workplaces as exemplary members of society, working hard to achieve fulfilling lives and the well-being of your families. Those who do so are victors in life.

## Become Liked and Trusted at Work

*Some people worry about how they will get along with their co-workers upon entering a company.*

Certainly, when working in a company—which is like a society or community all its own—it is important to create harmonious relations with your colleagues and superiors, using wisdom and discretion along the way. If you incur your co-workers' dislike by being selfish or egotistic, you will be a loser in work and society. Wisdom is vital to being successful at work.

Nichiren writes, "The wise may be called human, but the thought-less are no more than animals" (WND-1, 852).

Society, in many ways, is filled with contradictions. Some parts are quite ugly, and others are pretty harsh at times. I hope you will not take a complacent attitude toward such things and let society get the better of you. If that happens, then, no matter what excuses you make, defeat is defeat. Each of you must forge your way adeptly through the rough seas of society, always keeping your head above water.

President Makiguchi said there are three types of people in the world: those you want to have around, those whose presence or absence doesn't make a difference and those whose presence causes problems. Please become people others appreciate having around. This means becoming liked and trusted at work. Also, you mustn't forget to do your best. This is the correct way of life for believers in Nichiren Buddhism, which teaches that Buddhahood is eternally inherent in our lives.

*Many students say they want to work for world peace or promote the human-istic principles of Nichiren Buddhism through their work and have asked what kind of job they should do.*

Aspiring to devote oneself to a humanistic cause, to upholding human rights and spreading the ideals of Buddhism out of a desire to work for the people's happiness and welfare, is a truly laudable ambition.

That does not mean, however, that you cannot contribute to peace unless you are in some special profession. Of course, while I highly commend anyone who wishes to work for the United Nations or become a volunteer worker overseas, there are many people striving for peace in their own, humble specialties.

I have met many such people, like Argentina's Dr. Adolfo Pérez Esquivel, a sculptor and architect who won the Nobel Peace Prize as well as the 1996 Global Citizen Award of the Boston Research Center for the 21st Century,[3] for his activities to protect human rights. And Rosa Parks, the mother of the American civil rights movement, who was working as a tailor's assistant in a department store when she became the catalyst for the famous bus boycott in Montgomery, Alabama, in 1955.

The main thing is to be proud of your work and your capacity, to live true to yourselves. Many revolutionaries throughout history have lost their lives in the struggle for reformation. Theirs, too, was a worthy vocation.

At any rate, I want each of you to be active in all fields. Activity is another name for happiness. What's important is that you give free, unfettered play to your unique talents, that each of you live with the full radiance of your being. This is what it means to be truly alive.

World peace and widespread understanding of the humanistic ideals of Nichiren Buddhism will be achieved by each of you excelling in your respective fields.

1. See Daniel Coleman, *Emotional Intelligence: Why It Can Matter More Than IQ* (New York: Bantam Books, 1995), front matter.

2. Maxim Gorky, *The Lower Depths and Other Plays*, trans. Alexander Bakshy and Paul S. Nathan (Chelsea, Michigan: Yale University Press, 1945), p. 14.

3. The Boston Research Center for the 21st Century changes its name to the Ikeda Center for Peace, Learning, and Dialogue on July 3, 2009.

# 6

## WHAT IS A GLOBAL CITIZEN?

Let's continue our discussion. Today's topic is what it means to be a global citizen.

*Yes. Today, we've invited an official SGI Japanese-English interpreter to join us.*

*To this question, high school students most frequently replied that a global citizen is a person fluent in a foreign language. Other answers included a person who can easily make friends with people from other countries, one who doesn't assume that the values of one's own nation apply everywhere else in the world, and someone who can adopt a global perspective, looking beyond the boundaries of their ethnicity.*

*Some students also identified as international a person who has direct connections with other nations, as well as anyone who is confident and self-assertive and can view things fairly and objectively.*

Those are excellent responses. I agree with all of them. But I'd like to add that all those working for kosen-rufu, people like your parents, for example, are also truly global citizens. They are praying earnestly for the happiness of all humanity and selflessly working for the sake of others.

In spite of their busy day-to-day schedules, they are studying Nichiren Buddhism, a great universal philosophy. Even if they never leave their countries, such people are respected around the globe. Such a way of life is an inspiration to people everywhere. The international praise and recognition bestowed on the SGI demonstrate my point.

*The many awards and honorary degrees you have received are certainly proof of that, aren't they?*

I accept those awards and honors as a representative of your mothers and fathers. When I receive such awards, it is just as if they were being conferred on them. In effect, people all around the world are applauding their efforts and achievements.

INTERPRETER: I have traveled to many countries, and I'm always astonished at the high expectations people have for the SGI. In 1996, I went to India as a member of an SGI youth delegation. When we visited the president of the West Bengal Federation of the United Nations Association, one official said out of the blue: "I always read SGI President Ikeda's annual peace proposals with great interest.' Why don't we discuss them today?" He asked us to tell him more about President Ikeda's philosophy. I was surprised at this because it was not part of the agenda.

*I think people who feel a sense of responsibility toward the world's future can understand those who are earnestly taking action based on the same concern.*

Your parents and seniors in the SGI never sought fame or honors, nor did they seek ease or comfort. They simply remained true to the principles they believed in, devoting their energy to working for the happiness of others along with themselves. That is the noblest life a person can live. The foremost requirement to be a true global citizen is outstanding character.

*People deficient in such human qualities, even if they are proficient in a foreign language, can never hope to win respect or admiration, no matter where they go in the world. People are more likely to dismiss such people.*

Of course, language ability is important; but remember that language is only a means, not an end. What matters is the use to which you put this ability.

I have heard the opinion many times that Japanese people lack altruism. This must change. Not only will other nations not trust us, but we will isolate ourselves from others and become spiritually impoverished.

To work for the welfare of people and society is the most basic path of humanism. Yet this is something today's Japanese educational system fails to teach. Your fathers and mothers in the SGI, however, are doing just that. They are truly noble.

*So, essentially, to become a global citizen, you must develop your character and humanity.*

When I visited the United Kingdom, someone remarked offhandedly, "When a bomb drops, the British rush to see if anyone is hurt, but the Japanese run away from the scene." Another commented, "The Japanese believe everything they hear, but people from other countries think seeing is believing."

Many Japanese people seem to lack independence and a solid sense of self. They accept things at face value without thinking for themselves or acting on their convictions. They appear to be more worried about how they will look, what others will think and how it will affect their standing.

INTERPRETER: A diplomat posted in Japan once told me he really disliked the way Japanese people changed their attitude toward him when they learned of his position. Apparently, on weekends, he would dress casually, go fishing or eat at small local restaurants with the desire to get to know the people. Of course, he never mentioned to anyone he met on these excursions that he was a diplomat.

At a restaurant, he once had a long, interesting talk with a fellow diner. After the meal, the Japanese man insisted on exchanging business cards. Reluctantly, the diplomat agreed. When the man saw he was a high-ranking diplomat, he began apologizing so vehemently that it seemed he might drop to the floor and start groveling right there. The diplomat was both surprised and saddened to discover how far Japanese education still has to go.

*That's a telling story.*

It is time that Japan becomes a country of more broad-minded, open people.

There is a famous story about Chiune Sugihara (1900–86), who helped Jewish refugees escape the Holocaust during World War II. In 1940, when the Nazis were exterminating European Jews, Mr. Sugihara was vice consul at the Japanese Consulate in Lithuania. A wave of Jewish refugees from Poland, where Jews were being massacred, came to Mr. Sugihara to apply for transit visas to pass through Japan to a third country.

Mr. Sugihara asked the Japanese Ministry of Foreign Affairs three times to give him the green light to issue the visas, but each time the ministry refused. He was deeply troubled but finally came to a decision: "I couldn't abandon those who have come to me for help. If I did, I would be turning my back on God."[2] So he ignored the orders and issued the visas, saving nearly six thousand lives.[3]

His wife, Sachiko, said: "The lives of all people are precious, irrespective of race. My husband believed it was not right for a human being to refuse to help those in need, especially when in a position to do something... Today Japan is wealthy and at peace. But I hope people will not grow complacent and forget to think about the rest of the world. If young people only think of their own enjoyment, Japan is bound to go downhill."[4]

*That is so true. Why do so many Japanese refuse to open their hearts and minds to the world around them?*

*I think problems within the Japanese educational system have a lot to do with it. Also, since the Meiji Restoration [1868], the Japanese have had a warped, unbalanced view of the rest of the world, having suffered from an inferiority complex toward Westerners while feeling superior to other Asians and Africans. As a result, we have failed to interact as equals with people of other nations.*

There are many different viewpoints on this subject. Without going into detail, I will share something that the Russian writer Leo Tolstoy said: "The religion of men who do not acknowledge religion is a religion of submission to everything which the vast majority does, that is, more briefly, the religion of obedience to the existing power."[5] By religion, I believe Tolstoy means philosophy in the broadest sense.

*Mr. Sugihara refused to obey those in authority in Japan because he felt that by failing to help those who came to him, he would be betraying his faith and most cherished beliefs.*

*He had the courage to act in accord with his conscience, with what he believed was right, no matter how severely he was pressured. That kind of courage comes from deep conviction, from the philosophy or religious beliefs one holds dear.*

## PHILOSOPHY MEANS TO STAND UP FOR YOUR PRINCIPLES

Philosophy might seem like a difficult topic, but what it really refers to is an intrinsic belief that cannot be compromised.

My mentor, Josei Toda, had an interesting perspective:

> Philosophy isn't as complicated or hard to understand as Descartes or Kant. Some may say they don't know anything about philosophy because they didn't go to university, but to philosophize is simply to think.
>
> One basic example of philosophy can be found in the travel diary of Mito Mitsukuni [a feudal-period lord who traveled throughout Japan in disguise, righting wrongs and defending the helpless]. During his travels, he once asked an old peasant woman for some water and then sat down on a bale of rice. The woman, not recognizing who he was, flew into a rage, saying that he was sitting on a bale of rice that was to go to Lord Mito. Abashed, Lord Mito bowed his head and apologized.
>
> It was an ironic situation, of course, but for the old peasant woman, proudly offering this rice she had carefully harvested to the lord of her domain was her philosophy.

> Philosophy comes down to standing up for the principles you believe in, no matter what.

Though thrown into prison by the military authorities, Mr. Toda refused to compromise his beliefs, holding fast to his commitment to peace. The same is true of the founding Soka Gakkai president, Tsunesaburo Makiguchi. Today their life-and-death struggles have earned them respect worldwide. Neither of them ever left Japan, but more than ninety years ago, Mr. Makiguchi declared himself a global citizen. And in the 1950s, Mr. Toda, focusing on the future of Asia and the entire world, spoke of humanity as a "global family."

The bottom line is that it makes no difference what a person's nationality is. The true global citizen can share, as a fellow human being, the sufferings and sadness as well as the happiness and joy of others. This person can unite with others to promote common human interests.

*I feel I'm getting a clearer picture of what it means to be a global citizen. Before, I shared the shallow interpretation of many in Japan—that being a global citizen means being fluent in a foreign language, outgoing, fashionable and sophisticated.*

*When you think about it, there's not much value in knowing a foreign language if one only uses it to hurt people.*

Keeping one's word is an important responsibility of a global citizen. Japanese politicians have a reputation for making promises when they visit other countries, then forgetting them as soon as they step back on Japanese soil. That's certainly no way to earn others' trust.

*I'm sure that the absolute trust and friendship that people outside Japan feel toward you, President Ikeda, is because you have always kept the promises you have made.*

Friendship is key. I have found that people in other countries treasure friendship far more deeply than most Japanese are aware. It is a core part of their lives. To never betray one's friendship, to nurture and develop strong, amicable ties—these are the qualities required of a global citizen.

Perhaps some among you think: "I hate studying foreign languages" or "What's being a global citizen got to do with me?" But, like it or not, in the coming century, when you take your place in society, the world is going to become even more integrated.

Egyptian President Hosni Mubarak shared with me the following observation by Poland's president: No country today can produce even a box of matches by itself. The matchstick comes from one nation, the sulfur from another, the box from another and the glue from yet another. Many, many countries must cooperate to produce even a single box of matches.

The globalization of goods and production is taking place incredibly swiftly, as is the globalization of information, especially with the growth of the Internet. For these reasons, the globalization of heart-to-heart, grassroots exchange is absolutely critical in guiding these rapid changes in the direction of peace. That is why the SGI is working to promote peace, culture and education around the world.

*I think it's precisely because such efforts are needed that the SGI is praised around the globe. The way many Japanese, on the other hand, unjustly criticize our movement—without even trying to understand it—is evidence of just how far behind Japan is in the process of internationalization.*

This is where the importance of language ability comes in. Proficiency in a foreign language is necessary so that all of you, who embrace a global philosophy, can play an active role on the international stage.

I have visited more than fifty nations and made friends in all of them. If you were to ask me what I regret the most, I would probably have to say not being able to converse with the leading figures of those various countries in their languages. In fact, when I was a young man, I realized the importance of gaining proficiency in a foreign language and made an effort to study English. But in wartime, English was the language of the "enemy." We weren't allowed to speak it in Japan.

After the war, I still suffered from tuberculosis. I started working for Mr. Toda, whose business was failing. In those days, I never seemed to have enough to eat. In fact, I was so thin my ribs stuck out, and I often coughed up blood. Even so, I poured all my energy into working for Mr. Toda, taking only a little time to sleep.

Under such circumstances, it was impossible for me to go to university. So Mr. Toda decided to teach me. And for ten years, every morning, he instructed me in a variety of subjects. He had an excellent grasp of the basics of many areas of learning, including mathematics. Genius though he was, he was not very strong in English. When he was a young man in the early part of this century, it was not a required subject.

I hired a private instructor, but he was only interested in money and wasn't a good teacher. Ultimately, I became so busy with other duties that I finally had to be content with relying on interpreters.

All of you, on the other hand, are fortunate to be in an environment that allows you, if you wish, to study foreign languages to your heart's content. It's all up to you.

INTERPRETER: I am often invited to speak at junior high and high school meetings. When I ask, "Who likes English?" only a few students raise their hands. But when I ask, "Who doesn't like English?" almost the entire room replies, "Me!"

You graduated from Soka University and also studied at the University of Arizona, didn't you?

INTERPRETER: Yes, that's right.

Could you please share with us a few of your "secrets" for learning English?

INTERPRETER: Certainly. But as an interpreter, I'm still in training. I have a lot more to learn.

How did you come to like English?

INTERPRETER: Actually, it was through music. I used to listen to Beatles albums over and over and to Far East Network (FEN) radio broadcasts in

English—though I could hardly understand a word of either!

After a while, I noticed that the pronunciation on records and the radio was different from what I was learning in school. I also used to sing along with my records, following the lyrics in the liner notes.

I read my school textbooks over and over, too, until I memorized them. Reading aloud is very useful, I think. We had weekly tests in school that helped me build my vocabulary. It's a gradual, cumulative process. Keeping at it is important.

After going to university, I listened to the brief FEN news broadcasts and use them as dictation exercises. A friend I respected told me I shouldn't give up trying to understand a broadcast until I had listened to it at least one hundred times.

I also watched many movies in English. I would go to the first showing and sit through a film as many as three times. By the third time, I generally had the feeling I understood most of the dialogue without the subtitles. It's a lot easier today with electronic media.

*Even so, we don't use a foreign language every day. Is there some trick to mastering it?*

## PATIENT, INTENSIVE EFFORTS
## LEAD TO A BREAKTHROUGH

INTERPRETER: I think the secret is to study intensively for a certain period. You have to keep trying, keep working at it, until it suddenly clicks. Learning a language is not a passive activity. Casual efforts will get you nowhere. Find a book you are already familiar with in your language, like *The Little Prince* or a well-known fairy tale, and read it in the foreign language you're studying. Videos are good learning material, too—anything you're interested in and care about is a good starting point.

*How much time do you recommend should be set aside for such concentrated study?*

INTERPRETER: It's different with each person, but I can say that at some point, you will definitely make an unexpected breakthrough. You have to keep up your intensive efforts patiently until that moment. It happens much the same way a baby starts forming words all of a sudden, after months of only making sounds.

There are all sorts of textbooks and learning materials, but it is important not to skip from one to another. Follow through with one until you've really mastered it.

*I have heard that completely memorizing a junior-high-level language textbook can be helpful for high school students who feel they just cannot keep up with their class.*

You mustn't let your aversion to a subject get the better of you. No special talent is needed to learn a language. You're all fluent in your native language, aren't you? You have to decide, first, that you can do it. And then just challenge yourselves, one step at a time.

*More and more students think they have a better chance to learn a foreign language if they study abroad. Many students have asked recently if it's a good idea to study overseas while still in high school.*

Living in another country can be meaningful—it can broaden your horizons. I don't by any means oppose studying abroad. But it's all too easy to be swept away by your environment if you don't have a clearly defined purpose and objective to achieve.

If you are going to a school or university overseas just because others are doing so, you probably won't stick to your studies and won't gain anything to make you outstanding in your field in the future. You should always give the matter of studying abroad careful thought. There is no need to rush going abroad either. There will be plenty of time to do so later if you wish.

*Many complain that the English taught in Japanese schools today is useless.*

INTERPRETER: I thought that before I went abroad, but later found I was seriously mistaken. Unless you have the basics under your belt, including grammar, you won't learn any foreign language properly when you go abroad. Of course, study in a foreign country will help you gain proficiency in everyday conversation. But without a strong foundation, it's difficult to progress beyond that level. And if conversational ability is all you're aiming for, you can easily accomplish that without leaving your home country.

*What should we do about our friends who, in spite of everything we have said today, insist that foreign language is the one subject they just cannot learn to like?*

That's a tough question. We cannot expect people who don't speak our language to understand us through some kind of telepathy. They won't. We have to express ourselves clearly and correctly to get our point across.

But for those who really dislike learning languages, there are other ways of communicating with people around the world. Music and other art forms constitute nonverbal communication. So do sports. Mathematics is a universal language. You can master an art or science and gain respect for achievement in that field. The important thing is to acquire some skill, some means to enable you to hold your own on the world stage.

My dream is for all of you to be active and successful in every corner of the globe. But everything has a proper order. A novel must be read page by page, or you won't understand the story. In the same way, this is the time in your lives for building a solid foundation. I hope all of you can open your minds and challenge yourselves to develop ability in a foreign language.

1. See www.sgi.org/proposals.html. SGI President Ikeda's peace proposals explore the interrelation between core Buddhist concepts and the diverse challenges global society faces in the effort to realize peace and human security. In addition, he has also made proposals touching on issues such as education reform, the environment and the United Nations.

2. Sachiko Sugihara, *Rokusen-nin no inochi no biza* (Visas That Saved 6,000 Lives) (Tokyo: Asahi Sonorama, 1990), p. 204.

3. After the war, Chiune Sugihara was forced to resign from the ministry for disobeying orders. In 1991, the ministry posthumously restored his good name.

4. "Sunday Interview," December 15, 1991, *Seikyo Shimbun*.

5. Translated from Japanese: *Torusutoi zenshu* (Complete Works of Tolstoy), trans. Toru Nakamura (Tokyo: Kawade Shobo Shinsha, 1974), vol. 15, pp. 135–36.

# 7

## Bringing Out Your Best

Today, our discussion is on personality, something that greatly affects our lives. It has been said that personality is determined by fate, that there is nothing we can do about it. Most people, in fact, agonize over some aspect of their personality. This agonizing can actually lead to growth. But it is also true that just worrying about it won't change anything.

Although the human race has made incredible advances in science, in reality we still understand very little about ourselves and the workings of the human mind.

*One student came to me upset, saying: "My mom told me that I inherited my father's unattractive qualities. What can I do to change?"*

*There are different types of personalities: extroverted and introverted, levelheaded and hotheaded, fickle and persistent. Is it impossible to change our personality?*

Buddhism views a person's innate personality or nature as essentially unchanging.

People's personalities are truly diverse. The Buddhist term for society (Jpn *seken*) also has the meaning of "difference" or "distinction." In other words, society comprises a gathering of people who each possess unique, distinct personalities.

There is a vast vocabulary to describe the various personalities and character traits people have. The English language is said to have as many as eighteen thousand words for that purpose. Some people break personalities down into separate groups.

In the multitude of personalities, we see at work the Buddhist principle of diversity, expressed as "the cherry, the plum, the peach, the damson" (OTT, 200). Just as each blossom is beautiful in its own way, each person is endowed with special qualities.

Being introverted doesn't make someone incapable, just as being quick-tempered doesn't make a person useless. We should live in a way that is true to ourselves. That is the fundamental aim of Buddhism.

Once, when encouraging a member who had begun practicing Nichiren Buddhism to change his angry nature, President Toda said: "You don't have to worry about changing your personality. All you have to do is chant Nam-myoho-renge-kyo and live the best you can. Then, very naturally, you will see the negative aspects of your personality disappear, leaving you with the positive ones. You must have a clear purpose and work for the betterment of society."

That member ended up being loved and admired by everyone and living a truly happy, fulfilling life.

*So you mean that even though our basic personality may be difficult to change, we can bring out its positive traits?*

It's like a river. At a certain point, the river's banks are pretty much fixed. In the same way, the identity of a person doesn't change much. But the quality of the water in the river can vary. It may be deep or shallow, polluted or clean, have an abundance of fish or none at all.

The content, in other words, can change. It is the same with us. Our personality doesn't determine our happiness or unhappiness. Rather, it is the substance of how we've lived that decides our happiness. The purpose of Buddhism and education, as well as all our efforts toward self-improvement and growth, is to enhance that substance. This is what life is all about.

*So, are you saying that while our river cannot become a completely different river, we can, through effort and hard work, clean and purify it so that lots of fish will be happy to swim in it?*

Exactly. By chanting Nam-myoho-renge-kyo, we can cleanse our lives of negativity and impurities. We can push everything in the direction of happiness. For example, a person's shyness can be transformed into valuable qualities such as prudence and discretion, while someone's impatience might be transformed into a knack for getting things done quickly and efficiently.

A river meanders but never stops. This is the natural way of things. Similarly, if you make continual efforts, your personality will improve slowly and steadily. The key is to keep moving forward and never stop.

No one's personality is flawless. All, without exception, have some karma that renders them less than perfect. Inevitably, there will be aspects of your personality you don't like. But it would be foolish to become obsessed with such things, which could lead to feelings of self-hatred and unworthiness and consequently hinder your growth.

*A member told me that his mood swings were taking a toll on his friendships and causing him a lot of grief.*

In this unfeeling age, being a bit emotional might not be such a bad thing! You are young, so it's natural to have passionate feelings.

Getting along well with others is of course important, but doing so to the point of suppressing your individuality will only bring you misery. Furthermore, a strong character is almost a requirement to survive in this tumultuous, ever-changing world. And having intense emotions enables you to understand the feelings of others. It is not bad to be passionate, but if it is driven by egotism and hurts others, it can be dangerous. A race car that can reach hundreds of miles an hour also needs extremely powerful brakes.

The point is to develop self-control. And that comes from chanting Nam-myoho-renge-kyo and developing a strong life force. When you bring forth your innate Buddhahood, your passionate nature will become an impetus for progress, a strong sense of justice and a burning desire to help other people.

## LIFE IS A STRUGGLE WITH OURSELVES

*How would you encourage those who get down on themselves for settling for second-best, for not applying themselves seriously, for giving up easily, or for looking immediately for a way to get out of anything unpleasant?*

I think half the problem's already solved, because they know what the problem is!

People tend to lack willpower. To take the path of least resistance is human nature. Outstanding individuals didn't become great overnight. They disciplined themselves to overcome their weaknesses, conquering apathy and inertia to become true victors in life.

Life is a struggle with ourselves. It is a tug-of-war between moving forward and regressing, between happiness and unhappiness. Those short on willpower or self-motivation should chant Nam-myoho-renge-kyo with conviction to become people of strong will, who can tackle any problem with real seriousness and determination.

Perhaps they should try challenging some task at hand—it can be anything—and keep at it until they're absolutely satisfied they've done their best. Taking the first step leads to the next one.

*One student really got down on herself because, though she tried hard to overcome her laziness, her resolve never lasted long. Soon she would find herself slacking off again.*

Anyone who has ever made a resolution discovers that the strength of that determination fades with time. The moment you feel that is when you should make a fresh determination. Tell yourselves: "OK! I will start again from now!" There is a saying that if you fall down seven times, get up an eighth. Don't give up when you feel discouraged—just pick yourselves up and renew your determination each time.

The important thing is not that our resolve never wavers, but that we don't get down on ourselves or throw in the towel when it does. The fact that we realize we've become lazy is evidence we are growing.

*Another student told me she feels alone and isolated even when she's with others. She is quiet by nature, but other people think she's depressed.*

If you are not talkative, how about becoming an excellent listener? You can say to others: "Please tell me about yourself. I want to hear all about you." If you try to make people think you're something that you're not, then speaking will be nothing but torture. You are fine just the way you are. You should let people get to know the real you, including your strengths and weaknesses.

Some people just ramble on mindlessly without saying anything. A person of few words is likely to have far more substance and depth than those who talk just to hear their own voice! Someone who takes action swiftly and effectively is a great deal more trustworthy than someone who is all talk.

Of far greater importance than whether one is quiet or talkative is whether one possesses rich inner substance. The beautiful smile or small, unconscious gesture of a person who, even though reticent, possesses a rich heart, will speak more eloquently than any words. And often such people will speak out with authority and confidence at a crucial moment.

In Buddhism, we say the voice does the Buddha's work. Fundamentally, this refers to chanting Nam-myoho-renge-kyo. Those who chant Nam-myoho-renge-kyo are, in essence, the most eloquent of all. Start with expressing whatever you want to the Gohonzon while chanting. It's important to pray for others' happiness as well. Then, quite naturally, you'll develop the ability to freely and confidently say what you want to say.

*What about people who dwell for a long time on things that upset them?*

It's not necessarily good to get over things easily. Injustice, for example, must never be excused. In Japan, people tend to think that letting things go, like water under a bridge, is the noble thing to do. But such an attitude can hinder society's progress. It allows mistakes to be repeated. Where injustice and evil are concerned, we should keep our anger alive and continue to fight against them tenaciously and courageously. Those who have done so have effected positive change for their fellow human beings. It is also vital that we strive toward our goals with fierce perseverance and determination.

In short, it is important to become people who view things not in terms of tiny, selfish concerns but from a larger, more generous perspective. We have to pray to the Gohonzon to become more broadminded and tolerant. We have to chant and look unflinchingly at the people and things in our lives that are making us unhappy. Running away from things we find unpleasant is what causes suffering. But if we face and challenge such situations, they will enrich our lives.

*Some students complain that they can only see their own faults, and ask how they can find their good points.*

People who are strict with themselves often feel that way—it's a sign of a sincere and admirable character.

It's difficult to see ourselves objectively. Nichiren writes, "We ordinary people can see neither our own eyelashes, which are so close, nor the heavens in the distance" (WND-1, 1137). Perhaps you could ask someone who knows you well, like a friend, parent or sibling, what strong points he or she thinks you have and should develop. I'm sure that person will name many admirable qualities.

No one has only faults or only merits. We all have a mixture of both. Therefore, we should strive to develop and polish our positive attributes. As we do, our shortcomings will fade until they are no longer apparent.

Also, if someone should point out our faults, rather than getting offended or upset, it is to our benefit to listen calmly and objectively to what they have to say and regard it as constructive criticism. Once you take your place in society, few will be so honest with you.

## TAKE ACTION TOWARD YOUR GOALS

*Many young people worry about what others think of them. Although they tell themselves that no one is paying attention, they feel intimidated. They have no confidence in themselves and think that others are talking about them behind their backs.*

Timidity and shyness are signs of a gentle, sensitive nature. Perhaps you've heard of the first lady Eleanor Roosevelt (1884–1962), who remains one of the most respected women in the United States. She once wrote: "Looking back, I see how abnormally timid and shy I was as a girl. As long as I let timidity and shyness dominate me I was half paralyzed."[1]

Through self-discipline, Mrs. Roosevelt conquered her fear. What concrete measures did she take? Like most shy people, she was plagued by fears about herself, so she applied herself earnestly to break those chains. First, she stopped worrying about making a good impression on others and caring what they thought of her. Rather than thinking only about herself, she began thinking of the well-being of others. Second, she pursued wholeheartedly that which interested her and exerted herself to accomplish what she chose to accomplish. She learned that people don't pay much attention to what others are doing and that the amount of attention we pay ourselves is actually our greatest enemy. Realizing this, Mrs. Roosevelt put great effort toward disregarding herself. Third, her sense of adventure and desire to experience life were helpful in overcoming her shyness. She maintained a lively spirit to discover what life had to offer.[2]

By continuing to challenge herself, Mrs. Roosevelt gradually gained confidence. She was later involved in historic initiatives, such as the drafting of the United Nations' Universal Declaration of Human Rights. And she was loved by many people.

The important thing is to take that first step. Bravely overcoming one small fear gives you the courage to take on the next one.

Make goals, whether they are big or small, and work toward realizing them. You must be serious about and dedicated to your goals— you'll get nowhere if you just take them lightly. An earnest, dedicated spirit shines like a diamond and moves people's hearts. That is because a brilliant flame burns within.

If we are sincere, people will understand our intentions, and our positive qualities will radiate. It is pointless to be caught up in outward appearances.

The German poet Johann Wolfgang von Goethe (1749–1832) writes: "How may one get to know oneself? Never by contemplation, only, indeed, by action. Seek to do your duty, and you will know at once how it is with you."[3]

It's all about taking action, taking that first step. If your aim is to swim across a wide expanse of ocean, it will do you no good to get cold feet before you even get in the water. Rather, you've got to make a move, keeping your sights on your goal in the distance. Hindsight can be valuable to one's growth, but to set oneself up for failure before even trying is self-defeating.

*What about those who can only see faults in other people?*

It's much more valuable to look for the strengths in others—you can gain nothing by criticizing people's imperfections. To develop a bigger heart, please try chanting, even a little at a time, for the happiness of your friends. Gradually, you will cultivate tolerance and broad-mindedness.

I'm sure there are many other ways in which people's personalities cause them unhappiness. That we are troubled means we can change those things causing us suffering. Adults tend to resign themselves to fate and give up on improving their character altogether! Once they do so, however, their growth ends.

As long as we move forward and continue to grow, we will inevitably face a variety of problems and inner struggles. Even President Toda confessed that he made great efforts to overcome his docile nature. You cannot achieve human revolution without working hard at it. If you keep challenging yourselves without giving up, you will definitely develop courage and strength.

*Is our personality or character determined by our genes, our environment, or both?*

I imagine it's a little of both. Many studies have in fact been conducted on this topic. Essentially, however, we are the architects of our lives.

The word *character* derives from the Greek *charakter*, meaning to engrave or make an impression. From a scientific standpoint, personality and physical constitution may be determined to some extent by genetics. But knowing that alone won't change anything. What matters is what we do practically to improve ourselves.

Buddhism stresses the importance of the present and future. These are what matter. It teaches us to always challenge ourselves from this moment onward.

Psychology also views personality a number of ways. One view looks at it in terms of concentric circles. Our most basic nature constitutes the core or innermost circle. Around that is the aspect of us shaped by habit and custom, and surrounding that is the part we have formed to cope with various situations and circumstances.

*This idea has also been explained using layers: The deepest layer represents one's inherent nature, the next portrays the basic personality developed during childhood, and so on.*

The core personality isn't easy to change. Yet other aspects can sometimes change so much that people may comment that one seems like a completely different person.

In any case, we have to be true to ourselves. We have to follow our path and do our best to contribute to society. Education equips us with what we need to do that. And faith fuels our efforts.

*In other words, we become our best selves when pursuing a goal that allows us to fully develop and make use of our uniqueness.*

Those who practice Nichiren Buddhism are fortunate to chant Nam-myoho-renge-kyo to the Gohonzon. And those who don't practice can also lead good, fulfilling lives if they aim and work toward a great goal or purpose that embodies the values of beauty, benefit and good.[4] Indian political and spiritual leader Mahatma Gandhi (1869–1948) was an excellent example.

As a boy, Gandhi was excruciatingly shy. He was unable to sleep without a light on, haunted by imaginary thieves, ghosts and serpents. He was introverted and always worried that people would make fun of him. He struggled this way for many years.[5]

*That's so hard to imagine. I always think of Gandhi as a courageous figure who feared nothing.*

Let me add, however, that even as a young man, Gandhi possessed a strong sense of justice and an aversion to anything underhanded or morally wrong. Once, during his first year in high school, his class was paid a visit by an education inspector who told the students to write the word *kettle* to test their spelling. Gandhi misspelled it. His teacher, noticing Gandhi's mistake, gestured for to him to copy the correct spelling from his neighbor's slate. But the concept of cheating was alien to the young Gandhi. Consequently, he was the only boy in the class who got the word incorrect.[6]

*Gandhi's unyielding sense of right and wrong didn't change throughout his life.*

Nonetheless, even after passing the bar and qualifying as an attorney, he was still quite timid. When he finally had to present his first case in court, and the time came to cross-examine the witness, he became nervous and confused, and the room started spinning. He completely forgot what he was going to say and had to leave the courtroom.

A major turning point occurred when Gandhi was in South Africa. Indian residents there faced severe discrimination. On one occasion, Gandhi was riding in a first-class car on a train when a white person brought over the train conductor, who ordered him to move to the freight car. Gandhi wouldn't budge, so the conductor called a policeman, who forcibly pushed him off the train.

In the waiting area at the train station, Gandhi sat shivering in the cold and dark. He stayed awake all night lost in thought, pondering whether he should return to India or endure the hardship of taking a stand and fighting for human rights. He finally came to the conclusion that it would be cowardice to run from his fears and disregard those being discriminated against. From that moment, with the determination to save people from injustice, Gandhi faced and challenged his timid nature.

After a twenty-year struggle, the Indian people in South Africa gained concessions toward freedom. And, as is well known, Gandhi then returned to India where, through his movement of nonviolent civil disobedience, he achieved the independence of his home country.

Gandhi held the conviction that we can become anything we want to be. It all depends upon the strength of our determination.

Each of us embraces Nichiren's great philosophy, which expounds the principle of "three thousand realms in a single moment of life." It is the Buddhism of human revolution. Therefore, there is absolutely no reason for us to put ourselves down.

Nichiren Buddhism enables us to reveal our most intrinsic nature—to fully reveal our unique potential, to develop our character and bring our true self to shine. To do this, we need life force. A strong life force will bring forth the most positive aspects of our personality.

All rivers, irrespective of their differences, flow unceasingly to the sea. If we, too, continue to make persistent efforts, we will eventually reach the great ocean of happiness, for ourselves and others. We will savor boundless freedom and potential, shining brightly while celebrating and encouraging others' individuality.

The important thing is to accomplish everything you possibly can. You'll be more surprised than anyone at how much you can achieve. All of you possess such unlimited potential!

1. Eleanor Roosevelt, *You Learn by Living* (Philadelphia: Westminster Press, 1960), pp. 31–32.

2. See *You Learn by Living*, p. 32.

3. Frederick Ungar, *Goethe's World View: Presented in His Reflections and Maxims*, trans. Heinz Norden (New York: Frederick Ungar Publishing Co., 1963), p. 65.

4. *Education for Creative Living*, trans. Alfred Birnbaum, ed. Dayle M. Bethel (Ames, Iowa: Iowa State University Press, 1989), p. 75.

5. *Mahatma Gandhi and His Apostles*, Mehta, Ved (New Haven, Connecticut: Yale University Press, 1993 [Reissue]), p. 79.

6. *Mahatma Gandhi and His Apostles*, p. 77.

# 8

## WHAT IS KINDNESS?

*Today's topic concerns what it means to be kind.*

*When asked in surveys what qualities they look for most in a person, many people, male and female alike, are found to respond, "Someone who is kind." And when questioned as to what type of person they themselves hope to become, a large proportion give the same response.*

*However, many people have no idea what being kind is; they think it's keeping a safe degree of distance from others so as not to hurt them or be hurt.*

*The other day a friend told me about a mutual friend who was moping around at home by herself, thinking about quitting her job. My friend suggested that the best thing we could do right now would be to leave her alone. I was shocked and told her she was wrong—that if we didn't offer her support when she needed it most, we weren't being good friends.*

I see. It seems that, on the one hand, people treasure kindness in others and want to be kind, but at the same time, don't want to get too involved. Many of our readers may share such conflicting emotions.

Being kind is a matter of the heart. The heart is not something we can easily comprehend; it is subtle, complex. Therefore, it would be difficult for anyone to describe what it means to be kind in a few words. It is a profound question, tantamount to "What does it mean to be human?"

Someone pointed out that the Chinese character used to depict the word *kindness* in Japanese is made up of the pictographs for "person" and "concern." Thus, to be kind is to have concern for other people. It is to empathize with the sadness, pain and loneliness of others. This Chinese character can also mean excellent. A genuinely kind person, one who understands others' hearts, is an exceptional human being, an honors student in life. To possess such concern for others is to live in the most humane way. It is a sign of outstanding character.

When I was about twelve or thirteen, I worked as a newspaper delivery boy. I wanted to build up my strength and do whatever I could to help my family, since my brothers had gone off to war [World War II]. Our family business was farming seaweed, so there were many chores to do, starting early in the morning. Afterward, I would go on my paper route while the rest of the town still slept soundly. In winter, as I rode my bike in the bitter cold wind, my fingers froze, and my breath came out in white puffs.

There were many families on my paper route. I rarely saw their faces, but on the odd occasion when I did, they usually weren't friendly. I was also tormented by barking dogs.

It was difficult, but I will never forget the warmth and kindness shown to me by one young couple. They lived in a single-story apartment building, home to twenty families. One day, as I entered the building, the young wife was bringing a small charcoal stove into the corridor to cook rice. You are probably too young to know what a charcoal stove is, but it's like a portable earthenware cooking range. Anyway, I said, "Good morning" and handed her the paper. Greeting me with a warm smile, she said thank you and commented that I was always in high spirits.

As I turned to leave, she asked me to wait and handed me a bundle of thick slices of dried sweet potatoes, which we called *imokachi* in those days.

"I hope you'll enjoy these," she said, explaining that they had been sent from her hometown in Akita Prefecture in northern Japan the previous day. She then offered her regards to my parents. Her husband, a tall man as I recall, said: "It must be tough delivering papers in this cold weather. Study hard and you will achieve great things."

On another occasion, after I finished my evening paper route, the couple invited me to stay for dinner. They asked me many questions about my family. I told them about my father, who had fallen seriously ill and was bedridden. The husband then began to encourage me, sharing an anecdote about the American inventor Thomas Edison (1847–1931): When Edison was a boy, he sold newspapers, and at the same time, he kept up with his studies. The husband said, "People who struggle when they're young are truly fortunate." The young couple moved away not long after that.

Though these incidents took place more than fifty years ago, the great kindness and concern this couple showed me remain etched in my heart to this day. There was nothing arrogant or pretentious about them.

## VALUE AND RESPECT
## HUMAN DIGNITY OVER APPEARANCES

Buddhism teaches that "calmness is [the world] of human beings"[1] (see WND-1, 358). It is a tranquil state where one embraces all people warmly, without discrimination. The flip side of humanity is arrogance—arrogant people cause others to suffer. They flatter those stronger than them and intimidate those weaker. Such people live in the lower worlds of hunger and animality. Their behavior is despicable.

I understand that in British public schools, there is a tradition of evaluating character by giving students positions of authority or leadership. They say a student's character is revealed by how he or she behaves toward juniors.

*That's a good point. A friend of mine who works at a publishing company and has a lot of interaction with influential people like professors and celebrities said that such people are often full of themselves. He said it's amazing how many times he's seen them fly off the handle over the slightest mistake, and that one even threatened him, saying, "Do you know who you're dealing with?"*

*That's hardly the behavior one would expect from people in their position! Of course, there are also many humble professors.*

Being kind means valuing and respecting each person's dignity.

An acquaintance told me about an educator who taught for thirty-eight years in Kumamoto Prefecture in Kyushu [the southernmost of Japan's four main islands]. He was a warmhearted teacher deeply loved by all his students. What was the decisive turning point in his life? When he was in the second grade, one cold day during winter vacation, a mother and daughter came to his house. The two performed in the streets for donations, the mother playing the *shamisen*, a traditional Japanese stringed instrument, and singing, while the daughter danced. A light snow was falling, and the young boy sat casually eating pastries as he watched them. When the song ended, he handed the girl a half-eaten pastry.

Seeing this, his father, who had been close by getting his ox ready for work, ran over angrily and smacked him, knocking him to the ground. The father turned to the performers, who were a bit surprised by this, bowed deeply and apologized for his son's bad manners. He also made his son bow and apologize. In addition to giving the mother and daughter some grain, he seized the entire bag of pastries from which his son had been eating and handed it to the girl. Then, without even looking at the boy, who sat on the ground crying, he took his ox and went into the mountains to work.

The father wanted to drive home that all people are equal and worthy of respect. When the boy grew up, he was continually grateful for this lesson.

In Japan, it is rare these days to find fathers who are actively involved in raising their children.

It's important never to judge people by appearances. As a young man of twenty, Josei Toda left his home in Hokkaido and came to Tokyo to pursue his dream. However, carving his niche in Tokyo was harder than he had anticipated.

One summer day, having reached his wits' end, Mr. Toda visited the home of one of his mother's distant relatives, an army general. He arrived at the doorstep wearing a dark blue-and-white padded jacket over a threadbare *hakama*, a traditional pleated garment for men. Though he was shown into the living room, it soon became apparent that the general was patronizing him, only pretending to be interested. Far from empathizing with the young man's hopes and dreams, he did everything possible to keep his distance.

Mr. Toda was at first oblivious to this. Having been received courteously, he began talking enthusiastically about his goals. But when he realized his relative was only being polite, he prepared himself to leave.

As he did so, the general's wife wrapped in white paper some cakes that were sitting on the table and handed them to Mr. Toda, but he refused them, saying, "I didn't come here for your charity!"

Mr. Toda never forgot that humiliation as long as he lived. Whenever he recalled the incident, he would admonish his wife: "One must never judge people by what's on the surface! It's impossible to make a decision about a person's future or know what their mission is based on their appearance. Evaluating others at first glance is forbidden in our house!" Josei Toda was stronger than anyone; he was also limitlessly kind. He showered everyone, no matter how poor or unfortunate, with all the loving kindness he possessed.

The founding Soka Gakkai president, Tsunesaburo Makiguchi, whom Mr. Toda chose as his mentor, was also a strong, warmhearted person. As an elementary schoolteacher in Hokkaido, he would go out to meet students walking to school when it was snowing, and would walk them home after school. When he did so, he tried to make sure that the weaker students didn't fall behind the others, carrying the small ones on his back or leading the bigger ones by the hand if necessary. He would also always have warm water ready to gently soak the children's chapped hands. He would ask them: "How's that? Does it feel better?" And the students would say, "Uh-huh, it just stings a little." What a beautiful scene!

Later, Mr. Makiguchi became a noted school principal in Tokyo, but the education authorities kept close tabs on him because he refused to ingratiate himself with them. He was constantly being moved around and sent to schools where no one else wanted to go.

At one point, he was transferred to Mikasa Elementary School. All the students came from poor families. Some were so destitute they didn't even have umbrellas to shield them from rain. Out of his own pocket, Mr. Makiguchi would prepare lunch for the children who came to school without one. This was more than ten years before lunches were supplied in Japan's schools.

There were eight members in his own family to feed, so you can imagine how difficult it must have been. He was also so kind that he would place the prepared lunches in the janitor's room, where the needy children could get them easily without having to feel ashamed or embarrassed.

*If he had placed the lunches in the staff room or in the classroom in front of the other teachers or children, those students would probably have been embarrassed and hesitant to take them. How thoughtful of him!*

Mr. Makiguchi would have done absolutely anything for his students' happiness. That's how kind he was. He once wrote that when he thought of the Japanese system of teaching by rote learning, which only stifled the children's individuality, he wanted so desperately to free them that it nearly drove him insane.

For his students' sake, Mr. Makiguchi would readily confront and indignantly challenge any authority. Once, he even declared to the school inspectors, who wielded immense power over education at that time, that the inspection of classes was unnecessary, since it only led to the undesirable forced standardization of education. That's why he was closely targeted by the authorities.

That's also why everyone else loved and respected him. Whenever he was transferred, the students at the school where he'd been principal would burst into tears. Even the parents and teachers would break down.

Mr. Makiguchi later defied Japanese militarism and subsequently died in prison, a martyr for his convictions. No matter what might happen to him, he couldn't look on while oppressive government authorities inflicted suffering on the people. Nor would he accept an incorrect philosophy.

People with concern for others stand firm when faced with injustice. Buddhism teaches that anger can be constructive or destructive. When justice or good is imperiled, anger becomes necessary. On the other hand, anger that arises from emotionalism is a manifestation of animality. The greater the person, the more all-encompassing that person's love for others. This love is the source of strength and compassion.

## DEVELOP GENUINE CONCERN FOR OTHERS

*Precisely because one cares for others, one should never betray one's beliefs, even if imprisoned. That is noble! This is a little different from our usual understanding of what it means to be kind.*

Just being nice by nature does not mean one is truly kind. To fail to fight against injustice or to lack the strength to act when it is called for is merely weakness.

*Someone pointed out recently that human relations today seem to be pervaded by the desire to not make waves, to keep the status quo. Many feel that opening up too much to others puts one at risk of being hurt. In a recent public opinion poll in Tokyo, approximately 70 percent of the respondents said they didn't want to get too close to others. More than 50 percent said they were reluctant to help others because getting involved could produce unforeseen problems; they could be held responsible in some way [according to a September 1996 survey by the Tokyo Metropolitan Government].*

It's certainly a tough world we live in. I can see why some might want to shut themselves up in their shells. But those who do so are deluding themselves if they think they can live without other people. They have forgotten that they have been, and continue to be, surrounded and supported by the kindness and generosity of many people.

We would never have come into this world, or grown into what we are, without the love and concern of our mothers. And what about our fathers, brothers and sisters, grandparents, relatives, friends, teachers and seniors in faith? Haven't countless people embraced us with their warmth and kindness throughout our lives?

*Yes. One student shared with me her feeling of deep gratitude when, a month before her high school entrance examination, she found that her mother was getting up early to chant for her to do well. She said that this was the most thoughtful thing anyone had ever done for her.*

*Another student said: "I can see how much my mom loves me. Since I was a little girl, she has always been telling me to be considerate of others' feelings.*

*She's raised me alone since I was in the third grade, but my mom's love gives me courage, because she's always concerned and takes good care of me."*

That's heartwarming. Mothers are the strongest, most caring people!

*Another young woman told me that in her first year of high school, she hated school, because she couldn't make friends. She decided to drop out at the beginning of the second semester because she was miserable, but then a classmate called to cheer her up and invite her to have lunch together at school. Touched and encouraged by the classmate's kindness—and not wanting to let her down—she went to school every day from then on. Now, she says, they are best friends who talk to each other about everything.*

True concern for others manifests itself as unconditional friendship. To be kind means that the more someone is suffering, the more love you show that person. It gives you the courage to help another stand up. And it means recognizing another person's unhappiness for what it is, trying to understand and share that person's suffering. This will enable you to grow and at the same time help the other person become strong. Kindness means training ourselves in the art of encouraging others.

The important thing is not just pitying others but understanding what they are going through. Empathy is crucial. Sometimes having someone who understands can give us the strength to go on.

*Concern for others isn't tangible. For that reason, we cannot reach another person with our kindness unless we do something that expresses it. However, people often either cannot muster the courage or are afraid of being rejected if they do extend a helping hand.*

*One student told me she had hesitated to offer her seat to an elderly person on the train because she feared that person would be offended by being treated like an old person. She was afraid of being thought a do-gooder."*

Certainly, there's no knowing how another will respond. Sometimes your sincere intentions will be completely rejected, or you may be laughed at or even ridiculed. But turning around and getting mad at the person you're trying to help does nobody any good. Letting fear paralyze you is foolish, too.

What matters is what you want to do. You must have the courage to follow your instincts when it comes to helping people. Your life will expand only as much as you take action on behalf of others, regardless of how they may react toward your kindness. Kindness equals strength, so the more kind toward others you are, the stronger you will become.

Tsunesaburo Makiguchi was strict with people who lacked courage and just stood by and did nothing. The good but fainthearted, in failing to fight evil, are ultimately defeated by it. Mr. Makiguchi often said: "Not doing good is effectively the same as doing bad. Let's say someone places a huge boulder in the middle of the road. This is malicious, as it will cause trouble for those who pass by later. Then, someone comes along and sees the large obstruction, but, while knowing that it will cause serious problems, leaves it there with the attitude 'Well, I didn't put it there.' This may seem like simply not doing a good thing, but actually, not moving the boulder is causing the same inconvenience for future passersby as putting it there in the first place."

## COWARDICE BEGETS CRUELTY, COURAGE BEGETS KINDNESS

Most people have a spark of warmth or human kindness in their hearts. I don't think anyone is born completely coldhearted. But if, as time passes, people bury their warmth deep in their hearts for fear of being hurt, they will become cold and hard. Similarly, those who are self-centered and think everyone is against them gird themselves with the armor of authority, fame, status, callousness or conceit. Such behavior is devoid of humanity—a sign of animality.

Shakyamuni always initiated dialogue with people. He didn't wait arrogantly for others to speak to him first, nor did it ever occur to him to worry about what they might think of him. He addressed people warmly and with ease.

*To be concerned about others' welfare requires courage, doesn't it?*

Exactly. Cowardice begets cruelty. Courage begets kindness.

Here's something that happened to the famous Austrian writer Stefan Zweig (1881–1942) when he was a high school student.[2] One of his classmates was an excellent student and very popular. One day, this classmate's father, who was president of a large company, was arrested for some incident. The media got hold of the story and printed sensational reports about the father, going so far as to print photos of the family in the newspaper.

The classmate was absent from school for more than two weeks. Then, one day, he unexpectedly showed up and sat down at his desk. He buried his face in his textbooks and didn't look up. Even during the break, he sat by himself and stared out the window, avoiding eye contact with everyone.

Not wanting to embarrass the classmate or hurt his feelings, Zweig and his friends kept their distance. Zweig could see that his friend could use a kind word, but while he was wondering what he should do, the bell rang, ending the break. The classmate didn't show up for the next class. And he never returned to school.

This must have weighed heavily on Zweig. He must have regretted not acting on his instincts when he had the chance.

Some people may often take slanderous rumors about people as truth and spread them without checking the facts. This is the opposite of being kind. To be kind also means to be fair. It means being open-minded enough to find out the truth for oneself.

*It seems that the way we show or express kindness for others takes different forms depending on the situation.*

Yes. What's crucial is the sincere wish to see others become happy. President Makiguchi talked about the idea of small, medium and great good. This can be applied to kindness as well: small, medium and great kindness.

Mr. Makiguchi once said: "Friendship can be divided into three levels. Say you have a friend who needs about a hundred dollars. Giving your friend the money needed is an act of small good, whereas helping him or her find a job is an act of medium good.

"However, if your friend is suffering because of a basic tendency to be lazy, then a gift of money or a job will only cater to and perpetuate that negative habit. True friendship means helping that person uproot the indolent nature that is the source of suffering—in other words, teaching a correct belief system." In this sense, sharing Nichiren Buddhism with as many people as we can is the most kind, most humane thing we can do.

Often, attempts to do great good are misunderstood, like the way children sometimes cannot appreciate the way their parents try to discipline them. No doubt, you, too, will meet resentment when you try to help someone through your great kindness.

But, surely, the ultimate act of kindness for others is chanting for their happiness and doing everything you can for them. Though your efforts may not be valued now, as long as you act with the utmost sincerity, people will come to trust and rely on you. They will in time be truly grateful for the love and kindness you have shown them.

*It seems from what you're saying that individuals are only as great as they are kind toward others. I think it's important that we strive to become people who don't just wear generosity on the surface, but who can really touch people's lives.*

The noble side of a person is manifested in kindness and consideration to others. Kindness and consideration for others resonate with both the Buddhist concept of compassion and the core Western concept of love. I said earlier that every person has grown up supported by the warmth and kindness of many people. Actually, when viewed from a larger perspective, we exist thanks to the support not only of the people around us but of everything on this earth and in the entire universe.

Every thing—flowers, birds, the sun, the soil—supports every other thing in a beautiful symphony of life. Since the birth of this planet more than four billion years ago, without interruption, life has nourished life, life has sustained life, leading to the emergence of human beings. If at any point a link were missing from this chain of life, none of us would be alive today.

*I guess we are all proof that the chain hasn't been broken!*

Life produces new life—surely this is kindness in its most basic form. Delving deeper into this idea, I think we can say that the earth itself is a giant living organism and is great kindness incarnate. President Toda once said that the activity of the entire universe is essentially a function of compassion.

*A popular slogan goes "Be kind to our planet," but in reality, the planet has been kind to us.*

Behind each of us stands not just four billion years of kindness from the earth, but the compassion of the entire universe since time without beginning. Therefore, we mustn't slander or devalue our lives. Life is the most precious of all treasures. Each of you has been given this invaluable gift and each of you is irreplaceable. Those bearers of life—the universe, the earth and mothers—cherish their children. The most important thing for the twenty-first century is that we expand throughout society that absolute, fundamental kindness, that profound compassion toward life.

*If we do so, war and the oppression of human rights will disappear.*
*It will also put a stop to the destruction of the environment.*

That is why we must first develop ourselves. Truly commendable people possess the spirit to improve and grow, and this is, in itself, true kindness toward others.

In contrast, to be completely self-absorbed and utterly indifferent to other people's happiness shows arrogance and a mean-spirited nature ruled by the world of anger.

I hope that all of you—the leaders of the twenty-first century—will work diligently to become people of great strength and genuine kindness.

1. The Buddhist concept of the Ten Worlds delineates ten states of life that we experience within ourselves and that are then manifested throughout all aspects of our lives. From lowest to highest, they are: hell, hunger, animality, anger, humanity, heaven, voice-hearers (learning), cause-awakened ones (realization), bodhisattvas and Buddhahood. For more information, please see the booklet *The Winning Life*, available through SGI-USA (see www.sgi-usa.org).

2. From: Masataro Miyake, *Saiban no sho* (The Book on Trials) (Tokyo: Makino Shoten, 1942), pp. 184–85.

# 9

## The Essence of Human Rights

Spring is near. The plum trees have bloomed, the peach trees have flowered, and soon it will be time for the cherry blossoms. The English Romantic poet Shelley said, "If Winter comes, can Spring be far behind?"[1] No matter how long and bitter the winter may be, spring always follows. This is the law of the universe, the law of life.

The same applies to us. If we seem to be weathering an endless winter, we must not abandon hope. As long as we have hope, spring will come without fail.

Spring is a time of blossoming. Buddhism, as I have mentioned many times, teaches the principle of cherry, plum, peach and damson (see OTT, 200)—that all things have a unique beauty and mission. The cherry has its distinct beauty, the plum its delicate fragrance. The peach blossom has its lovely color, and the apricot has its special flavor. Every person has a singular mission, unique individuality and way of living. It's important to recognize that truth and respect it. That is the natural order of things. That is how it works in the world of flowers: Myriad flowers bloom harmoniously in beautiful profusion.

Unfortunately, in the human world, things do not always work this way. Some find it impossible to respect those who are different, so they discriminate against or pick on them. They violate their rights as individuals. This is the source of much unhappiness in the world.

All people have a right to flower, to reveal their full potential as human beings, to fulfill their mission in this world. You have this right, and so does everyone else. This is the meaning of human rights.

121

To scorn and violate people's human rights destroys the natural order of things. We must become people who prize human rights and respect others.

*Discrimination and bullying exist in our immediate surroundings. At the extreme end of the scale we have war and oppression. Do you think it's safe to say that these share a common root?*

Yes. Some have said that bullying is just war in miniature. I remember something that happened during World War II, when I was about your age or maybe a little younger. Someone was selling hard-boiled eggs in front of Kamata's Otorii Station in Tokyo's Ota Ward. I wanted one very badly, but I didn't have any money.

A soldier came walking by with a woman. It just happened that an army officer was there, too. When the soldier walked past him, the officer shouted, "You didn't salute properly!" and began kicking and beating the soldier viciously.

The soldier had saluted correctly, but the officer seemed jealous that the soldier had a female companion, and he took it out on the poor man. That's why he beat the soldier in front of his girlfriend and a large crowd of people.

The soldier, of course, dared not resist. I will never forget the face of the woman, who was in tears. I remember thinking how much I disliked people who mistreat others. I knew even then that the military was vicious and wrong.

Pettiness, arrogance, jealousy and self-centeredness—all those base and destructive emotions violate human rights. On a larger scale, they manifest as war and crime.

*I understand that in most European countries, discrimination is a crime. Japan is still an underdeveloped country as far as human rights are concerned.*

Many, many people have said as much. Our distorted society is responsible in no small part for the bullying that plagues our schools.

*May I read a few passages written by students about the problem of bullying?*

*One writes: "There's a boy in our class who only picks on those he thinks are weaker than he is. Whenever he's with someone he thinks is stronger, he flatters and plays up to them. I think people like that are despicable."*

*Another says: "I have experienced being bullied, but I had friends, and that made a world of difference. Because of them, I didn't lose hope. The advice I can offer to students being victimized is to fight back against those doing the bullying. If you have the courage to stand up to them, they'll stop picking on you after a while. It's also important, I think, not to wallow in self-pity. I decided I wouldn't let them beat me! I wouldn't let them ruin my life!"*

*There's also a student who writes: "I have been bullied, but I have a friend I can talk to about everything. And my parents have been really supportive with their encouragement and advice, too. Above all, I have the Gohonzon. Many times, I found myself crying before the Gohonzon as I chanted to change the situation. Fortunately, I did change it, and I'm determined never to forget that experience. I want to become a strong, broad-minded and compassionate person, who can make a difference in preventing bullying."*

*Another writes: "I used to bully others, but I realized what a terrible thing I was doing, and I apologized. Now we get along very well."*

Whatever the reason, bullying is wrong. Maybe those who bully others have their excuses—maybe they want to take out their pain on others. But whatever the reason or motive, bullying and discrimination are impossible to justify.

We all need to come to an agreement that bullying is a crime against humanity. Part of the fight for human rights is standing up to those doing bad things. Another part of that fight is protecting good people.

## Needed Is a Solid Philosophy of Life

*I've heard students say that when they try to put a stop to bullying, they end up being bullied themselves. Fear immobilizes them, and then they get really depressed and down on themselves because they cannot change things.*

When you cannot get the bullies to stop picking on others through your own efforts, talk to your principal, your homeroom teacher, older students whom you trust or your parents. Think of some way to improve the situation.

If that doesn't work, pray to the Gohonzon. But whatever happens, you must not get down on yourself if you cannot solve the problem. Even if you find you cannot do or say anything right now, it's important to recognize that bullying is wrong.

Rather than deciding there is something wrong with you, concentrate on developing yourself so that you can effect a positive change in the future. If you end up in a fight and only get beaten up yourself, it won't solve anything. You have to find a long-term solution.

Basically, unless we cultivate an awareness of human rights in society, we cannot begin to prevent abuse. I hope that each of you will be aware of your own and others' rights, so that Japan can become an ideal nation in its respect for human rights.

*Why do people discriminate against one another? A book I read quotes a student from Laos who was living in Japan and studying at a Japanese junior high school: "When I was in fifth grade, some Japanese newspapers and television stations did stories on me, because I was from Laos. I remember a Japanese student coming up to me and saying: 'It's stupid for you to be on television. You're not a star or anything.' I didn't know what she was talking about, so I asked why she said that. 'You're lucky we let you stay here in Japan,' she said, 'so you shouldn't show off.' I felt miserable."²*

Those unable to see people of other countries as human beings the same as themselves are spiritually impoverished. They have no sound philosophy of life. They do not ponder life's more profound questions.

They care only for their own petty concerns. Our society is filled with people who are consumed by hunger and at the mercy of unrestrained greed and animality, picking on the weak and fawning on the strong. These negative tendencies are what make our society discriminate against people and ignore human rights.

We are all human beings. That is what matters. But most Japanese think of themselves as Japanese first and members of the human family second. Such is the narrow-minded, island-nation mentality of Japan. There is a tendency to reject and attack anything the least bit different. That same closed-mindedness isolates Japan in the international community.

For example, there is a large Korean minority living in Japan. The only way that second- and third-generation Koreans can learn their parents' language and Korean history and culture is to attend private Korean schools. But the Japanese government treats those schools as special schools. For the longest time, Korean school students were not allowed to participate in interschool sports competitions with Japanese high schools.

Korean school students also weren't eligible for discount student passes for public transportation. Even today, except at a few private and public universities, those students are not permitted to sit for university entrance examinations because the Japanese Ministry of Education does not recognize their high schools. This is just one example.

*Japan's constitution guarantees respect for basic human rights, but there is still a deeply entrenched, structural discrimination that violates those rights.*

## PEOPLE ARE THE END, NOT THE MEANS

We must teach all Japanese to see both themselves and others first and foremost as human beings. We have to raise people's awareness of human rights through education. Our schools must teach human rights, our religions must teach human rights, and our government must respect human rights.

Unless we can build a society that regards human beings not as a means to an end but as the end itself, we will remain forever a society of discrimination, unhappiness and inequality—a realm of animality where the strong prey upon the weak. We will simply repeat the same patterns.

You may have heard of Minamata disease,[3] one of the worst pollution-related diseases of postwar Japan. People afflicted with Minamata died in agony, their arms and legs stretching pitifully upward. They lost the ability to speak. Many lapsed into comas and never awoke. Many were babies who had been exposed to mercury poisoning—from the industrial-waste-polluted waters of Minamata Bay—while still in the womb.

A group of Minamata disease victims went to Tokyo, to the head-quarters of the Chisso Corporation, which was responsible for the deadly pollution. They made the long trip from Kumamoto, Kyushu, in spite of being severely disabled by the disease. Their purpose was to discuss a compensation settlement with Chisso executives.

One victim asked them: "As human beings, how do you feel about what happened? You are human, and so am I. You may have graduated from Tokyo University, but if our skin is cut, we bleed the same way."[4]

The executives, many of them indeed graduates of Japan's most prestigious national university, answered: "Yes, that's true. But we're just here today to discuss the settlement."

They didn't get it. Not only did they not get it, they had the nerve to tell the victims not to make a fuss, because the failure of Chisso as a company would have serious negative social repercussions. They began to threaten the very people whose lives they had ruined!

"As human beings, how do you feel about what happened?" The executives wouldn't answer that question, wouldn't even entertain it. They were incapable of feeling the pain and suffering of real flesh-and-blood people. If that is the product of Japan's elite schools…well, then we really are in trouble.

*I agree. There is a terrible problem with the Japanese educational system. Control and order are valued above all, creating an environment where it's difficult for students to voice their opinions.*

*In addition, too much emphasis is placed on grades. Students are treated as inferior if their test scores aren't good. Some teachers even take the attitude that students who cannot keep up have forfeited their rights. But the truth is that test scores measure only a tiny part of our worth as human beings.*

Studying is important, of course, but the real purpose of study is to enrich oneself as a human being in order to make valuable contributions that will benefit many people. Grades are just one way of measuring progress toward that goal. If study ends up robbing people of their humanity, its purpose is completely destroyed.

Remember, test scores never tell us anything about what a person is really like.

The classic tale *The Little Prince* has been called one of the master-pieces of the twentieth century. There is a passage in that lovely story that I'll share with you: "When you tell them [adults] about a new friend, they never ask questions about what really matters. They ask: 'What does his voice sound like? What games does he like best? Does he collect butterflies?' They ask: 'How old is he? How many brothers does he have? How much does he weigh? How much money does his father make?' Only then do they think they know him."[5]

This depicts the foolishness of adults, who try to understand a person in terms of numbers. In the process, the person completely disappears!

A child's heart does not discriminate. If parents don't teach them to discriminate, children of all races play happily together.

And little children are not the least bit interested in how well-off the families of their playmates are or what kind of work their parents do. They know that all human beings are equal.

*I think that the purpose of education is to nurture and solidify this spirit in young people. But it is coming to have just the opposite result, isn't it?*

It is up to you, the youth of today, to change that direction. You must not give up. You are going to change the country and the world in the coming century.

Tsunesaburo Makiguchi argued that the times would evolve from military competition to political competition, and from there to economic competition, until finally we would arrive at humanistic competition. I think that is true. If that doesn't happen, the future of the human race is very dark indeed.

Many of the world's leading thinkers lament that there is no country that can serve as an ideal for human rights. Today, Japan is an underdeveloped nation in terms of human rights, but with our peace constitution, we are in a unique position to win that humanistic competition—the contest for human rights—and serve as a world model. I hope our political leaders and educators will work toward that goal.

In the long history of humanity, there has been no true happiness, no true peace. Both leaders and great thinkers have pursued these, but they have not attained them. Unless things change, the future promises to be an endless repetition of the present dilemma. One of the main reasons for this lamentable state of affairs is our failure to securely establish human rights.

It is true that many organizations have talked about the importance of guaranteeing human rights. But all too often, support for human rights stops at words.

*Unless our commitment to human rights has a basis in a profound philosophy and view of humanity, our words ring hollow.*

Yes. To study human rights, we must study philosophy. We must study Buddhism. And just as important as studying philosophy is the willingness to stand up for our beliefs and take action. Human rights will never be won unless we speak out, unless we fight to secure them.

Even if human rights are protected and guaranteed by law and government policy, ceaseless efforts are necessary to ensure that they are indeed upheld. Otherwise those rights will become empty, real in theory only.

Why is this? Power is a demonic force that despises human rights, whether it be power of national governments or any other institutions or organizations. Securing human rights protects the individual, based on the awareness that each person is precious, irreplaceable. The purpose of upholding human rights is to enable all people to live with dignity and realize their potential.

Power, instead, looks on people as a mass, not as individuals. It treats them as objects, numbers, statistics.

The SGI fundamentally seeks to transform this thinking. Ours is a struggle for human rights that values each individual.

What was the turning point in Josei Toda's life? Mr. Makiguchi's death in prison. Whenever he spoke of it, tears welled up in his eyes. He would clench his fists in rage. Why did his mentor have to die? Why did such a good, just person have to be persecuted? Why had such a foolish, destructive war not been prevented? His pain and grief knew no bounds.

Mr. Makiguchi died in prison. Mr. Toda left prison alive. President Toda's awareness of his mission was acute—he would vanquish the demonic powers that caused Mr. Makiguchi's death. Changing Japan's social system and form of government would not be enough to achieve that. Change would have to start from the people. They would have to become stronger, wiser. And all the world's people would have to reach out to one another and forge solid bonds of friendship.

## HOLDING A PRISTINE IDEAL AMID A PERVERSE SOCIETY

The Soka Gakkai's movement is a human rights struggle—by the people, for the people. Our movement's history is one of extending a helping hand to those suffering, those lost and forgotten—to people exhausted by sickness and poverty; people devastated by destructive relationships; people alienated and forlorn as a result of family discord or broken homes. We have shared people's sufferings and risen together with them.

Many of your parents have devoted their lives to this struggle for humanity. Desiring neither fame nor status, they strive with a selfless love for humanity, for the benefit of all. They live in the muddy pond of this perverse society but hold a beautiful, pristine ideal above it. They are noble men and women.

I hope you will inherit their commitment and continue to send a great tide of love for humanity around the globe.

*Valuing the individual is the basis of democracy, in my opinion. And without respect for human rights, democracy will crumble.*

When there is little respect for human rights, the way is paved for the tyranny of dictatorship and mob rule. Society will not prosper. That is why in Japan we must fight for human rights, defending freedom of thought and religion and raising people's awareness.

Human rights, democracy and peace are a single entity. When one disintegrates, they all disintegrate. Leaders in all spheres of society must engrave this truth in their minds.

In a society where there is no fundamental respect for human rights, reputation and standing are nothing.

The most important thing is whether we have genuine love and compassion for others.

More than three decades ago, in 1962, a delegation from Japan's Buraku Liberation League visited China.

[The Buraku Liberation League is a grassroots organization formed by descendants of Japan's old untouchable caste, which was originally composed of those engaged in such so-called unclean occupations as being butchers and tanners, and who were known as *burakumin*. For centuries, contact with *burakumin* was shunned. They were forced to live in segregated ghettos (Jpn *buraku*). Discrimination and prejudice against descendants of this group remain deeply ingrained in Japan even today, despite a number of government measures to promote equality and integration into the mainstream of Japanese society.]

When its members met with Chinese Premier Zhou Enlai, the delegation leader expressed his gratitude that the premier had made time in his busy schedule to see them. Zhou Enlai replied: "What are you saying? Any premier who would not meet with the most oppressed and suffering of all the Japanese people, when they've come all the way to China, would not deserve to be China's premier!"[6]

Premier Zhou [who attended university in Japan] cared as much about the Japanese people as he did about the Chinese. He strove to build a new China by reaching out to form alliances with suffering and oppressed peoples the world over.

Buddhism expounds a great, undifferentiating wisdom—the recognition and insight that all living beings are equal, that the Buddha and living beings are one. The highest state of being, Buddhahood, resides in all people. That is why our every effort must be for people and why everything depends on people. Human rights are the distillation of this essential truth.

Every sphere of human endeavor—education, culture, science, government, business and economics—will either guarantee and foster human rights or come to a dead end. In education, for example, schools should exist for the sake of the students. Yet today, it is as if the students exist for the sake of the schools.

We need to refocus on the importance of benefiting humanity and make a fresh departure from there. That is how human rights will be established.

## Human Rights Means
## To Be Strong! Be Proud!

*A high school student says: "I suffer a physical disability. People at my school and in the streets make fun of me. I don't know what to do. Could you give me some advice?"*

Essentially, you have to become stronger. That, too, is part of the human rights struggle. Having your rights as a human being recognized by others is not just having people behave sympathetically toward you. Be proud of yourself as an individual, regardless of your disability. You must be proud of your mission.

Those who laugh at you and make fun of you are cruel and wrong. They create a terrible burden of negative karma for themselves by ignoring your right to be treated as a human being.

Letting their taunts get to you is a defeat for human rights. Your strength, however, is a victory for human rights.

*The last time we talked, you taught us that to be considerate we need to be strong. So we also need to be strong to defend human rights, our own and those of others.*

I have spoken with champions of human rights the world over: Linus Pauling of the United States, Austregésilo de Athayde of Brazil, Adolfo Pérez Esquivel of Argentina, B.N. Pande of India. I cannot count how many I have spoken with. All of them were gentle people, and all of them were strong. They had the strength to endure the hardships of persecution or imprisonment, yet just by meeting them you sensed a warm responsiveness and sensitivity to others' feelings.

Rosa Parks fought against racial discrimination in the United States. She is another of these gentle yet strong people I have met. Even at the height of discrimination against African Americans, she refused to ride in the elevators marked "Colored." Unable to compromise with such discrimination, she took the stairs. She disliked riding on the buses where the seating was segregated and often chose to walk long distances instead.

One hot summer day, although her throat was parched, she went thirsty rather than drink from the "Colored" water fountain. Mrs. Parks writes: "I have never allowed myself to be treated as a second-class citizen. You must respect yourself before others can respect you."[7]

One must live with dignity. Character is the foundation of human rights. It is far more valuable than money.

No true peace can be achieved as long as we seek only material wealth.

We must make the twenty-first century a century of human rights. We must build a society with more than short-term profit as a goal. To do that, the first step is respecting ourselves, living with dignity, self-confidence and pride. Such people can then treat others with respect. A great river begins with a tiny drop of water and, from that humble beginning, flows into the sea. The current toward a century of human rights has just begun.

*How do I become the kind of person you're talking about?*

You can start by reading good literature. You will find many human rights issues explored in the pages of such works.

You can also learn to recognize the positive qualities in others. One of the first steps in achieving human rights is appreciating and embracing individuality.

It's also important to develop a solid perspective about humanity, realizing that though others may be different from you, we are all members of the same human family. According to one scientist, ability to differentiate operates at a very shallow level of the brain, while ability to find commonalities involves highly sophisticated information-processing—a much deeper level of the brain.

Those who can get along with all kinds of people, seeing them as equals, as fellow human beings, manifest the true excellence of their character. They are people of genuine culture and education.

The richer our hearts, our humanity, the more we can recognize and value others' humanity. Those who bully and belittle others only diminish their own humanity.

Please allow me to share a poem, "Light," by Francis William Bourdillon:

*The Night has a thousand eyes,*
*And the Day but one;*
*Yet the light of the bright world dies*
*With the dying sun.*

*The mind has a thousand eyes,*
*And the heart but one;*
*Yet the light of a whole life dies*
*When love is done.*

Human rights are the sun illuminating the world. So, too, are love of humanity, kindness and consideration. All these things light our world. Their light brings "cherry, plum, peach and damson" (see OTT, 200) into glorious bloom in society, enabling everyone to reveal their unique potential.

Your mission is to make the sun of human rights rise over the twenty-first century. To do that, you must make the courageous sun of love for humanity rise first in your own hearts.

1. "Ode to the West Wind," *Shelley—Selected Poetry*, selected by Isabel Quigly (London: Penguin Books, 1956), p. 162.

2. Akito Kita, *Watashitachi no dokuritsu sengen* (Our Declaration of Independence) (Tokyo: Popurasha, 1992), p. 153.

3. Minamata disease—A crippling disease of the central nervous system that affected thousands of people in the 1950s and 1960s in and around Minamata,

a city in Kyushu. The waters off Minamata were polluted by highly toxic industrial discharges from a local carbide plant owned by Chisso Corporation. The disease resulted from consumption of seafood contaminated with high concentrations of mercury. Many children were born with terrible birth defects for years afterward. A final settlement in lawsuits by the victims and their families against Chisso Corporation was only concluded in 1996.

4. Quotes here and below from Michiko Ishimure, *Hi no kanashimi* (Sorrow of the Sun (Tokyo: Asahi Shimbunsha, 1991), pp. 89–91.

5. Antoine de Saint-Exupéry, *The Little Prince*, trans. Richard Howard (New York: Harcourt Inc, 1971), pp. 10.

6. Saichiro Uesugi, *Jinken wa sekai o ugokasu* (Human Rights Move the World) (Osaka: Kaiho Shuppansha, 1991), pp. 127–28.

7. Rosa Parks with Gregory J. Reed, *Quiet Strength: The Faith, the Hope, and the Heart of a Woman Who Changed a Nation* (Grand Rapids, Michigan: Zondervan Publishing House, 1994), p. 72.

# PART THREE

# YOUTH AND
## *Self-Improvement*

# 10

## THE JOY OF READING

*This time, we'll discuss the joy of reading.*

OK, but I think many people nowadays find reading a chore rather than a pleasure.

*That's true. Perhaps it's because computers are now so popular that many youth have an aversion to books.*
*And if they do read anything, it seems to be mostly lightweight, entertaining reading matter. But I guess that's better than not reading at all.*

I'm sure there are all kinds of young people—some who like reading and some who don't. Even so, one thing is clear: Those who know the great joy of reading have richer lives, broader perspectives, than those who don't.

Encountering a great book is like encountering a great teacher. Reading is a privilege known only to human beings. No other living creature on this planet has the ability. Through reading, we come in contact with hundreds and thousands of lives, and commune with sages and philosophers from as long as two millennia ago.

Reading is a journey: You can travel east, west, north and south, and become acquainted with new people and places.

Reading transcends time. You can go on an expedition with Alexander the Great or become friends and hold dialogues with people like Socrates and Victor Hugo.

In his *Essays in Idleness*, Yoshida Kenko writes, "The pleasantest of all diversions is to sit alone under the lamp, a book spread out before you, and to make friends with people of a distant past you have never known."[1] How sad to not know this joy! It's like standing before a mountain of precious jewels, all there for your taking, and returning home empty-handed.

Almost without exception, the great people of history had a book they held dear during their youth—a book that served as their guide and as a source of encouragement; as a close friend and mentor.

Books introduce you to the fragrant flowers of life, to rivers, roads and adventures. You can find stars and light, feel delight or indignation. You are set adrift on a vast sea of emotion upon a ship of reason, moved by the infinite breezes of poetry. Dreams and dramas evolve. The whole world comes alive.

To gain true satisfaction and pleasure from anything requires some kind of practice, training and effort. You cannot fully enjoy skiing without working at it. The same goes for playing the piano or using a computer. It also takes effort, perseverance and patience to appreciate reading. Those who have tasted this joy, who have looked on books as friends, are strong.

Reading gives you free access to the treasures of the human spirit—from all ages, from all parts of the world. One who knows this possesses unsurpassed wealth. It's like owning countless banks from which you can make unlimited withdrawals.

*That sounds great! How exactly can you cultivate such an appreciation for books?*

The first step is to get into the habit of reading. Those who have, you'll find, will utilize every spare moment to read, whether while commuting by train or before going to bed.

As a youth, Josei Toda had a job in which he had to transport goods on a large two-wheeled cart. Reminiscing about that time, he once said, "I would finish my work as quickly as possible and hurry to an open field nearby, where I would toss the cart aside, lie down on the grass and read."

The French philosopher and mathematician Blaise Pascal (1623–62) described the human being as a "thinking reed."[2] Reading is essential to thinking. Perhaps we can even say that reading is a sign of our humanity.

*President Ikeda, many students are wondering how on earth you have found the time to read as much as you have despite your busy schedule.*

The foundation for everything in my life was forged during my youth. I devoted every minute I could spare to reading.

One summer, I would even go down occasionally to the Zoshigaya Cemetery [in Tokyo's Toshima Ward] to read. Sitting outside on a straw mat under the moonlight, with a flashlight, I would read books such as Hugo's *Les Misérables*. It was cool and quiet there. We had no air-conditioning in those days, you see. The mosquitoes were quite a nuisance, though!

*You really got into the habit of reading!*

I was a voracious reader. I devoured every book I could get my hands on.

From a young age, probably because I was sickly, books were my greatest treasure. During World War II, there were times when I would take them into the air-raid shelter to shield them from the bombings.

When the war ended, I was seventeen. As far as the eye could see, Tokyo was in ruins. The only serenity to be found among the destruction, on the rubble-filled streets of a defeated land, was the sprawling clear, blue sky overhead. I still remember vividly the color of that sky.

Though we had nothing, lacking even basic necessities such as food and clothing, I had boundless hope—peace had finally been restored! Now I could study as much as I wanted. I could read at last, and books were a wonderful feast.

Around this time, twenty or so of us youth living in the same neighborhood formed a reading group. We would meet to discuss books like Dante's *The Divine Comedy* and topics such as the German economy.

Japan's defeat had completely shattered everything we had believed in. Young people were desperately searching for the truth, the real meaning of life, an understanding of the world. Books were our only reliable guide. Whenever I had spare time, as though I were in my own personal library, I would browse used bookshops in Tokyo's Kanda area, asking myself, "I wonder if there are any good books today?" or thinking, "I hope they still have that one I had my eye on."

Often I rushed down there with money I saved from my meager wages. I can still clearly remember the exhilaration I felt when I finally purchased a book I long wanted, which the store still had when I got there.

*Nowadays there is an overabundance of books, but many people just aren't reading. How spoiled we've become!*

## READING IS A REQUIREMENT OF GENUINE LEADERS

You cannot imagine how strict Mr. Toda was when it came to reading. Seeing youth engrossed in tabloid publications, he would become furious, sternly rebuking them: "How can you enjoy that garbage? Do you want to be nothing more than a third- or fourth-rate person? You must read epic novels, you must read the classics! You can never hope to forge your character if you don't read them while you are young! You will never become a leader in the future!"

Mr. Toda was also always checking on me, asking, "What are you reading now?" If I were to answer, "Rousseau's *Émile*," for example, he would ask me about the content—there was no way I could pretend to have read something I hadn't!

Even just two weeks before he died, Mr. Toda was still inquiring about my reading. He said: "A leader must never forget the importance of reading, no matter what may happen. I'm up to the third volume of the ancient Chinese work *Compendium of Eighteen Histories*." Even in his weakened physical state, Mr. Toda devoted every spare moment to reading and contemplation.

At our young men's division Suiko-kai[3] meetings [a training group, named after the Chinese novel *The Water Margin*, which met twice a month to discuss great works of world literature], Mr. Toda would lecture on leadership and human character through such classics as *The Water Margin*, *The Romance of the Three Kingdoms*, *The Count of Monte Cristo* and Nikolai Gogol's *Taras Bulba*.[4] He would stress: "Study while you are young. Otherwise, as you get older, you will be ridiculed not only by your peers but by children. What you read while you are young will remain with you throughout your life."

I feel the same way. I want each of you to savor the great joy that reading brings. I hope you will work at reading until it becomes something you cannot live without. You are the only one who will lose out if you don't try your hardest.

*People often complain that they just don't have time to read.*

Mr. Toda said, "Youth, make time in your heart to read and think seriously about things!"

It's a matter of setting your mind to it. Those who claim they have no time haven't really made room in their hearts to do so. If the desire to read is there, there is no way you cannot find ten or twenty minutes.

You don't have to be sitting at a desk to read. An old saying goes that there are three places suitable for writers to mull over their ideas: on horseback, in bed and in the bathroom. The same can be said about reading today if we substitute public transportation for horseback.

When you're head over heels for someone, for instance, you want to see him or her whenever and wherever you can—even if it's only a brief glance or just for five minutes, right? That should be our attitude toward reading.

If you make the time—for example, ten minutes in the morning, ten in the afternoon and ten at night—you'll be reading a total of thirty minutes each day. And you'll often find that you read with much greater concentration in those precious moments set aside in a busy schedule. It usually leaves a deeper impression than reading done at a more leisurely pace.

I'm sure there are some of you who at the moment think you haven't the time to do anything other than study for exams, but reading actually serves as the foundation for all your studies. Your results in school will surely reflect your reading in the long run. Naturally, you have to use your wisdom to decide when your time is best spent reading a book.

*Do you have any advice for people who want to read but don't know where to begin?*

Rather than worrying about what to read, it's probably best just to read even one page of something. Indecision will get you nowhere. At least if you read one page, you'll have made progress.

*Many students find epic novels and the classics rather daunting.*

Just as there are good and bad people, there are good and bad books.

All of us live in an intricate web of interrelationships. If we associate with good people, our lives will be positively affected. If we spend time with bad people, our lives will be negatively affected. Even those who are essentially good stand a 20 to 30 percent chance of being corrupted if they spend enough time in a dishonest environment.

Reading good books cultivates and nourishes one's life. A classic never grows old; it is always refreshing and new. And its message is just as valid in the twenty-first century. Encountering such a work is a lifelong treasure.

There is an episode involving the British playwright George Bernard Shaw (1856–1950). Upon discovering that he was unfamiliar with a certain popular novel of the time, an acquaintance said to him: "Mr. Shaw, this book has been a bestseller for five years! How can you not know it?" He calmly replied: "Madame, Dante's *The Divine Comedy* has been a bestseller throughout the world for more than five hundred years. Have you read it?"

Ralph Waldo Emerson (1803–82) said that a book that's been in print for less than a year isn't even worth reading. A book that is still read decades or centuries after it was published is a masterpiece.

Life is short. So we should make a point of reading good books. One way to find the time to do so is simply to stop reading bad books. In Buddhist terms, bad books are those that bring forth the lower of the Ten Worlds—the life-conditions of hell, hunger, animality and anger. They are like poison or drugs that produce misery.

On the other hand, good books point your life toward happiness, wisdom and creativity. They possess sound substance that enables you to think and grow.

*Some say that they've read some of Goethe's or Tolstoy's works, but couldn't make heads or tails of them. Or they were left feeling unimpressed.*

At least they're honest! But it's not Goethe's or Tolstoy's fault if their works don't impress you. Reading classic literature is like striking a large bell. A weak stroke will produce a weak sound, but if you pound that bell with all your might, you will get a resounding response. It all depends on the reader's effort.

If, when reading the classics, you reach a part that seems over your head, it's perfectly fine to skip twenty or thirty pages until you get to a section that's easier. Once you've figured out the story, you can always go back and reread those pages. I stress that if you have the desire and the will to learn, you will definitely find some gem in whatever you read.

## READ THOUGHTFULLY, NOT PASSIVELY

Reading is like mountain climbing. There are high and low mountains. Ascending a steep summit is quite difficult, but how great is your exhilaration when you've successfully conquered it. Vast vistas stretch before you. From your vantage point, you can see how low the other hills and mountains are.

The greater the struggle, the more enriching the experience. That said, if you immediately set out to climb a high peak without preparation, the challenge could be beyond you. You may be forced to abandon your ascent, losing your way or suffering altitude sickness! It might be better to first attempt a goal suited to your level.

You could start with a book about something that interests you. Once you've mastered the basics of reading and developed some degree of confidence in your ability, then you can go on to reading more challenging books.

If some books are beyond you right now, it's fine to wait to read them until you are in college or until later in life. Learning is a lifelong process. Crucial is the determination to make the wisdom passed down through the ages your own. "I'm going to read thousands of books"— that's the kind of enthusiasm I want you to have.

You all have a mission in the twenty-first century. No matter how talented you may be, without culture, wisdom and rich character, you will never be respected in the world arena. In fact, like many Japanese today, you might be dismissed as a money-driven automaton.

Reading makes us human. We mustn't limit our lives to one field of narrow specialty to the exclusion of all else. No matter how high people's positions are, if they haven't read great novels by the world's renowned authors, they can never hope to become outstanding leaders. To build a humanistic society where people live with dignity, we must have leaders acquainted with genuine great literature. This is extremely important.

People in other countries tend to read far more than the Japanese, who for the most part just pretend to be well-read.

*Are there any other pointers you could give us?*

"Read thoughtfully, not passively!" I jotted these words down in the reading notebook I kept in my youth.

I diligently wrote my thoughts and impressions about books I had read in a notebook made of cheap, coarse paper, over the period of about a year, between 1946 and 1947. In those days, paper was an extremely precious commodity. How I treasured that humble notebook! When I read something that touched me, I would write it down immediately.

Unfortunately, because the paper was so cheap, the ink would run easily, rendering parts of my notes illegible. But I constantly told myself, "Read thoughtfully, not passively!"

We must read in a way that nourishes and cultivates us. Food will only nourish us and contribute to healthy bone and muscle growth if digested and absorbed properly. Similarly, digesting what we read requires serious reflection and contemplation.

President Makiguchi said: "Don't read carelessly. You must ponder everything you read. It seems that many young people read but fail to think about the content. Thinking about what you read makes it part of you."

And President Toda offered more specific advice, saying: "There are many ways to read a book. One is to read only for pleasure, simply following the plot—this is a very shallow way to read. Another is to think about the author's motivation for writing the book, its historical backdrop, the societal elements of the time, the characters in the story, and the ideas and intention that the author is trying to express. And yet another way is to try to understand through the work what kind of person the author is or was, to grasp the writer's true character, ideals, beliefs and views on life, the world and the universe. If you don't take it this far, it cannot be called reading."

In any case, it's important to have a good book always at your side. A friend once suggested that I read *A Teacher Called Takezawa*[5] by Yoshiro Nagayo (1888–1961). That book taught me many things. My friends and I chose good books and then recommended them to one another.

*In order to internalize what we've read, do you suggest that we, too, keep a reading notebook as you did?*

For those so inclined, I highly recommend it. It will serve as a record of your spiritual development. If you don't wish to keep a full-length journal, perhaps you could just jot down your impressions in three or four lines on the inside back cover of the book. If you thought it was interesting, what made it so? If it was boring, why? You could also underline the parts that struck you and write down your thoughts or counter arguments in the margins.

Of course, this wouldn't go over too well if it's a borrowed book! Anyway, taking notes on what you read sets the wheels of your mind in motion.

# As Foods Nourish the Body, Books Nourish the Mind and Spirit

A saying goes that genius derives from study. I understand Napoleon (1769–1821) also kept a reading journal. He was certainly an avid reader. When he was a child, one of Napoleon's favorite books was Plutarch's *Parallel Lives*, and he dreamed of growing up and becoming just like those heroes whose lives were depicted. A biography of some famous person would be a good place for you to start, too.

In later years, when on expedition to Egypt or Spain, Napoleon always took along books covering a wide variety of subjects. It's been said that he even had a bookshelf built into his horse carriage. Reading was Napoleon's driving force, giving him the energy to press onward.

Incidentally, Stendhal (1783–1842), a French writer who held Napoleon in high esteem, said that just as a locomotive could not run without fuel, he could not get into the right frame of mind without reading at least a few hundred pages first thing in the morning. For both of them, reading was fuel for the mind and soul. It gave them the inspiration to generate new ideas, challenge their obstacles and continue forward.

In the same way that having a healthy body requires nourishing food, having a healthy mind requires reading. You will become ill if all you eat are sweets and soft foods that don't require much chewing. And it is unhealthy to turn one's nose up at nutritious food or just eat the same foods all the time.

Likewise, we shouldn't avoid good books that enrich our minds.

Someone once described bad books as "messengers of degeneracy, guides to delinquency, traps to misery and an insidious poison." Good books, on the other hand, are as wonderful as an amazing teacher, a trusted confidant or a parent. They contain a wellspring of wisdom, a fountain of life, bright illumination and human goodness.

*By the way, some students were wondering if they should steer clear of comic books.*

If you read nothing but comics, of course it would hardly be beneficial! The most important thing is to develop yourselves. Some comic books do have positive messages that could change your life, open your eyes or move you. Sometimes a comic book has a more profound message than a dull, monotonous book. One I've mentioned before is the Japanese comic book *Tomorrow's Joe*. This was the inspiring story of a young boxer who gave his absolute best, pushing himself to his limits to achieve his dream.

There is also the argument that comic books, along with television, stifle one's imagination. Both media provide the viewer with a prepackaged image. The strong point of literature, however, is that it lets you develop your imagination and ability to think.

There is a fundamental difference between the way you receive information from television and from books. Reading something in a book engraves it in your mind, in your life. It provides you with sustenance to grow. Just looking at something leaves you with only a surface impression—it's easy to do, and it gives you the illusion that by merely seeing something, you know all about it. This is only superficial understanding, though; it hasn't become a living, breathing part of you.

Taking shortcuts has become the undercurrent of Japanese culture, as indicated by the many convenient instant foods on the market. Getting swept up in this kind of social trend—and turning your back on the challenge of reading literature—leads you to a shallow and empty existence. That is a terrible tragedy!

I was once asked if I had any regrets. I replied, "Only that I didn't read more books during my youth."

*If you feel that way, President Ikeda, there's not much hope for the rest of us!*

No matter how much we study, it can never be enough. I hope all of you will develop into great individuals in the twenty-first century. Now it's time for you to cultivate your minds through reading. That will decide everything.

There is no limit to your potential if the earth of your minds is cultivated and well-nourished. Within each of you lies a vast field of infinite possibility. And reading is the hoe with which to till that boundless frontier.

I hope you will all become people who can wholeheartedly, honestly say of your youth that you read as much as you could and gave your all to your studies!

1. *Essays in Idleness—The Tsurezuregusa of Kenko*, trans. Donald Kenne (Tokyo: Charles E. Tuttle Co., 1967), p. 12.

2. Blaise Pascal, *Pensées: Notes on Religion and Other Subjects*, trans. John Warrington, ed. Louis Lafuma (London: J.M. Dent & Sons Ltd., 1960), p. 58.

3. Suiko-kai: A training group for young men's division members formed in 1952, which met twice a month with second Soka Gakkai president Josei Toda to discuss the great Chinese Ming dynasty epic novel *The Water Margin* (*Shuihu zhuan*: Jpn *Suiko den*), from which the group takes its name, and other great works of literature from around the world.

4. *Taras Bulba*: A historical novel by Russian author Nikolai Gogol (1809–52).

5. Japanese title: *Takezawa Sensei to iu hito*.

# 11

## KNOWING HISTORY IS KNOWING YOURSELF

*Today's theme is history. There are some who love to study history, who find it engrossing. Then there are others who dislike it, who find history classes boring because of the emphasis on memorizing long lists of facts and dates.*

*A lot of students are critical of their history classes. There are a few teachers, though, who give vivid, inspiring accounts of various historical episodes or use audiovisual presentations to try to make history come alive.*

*What can we gain from studying history?*

One important thing is a broader point of view. If we're always looking at the ground when we walk down the street, we're likely to get lost. But by looking up, choosing something big by which to orient ourselves, we can make sure we are heading in the right direction.

Another way of thinking of it is to imagine yourself looking down from a high mountain. From an elevated vantage point, it is easy to pick out the road on which to proceed.

The same is true of life. If you always have a shallow perspective and only pay attention to trivial things, you are sure to get bogged down in petty concerns and not be able to move forward. Even relatively minor hurdles or problems will seem insurmountable. But if you look at life from a broad viewpoint, you will naturally discover the solution for any problem you confront. This is true when we consider our personal problems as well as those of society and even the future of the world.

President Toda always said that leaders should study and read books on history. History helps us see the direction in which society and the world are heading, how we can steer the times in the best direction. The German poet Goethe wrote:

*He who cannot be farsighted,*
*Nor three thousand years assay,*
*Inexperienced stays benighted,*
*Let him live from day to day.*[1]

That's why I want to say: Don't get tied in knots over unimportant things. The more problems you have, the more you should read history. Studying history takes you back to the events and lives you are reading about. You meet passionate revolutionaries and base traitors. You encounter vainglorious tyrants and tragic heroes. You come to know people who sought only to lead peaceful lives but were forced to go through difficulties in their lives. You experience the brief moments of peace between seemingly endless stretches of war, like sweet shade from the burning sun.

You see large numbers of people sacrificed for what we now know was foolish superstition, as well as men and women of principle who gave their lives for the love of humanity. You meet great people who pulled themselves up from the depths of suffering to make the impossible possible. You watch this unfolding drama from a distance, or view it as in its midst—history is played out inside the human mind.

Watching this drama unfold in our minds, we naturally learn to see life from an expansive point of view. We can see ourselves riding the crest of the grand river of history. We see where we have come from, where we are and where we're going.

History is our roots. Those who have studied history in depth have become aware of their origins, their heritage. Knowing history is knowing oneself. At the same time, the better one knows oneself and human nature, the more accurate picture one gets of history. This is how we acquire an insight into history.

*Some say history repeats itself. Others say it doesn't. Which do you think is true?*

History is a record of human probability, human cause and effect, and the science of human activity. We might call it the statistics of the human race.

For instance, though we cannot predict the weather with complete accuracy, we can forecast trends based on statistics, on probability. The human heart is also unpredictable, but if we look at history we see trends, probabilities in human actions.

The study of history, then, is the study of humanity. Although not everyone can be a professional historian, it is important to use history as a mirror to guide us in shaping the future. You are the protagonists who will write a fresh history.

Without a mirror, it's impossible for you to see your own face or full appearance. Similarly, armed with the mirror of history, you can see what needs to be done. It's interesting, by the way, that many Japanese works of history have been called mirrors—for example, *Okagami* (The Great Mirror), *Imakagami* (The Mirror of the Present), *Mizukagami* (The Water Mirror) and *Masukagami* (The Clear Mirror).[2]

Mr. Toda stressed the importance of history. He said history is a signpost to help us move with greater certainty from past to present, from present to future, toward the goals of peace and the harmonious coexistence of all humankind.

There is so much recorded history now that one person cannot absorb it all. That is why it is necessary to have a firm historical perspective, an understanding of basic historical principles, even if we cannot know every fact and detail. If we are aware, through our knowledge of history, of humanity's negative tendencies, we can be on the lookout for them and avoid a repetition of our dark and destructive history. Repeating history's abominations signals a failure to learn the lessons that history teaches.

## HISTORICAL ACCOUNTS
## DON'T ALWAYS CONVEY THE TRUE PICTURE

*It is certainly true that if all you focus on is names, events and dates, history loses much of its interest.*

It is important to master the basics of history, of course, but it is more important to use it to acquire the ability to see the truth. Napoleon described history as the "version of past events that people have decided to agree upon."[3] That is true in some respects — the history that is recorded and passed on does not always accurately reflect the truth. Of course, we know the dates on which certain events took place. I am not talking about such unarguable facts and details. At times, the exact opposite of the truth becomes the recorded historical opinion. And far more important truths are not recorded or transmitted at all.

*That reminds me of a passage in* A Youthful Diary. *"History books are filled with errors," you wrote. "But in our own history, the history written only in our hearts, one cannot record a single falsehood or embellish anything" (June 15, 1950).*

History is never definitive. It can be interpreted in many different ways, which is why we mustn't simply accept everything that is written in history books.

For example, let's look at the Crusades launched by Christians in Europe, primarily against Muslims during the Middle Ages. European and Islamic accounts of the Crusades have almost nothing in common! And most of the world history we study in Japan derives from European accounts. Though it's natural if you think about it, Islamic history books don't use the heroic-sounding term *crusader* to describe the aggressors who invaded their lands.

In fact, at the time, Islamic civilization was far more advanced than that of Europe. The crusaders invaded Islamic states, looting and pillaging, leaving a trail of destruction. At least that is how Muslims see it. Islamic histories record the horrible atrocities that the crusaders committed.

The true history of the Crusades is not simply a matter of the past, either. A strong prejudice against Islamic civilization persists today, casting a dark shadow over our chances for world peace. It is a problem of today. It is a problem of the future.

Another example: In the past, it was widely taught that Christopher Columbus discovered the Americas. But people had already been living there since long before. It was a discovery from the European perspective but not from that of Native Americans.

The problem is that the concept of discovery inherently demeans and discriminates against the Americas' original inhabitants. The conquerors of the so-called New World were so self-centered that they didn't even regard the indigenous peoples as human!

As Europeans moved from island to island, they slaughtered the inhabitants or rounded them up for slave labor, nearly wiping out entire populations. While the inhabitants had welcomed them with open arms and helped them, the European invaders repaid them with betrayal and violence. What can we say about this historical truth? The view that Columbus discovered America legitimizes the "discoverers." At the same time, it legitimizes similar actions by others. Within the word *discovery*, we can detect a self-righteous historical view, a view of humanity that justifies the subjugation of other peoples in one's own interests.

Perhaps we can call this the colonial viewpoint. This gave birth to tragedies the world over—not only in North and South America but in Africa and Asia as well—for five hundred years. This is why one's view of history is important. From a history of "discovery" comes a future of subjugation. It leads to misery and tragedy.

This colonial view of history lay behind Japan's invasion of Asia as well. From the Meiji period, beginning in 1868, we Japanese were intent on catching up with Europe and aimed at becoming the "Europeans of Asia." We treated our fellow Asians in the same way that the Europeans treated the indigenous peoples of America after Columbus' arrival. While on the one hand the Japanese became subservient and fawning to white people, we became arrogant and cruel to all other races. This Jekyll-and-Hyde nature of the Japanese, which persists today, comes from this distorted historical viewpoint.

What we should have done, of course, was build friendly ties with our fellow Asians and work with them toward world peace. If Japanese leaders had possessed such a view—and vision of the future—Japan's modern history would have been entirely different.

One's view of history is crucial. Chancellor Wang Gungwu of the University of Hong Kong spelled it out clearly: "When leaders have a mistaken view of history, many decisively negative influences result, and they in turn push society in an even more mistaken direction."

*Columbus didn't discover anything, then. The people of Europe and the Americas simply encountered one another.*

Yes. A view of history based on the idea of encounters is one in which all parties are equal. At the very least, it shows respect for one another. The reality in this case, however, was that the Europeans invaded the Americas.

As another example, a history of the Age of Exploration that teaches only of Magellan[4] the heroic explorer and not Magellan the invader, that fails to teach of the courageous struggle of the Filipino chief Lapu-Lapu[5] to defend his homeland, the Philippines, ends up propagating the historical viewpoint of "discovery" of one people by another.

## Perspective Changes Everything

*So a single historical event can take on opposing meanings depending upon how it is interpreted or explained.*

Yes, this applies not only to history, but to present-day events.

Much depends on the angle from which things are viewed as well as the viewer's personal agenda. For example, let's say that there is a demonstration in a certain country. The police try to stop it, and a fracas ensues. If the television camera is within the group of demonstrators, it will show the fierce faces of police officers swinging their batons. Those who see the image will sympathize, naturally, with the demonstrators. But if the camera is on the side of the police, it may well show the protesters as an unruly mob, angrily throwing stones and resisting police efforts to keep the peace and order.

*Watching that latter image, one could decide it is a riot.*

Depending on which side you are on, the information could be interpreted in contrasting ways. Both images may be factual, but where the overall truth actually lies is an entirely different question. Even the fact that a demonstration occurred cannot be understood without knowing why it took place, why it may have been suppressed. Knowing this background is essential in knowing the truth of the event.

*We live in what we call the information age, but though enormous quantities of information are available, I think its quality is often questionable. Does the information come from the side of the people or the side of the authorities? In far too many cases, the intent behind the information is only to make money or create scandal.*

This reinforces my point about how difficult it is to learn the full truth of past events. The history is written by the victors, they say. Might makes right—the losers are often portrayed as wrong, as evil. We must always be aware of this. And we must leave a record of true, correct history.

That is also why it is important for us not to lose in our struggle. We must create a history in which those who champion justice, truth and integrity prevail.

Both a solid historical perspective and insight are important. A pile of bricks is not a house, and you cannot write history by just gathering a pile of facts. A history reflects the perspective of its historian through the way its combined facts represent reality. We need to be aware of this as well.

In reading a work of history, you must cultivate your historical sense by always remaining critically aware, by searching for the truth. Sometimes you will agree with the writer, sometimes not. There is no simple method to achieve this sense of history.

The only way is to study many things, think about many things and experience many things. And it is crucial to remain objective. You must always seek the facts, the truth, without succumbing to personal biases or self-interest. Never accept a lie.

The way in which World War II is presented in Japan has long been a problem. Whatever shameful acts took place, it is extremely important for the Japanese people and the world that the truth be recorded and passed on. That period may be a single frame in the long reel of human history, but our view of history will be distorted unless the truth is recorded. Not only that: Falsified or incomplete history causes future misfortune.

Creating a true historical record is creating the road to peace and happiness for all humanity. History must not be warped and distorted. Fabricated history is no more than fiction. Hiding unpleasant things and only recording favorable achievements isn't history—it's no more than a forged résumé. History must be recorded objectively and accurately, based on formal evidence and reliable firsthand accounts.

*In the former West Germany, it was recommended that sixty classroom hours be devoted to the Nazi period, and visits to the concentration camps were also strongly recommended. In this, we can clearly perceive the German people's sincere determination to face and learn from past mistakes.*

I once met the first president of the unified Germany, Richard von Weizsäcker in 1991. He was a great man. He made the well-known remark "Anyone who closes his eyes to the past is blind to the present."[6]

*Even in our personal relations, we don't trust those who lie. So it is sad to hear the excuses Japanese officials give for Japanese schools not teaching students the truth about what the Japanese military did in World War II.*

During the war, my eldest brother was sent to the front to fight, and I remember clearly that once, when he came home on furlough, he told us angrily that Japan definitely was in the wrong. "Japan's behavior is abominable," he said. "What we are doing to the Chinese is unforgivable." My brother died in the fighting in Burma [now Myanmar]. He was a person of fine character. It was a terrible waste.

The Japanese soldiers sent to invade Asia were also victims of Japanese militarism and imperialism. We must teach the unvarnished truth about the war to the next generation, so that such a tragedy will never be repeated.

As part of that effort, the Soka Gakkai has collected accounts of people's war experiences and published them in more than one hundred volumes. The experiences of victims as well as remorse-stricken former members of the armed forces involved in the slaughter are documented. Our antiwar books have been published in English, French, German and Romanian, and in children's editions. We have also sponsored antiwar exhibitions that have toured the world.

*Because we have sincerely confronted and acted on this issue, the Soka Gakkai is trusted in Asia.*

   *I was surprised to learn that the foreign students center at the University of the Philippines is called Ikeda Hall. The Japanese forces occupying the Philippines during the war were incredibly brutal, and anti-Japanese sentiment is strong there. I heard that this was the first public building ever to be named after a Japanese.*

José Abueva, the former president of the university, is a dear friend of mine. Both his mother and father were killed by the Japanese military. They were tortured and murdered, and their bodies discarded. Every Asian country has an infinite number of such unspeakable tragedies in its past.

   Dr. Abueva said of the situation that continues in Japan decades later: "Japanese leaders still stubbornly refused to admit, and apologize for, the grievous wrongs they had committed in the countries they invaded in World War II. Japanese history textbooks purposely concealed the truth or justified the wrongs. Fellow Asians were outraged by the insensitivity and dishonesty of the Japanese. How could they gloss over the sordid truth that so many had witnessed and endured, recorded and remembered?"[7]

   I will never forget these heartrending words.

## YOUTH ARE THE LEADERS OF A NEW AGE

*Let me share the opinion of a high school division member about the war: "What Japan did to the other countries of Asia was really terrible. Unless we sincerely apologize and make amends for those actions, relations between Japan and its Asian neighbors can never be healthy and strong. I wish our political leaders would realize that this is not a matter that can be solved by throwing money at it."*

That is so true. The high school division members are astute. Remember, the hope for peace rests in your hands.

To have a true vision of history, one must have a true vision of humanity, of society, of life. It is important to rethink everything from the viewpoint of whether it is in the interest of the people, whether it contributes to their happiness.

Until now, history has almost always been centered on the interests of the powerful, on politics and the state. We must rewrite history so that it is centered instead on the people and their lives, so that it reflects all of humanity's viewpoint.

A few years ago [in 1992], a textbook of European history written from a pan-European perspective was published. It was unlike any previous history textbook where the focus was on only one nation's story, where everything was viewed from a national perspective. This represents the beginning of a trend to abandon national histories for those written from a broader point of view.

I think the time has come to seriously contemplate writing a pan-Asian history textbook and, after that, a pan-human or global history textbook—one written from the perspective of all humanity.

*You were a pioneering figure in reestablishing official relations between Japan and China at a time when relations were still fraught with difficulty. I think that shows a visionary wisdom.*

*You also opened the way to personal friendships and ties with the former Soviet Union, even during the Cold War. You were one of the first to predict that the Soviet Union and China, their relations extremely frosty at the time, would once again be friends. And you acted on that vision. How have you acquired the ability to read the future in this way?*

I think it's just a matter of my never having lost my faith in the people. They are the main protagonists in history. In the long run, the people's awareness, their actions and wishes, are the strongest forces of all. Mahatma Gandhi once said: "When I despair, I remember that all through history the way of truth and love has always won. There have been tyrants and murderers and for a time they can seem invincible but in the end they always fall."

So the basic task of making history is changing the consciousness of the people. For example, as part of the civil rights movement, African Americans staged sit-ins at lunch counters. This kind of protest began in 1960 with four students at a North Carolina agricultural college. At the time, lunch counters and diners in the town refused to accept orders from African Americans. Then one day, four African American students, indignant at this treatment, entered a retail store, sat down at the lunch counter and ordered coffee and doughnuts.

The store manager came, and an argument ensued. A crowd gathered. The students were called every name imaginable and struck. But they refused to budge. They sat there through it all, and they kept up their nonviolent protest, staying until the store closed.

The next day and the next, they sat at the lunch counter. Eventually, white students joined them.

The movement they started began to spread and, by September 1961, more than thirty-six hundred protesters had been arrested. Some seventy thousand black and white college students participated. This movement, an embodiment of courage and conviction, began with the actions of just four students. But it surely made a substantial contribution toward eliminating racial discrimination in the United States.

*We must take this as an example as we create history, too.*

It is all up to young people. Political scientist and author Masao Maruyama declared that "Japanese history is the story of the passive resignation of the people to their fate." We must change this. To do so, we need the wisdom to distinguish truth from falsehood and the moral courage to publicly declare the truth.

Many years ago, I met the famous French journalist Robert Guillain, who was the Far East Bureau chief of the newspaper *Le Monde*. He was in Japan during the war and observed the Japanese close up. One reason, he concluded, that the Japanese could not call an end to the war was that, while they had physical courage, they had no spiritual courage. He also said that the Japanese lacked the important virtue of respect for the truth. As a result, they were easily manipulated by evil forces.

You, today's youth, are the new leaders of a new age. You must create a history of human unity for the dawning of this new age on our planet. Perhaps you think that there is little you can do as individuals. But, as Victor Hugo observed, "An invasion of armies can be resisted; an invasion of ideas cannot be resisted."[8] We are moving toward an ever-expanding humanism.

I am convinced that whatever twists and turns there may be along the way, that is the direction. You, my young friends, embracing a philosophy of humanism for which the world so hungers, are the front-runners who will lead the way.

1. Johann Wolfgang von Goethe, *Western-Eastern Divan*, trans. J. Whaley (London: Oswald Wolff Publishers Ltd., 1917), p. 91.

2. These are from the eleventh through fourteenth centuries.

3. See quotationspage.com.

4. Magellan: Ferdinand Magellan (c. 1480–1521), the Portuguese navigator and explorer, who undertook sea voyages for both Portugal and Spain.

5. Lapu-Lapu: the Filipino chief Lapu-Lapu, who killed the Portuguese explorer Ferdinand Magellan in the battle of Mactan Island in April 1521.

6. From a speech given in the then West German parliament on the occasion of the fortieth anniversary of Germany's defeat in World War II, May 8, 1985.

7. From a personal unpublished account of his family history titled "Our Family Story of War and Peace, Love and Remembrance."

8. Victor Hugo, *The History of a Crime*, trans. T.H. Joyce, Arthur Locker (New York: Mondial, 2005), p. 409.

# 12

## APPRECIATING ART AND CULTURE

*Today we're going to talk about art. I think for some people the word art conjures images of something stiff or formal.*

That may be true. But surely no one regards a bird's song as stiff or formal. Nor, I'm sure, does anyone gaze at a meadow of flowers and feel intimidated. Who can fail to be captivated by the beauty of cherry blossoms in full bloom in the moonlight? And on a fine, clear day, I'm sure we all look up at the blue sky and think, "How wonderful!" The bubbling of a stream certainly delights the ear, cleansing and refreshing our senses. These are all examples of our intuitive love of beauty and the spirit of art and culture.

Art is by no means unusual or extraordinary. Great works of art, just like the beauty inherent in nature, are a relaxing, refreshing balm for the spirit—a source of vitality and energy.

Many of our daily activities resonate with the spirit of art and culture. For instance, when we try to look our best, we are seeking to create beauty. When we tidy and clean a room, we are striving to create beauty. Just one flower in a vase can completely transform a room, giving it a warm and gentle touch. Such is the power of beauty.

Art should calm and soothe us, not put us on the defensive or make us feel uncomfortable. It should encourage us when we are run-down, relax and uplift us when we are tense.

*Some young people may feel put off by art, since it is a required subject in school.*

To begin by simply enjoying art is most important. If you start out with a scholarly or analytical approach, you're likely to end up confused and in the dark about what art really is. I doubt very much that people listening to a bird's song or gazing at a meadow of flowers analyze such beauty intellectually.

Of course, to fully appreciate some great artworks, one needs to concentrate and make a degree of mental effort. But appreciation starts with simply experiencing the work. With music, for instance, we begin by just listening. With a painting, we start by looking. Too many people, I'm afraid, are so intent on analyzing art that they don't really see it.

In Japan, for instance, even visiting an art museum is for most a rare and special event. But in Europe, people visit art museums frequently from the time they are young. They are used to museums, so they don't find them intimidating.

One reason may be that museums in the West are products of a democratic society. In earlier centuries, only the aristocracy or the very wealthy could collect and enjoy objects of art. Public art museums were born when the people insisted that they, too, had a right to have access to the great works of art. That simply is how museums came about—out of the public's growing demand for the opportunity to enjoy art.

In Japan, on the other hand, museums were first established in the Meiji period (1868–1912), when Japan opened itself to the world after centuries of seclusion. The Japanese government then established museums imitating Western ones, believing Japan would be thought backward by Western powers if it didn't have them. As institutions of the Imperial government, Japanese museums inevitably carried the condescending message "Here—we will allow you to see these works of art."

*"And you should be thankful that we do so" is what was communicated.*
*That atmosphere contributes to making a museum visit an unpleasant, even daunting, experience.*

162

Although things have changed considerably in Japan, that attitude still persists in the realm of art and culture, coloring the way we react to them. Culture actually exists to make people feel happy and at ease. Art is not meant to intimidate us, but many people don't seem to recognize that truth.

True art, true culture, strives to enrich the individual and encourage self-expression, while seeking to reach out, touch, communicate and bring people together. It arises from the spirit to bring joy to others and not from a desire for fame or profit. Genuine art and culture mean to foster that spirit, but intellectuals and political leaders in Japan today seem to have missed that point. They tend to view art as something to serve their interests. Consequently, they may never come to know the essence of art and culture.

I hope, therefore, that all of you, the high school division members, will become individuals who appreciate the true spirit of culture. Visiting museums and attending concerts are important ways to cultivate that spirit. At the same time, you might try your hand at an artistic pursuit, perhaps singing or painting or doing some craft. In that way, you will gradually become a cultured person who can appreciate and enjoy art and culture.

If you spend all your time only studying for university entrance exams, your life will be limited. Of course, it is necessary to study for exams, but you mustn't forget what is important in terms of the larger, lifelong goal of cultivating your individuality and self-expression.

Taking time out to acquaint and familiarize yourself with art is important. Studying for exams is little more than processing information. Art and culture enrich our lives and make them truly worth living.

Art classes at school are also important, because they can expand, deepen and enhance us as individuals.

# Arrogance Is the Antithesis of Culture

*Many members complain that their art classes are boring and dull.*

That may be true. One scholar said that, in Japan, many art teachers are unreasonable and conceited. He asked why it wasn't possible for them to conduct classes in a more straightforward, accessible way for students. One problem may be that Japan lacks the spiritual soil in which a heartfelt appreciation for the true essence of art can be cultivated.

Under such circumstances, sometimes teachers become arrogant, forgetting that their professional skill is nothing more than that—a skill. For example, there are haughty, condescending English teachers who imagine themselves somehow superior because they can speak English, and their students cannot. In the same way, there are art teachers who, because they can paint or sculpt well, look down on their students who cannot.

Surely an art teacher's merit can only be judged by whether he or she strives to nurture and encourage an understanding and appreciation in students of art and culture. Unfortunately, the culturally poor soil of Japan produces far too few such individuals.

Since culture is ultimately the cultivation of the spirit, artistic skill or lack thereof aside, "It is the heart that is important." Culture is an expression of the inner impulse to cultivate the earth of the hearts of people, who are bound by karma, so that more beautiful flowers can be brought to bloom and abundant fruit brought to ripen.

Arrogance is the opposite of this spirit. Someone has said that an artist who is arrogant is not a true artist—such a person is only a purveyor of art, someone who makes a living from art. Likewise, a seemingly cultured person obsessed with publicity and fame is only a purveyor of culture.

All of you, the leaders of the future, should know that genuine artists, people who appreciate culture, are those who can foster a shared understanding among the people, who always humbly maintain a sense of gratitude and respect for others.

*I have an example of how the arts—in this case, music—can uplift people's hearts and bring them release. A high school division member played the violin at a meeting I attended. As music filled the room, those present, some of whom had been looking down at the floor, withdrawn, all raised their heads, eyes shining, and listened. The change of mood was astonishing.*

*The Tohoku (northern part of Japan's main island) young men's high school division leader, a music teacher, has had the same experience. He often plays the piano at meetings. By playing what he describes as "music from the world of bodhisattvas," it is his wish to encourage and inspire the members in some small way.*

That's wonderful. A world without art is gray and lifeless. Only when the flowers of culture flourish does our world become bright and colorful. The SGI's movement to promote culture, reaching from the grass roots to the global level, is also a bright, colorful garden of flowers spreading around the globe.

*That's true. Actually, the Tohoku high school leader's first encounter with music was when he joined a Soka Gakkai future division chorus. [The Soka Gakkai's future division collectively comprises the elementary, junior high and high school divisions.] From his second year in high school, he began to study music in earnest. He once said to me: "I believe that art is the joy of self-discovery. My happiest moments are when I am teaching children, and some new aspect or side of them comes to light through music. In this sense, art is the pursuit of our humanity."*

I agree. It is the pursuit of our humanity, not the pursuit of fame, riches or honors. The great works of art from around the world, from throughout history, have survived and continue to inspire us and communicate to us precisely because their creators sought to leave behind a legacy of their spirit, without any thoughts of fame or wealth. Art created from ignoble motives is like brass when compared with the gold of great art.

Great art is infused with powerful vital force. It is alive, endowed with the creator's life and spirit. The renowned French sculptor Auguste Rodin (1840–1917) said that the important thing for artists is to feel, to love, to hope, to tremble, to live. It is to be, before an artist, he said, a human being. These human feelings—hope, love, anger, fear—are communicated to us through the artist's work. The vibrations of the artist's spirit set off similar vibrations within our hearts. This is the essential experience of art. It is a shared feeling that links the creator and the viewer, transcending boundaries of time and space.

*As Nichiren writes, "It is the heart that is important" (WND-1, 1000).*

Dunhuang in western China has been called a great art museum in the desert. It is a marvelous storehouse of Buddhist artworks spanning a thousand years, dating back to the fourth century. The late Chinese painter Chang Shuhong (1904–94) made it his mission to protect that valuable treasure and introduce it to the world. He was a remarkable person whom I met on several occasions. In fact, we published a book of our dialogues in Japanese under the title *Tonko no kosai* (The Radiance of Dunhuang).[1]

In his youth, Mr. Chang studied Western art in Paris and was on his way to becoming a leading artist. He had won many prizes, and his future was quite promising. Then, one day, he happened upon a book in a used bookshop along the banks of the Seine—a collection of illustrative plates of the grottoes of Dunhuang.

His homeland of China possessed such magnificent art! And it had been plundered by foreigners! He decided then and there to return to China and guard these great treasures with his own hands.

The young Mr. Chang abandoned his budding career and Paris life, and traveled to Dunhuang in the desert. In what others might regard as a life sentence of hardship and suffering, he gave his all, right up to the end of his life, to protect and restore the Dunhuang paintings.

His struggle was grand, heroic. Life in the desert was so hard that his first wife left him. Mr. Chang's dedication to preserving Dunhuang's beauty and making it available to the people was such that he needed nothing for himself. His was the true spirit of art.

Mr. Chang once said: "The paintings of Dunhuang are so fresh and vibrant even today because their creators painted from their souls. The creative energy that comes from the depths of the soul is always genuine. True works of art never lose their power to move us, even after thousands of years. Works of art that may be beautiful at first glance are sometimes revealed as fakes upon closer examination."

No doubt that is correct. In today's art world, there is the tendency to judge works highly if the creator is famous or if the work has a high price. This is a warped, unfortunate attitude. But whatever our present situation may be, the pursuit of culture is an eternal concern. Culture is indispensable to making our lives richer, more enjoyable and more worthwhile.

There is no denying that humans have the cruel aspects of rivalry, war and jealousy. But we also have another side—our wish to live richer, more beautiful and brighter lives. The interaction of these two tendencies is the story, the history, of our species.

That's why culture and art are so crucial. They encourage our better aspect, helping us enjoy the most fulfilling lives we can. And they nurture the virtue of goodness, the desire to make this earth a paradise. This is the ideal way to live as human beings. It's what distinguishes us from other animals.

*Art that comes from the soul often also expresses religious faith. Great religions give birth to great culture.*

That is true as long as the religion does not ally itself with authoritarian forces.

Without the backing of a sound philosophy rooted among the people, a culture will not flourish long. Religions—Buddhism in particular—are indivisible from culture. Religion and culture are two aspects of the same thing. Both culture and Buddhism aim to inspire people from within. As Mr. Chang said: "The source of the creative inspiration for the art of Dunhuang seems to have been religious. If the painters had not believed in Buddhism, they could not have created the wall paintings that they did."

*Oppressive authority and arrogance are fatal to culture, aren't they?*

# PEOPLE OF CULTURE VALUE PEACE

Yes. When I was a boy, all Japan rushed headlong to war. In that atmosphere, anything artistic was widely regarded as unpatriotic. The only music we had was military songs. At school, we were taught only to draw soldiers and tanks or nurses tending the wounded on the battlefield. Strong oppressive forces were brought to bear on our culture. Such is the demonic nature of tyranny.

While art and culture liberate people from within, authoritarianism oppresses people from without. These are opposing forces.

*Not many leaders in our society have a real understanding of beauty. Rather, they try to exploit culture to realize their ambitions.*

That is why it is important for the people to support and encourage culture. In a certain sense, the art of the European Renaissance articulated the people's liberation from the oppressive authorities of church and state. "This is the way people are meant to live!" it expressed. It was an assertion of the tremendous power of the people. And the eternal worth and beauty of Renaissance art are still recognized today.

That those in power don't try to understand art and culture is frightening, actually. Their lack of appreciation for the finer aspects of life makes it easy for them to go to war, to lean toward fascism.

Of course, there are also examples of leaders who understood and appreciated art. Albrecht Dürer (1471–1528) was a great German Renaissance painter and printmaker. One day, he climbed a ladder to work on a large painting in the palace of the Holy Roman Emperor Maximilian I. The ladder began to wobble, and the emperor, looking on, called for one of the aristocrats in the room to steady it. No one made a move. The social status of a painter at the time was low—they would not stoop to help Dürer. The emperor himself rose from his throne and steadied the ladder.

One of the courtiers began to grumble, commenting how inappropriate it was for the emperor to assist a lowly painter. When the emperor heard the complaint, he said: "I can make any number of aristocrats at my choosing. I cannot, however, make another great artist like Dürer."

*I guess he knew what kind of person is important.*

People who appreciate art and culture are important. Cultured people value peace and lead others to a world of beauty, hope and bright tomorrows. Tyrannical authority, on the other hand, only leads people to darkness—the opposite of art.

For that reason, nurturing and spreading an appreciation for art and culture are crucial in creating peace.

*I realize that being a person who appreciates art and culture will be very important in the upcoming century, but how does one go about it? I'm sure there are many who think: "I'm not a good singer," "I cannot draw or paint," and who feel insecure about their artistic abilities.*

I myself was not good at drawing or calligraphy, but I made an effort to seek out and view fine paintings and calligraphic works. That effort paid off very well in my life.

We must live our lives wisely and thoughtfully. Many people tend to give up on the way to reaching their goal, thinking they've hit a dead end. Though it may be long and difficult, however, there is always another route to follow.

*I think people do the same with their studies. Some people give up on the subject they're studying, convinced that they'll never get it.*

When in fact that's simply not the case. Such people find themselves at a dead end only because they decide they are. The greatest enemy of learning is fear. This is true of language, of art, of every area of study. When we're afraid of being laughed at, of embarrassment, of being looked down on by others for our mistakes, shortcomings or limitations, progress becomes very difficult. We must be brave. So what if others laugh? Whoever makes fun of those trying their best are the ones who should be ashamed.

There's no need to compare ourselves with others. What's important is our own growth, even if it is just a little at a time. The better the teacher, the more at ease the students are made to feel. That's because the teacher understands that fear is the greatest hindrance to the development of a student's full potential.

## Culture and Art Should Be Enjoyed by All

*Intimidation certainly kills culture. The atmosphere in some museums and concert halls makes people feel tense and uncomfortable, when such places should actually make us feel relaxed and energized.*

Culture and art should be shared and enjoyed by all. They do not discriminate. When we encounter beauty, we return to the essence of our humanity, where all people are equal. From that standpoint, there is no distinction between company president and employee. There are no teachers or students, no specialists or amateurs. Such distinctions exist in society, but we need a place where we can restore our humanity. That place is built by art, by culture. Creating that place is also one of the fundamental roles of religion.

The problem is how to foster a truly cultured mind in those who come into contact with art and culture. For example, those who are boastful of their expertise in world art or culture are most likely using culture only to gain personal prestige. Such people are not cultured in the genuine sense.

*It is often said that the Japanese people are well-schooled but uncultured. This again seems to be a matter of developing a heart or spirit capable of cherishing culture.*

Some say Japan is a third-rate cultural power; others say it is fifth-rate. Japanese leaders, teachers and students for the most part are not yet cultured individuals. They don't even try to appreciate the importance of culture. They don't make any real effort in that regard. Caring only about appearances—about culture as a formality—they have no genuine experience of culture.

Until now, Japan emphasized economic achievement. Culture was always just an "accessory." We Japanese have also tended to judge the value of culture in monetary terms, and this has become a national trait. Japan's future is dark unless we change this.

*Isn't the idea that culture is somehow an accessory still rather firmly rooted in Japan? We seem to think that now that we've achieved a strong economy, it's time to turn our attention to culture, but that view treats culture as a mere decoration, something only for show.*

*Most Japanese don't seem to realize that culture is not an accessory; it is a vital necessity for human beings.*

The Meiji-period writer Natsume Soseki (1867–1916) wrote in *The Three-Cornered World*: "Approach everything rationally, and you become harsh. Pole along in the stream of emotions, and you will be swept away by the current. Give free rein to your desires, and you become uncomfortably confined. It is not a very agreeable place to live, this world of ours.

"When the unpleasantness increases, you want to draw yourself up to some place where life is easier. It is just at the point when you first realize that life will be no more agreeable no matter what heights you may attain, that a poem may be given birth, or a picture created."[2]

We have to live. We work, we eat, and we grow old. Our lives are a constant repetition of little deeds. Against that backdrop, we progress, we seek a more fully human existence, we desire to make a flower bloom. From that feeling, culture and art are born.

Life is painful. It has thorns, like the stem of a rose. Culture and art are the roses that bloom on that stem.

*A life without art is like nature without flowers.*

The flower is yourself, your humanity. Art is the liberation of the humanity within you.

The institutions of society tend to treat us as parts in a machine. They assign us ranks and place considerable pressure upon us to fulfill our defined roles. We need something to help us restore our lost and distorted humanity. Each of us has feelings that have been suppressed and have built up inside. We have a voiceless cry resting in the depths of our souls, waiting for expression. Art gives those feelings voice and form.

We can also vent those feelings through pleasures and play, which may suffice for a while, but in the long run such distractions bring no true satisfaction or sense of fulfillment. Our lives will grow dull and lusterless, we will feel empty inside, because our true selves, our true heart's desires, have not been set free at the deepest core. Art is the cry of the soul from the core of one's being.

Creating and appreciating art set free the soul trapped deep within us. That is why art causes such joy. Art, quite aside from any questions of skill or its lack, is the emotion, the pleasure of expressing one's life exactly as it is. Those who see such art are moved by its passion, its strength, its intensity and its beauty. That is why it is impossible to separate a fully human life from art.

The Buddhist concept of cherry, plum, peach and damson (see OTT, 200)—that each person should live earnestly, true to his or her unique individuality—has much in common with culture and art. Culture is the flowering of each individual's true humanity, which is why it transcends national boundaries, time periods and all other distinctions. Likewise, correct Buddhist practice means cultivating oneself and serving as an inspiration for leading a truly cultured life.

*I can see now what a profound role culture plays in human existence. A society that regards culture as a mere accessory is not a fully humanistic society.*

## THE VALUE OF BEAUTY LEADS TO PEACE

A society that values culture is a society that values human happiness. President Makiguchi said that happiness lies in the pursuit of three forms of value: benefit, good and beauty.[3] Benefit is the pursuit of all that is rewarding, in the broadest sense. Good is the pursuit of justice and opposition to injustice. Beauty is the pursuit of art and culture. All three of these contribute to our happiness. When any one is lacking, there is imbalance. When people become unbalanced, society becomes unbalanced, and people cannot attain happiness.

Today's Japan is unbalanced in favor of political and economic interests and technology, which makes it all the more crucial to restore balance by emphasizing the importance of art and culture and supporting their development. Such efforts will make Japan more humanistic, a nation that other nations can safely trust, and consequently we will be able to contribute to world peace.

*You have long been fighting to achieve just that. Despite your endeavors, unethical people with no understanding of the importance of art and culture have attacked you and tried to undermine your efforts. This makes us very angry.*

From the time I met Josei Toda, when I was nineteen, I realized that the only route for Japan was to become a cultured nation. Only through culture and the arts would Japan rise spiritually from the ashes of war. This is true of any country.

I have stuck to this belief over the years, and that is why I, though an ordinary private citizen, could meet with so many people around the world and have earned their trust and support. It has all been due to the power of culture.

I held a dialogue with Dr. Arnold Toynbee (1889–1975), the great British historian, some twenty-five years ago [in 1972 and 1973]. We spoke about many topics, including the importance of culture. In the midst of our discussions, there was some exciting political news of a meeting between two world leaders. At that time, Dr. Toynbee said to me that though our discussions might not be attracting much attention at the moment, in ten or twenty years, people all around the world would agree with and laud what we had said. His prediction came true.

[Today the dialogue between President Ikeda and Dr. Toynbee has been published in twenty-seven languages.]

The power of culture may be hard to detect at times, but it is a fundamental force, since it transforms the human heart. Political and economic developments make the news more often, but culture and education are the forces that actually shape any age. We must not make

173

the mistake of looking only at the shallow waters that bubble noisily over the rocks; the deep currents are even more important in knowing the true nature of the river.

*To return to an earlier point, you said that whether one has skill makes no difference. Could you elaborate on that?*

Yes. Whether or not one is skilled, it's important to come into contact with great art. The wonder and excitement one experiences from great works is the heart of art. The essence of art is seeing, hearing, feeling and then discovering.

*Though we know we should experience great art, many of us may not feel confident that we know what art is great and what isn't. We may not appreciate what others agree is a great work. How can we recognize great art?*

A great work of art is one that truly moves and inspires you. You are the one who must be moved. Don't look at art with others' eyes. Don't listen to music with others' ears. You must react to art with your own feelings, your own heart and mind. If you allow yourself to be swayed by the opinions of others—"It must be good, because everyone else likes it," "It must be bad, because no one else likes it"—your feelings, your sensibility, which should be the very core of the artistic experience, will wither and die.

To enjoy art to the fullest, you must abandon all preconceived notions, leaving a blank slate. Then confront the work directly, with your entire being. If you are deeply moved, then that work is, for you, a great work of art.

*Then what is considered a great work of art is different from person to person?*

Though one's subjective responses are very important, we must not lose sight of objectivity, either. It is necessary to nurture, through effort, the ability to appreciate truly great art. As we progress in our degree of understanding, art that we thought was good in the past may no longer seem so satisfying, and works that once left us cold suddenly have a tremendous power to move us.

For example, artworks that are recognized around the world and have moved many, many people over the centuries do possess qualities that merit their being identified as great, universal works of art. Art that lacks those qualities, though it may be popular for a time, tends not to last. There are certain experiences that almost all human beings are inclined to agree upon: When we look up at the clear blue sky, we all think it is marvelous; when we gaze at cherry blossoms, we all find them beautiful.

The great works of art also possess a universal quality. They possess a life force similar to that of nature itself. To instill that life in their work, the great artists suffer immensely, pouring their whole life energy into their art.

*In what way can we nurture our ability to recognize great art?*

Probably the best way is to see and hear as many of the generally agreed-upon masterpieces of world art as you can, which will cultivate and refine your sensibilities. You will naturally learn to distinguish good from bad.

Looking at second- and third-rate art will not help you understand first-rate art, but once you know first-rate art, you will immediately apprehend what is second and third rate. Your critical eye will emerge. That is why you should make an effort to come into contact with the best from the very start.

You can see great art in books, of course, but seeing the real thing, when you have a chance, is an entirely different experience. I still remember how tremendously moved I was when I first saw the great paintings in the Louvre. It's the difference between seeing someone's photograph and the person himself.

View good paintings. Listen to good music. Experiencing fine art will develop and nurture your mind.

*We are not all meant to be professional artists, so I guess the important thing is to foster a love of art and culture.*

To enjoy painting or singing as a hobby can also be a way of participating in the movement to spread culture. Recently, we have even seen Japanese companies seeking to recruit employees who have mastered an art. There are many reasons for this, but one is that they value the kind of personality that pursues art and culture. We should all develop the mind to rejoice in, praise and share in the gift of those who have artistic talents and a richness of heart, whether they achieve wide recognition or not. Cultivating such a beautiful mind is a very worthy effort.

Culture and art are not just decorations. They are not just accessories. What matters is whether culture enriches the essential substance of our lives.

*I understand that the important thing is to enrich our inner selves. The leader of the high school girl's division in Kyoto is working in a uniquely Japanese field of textile dyeing, in which complicated patterns are hand-painted or stenciled on silk. She says: "My feelings find expression in the colors I use. For example, if I am thinking of the happiness of others, that will appear in the designs and the colors. That's why I need to continue developing myself."*

*She also said: "I hope to look out to the larger world and breathe the fresh air of change, infuse my craft with that inspiration, and then share it with the world as an example of Japanese culture. My aim is to create beautiful art for the world, for others."*

That's wonderful. I hope we can inspire many who also respect culture and love art. When many such individuals come together, and when nations are linked in that spirit, our world will be ideal, and the century of true humanity will dawn.

*That will surely be the century of peace.*

## INNOVATION COMES FROM EFFORT

Peace and culture are one. A genuinely cultured nation is a peaceful nation, and vice versa. When conflicts multiply, culture wanes and nations fall into a hellish existence. The history of the human race is a contest between culture and barbarity. As we leave the tensions of the Cold War behind, the pressing question becomes "What will the coming century be like?" Only culture is a force strong enough to put an end to conflict and lead humanity in the direction of peace.

*You had enormous foresight in establishing so many cultural institutions, such as the Min-On Concert Association, the Fuji Art Museum [in both Tokyo and Shizuoka], Soka University and many others. You have contributed greatly to that cultural force you speak of.*

At the time, everyone opposed those projects! No one understood what I was doing.

*To pursue such a vision on your own, against opposition, and actually carry it out reflects great artistry in its own right.*

*In culture and other fields as well, people often say that the Japanese are good imitators but poor innovators. How do we learn to innovate?*

The pursuit of beauty, like most other human activities, often starts with imitation. All learning begins as imitating; one cannot innovate without first learning the basics. Someone plunking around on the piano without having first mastered the keyboard is not what we call an innovator. Imitation is the first step toward the creation of new art.

But one cannot remain an imitator forever. In Japan, most artists never get beyond imitation, never reach the stage in which they are creating something of their own. We are a nation of imitators; in technology and many other fields, we have used our ability to imitate to make money and created the Japan we see today. But though we are clever imitators, we don't seem to have the ability to take the next step, to break through the wall that leads to innovation. The only way to surmount this restrictive tradition is human revolution.

*What is essential for advancing from imitation to innovation?*

If we only repeat what we have seen and heard, we will never advance beyond imitation. The heart is crucial. We have to experience with the heart and express with the heart in order to innovate. That requires blood, sweat and tears. It requires relentless searching and continual effort. Only then do we gradually acquire the ability to express ourselves fully and naturally.

Effort is key. Leonardo Da Vinci (1452–1519) wrote in his manuscript notes: "Poor Leonardo! Look how much you suffer!"[4] And Beethoven, on his deathbed, while eagerly continuing to study the music of George Frederic Handel (1685–1759), is said to have declared that he still had much to learn.

*Beethoven said that? I always thought Beethoven was a very proud man who regarded himself as a genius who could learn from no one.*

He may have been proud, but all great people are also humble, in the truest sense. They know what it is to respect and look up to others. The pettier the individual, the more prone he is to envy.

Beethoven once wrote to a young girl: "The true artist has no pride; unhappily he sees that Art has no bounds. Obscurely he feels how far away he is from his aim, and even while others may be admiring him, he mourns his failure to attain that end which his better genius illumines like a distant sun."[5]

*This profound humility must be what allowed Beethoven to create the great works he did.*

In the same letter, I believe, Beethoven wrote: "I know of no other advantages of human beings than those which place them in the ranks of the good and the superior; wherever I find these, there is my home."[6]

*It's who we are as people that is important. There have been, certainly, famous artists who were not especially good human beings.*

Yes. Appreciating an artist's music or painting is quite different from respecting the artist as a human being. We must be careful not to confuse the issues of artistic skill and talent with respect for the artist as a person. It is not at all rare to find "cultured" people who have lived degenerate lives or have committed atrocities. It may be an extreme case, but Hitler regarded himself as an artist. Many of his paintings survive, and though opinions vary, it is probably fair to say that they are not inferior from the standpoint of technique. Yet Hitler can never be regarded as a civilized, cultured person. He was a barbarian, an incarnation of the evil nature of corrupt power.

An example of an artist who was very good-natured was the French painter Jean Baptiste Camille Corot (1796–1875), a precursor of the Impressionists. After achieving some success as a painter, he was always kind to those around him. When one of his models married a poor man, he gave her a dowry. When a painter friend was about to be driven from the house he was renting, Corot bought the house and gave it to him.

A woman who knew Corot is said to have remarked, "I don't know if his paintings are masterpieces, but he himself is a masterpiece created by God."

*Even artists must examine themselves as human beings. They cannot allow themselves to become self-centered.*

Being creative is very different from being self-centered, just as genuine individuality and an invented, eccentric persona are different. In fact, it may well be that truly unique individuals express their uniqueness without even trying. They seek and accept nature, life and truth and try to convey them exactly as they are. In the process, their individuality naturally shines through. That is true creativity, true innovation.

I think the French sculptor Auguste Rodin (1840–1917) meant the same thing when he said that life is more important than individuality in the creation of art.

*Real creativity is important for all of us, not just for artists. In the future, Japan cannot get by with mere imitation.*

That's probably true. It will be a time of "creative competition." But it's far easier to talk about creativity than actually to be creative. Being creative is a fierce struggle. Creative people always face opposition from those intolerant to change, and they must endure the loneliness and isolation that comes with being misunderstood. They need courage. They need tenacity. They need to have faith in their endeavor that isn't swayed by petty considerations of gain and loss.

*When people say the Japanese are not creative, they may be pointing to the fact that many Japanese lack such faith and courage.*

I would like you, our young people, to make Japan and the world into a creative, culturally rich society. The twentieth century killed far too many, beginning with its two world wars. Though it is spoken of as the century in which civilization made its greatest advances, it has also been the century of the most barbaric massacres. Auschwitz, Hiroshima, Nagasaki, Nanking and the Stalinist purges are all symbols of that barbarism. They are lessons to us all: Even an apparently civilized society will never have peace without truly cultured individuals who love humanity. Without that, the products of modern civilization become the tools of demons.

Mr. Makiguchi taught that education is the highest of all arts, the art of creating the values of fine character. His words are golden. Art does not belong to a select few. Nurturing people, cultivating the self is also art. Art is displayed in a beautiful life, beautiful actions, beautiful prayer.

The wonderful art of peace is being devoted entirely to linking beautiful human hearts to one another. When cultivated lives and culture itself are joined, the truly humane culture of the twenty-first century will be born. When fully realized humanity and art come together, a truly humane art will be born. It is your mission to forge that spectacular and creative future.

1. Chang Shuhong and Daisaku Ikeda, *Tonko no kosai* (The Radiance of Dunhuang: On Beauty and Life) (Tokyo: Tokuma Shoten, 1990). To date, not available in English.

2. Natsume Soseki, *The Three-Cornered World*, trans. Alan Turney (Tokyo: Charles E. Tuttle Co., 1965), p. 12.

3. *Education for Creative Living*, trans. Alfred Birnbaum, ed. Dayle M. Bethel (Ames, Iowa: Iowa State University Press, 1989), p. 75.

4. *Reonarudo da Binchi no shuki* (The Notebooks of Leonardo da Vinci), trans. Mimpei Sugiura (Tokyo: Iwanami Shoten, 1977), vol. 1, p. 31.

5. Michael Hamburger, *Beethoven: Letters, Journals and Conversations* (London: Thames and Hudson, 1951), p. 115.

6. *Beethoven—Letters, Journals and Conversations*, p. 115.

# *13*

## DIALOGUE WITH NATURE

*The subject of many of your photographs, President Ikeda, is nature. When I look at them, I'm always surprised at how you've captured the beauty of even the most familiar scenes.*

*What do you feel as you take those photos?*

I always click the shutter with the feeling that I am engaging in a dialogue with nature. Through that dialogue, I see my true self—I see the true image of humanity and life.

Nature is like a mirror. It remains still, but we move. It seems unchanging, yet we are constantly changing. The mirror of nature reflects our inner world, the essence of humanity, and the great, all-embracing expanse of life itself.

*One high school student wrote: "I feel good on a beautiful day. I think it's because the wonderful sun, the wind, the grass and trees are completely natural, existing as they are without pretense or artificiality." I think, in her own way, she is engaged in a dialogue with the blue sky, a conversation with the sun.*

Yes, no doubt she is. Only when we are connected to nature, engaged with nature, are we truly alive and vigorous. To really be alive, one must be under the sun, the moon, the shining stars and surrounded by the beautiful greenery and pure waters of the natural world. A dirty, foul environment is not natural. When people live in such surroundings, their hearts become polluted, too. That is the "oneness of life and environment."

*The "oneness of life and environment" is the Buddhist principle that explains that that the environment and all living beings within it must be regarded as inseparable, as a single, whole entity.*

Yes. People cannot exist apart from nature. And the destruction of nature is nothing but a sign of the arrogance and ignorance of humanity.

I have always loved the writings of Japanese author Doppo Kunikida[1] (1871–1908), which are filled with magnificent descriptions of nature. I still remember many. A passage in *Musashino* (The Musashi Plain) reads: "The clear blue sky beyond the tree tops, the sun's light scattered by leaves swaying in the breeze; no words can describe the beauty."[2]

*When one experiences such natural beauty, one's heart is cleansed. That's what we mean by having a dialogue with nature, isn't it?*

I take photographs because I want to record such a dialogue, so that together we may experience nature's beauty and wonder. Photographs are taken with the heart.

Robert Capa (1913–54) photographed the tragedy of war from the battlefield and left a record of it for us from which we can learn. I want to leave behind a record of nature's importance.[3]

Today, there is little interest in pursuing the profound life inherent in nature. Far more energy is devoted to the exploration of other subjects. Comprehensive though it may be, however, when learning is removed from the essence of life, it has little true value.

All of the greatest artistic and cultural achievements of the past were born of a love of nature and from intimate experience of it. As nature has been progressively destroyed, art has become more and more artificial.

*The Kansai Soka schools are well known for raising fireflies. Both teachers and students there are making efforts to breed and protect these luminous wonders of nature. I understand that you proposed this project, President Ikeda.*

*I've heard that the students work hard taking care of the firefly lar-vae, feeding them every day, no matter what the weather. Caring for living things is a strenuous effort.*

*I remember hearing that once the students used a photographic develop-ing pan to house the larvae. Though they had washed the pan carefully, it seems some chemical residue remained, and all the larvae died.*

Sad as it is, I'm sure the students learned the fragility and value of life from that experience. Fireflies live only two weeks in their adult form, during which they glow and shine beautifully. Their brief lives demon-strate the drama of nature.

When I was a boy, there was a pond next to the cherry tree that stood by our house in Tokyo's Ota Ward. In summer, clouds of fire-flies would dance in the night skies over the little stream that ran from the pond.

Where there are fireflies, humans and nature are in harmony. Fireflies are symbols of peace.

I heard a report that the students who were involved in the firefly project are now growing into kind and considerate adults.

*Fireflies can be found all around the world, right?*

Yes. As a matter of fact, there are beautiful fireflies at the SGI-Italy Culture Center in Florence.

I heard that when the Brazilian poet Amadeu Thiago de Mello visited the Kansai Soka schools, he shared with the students a child-hood memory of fireflies. It was night in the Amazon, and the sky was filled with stars that were reflected perfectly in the gleaming, jet-black surface of the river, clear as a polished mirror. Stars in the heavens and stars in the river, and in between, a twinkling cloud of fireflies. He said it was unforgettable.

## Preserving the Environment
## Is the Greatest Honor

*What a magical vision!*
  *Mr. Mello is known as a protector of the Amazon. By the way, the SGI is carrying out a tree-planting program in the Amazon region.*

Reforesting the Amazon is a tremendous art form in itself. It is back-breaking, dirty work, far out of the limelight. Yet the volunteers, with great patience and determination, stick with it, because they believe in what they are doing. They all deserve commendations.

Our world should be one in which people like that, those committed to preserving nature, are honored. It makes no sense giving medals and decorations to politicians just because they have been in government for a long time. I'd like to see any one of them speak in the legislature out of a love for the environment and in favor of protecting it.

Government must be dedicated to the good of the people. It is a tragedy that the beautiful natural environment people have cherished and protected for generations is being destroyed in the name of economic growth, political advantage and scientific progress. Because human beings have the capacity to be aware of the balance of nature, it is our duty to work to preserve it.

I once suggested to someone that each railway station in Japan should cultivate a unique natural character. One could be planted with cherry trees, another with azaleas, another with wisteria and so on.

I think, too, that we should plant more trees along our streets. China has many beautiful tree-lined streets and avenues. At Soka University, I made sure that many azaleas were planted because I believe that humanistic education can only occur in a rich, beautiful natural environment.

I also had many cherry trees planted at the head temple, Taiseki-ji. Later, as you know, they were cut down by those who lack respect for the environment.

The Nichiren Shoshu priesthood cut down more than two hundred eighty cherry trees donated by the Soka Gakkai and planted on the grounds of Taiseki-ji.

*When someone outside Japan heard that story, they said that this itself is proof of the evil nature of the Nichiren Shoshu priesthood. They couldn't believe that anyone would commit such a hate-filled act.*

In countries with an advanced appreciation of the environment, there are many laws protecting it. In Brazil, for example, you cannot cut down a tree—even if it's on your property—without permission from a supervisory agency.

A saying goes that planting a tree is planting life. I think we should all consider the full significance of that.

*We are facing an environmental crisis on a global level, and it is a fundamental problem that concerns all humanity.*

Yes. Buddhism explains life in a system of ten stages or states of being known as the Ten Worlds—the states of hell, hunger, animality, anger, humanity, heaven, voice-hearers (learning), cause-awakened ones (realization), bodhisattvas and Buddhahood. The state of humanity is right in the middle, with nobler states of life above and uglier states below. Those states below are unnatural states of being, states at odds with nature. The four stages above humanity all value nature and strive to create a paradise where its beauty flourishes in abundance.

The question is, will we allow ourselves to be dragged down to the lower states, or will we advance to the higher states? Only intelligence, culture and religious faith can lead us out of the baseness that thoughtlessly consumes nature, leaving a barren wasteland. Because of the "oneness of life and its environment," a desolate, destructive heart or mind produces a desolate, devastated natural environment. The desertification of our planet is linked to the desertification of the human spirit.

War is the most extreme example of this destructive impulse. War destroys both nature and the human spirit. The twentieth century has been a century of war. We must make the twenty-first century a century of life, a century in which life is the top priority in all spheres of human activity—in commerce, in government, in science.

*Environmental destruction is going on right around us, as well. Where I live, green hills and empty lots are all being "developed" into apartment complexes and other buildings. There is no longer any place you can walk your dog without a leash. It feels extremely cramped and binding.*

The destruction of nature is the destruction of humanity. Nature is our home. All life on this planet, including of course human life, was born from the natural environment. We don't owe our existence to machines or science. We are the products of nature. Life on this planet was not artificially created.

There are many theories about the origins of humanity. Some say that the first humans appeared in Africa; others say that human beings appeared in various locations around the world at the same time. Whatever may be true, it is indisputable that the human species was born of nature.

Because of that, the further we alienate ourselves from nature, the more unbalanced we become. Our future as a species is grim unless we recognize this.

The eighteenth-century French philosopher Jean-Jacques Rousseau (1712–78) called for a return to nature. Civilization even in his time had become too mechanical, too reliant on science, too concentrated on profit, distorting human life into ugliness. Rousseau protested this unfortunate development.

President Toda used to tell young people to walk barefoot upon the soil and plant trees. He was trying to teach them to root their lives in the natural world.

Indeed, we all want to be healthy. For that reason, we want to breathe clean air, to see beautiful flowers and greenery. We turn to nature for this, just as a sunflower turns to the sun. We must recognize that any action that disrespects or destroys our right to do so is a terrible mistake. All the money in the world cannot buy the blue sky. The sun and the breeze belong to everyone.

Human beings can either destroy nature or live in harmony with it. We must never forget that we are a part of nature.

*It is true that our lives today are far more convenient than they once were. We can buy almost everything we need, and we can get something to eat anytime we like, day or night. We have access to such a variety of goods that our biggest problem is choosing what we want. But we seem to be destroying the environment and ourselves for the sake of convenience.*

*When I was a student, I had a part-time job at a large fast-food hamburger chain. All of the food arrived frozen from the factory, and we warmed it so that we could serve it immediately. But whenever anything sat for thirty minutes, we would throw it out, wrapping and all, so that we could serve customers fresher food. I was shocked at how much food we threw away.*

That's symbolic of our gluttonous society. In the old days, it was considered a crime to leave even a single grain of rice uneaten in one's bowl.

Mass-producing fast-food hamburgers requires large quantities of cheap beef. And beef cattle need pastureland. To get pastureland, huge tracts of forest are cut down. According to one calculation, five square meters of pastureland in the tropics are required to produce the meat for one hamburger.

But when the trees are cut down and the roots that once held the earth together are gone, rains wash away the topsoil. As a result, a large proportion of all such pastureland becomes a wasteland after only a few years.

In fact, by 1985, two-thirds of all the accessible rain forests in Central America had been cut down, much of it for pasture. All of the plants and animals living there were killed. The indigenous peoples living in the forest lost their homes and their culture.

Any mass production that requires such a terrible sacrifice is wrong. Even more so if the product is thrown away casually. Is this a sign of real wealth and a good life? How can we condone this when tens of thousands of our fellow humans are dying of malnutrition every day?

# The Chain of Life Links All

*It seems to me that something is fundamentally wrong with the path the human race has taken.*

No one is denying that science has improved our lives. Thanks to science, we can use electricity instead of just oil lamps and candles. But we need to match the progress of science with progress in our commitment to preserve and protect our environment. We need a balance.

Let's talk some more about forests. Where does the oxygen that we breathe, that keeps us alive, come from? From forests, from sea plants. Plants have spent billions of years creating this oxygen.

What about water? Most of the water we use comes from river systems. Whether it rains or shines, water flows through rivers. Why? The trees and the soil around them absorb the water, storing it underground, from where it flows constantly, bit by bit, into the rivers. If there were no forests and the mountains were hard as asphalt, all the rain that fell in a day would run immediately into the rivers and flow out to sea, just like a bathtub emptying when you pull the plug.

Soil is another gift of the forest. Small animals and microbes help transform the dead roots of trees and their leaves into rich soil. Without that soil, we could not grow grains or vegetables. We would have no food, and humanity would perish.

Many other products come from forests. Without them, we would have no rubber bands, no paper, no wooden desks or furniture—no homes. All of these, too, are the forest's gifts.

*Forests produce the air we breathe, the water we drink, the soil in which we grow food—all of which we take for granted. Every aspect of our lives is made possible by trees.*

And that's not all. Unless we take care of the forests, we won't be able to catch fish in the sea.

*Why is that?*

As I said, without forests all the rain would flow away down the rivers to the sea. That rain would also carry large amounts of silt with it. The silt would cloud the seawaters, block the penetration of light and lower the sea's temperature, making it too cold for many fish. The forests also produce nutrients that eventually make their way to the sea and become food for marine life. The forests protect the life of the sea.

*Everything is linked, isn't it?*

Life is a chain. All things are related. When any link is harmed, the other links will be affected. We should think of the environment as our mother—Mother Soil, Mother Sea, Mother Earth. There is no crime worse than harming one's mother.

*It's important to have a philosophy that recognizes everything in the universe as living and sacred.*

We are dependent on the earth, not the other way around. In our arrogance, we have flagrantly overlooked this. The Soviet cosmonaut Yuri Gagarin (1934–68), the first person to see the earth from space, declared it a blue planet. This is a great testimony. The blue of the oceans, the white of the clouds—they are proof that earth is the water planet, a planet sparkling with life.

The essential teaching of Buddhism is that the life of the Buddha resides in every plant and tree, even in the smallest speck of dust. No philosophy has a more profound reverence for life.

Buddhism elucidates this both deductively and intuitively. I believe that science ought to be committed to the welfare of humanity based on induction, based on reasoning derived from the concrete facts of life. Everything must begin from such purpose.

The Gaia hypothesis, that the earth is a living thing, is well known. Dr. James Lovelock, who first formulated this idea, wrote in *The Ages of Gaia*, "Strangely, [the Gaia theory] is not a view inconsistent with the human values of kindness and compassion."[4]

# TREAT THE EARTH WELL

*If one were to possess such kindness, one would find it impossible to litter.*

Only someone who lives in the selfish state of animality could throw trash or aluminum cans by the road. This is an egoism that cares nothing for others. It is an unnatural way to live. A person who loves nature is simply unable to litter. Tossing one's trash away carelessly is to toss away one's humanity.

By the same token, one who loves nature can cherish other humans, value peace and possess a richness of character unfettered by selfish calculations of personal gain and loss. Those who live in a calculating way will end up calculating their own worth in the same manner. Such a life is limited in the extreme.

Nature, however, is infinite. Though it may seem beneficial to keep track of personal gain and loss, from nature's broader viewpoint, this is actually a poor, miserable existence. Such people only hurt themselves.

*People might think that there is no reward in picking up trash others have strewn about, but I think it's important to do things like that out of love for nature—without thinking about what one may or may not gain.*

Only through such selfless actions can we live the best way as human beings.

*I think that because technology has advanced to the extent it has, it's more important than ever for each person to develop the awareness to protect the environment.*

As science advances, it is only natural that we should become involved in many endeavors to preserve the environment. Each of us, as individuals, must make an effort not to be selfish; to save energy, for example. We must take better care of our environment. Any apparent material improvements are illusory unless we enhance the fundamental quality of our lives.

*Many members have begun pondering this subject. One wrote, "I think it's important to stop thinking that one person cannot make a difference." And another said, "We mustn't believe that we can make an exception for ourselves, that it's OK for us to pollute our environment."*

That's true. It is a lot easier to talk about environmental protection than to practice it. There are obstacles sometimes—and sometimes practicing it can even be life threatening.

I wonder if you've ever heard of the American marine biologist Rachel Carson. She wrote a groundbreaking book called *Silent Spring*, published in 1962, which attacked the problem of pollution.

At that time, very powerful insecticides such as DDT were being used all across the United States. They seemed to be effective at first, but gradually, beneficial insects, fish and birds were disappearing from the landscape. With no birds to sing, Ms. Carson wrote, a silent spring awaited us. People were beginning to show signs of being poisoned and getting sick from the chemicals, as well.

Her book announced these facts to the public and urged that dangerous pesticides be banned. Immediately after the book's publication, she was vehemently attacked.

*She was criticized, even though what she wrote was true?*

She was attacked *because* what she said was true—by the giant corporations that made huge fortunes from manufacturing pesticides, and by officials and politicians who were in the pockets of those companies. This happens all the time, whenever someone tells an unpleasant truth. We must learn to see through such charades.

Those linked to the pesticide industry joined in a campaign to discredit her. Agricultural magazines attacked her. One wrote, "Her book is more poisonous than the pesticides she condemns."[5] Even state research organizations joined the campaign—research organizations that, needless to say, received large amounts of funding from the chemical companies.

It was a campaign to silence *Silent Spring*. At one time, attacks on Ms. Carson were appearing on radio and television as frequently as once every fifty minutes. Even the American Medical Association came out with a statement that the effects of pesticides on human beings were precisely as described by the manufacturers.[6]

But she would not give up. And she went even further, declaring that pesticides were only part of the story of the poisons that were threatening our world. Eventually, she won the support of the people, and environmentalism began to spread across the United States and throughout the world. That torch of faith kept burning after she died in 1964 and has grown to dramatically transform public awareness.

Rachel Carson left these words in *The Sense of Wonder* for the younger generation: "Those who dwell, as scientists or laymen, among the beauties and mysteries of the earth are never alone or weary of life."[7]

A Kenyan saying goes that we should treat the earth well; it is not a gift from our parents but a loan from our children. But the adults of our day are leaving a dismal inheritance to today's young people and the children you will have. With their philosophy that making money is most important of all, they are selling off your legacy—the health, culture, environment and even life that nature has protected and nurtured for so many eons.

It is your legacy, so you must act. You who have not yet forgotten the beauty and wonder of the earth must speak out. Your struggle to protect the twenty-first century, your century, the century of life, has already begun.

1. Doppo Kunikida (1871–1908): Japanese poet and novelist who played an important role as a forerunner to naturalism in Japanese literature.

2. Translated from Japanese. Doppo Kunikida, *Musashino* (Musashi Plain) (Tokyo: Iwanami Shoten, 1939), p. 13.

3. Robert Capa is regarded as one of the greatest photojournalists of the twentieth century. He was on the front lines as a photographer in five wars and took more than seventy thousand photographs.

4. James Lovelock, *The Ages of Gaia: A Biography of Our Living Earth* (New York and London: W.W. Norton & Company, 1988), p. 240.

5. Paul Brooks, *The House of Life: Rachel Carson at Work* (Boston: Houghton Mifflin Company, 1972), p. 296.

6. *The House of Life: Rachel Carson at Work*, p. 297.

7. Rachel Carson, *The Sense of Wonder* (New York and Evanston: Harper & Row, Publishers, 1965), p. 88.

# 14

## Discovering Great Literature

*In this installment, we shall ask some questions about literature.*

*Earlier, we talked about the importance of reading. Many members were inspired by that discussion and are now reading with enthusiasm.*

*We often make excuses for not reading, such as being too busy, but actually, once we make a firm resolve to read, we find that we do have time. One student said that our discussion on that subject gave her a new appreciation of how much fun reading can be.*

Yes, literature is a very important subject, and it deserves our further discussion. By sparking the high school division members' interest in literature, I hope that we may help them lead rich and satisfying lives, to become engaging human beings who understand others' hearts.

In Japan today, great literature is far removed from most people's daily lives. It is viewed as something to be read only for school exams. What a sad waste. More effort needs to be made to show people how wonderful it is to explore literature. Life is a quest. We are always searching for the answers to the grand questions: What is it to be human? What is a good life? Literature is an excellent companion and guide on that quest.

*There are many ways to have fun. For example, computer games are definitely fun. But once the game is finished, there's little to show for it. Many people have experienced this. But the impression one gains from reading a really good book lasts forever.*

195

Yes. Watching an image may give momentary pleasure, but reading has a far more enduring impact. Reading requires mental effort and perseverance—we have to use our imagination and make our way through a book word by word, line by line, page by page.

It may be difficult, but we cultivate our hearts and minds only to the extent that we challenge ourselves. Those who read great literature have more depth. If we make an effort to read, it will eventually become second nature and a source of enjoyment.

*Whenever I read your book* A Youthful Diary, *President Ikeda, I am astonished by the incredible pace and scope of your reading. Even when Mr. Toda's business was going bankrupt, and you were busy taking care of the company's affairs, your reading schedule never slowed.*

*In your diary entry for February 8, 1951, you write: "Fourteen young religious revolutionaries gathered boldly under the leadership of our teacher, Mr. Toda. All participants were serious... Next, the participants discussed the book* The Eternal City.*"*

*The entry for February 21 says: "Youth, arise! Youth, advance! Youth, move! Onward, ever onward! Unafraid of towering precipices or raging waves. Like Bruno or Rossi. Like Napoleon, Alexander, Whitman or Dante."*

*The entry for February 24 states: "Finished reading the last volume of the* Romance of the Three Kingdoms... *The grand plot skillfully portrays the human spirit's subtleties. It conveys the felling of a giant scroll-painting depicting the heat of battles as well as the intrigues of generals and politicians' schemes, love, tears, high spirits, ability and moral lessons. The main character, Liu Pei Hsüan-te, is a youth of revolution—a man of construction."*

*Although you were then going through the most tempestuous of times, you continued to study, looking ten, twenty years ahead.*

*Your diary is filled with references to your love of literature. One day you write: "Read* The Count of Monte Cristo. *Had many thoughts." Another day you report: "Read* Scaramouche.*" In yet another entry: "Read* Parallel Lives *by Plutarch. Will read again tomorrow." And again: "To Kanda Avenue in the evening. Bought three secondhand books. The books I want to buy can be piled as high as a mountain. Difficult to afford."*

*I have heard that from the time you were a young man, President Ikeda, you knew you wanted to become a great writer. How did you come to be so fond of literature?*

I suffered from poor health when I was young, so I couldn't participate much in sports. Since one can read in bed or while lying down, I naturally spent a lot of time reading. That was the first step.

## LITERATURE IS THE STUDY OF HUMANITY

*One member said that he is a science major and has no interest in literature. He asked if he should make an effort to read anyway.*

Well, that's certainly an honest question. Actually, contrary to what he may think, reading literature can greatly enhance his study of science. If science is all he focuses on, his thinking will become very mechanical. We are only fully human when we possess not only intelligence but also emotion and sensitivity. Literature is the oil that greases the wheels of the mind.

Many tragedies have occurred because this has been largely forgotten. If national leaders know nothing but science, it may well be that they will think only of building weapons. Knowing great literature breathes life into our humanity. Literature derives from the human spirit.

*Speaking of science, wasn't Mr. Toda an expert mathematician?*

Yes, mathematics was his specialty, but he also knew a great deal about literature. He declared that one could neither understand mathematics nor religion unless one read literature. And he always urged the youth division members to read a great deal. The last time that Mr. Toda asked me what I was reading, I responded, "Rousseau's *Émile.*" I was reading this treatise on education because I was determined to found a school someday.

Literature is the study of humanity. It is the study of oneself and of the infinite realm of the human heart. Without an understanding of people's hearts, one cannot gain a profound understanding of any other

197

sphere of learning or endeavor. Human culture is the product of the human heart and mind.

Actually, dividing things into humanities and sciences is itself odd. As long as so many political leaders and educators remain caught up in their specialties and unaware of the vital importance of literature, we will never create a better society. It will be very dangerous if our society is made up of people who, like robots, possess knowledge but have no heart or conscience.

*Every day, when I ride the train to work, I am disappointed by what I see middle-aged men reading. Almost all of them have their heads in weekly gossip magazines or trashy tabloids. How spiritually impoverished Japan is, I always sadly think. Even people who at least sample the works of world literature during their student days stop reading them as soon as they graduate.*

*I hope today's high school students will grow into different kinds of adults—the kind who will continue to read literature and learn from it all of their lives.*

Does merely growing older make one an adult? No. What makes one a mature person is one's growth as a human being, one's richness of character and experience. Those are things that literature can indeed help us develop.

Learning languages allows us to expand our boundaries to encompass other nations and cultures. Reading literature further widens our horizons, enabling us to become acquainted with people and places all around the world. Sometimes an encounter with a great work of literature can change the course of our lives entirely.

Literature is the very pulse of life. Those who have learned to appreciate great literature during their youth are always vital and vigorous, because the pulse of literature beats within them. Those who haven't learned such an appreciation lack that vitality; their lives are spiritually drab and empty.

Looking up at the blue sky, for example, might be a different experience for someone who has read *War and Peace* than for someone who hasn't, for that person who has may be reminded of the peaceful blue sky that Prince Andrei gazed up at in the midst of a terrible bloody battle—one of the novel's climactic scenes. That same sky stretches above all our heads at this very moment.

[Prince Andrei, who had carried the Russian flag in the attack against the French forces, lies wounded on the battlefield. He looks up at the blue sky: "Above him there was now only the sky—the lofty sky, not clear yet still immeasurably lofty, with grey clouds creeping softly across it. 'How quiet, peaceful and solemn!... How was it I did not see that sky before? And how happy I am to have found it at last! Yes, all is vanity, all is delusion except these infinite heavens. There is nothing, nothing but that. But even it does not exist, there is nothing but peace and stillness....'"[1]]

Take also the example of a flowing river. Those who have read Hermann Hesse's *Siddhartha* may share the joy Siddhartha felt when, after a long regime of painful austerities, he regained his strength at the river's edge. A river flows endlessly, never for a moment ceasing. It is in constant motion, yet it is always there. It never changes, yet it is always new. In the same way, the world itself is also whole and complete each moment, and we attain happiness here and now—not in some other place, at some other time.

Literature also helps us relate to people's characters and dispositions. In one person, we may detect some of Hamlet's qualities; in another, Don Quixote; in another, Moliere's hypocritical Tartuffe. We may know a person who resembles the proud Julien Sorel from Stendhal's *The Red and the Black*, or a person like Sydney Carton from Charles Dickens' *A Tale of Two Cities*, who goes to the guillotine for the sake of friendship and love.

Similarly, a visit to the sea may remind one of the sea of obsession in Herman Melville's *Moby Dick*, or the drifting sea of Homer's *Odyssey*, or the sea of sadness in Bernardin de Saint-Pierre's *Paul et Virginie*. There is also the tranquil sea described in the *Man'yoshu* (Collection of Ten Thousand Leaves), a collection of ancient Japanese poetry.

Reading literature allows us to view the incredible kaleidoscope of human behavior and emotion. It also gives us an insight into the vast, deep ocean of life existing beneath the countless rolling waves.

# GET INTO THE HABIT OF READING
# WHILE YOU ARE YOUNG

*I was asked by one student if there is something to be gained from reading books when we are young that we won't be able to gain when we get older.*

I would say there is. It is more of a challenge to read when you get older. You have to battle with busy daily schedules and sometimes even increasingly poor eyesight! And you may find yourself starting to forget what you have read. This might be hard for you to believe right now, but it's true.

Everything has a time. What you read when you are young is etched into your memory. It becomes a part of you. What you learn as a result becomes a valuable experience and asset for forming your own ideas and philosophy, and acquiring different ways of looking at things.

Only human beings have the ability to read. I'm sure that some of our readers are probably thinking that they'll start reading later in life when they have more time. But chances are that if you neglect reading during your youth, you won't read later on either. For that reason, it's important to get into the habit of reading while you are young—this will establish the foundation on which to build the rest of your life. I cannot stress this enough.

Leading figures around the world frequently cite works of literature. Quite a few individuals even have a cursory knowledge of Japanese literature. If you read literature while you are young, you will be more familiar with what those people are saying.

I have talked about *The Tale of the Bamboo Cutter* [Taketori Monogatari] with the Russian minister of education, and about the *Man'yoshu* with Dr. Arnold Toynbee. With others I have talked about *Urashima Taro* [a sort of Japanese Rip Van Winkle]. Unlike discussions about politics or business, discussions about literature are beautiful; they don't cause arguments, and they lend quickly to striking a rapport.

Mr. Toda once encouraged a young woman to discuss not only the writings of Nichiren Daishonin when traveling overseas, but also Japan's many fine novels.

*There's something very likeable and attractive about people who have lots of things to talk about.*

I hope our youth division members will have sufficient knowledge of the famed stories and novels of their homelands to relate them with great expression and feeling. Every country has its folk tales and legends. The spiritual legacy of the people is woven into most of them. Stories that have been handed down through the generations have a value that has ensured their survival.

Time is the greatest critic. For that reason, I urge all of you to read literature that has stood the test of time.

*One member, who is a great fan of Japanese novelist Shugoro Yamamoto, said that he just cannot seem to find anything appealing about non-Japanese literature.*

Non-Japanese literature can be difficult to read in Japanese, usually because of the translation. From my experience, most such books are rather hard going for about the first quarter of the way through. But if you can stick with it and get past that point, you'll find yourself quickly drawn in and carried along. For example, Balzac's *Old Goriot* begins with a long description of the inn where the novel takes place and is a little slow in getting started. Yet no novel depicts a father's love for his daughter as wonderfully as this one does.

Though translated literature may be a challenge to get into at first, I hope you'll do your best to read such works. It's like hiking up a mountain—when you reach a certain height, the beautiful scenery begins to unfold all around you.

*Many students say that they want to read, but they don't have time. They are too busy with their studies, part-time jobs or extracurricular activities.*

We often say we don't have time, but all of us can spare at least five or ten minutes now and then. Being a reader doesn't mean that you have to sit down for three or four hours and read straight through. In fact, I think that in many cases, the things we read in brief spaces of time tend to stay with us longer. One method is to choose two or three types of books, like something easy and maybe a short story or an epic novel, and then read whichever one you want when you have a spare moment.

*Some say that they enjoy reading nonfiction but have no interest in fiction.*

Works of fiction can at times be far-fetched and inaccurate. That's why it's important to firmly establish and maintain your own critical awareness so that you are not taken in by everything you read. Truly great literature, however, is filled with the richness of forests, rivers, stars, the four seasons and the whole tumultuous panorama of human history.

Many of the popular novels today tend to be limited in scope. Works that can be classed as great literature, on the other hand, take one on a journey of much greater depth and breadth. Those who have never savored that vast realm are most unfortunate. They are like people who have never seen the sea and think that the shallow stream nearby is all the water there is on earth.

*Another student said that he hates reading. He struggles to read even one or two books a year, and as soon as he begins to turn the pages, he starts nodding off. He asked if there is any shortcut or secret method that he can use to become a better reader.*

I'm afraid there's no shortcut. The only way to become a better reader is to make active efforts in that direction. As long as you are looking for an easy way out, you'll never progress.

The same is true with physical exercise. If you hate running and make no effort to run, you'll never be a fit runner.

So if you get sleepy when you read, then perhaps it's best just to get some sleep; then resume your reading when you wake up. Without effort, you can never hope to grow or improve, nor can you realize your true potential. You'll just grow old without experiencing the depth and wonder of life.

Having said that, I hope that those who haven't yet gotten into the habit of reading will take up the challenge. For starters, perhaps you can select a short, accessible book, and just dive in. That will be the first stone in the foundation of your reading capacity.

## Appreciate Reading the Classics

*It's a real shame never to experience the pure joy of reading.*

Reading is fun. Shakespeare's plays, at the time they were written, were popular entertainment. They were like today's movies. When the eleventh-century Japanese novel *The Tale of Genji* was written, people used to vie to borrow a copy and read it, much like people pass around comic books today. It's a mistake to think of the classics as musty, difficult and boring. There's no need to be awed or intimidated by them, either. Once you have come to really appreciate them for what they are, you will find yourself a richer human being.

*One student said that she can see the important influence literature has on our lives, and wondered how that is different from what music and art teach us.*

All appeal to our senses in different ways. Literature by its very nature expresses thoughts and ideas in the written form. Without ideas, it would be impossible to write. Ideas are vast in dimension; they are unlimited. Ideas move us and change the way we think.

The Bible, the Lotus Sutra and the ancient Japanese chronicle *Kojiki* can all be considered literature. Literature occupies a very important place in the history of human thought. Its influence reaches into the depths of human experience. Humankind will suffer a tremendous loss if all we do is restrict ourselves and our concerns to the spheres of politics, business and science, without reading and pondering great literature.

Literature is a stage upon which many different realms of human experience are presented, such as philosophies of life, the relationship of the individual to society, war and peace, struggle, and love and death. Music and art can illuminate one part of that experience, of course, and religion illuminates it fully and completely.

Upon the foundation of literature unfold other aspects of culture such as drama, theater, film and music.

*There is a film of Tolstoy's* War and Peace, *for example, and a musical based on Victor Hugo's* Les Misérables. *Some people come into contact with literature by seeing such a film or musical first, and then going on to investigate the original literary work.*

*Reading gives us so much. Returning to your book* A Youthful Diary, *President Ikeda, I found this passage: "Gentle rain. Finished reading* The Count of Monte Cristo *at the office. Reading supplies one with wisdom, knowledge and leadership ability, and it helps in studying Nichiren's writings as well. Someone once said: 'Read throughout your life, even if only thirty minutes each day. In the course of a lifetime, this will add up to a tremendous amount of reading'" [February 18, 1954].*

Yes, I remember that time of my life fondly. Reading literature is an indispensable tool for understanding Nichiren's writings. Both the writings of Nichiren and literature depict the human experience. We find in Nichiren's words the profoundly compassionate wish to save all of humanity, a fierce anger toward evil and a warmth that enters into the hidden corners of people's hearts.

For example, to a follower who had first lost her husband and then her dearly loved son, Nichiren Daishonin writes, sharing in her grief, "It must be a dream, an illusion!" (WND-1, 1091). He goes on to say that if only her son had left word where she could meet him, "then without wings, you would soar to the heavens, or without a boat, you would cross over to China. If you heard that he was in the bowels of the earth, then how could you fail to dig into the ground?" (WND-1, 1092). Nichiren voices the mother's feelings for her son in his letter, empathizing with her pain.

*How comforted she must have been by that letter!*

Nichiren's writings contain innumerable descriptions of the human condition. The more experience we acquire in life, and the more great literature we read, the more we can appreciate the greatness of

Nichiren's writings. At the same time, by reading Nichiren's writings, we gain a deeper understanding of literature.

Literature portrays the complexities of the human heart. If we are determined to live our lives as true humanists, we must read literature. Cheap, carelessly written books or books that are solely for entertainment aren't literature, because they do not explore the meaning of life. Technical and nonfiction books are important, of course, and have their purposes, but literature is an irreplaceable lifeline for all humanity.

## Words of Genuine Concern and Compassion

*The question has been asked, "What good is literature to a starving child?" Some say that literature is just words; it cannot really change things or help those who are suffering.*

The most important kind of help we can give another is spiritual help. Only when spiritual help is provided first can monetary and material help really be put to good use.

Reading literature makes us think of others' situations and encourages us to address them with genuine concern and compassion. It enables us to speak from the heart. It is from such a sense of humanity that charity in its truest form emerges.

Great literature is a necessity both for the starving child and for those helping the child. Buddhism teaches, "The voice carries out the work of the Buddha" (OTT, 4). Our voices, our words, save people. Words that express a profound mind are in great need. The ability to express oneself well comes from an understanding of and a familiarity with literature. Because they lack this foundation, the words of most Japanese politicians are hollow and empty.

In his preface to *Les Misérables*, Hugo writes, "While ignorance and poverty persist on earth, books such as this cannot fail to be of value."[2] Literature, we might say, is what nurtures the will to save the starving child; then, from that will, action is taken and material and financial assistance is realized.

*How would you define "good writing"?*

I once posed the same question to a writer with whom I was engaged in a dialogue. He said, "When I flip through a book, I find that when the words (Chinese characters) line up beautifully, the writing is good; if they line up poorly or unattractively, the writing is bad." Be that as it may, I think reading good writing is like eating good food, a pleasurable experience.

Mr. Toda told me to always read the preface and afterword of every book I read. He said one could judge the writer's ability to some extent in those sections of the book.

*You have been designated a world poet laureate, President Ikeda. How do you write poetry?*

I try to express my thoughts exactly as I think them, to put them into words exactly as they are.

When you read lots of great literature, the words therein are naturally fused with your own. Then, when you see a beautiful scene, words come to you without effort. By reading a great deal, one's perception of nature changes. When animals see the beautiful green of the woods, for instance, they may not feel anything special. An artist, however, may be moved by its magnificence. And a gardener may see it as healthy and robust.

Imagine, for example, the moon shining on a beach. If you know the poem from the collection of Japanese poetry *Senzai wakashu* (Collection of a Thousand Years) that reads, "Moon on this autumn night: / How you have transformed / The sands of the vast shore / Into a plain of jewels," then, when you see that moonlit beach, its sands might immediately appear to you as a jeweled garden.

The Chilean poet Gabriela Mistral, in "To the Clouds," wrote:

*Ethereal clouds,*
*clouds like tulle,*
*transport my soul*
*through azure heaven.*[3]

After reading that poem, you may find that now the clouds and the breeze arouse the keenest, deepest emotions.

Beautiful poetry isn't simply a collection of fancy words and phrases. True beauty comes only from a beautiful spirit. I believe, too, that beautiful words come from a spirit that fights for humanity amid life's challenges. Poetry is the product of trying to express in words the emotion of everyday life. And so is literature.

All great literature, ancient and modern, is a bridge connecting one human being to another, one spirit to another. The quality of our lives is determined by how many of those bridges we can cross.

1. L.N. Tolstoy, *War and Peace*, trans. Rosemary Edmonds (London: Penguin Books, 1978), p. 326.

2. Victor Hugo, *Les Misérables*, trans. Norman Denny (London: Penguin Books, 1976).

3. "To the Clouds," *Gabriela Mistral: A Reader*, trans. Maria Giachetti (New York: White Pine Press, 1993), p. 45.

# PART FOUR

# YOUTH
## *and Faith*

# 15

## WHY DO WE CHANT EVERY DAY?

*Now, we want to talk specifically about our faith as SGI members, and present some questions we have heard.*

Faith is an issue of fundamental importance to all of us. You can become genuine successors of the Soka Gakkai and great leaders for the twenty-first century only by establishing a firm foundation of strong, unshakable faith. The single word *faith* encompasses everything. It contains truth, courage, wisdom and good fortune. It includes compassion and humanity as well as peace, culture and happiness.

Faith is eternal hope; it is the secret to limitless self-development. Faith is the most basic principle for growth.

*Yet, oddly enough, in Japan, admitting to having religious faith tends to draw strange looks from many people. If anything, such an admission ought to suggest that a person possesses firm convictions and a solid outlook on life—qualities that I'd say are pretty admirable. What precisely does the word* religion *mean?*

The Japanese word for "religion" (*shukyo*) is composed of two Chinese characters—one meaning "basic or root (*shu*)," and the other, "teaching (*kyo*)." In that sense, religion is that which attempts to teach the basics or fundamentals of life and the universe.

*Without being aware of these basics, our lives would be rootless and ungrounded.*

Religion is proof of our humanity. Of all the animals, only human beings have the capacity for prayer, a most solemn and sublime act.

Nature's colossal and wondrous forces inspired people from ancient times to worship things in their natural environment, such as mountains, fire and the ocean. We can assume, therefore, that a mixture of fear, awe and respect toward the natural world and its phenomena—infinite, vast, majestic and filled with mysteries—led to the human expression of prayer.

For instance, people instinctively wish for protection for themselves and their loved ones when faced with a sudden natural disaster or threat and at the most desperate and dire of times. When such a wish is powerfully focused, it becomes a prayer. It lies beyond the realm of logic or intellect. It transcends such things. Prayer is an act in which we give expression to pressing and powerful wishes in the depths of our being and yearn for their fulfillment.

## Prayer Gave Birth to Religion

*I think this is something everyone can relate to.*

Human beings have an undeniable inherent capacity for prayer. Religion first came into being in response to this. Prayer did not come into existence because of religion; it was the other way around.

There may be many instances when you might feel like praying: in hoping to score well on a test, for example, or to have fine weather the following day. Even those who consider themselves not religious pray for something. Just wishing for the good health of one's children or resolving to improve oneself in some way also constitutes a prayer, even if you don't want to call it that.

Prayer in Nichiren Buddhism—chanting Nam-myoho-renge-kyo to the Gohonzon—directly fuses all our diverse prayers with reality, based on the universal Law of life.

In short, religion came into being out of the human desire for happiness.

*This helps us understand the significance of prayer. But there are many different religions in the world. Why is this?*

Religion emerged out of the human impulse to pray, but later in history, various religions began to define or adopt different objects toward which to focus their prayers.

*People seem to worship and venerate all sorts of things, depending on their religion.*

What people take as their object of devotion is a very important issue. In Japan, some people worship foxes [which, in folk belief, are thought to have spiritual powers]. But by making a fox their object of devotion, they merely draw forth the state of animality from within themselves. This is because our lives embrace and respond to the object of devotion, manifesting a state resembling that embodied therein.

*We also see great divisions within the world's major religions.*

Yes, that is true. When we trace the various schools and denominations of the major religions back to their origins, we arrive at the teachings of such founders as Christ or Muhammad, for example. There are many different kinds of Buddhism, as well. But ultimately they all trace back to Shakyamuni Buddha.

*How did teachings from just one founder split into so many different groups?*

An important reason lies in people's exploitation of these original teachers for their own ends. As the religion developed, priests, scholars and others took advantage of the founder. They used that original teacher as a symbol with which to cloak themselves in authority and enhance their own prestige.

Their self-interest became central, not their teacher. This led to splinter groups and schools. This is where all distortion begins.

*Basically, they forgot the spirit of their religion's original teacher or founder.*

In Christianity, Martin Luther launched the Protestant Reformation in the sixteenth century, calling for a return to the teachings of Christ. Nichiren Daishonin in Japan made a stand, appealing for a return to the teachings of Shakyamuni.

*Now, the Soka Gakkai is forging ahead, calling for a return to the spirit of Nichiren Daishonin.*

In any event, Nichiren Buddhism is as vast and all-encompassing as the universe. It applies not only to this earth. It is not just for the present. It is a fundamental Law that can bring happiness to all life for all time.

Consequently, those of you who have encountered the Mystic Law, this sublime law of life, in your youth are the happiest and most fortunate people in the world. The question is whether you can fully appreciate this fact. The only way you can really awaken to the wonder of this practice is to experience it for yourselves.

We can understand neither faith nor life through theory or logic alone. Life is not an abstraction. It has to be lived and experienced. It is the history we write through our real-life efforts and struggles.

*I think the foundation of our faith is the practice of reciting the sutra morning and evening and chanting Nam-myoho-renge-kyo. Some have told me they recite the sutra because their parents tell them to, but they don't really have a clear idea what benefit it has or what its purpose is. Others admit they see no point in chanting when they don't have a particular problem.*

*One high school division leader shared with me a comment by a student who had recently joined the Soka Gakkai: "Reciting the sutra morning and evening somehow propels me in a positive direction. I'm happy with how my day goes; everything just seems to fall into place the way I hoped."*

*Would you explain the meaning and significance of reciting the sutra and chanting Nam-myoho-renge-kyo morning and evening?*

214

Reciting the sutra is a daily activity in which we purify and prime our hearts and minds. In the morning, it is starting the engine for our day, like grooming ourselves before we set out for the day.

Some people have powerful engines, and some have weak engines. The strength of the engine dramatically affects what we accomplish throughout the course of our lives. The difference can be enormous.

Diligently applying ourselves in our daily practice of the sutra recitation boosts the power of our engine.

## A CEREMONY BETWEEN ONE'S LIFE AND THE UNIVERSE

*When we recite the sutra twice daily, a strong life force comes welling forth. But why is this so?*

Reciting the sutra is a ceremony in which our lives commune with the universe. As we recite the sutra and chant Nam-myoho-renge-kyo, through our faith in the Gohonzon, we vigorously infuse the microcosm of our individual existence with the life force of the macrocosm, of the entire universe. If we do this regularly each morning and evening, our life force—or engine—is strengthened.

*Each of us is a microcosm—a mini-cosmos or universe unto ourselves.*

Yes, that's what Buddhism teaches. We exist; we have life. In the same way, the universe is a giant living entity. Buddhism teaches that life is the universe and that the universe is life. Each of us is a living entity just like the universe; we are our own little universe.

A number of Buddhist sutras have stressed the "oneness of our lives and the universe" by using the example of the human body. For instance, the roundness of our heads represents the celestial sphere. Our two eyes correspond to the sun and the moon. The opening and closing of our eyes are night and day. The hair on our heads represents the twinkling stars. Our eyebrows are the constellations.

*That correlation of our bodies to the universe is really interesting. Are there other examples?*

Our breath is likened to the wind: Soft breathing is like a gentle breeze blowing through a valley. The raging breath of someone who is furious or agitated might be likened to a gale or typhoon! As for the joints in our body, it is said we have three hundred sixty—which corresponds roughly to the days in a year. We have twelve major joints, corresponding to the months in a year.

*Is there some parallel for the four seasons?*

The warmth of our stomachs represents spring and summer, while the cool hardness of our backs represents autumn and winter.

Our blood vessels, meanwhile, both large and small, correspond to rivers. A fissure in an embankment that leads to flooding might be likened to a burst blood vessel or a stroke.

Our bones correspond to rocks or minerals. Our skin and flesh are likened to the land. The hair covering our body is like the woods and forests. The list goes on and on to include our internal organs and such. Buddhist writings set forth in great detail that our body is itself a small cosmos. (See WND-2, 848–49.)

*The human brain is also often referred to as a miniature universe of its own. This is because the brain has infinite potential.*

That's right. The key lies in how to draw forth that potential. When we look at how the body functions, we could say it resembles a giant pharmaceutical factory. The body produces its own drugs and medicines and has the ability to protect its own health and well-being. It is a truly wondrous microcosm.

The universe is made up of incalculable numbers of elementary particles—protons, electrons, neutrons and photons—as well as atoms of the chemical elements, such as hydrogen, oxygen and calcium. These same particles and elements compose our bodies.

One scholar observed that the human body is made of the same material as the stars, and called human beings "children of the stars." Our bodies are not only made of the same matter as the universe but are governed by the same basic principles of generation and disintegration. They are subject to the rhythm of life and death that pervades the cosmos. All physical laws—such as those of gravity and the conservation of energy—also affect and operate in the microcosm of each living entity.

It takes the earth 365 days, five hours and forty-nine minutes and twelve seconds to complete one revolution around the sun. There is a rigorous order to everything.

It is said that the human body comprises more than sixty trillion individual cells. When they function each day in a well-ordered fashion, correctly carrying out their respective jobs, we enjoy good health. The complexity and precision of the human body are mind-boggling.

*Yes, even bodily functions, such as perspiration that regulates body temperature when it's hot, are pretty amazing when you think about them.*

Great trouble would arise if our planet veered even slightly from its present orbit around the sun. And nothing short of catastrophe would result if the earth's axis were to shift even minutely. All life on this planet would be threatened with extinction. Everything hangs in a delicate balance, governed by the strict principle that life and the vast universe are one. The same principle applies to each individual life—to each microcosm.

Science, for its part, is devoted to the investigation of real, yet invisible, natural laws. Such investigation has led to the invention of many machines and devices that apply those laws. An understanding of the principles of buoyancy, for instance, led to the development of seagoing vessels.

Similarly, the discovery of the laws of aerodynamics led to the invention of aircraft, and an insight into the workings of radio waves paved the way for the development of radio and television.

These natural laws I have just mentioned, however, are but partial laws. In contrast to science, Buddhism is devoted to the investigation and exploration of the Mystic Law—the great Law of life itself that is the essence and source of all other laws and principles in the material and spiritual realms.

The Mystic Law, too, is invisible. Nevertheless, it exists without a doubt. Nichiren Daishonin revealed the object of fundamental respect, the Gohonzon, in the form of a mandala so that we could tap and manifest the power of the Mystic Law in our own lives. That is why the Soka Gakkai's second president, Josei Toda, put it in the following easy-to-understand way: "I apologize for using such a simplistic analogy, but the Gohonzon can be likened to a happiness-manufacturing machine."

When we recite the sutra and chant Nam-myoho-renge-kyo to the Gohonzon, the microcosm of our individual lives harmonizes seamlessly with the macrocosm of the universe.

*How is that so?*

The universe and our lives are manifestations of the Mystic Law, Nam-myoho-renge-kyo. The Gohonzon is also an embodiment of Nam-myoho-renge-kyo. Since all are entities of the Mystic Law, they are essentially one and indivisible. Therefore, when we focus on the Gohonzon while chanting Nam-myoho-renge-kyo, our lives and the universe merge like cogs in a great machine meshing together with perfect precision, and we begin to move in the direction of happiness and fulfillment.

We can be in rhythm with the universe 365 days a year—in spring, summer, autumn and winter—manifesting the vigor, wisdom and good fortune with which to surmount any problem or suffering. When we rev up the powerful, revitalizing engine of Buddhahood, we can break through any impasse and boldly steer ourselves in the direction of hope and justice.

# THE LANGUAGE OF BUDDHAS AND BODHISATTVAS

*I don't think I fully appreciated the significance of reciting the sutra and chanting Nam-myoho-renge-kyo until now.*

It is a solemn ceremony through which we open wide the doors of the treasure storehouse within. We mine the dynamic wellspring of life force that lies dormant in the vast inner reaches of our being, and we tap an inexhaustible source of wisdom, compassion and courage.

*One student asked why chanting Nam-myoho-renge-kyo and reciting the liturgy of Nichiren Buddhism should bring about benefit even though she doesn't understand what she's saying.*

An infant drinks and benefits from its mother's milk but does so without knowing the milk's composition. The same principle is at work when we chant Nam-myoho-renge-kyo and recite the sutra.

Naturally, it's all the better if we come to understand the meaning—but only because it can help strengthen our confidence in the Mystic Law. If such understanding is not accompanied by practice, however, then it is ultimately meaningless.

It is difficult to grasp fully the profound meaning of the Mystic Law purely through theory.

In the animal kingdom, each species has its own unique means of communication or language. We humans cannot understand it, but birds, for example, clearly understand the language of other birds, and dogs of other dogs.

Similarly, codes, abbreviations and foreign languages might be incomprehensible to those unfamiliar with them but are perfectly clear and intelligible to those proficient in them.

*Yes. I guess even if a Japanese person were to say the English phrase* thank you *without knowing what it means, an English speaker would immediately understand its meaning.*

In the same way, our voices chanting Nam-myoho-renge-kyo and reciting the sutra morning and evening are communicated to the Gohonzon
and unerringly understood in the realm of Buddhas and bodhisattvas.
You might say that when we recite the sutra and chant Nam-myoho-
renge-kyo, we are speaking the language of Buddhas and bodhisattvas.

So even if you don't understand the literal meaning of what you say,
your voices while reciting the sutra and chanting Nam-myoho-renge-
kyo to the Gohonzon reach all Buddhas, bodhisattvas and Buddhist
deities throughout time and space—the protective functions within life
and the universe. Unseen, the entire universe will be activated toward
fulfilling your prayers.

*Some students say they have to get up so early to go to school that they simply
find it impossible to recite the sutra in the morning. Is it OK in such cases to
skip reciting the sutra and just chant Nam-myoho-renge-kyo instead?*

Just chanting Nam-myoho-renge-kyo in such cases is fine. To borrow
the example of a meal, chanting Nam-myoho-renge-kyo might be likened to the main course, and reciting the sutra morning and evening
to the side dishes. Though one main dish might make for an adequate
meal, we need to eat from other food groups as well if we want to have
a nutritionally balanced diet. When we're busy, a carbohydrate meal,
for example, might be fine and give us the energy we need, but a balanced meal is ideal.

*So the important thing is to challenge ourselves?*

Yes, a spirit of challenge is important. Naturally, it's better if we can
recite the sutra and chant Nam-myoho-renge-kyo morning and evening in the manner prescribed. But the most vital thing is to maintain
faith in the Gohonzon your whole life and never abandon it.

It is self-defeating if for a time you practice passionately, with "faith
like fire," and then end up discarding your faith later on. Challenging
yourselves a little at a time is fine. It's important that you develop "faith
like water" that flows steadily and unceasingly, like a river that gradually grows in size and converges with the vast ocean.

*Some people feel guilty when they skip reciting the sutra.*

As long as we have faith in the Gohonzon, we are not going to suffer punishment or negative consequences on such account. So please put your mind at ease. Nichiren Daishonin says that chanting Nam-myoho-renge-kyo even once contains limitless benefit.

*Then chanting Nam-myoho-renge-kyo ten times must contain incredible benefit!*

Yes, so you can imagine the immense benefit you will obtain when you continue earnestly to recite the sutra and chant Nam-myoho-renge-kyo morning and evening. Basically, you do both for yourselves. Your practice of reciting the sutra morning and evening and chanting Nam-myoho-renge-kyo is not an obligation—it is a right.

The Gohonzon will never demand that you chant to it. An attitude of appreciation in being able to chant to the Gohonzon is the heart of faith. The more you exert yourselves in faith—in reciting the sutra morning and evening—the more you stand to gain.

Also, Nichiren writes nothing about the specific amount we should chant. It is entirely up to each individual's awareness. Faith is a lifelong pursuit, so there's no need to be unnecessarily nervous or anxious about how much you chant, or to put unnecessary pressure on yourselves. Buddhism exists to free people, not to restrain them. Doing even a little bit every day is important. The food we eat each day turns to energy for our bodies. Our studies, too, become a valuable asset when we make steady efforts on a daily basis. Our lives are created from what we do, how we live, every day. For that reason, we should strive to live each day so as to continually improve ourselves. The driving force for this is our morning and evening practice.

Simply offering prayers on a handful of occasions throughout the year—like the droves of Japanese who flock to Shinto shrines or Buddhist temples at New Year's to pray to various gods and Buddhas for protection in the coming year—is just empty ritual and ultimately meaningless.

Exerting ourselves in the practice of reciting the Lotus Sutra each day amounts to what we might call a spiritual workout. It purifies and cleanses our lives, gets our motors running and puts us on the right course for the day. It gets our bodies and our minds working smoothly and puts us in rhythm, in sync, with the universe.

*Yes, it's important to keep making efforts, however small, each day. A young women's high school division leader in Hokkaido said that many of the members in her area find themselves unable to recite the sutra regularly. But all seem to know that when they have problems, they should take them to the Gohonzon and chant about them.*

## FROM THE FIREWOOD OF PROBLEMS, THE FLAME OF HAPPINESS

The spirit to seat oneself before the Gohonzon is in itself very important. Those who have the spirit to continue to challenge themselves in this way are most worthy of respect. You might decide, for example, "I'm going to chant Nam-myoho-renge-kyo, even for just a few minutes" or "I'm going to chant to the Gohonzon every day." Buddhism teaches the principle that "earthly desires are enlightenment." To explain this very simply, "earthly desires" refers to suffering and to the desires and cravings that cause suffering, while "enlightenment" refers to attaining a vast and expansive state of absolute happiness.

Normally, one would assume that earthly desires and enlightenment are separate and distinct—especially since suffering would seem to be the exact opposite of happiness. But this is not the case in Nichiren Buddhism, which teaches that only by igniting the firewood of earthly desires can the flame of happiness be attained.

As a result, our lives are infused with the light and energy of happiness. Through chanting Nam-myoho-renge-kyo, we burn the firewood of our earthly desires.

*I guess you could say that earthly desires are transformed into enlightenment by Nam-myoho-renge-kyo.*

When we chant Nam-myoho-renge-kyo, our problems and sufferings all turn into energy for our happiness, into fuel for our advancement.

*So the greater our problems, the happier we stand to become.*

That's right. The wonderful thing about faith in Nichiren Buddhism is its capacity to transform people's lives from the direst suffering into the greatest possible happiness and turn the most daunting problems into a source of growth and a foundation for human greatness.

Problems come in all shapes and sizes. You may have some personal problem; you may be wondering how to help your parents live long and fulfilling lives; or you may be worried about a friend who is sick or depressed, wishing for that person's recovery. On a different level, you may be deeply concerned about the issue of world peace and its realization or humankind's direction into the coming century. These are very noble concerns.

Through chanting Nam-myoho-renge-kyo, you can turn all these worries and concerns into fuel to propel yourselves forward—you can transform them into life force, into greater depth of character and into good fortune.

I hope you will seriously concern yourselves with many things, chant abundantly and strive in your personal growth as you do so. Faith means setting goals and working to realize each one. If we view each goal or challenge as a mountain, faith is a process whereby we grow with each mountain climbed.

*One student admitted being uncertain about how to pray to the Gohonzon; he wanted to know whether he should just chant about one thing at a time— waiting for that prayer to be answered before going on to the next one—or whether it was all right to pray for many things at the same time.*

You can chant for as many things as you like. A person with many wishes and dreams should pray earnestly to fulfill each one. Buddhism is reason.

To use the analogy of shopping, you can buy many things when you have enough money in your wallet. To buy something that costs three hundred dollars, you need to have three hundred dollars. If you only have ten dollars, you can only purchase ten dollars' worth of goods. If you want to buy something, you need to bring along enough money to do so.

In faith, the same logic applies. You are the only one who can realize your desires; it's up to your own faith and practice, no one else's.

*Some members say that they have trouble concentrating or focusing on the Gohonzon when they chant; they get distracted, and their minds wander. What can they do about this?*

Because we are human, it's natural for our minds to wander, for all sorts of thoughts and memories to surface. You can just share all those thoughts with the Gohonzon. There is no set form or pattern for how we should pray. Buddhism speaks of being "uncreated" and "unadorned." In other words, it emphasizes being natural. Therefore, simply chant earnestly and without pretense, just as you are. In time, as your faith develops, you'll find it easier to focus your mind when you chant.

*Is it all right to chant mainly for ourselves?*

Yes, it's fine. It's natural for prayers to center on your own desires and dreams. There's no need to pretend that you're praying for something lofty when you're not. You're only fooling yourself if you do. By chanting naturally, without affectation or reservation, for what you seek most of all, you'll gradually come to develop a higher and more expansive life-condition.

Of course, it's also fine to chant with the resolve to become bigger-hearted or for the welfare of your friends and for kosen-rufu—the happiness and prosperity of all humankind. You are free to chant for whatever you wish. It's all up to you.

Reciting the sutra morning and evening and chanting Nam-myoho-renge-kyo are not obligations. They are a wonderful right you possess.

# Develop a Strong Inner Core

*A young women's high school division leader in the Chugoku area in Japan said that many students have asked her whether chanting Nam-myoho-renge-kyo and reciting the sutra would really help solve their problems. One member in particular was very despondent. Apparently, she had challenged a difficult problem by reciting the sutra and chanting earnestly, but failed to make any headway. She began to worry that she might never solve her problem, and then became lax in her daily practice. She wanted to know where she was going wrong.*

In Nichiren Buddhism, it is said that no prayer goes unanswered. But this is very different from having every wish instantly gratified, as if by magic. If you chant to win the lottery tomorrow, or to score 100 percent on a test tomorrow without having studied, the odds are small that it will happen. Nonetheless, viewed from a deeper, longer-term perspective, all your prayers serve to propel you in the direction of happiness.

Sometimes our immediate prayers are realized, and sometimes they aren't. When we look back later, however, we can say with absolute conviction that everything turned out for the best.

Buddhism accords with reason. Our faith is reflected in our daily lives, in our actual circumstances. Our prayers cannot be answered if we fail to make efforts appropriate to our situation.

Furthermore, it takes a great deal of time and effort to overcome sufferings of a karmic nature, whose roots lie deep in causes we made in the past. There is a big difference, for example, in the time it takes for a scratch to heal and that required to recover from a serious internal disease. Some illnesses can be treated with medication, while others require surgery. The same applies to changing our karma through faith and practice.

In addition, each person's level of faith and individual karma differ. By chanting Nam-myoho-renge-kyo, however, we can bring forth from within a powerful sense of hope and move our lives in a positive, beneficial direction.

*So even if we don't get immediate results, the important thing is to persevere in our Buddhist practice.*

It's unrealistic to think we can achieve anything of substance overnight. If we were to have every prayer answered instantly, it would lead to our ruin. We'd grow lazy and complacent.

*Yes, it certainly makes sense that if all our prayers were immediately answered, we'd probably stop making any real effort.*

You may have a passing interest in drawing, for example. But if you think you can simply dash off some paintings, suddenly hold an exhibition and have all your work snapped up by art collectors, you are hardly being realistic.

Suppose that rather than working, you spend all your money playing and are now destitute. Do you think someone giving you a large sum of money would contribute to your happiness in the long run?

*No, it is only likely to aggravate the problem.*

It would be like making superficial repairs to a crumbling building without addressing the root problem. Only by first rebuilding the foundation can we build something solid upon it.

Faith enables us to transform not only our day-to-day problems, but our lives at their very foundations. Through our Buddhist practice, we can develop a strong inner core and a solid and inexhaustible reservoir of good fortune.

There are two kinds of benefit that derive from faith in the Gohonzon: conspicuous and inconspicuous. Conspicuous benefit is the obvious, visible benefit of being protected or being quickly able to surmount a problem when it arises—be it an illness or a conflict in personal relationships.

Inconspicuous benefit, on the other hand, is less tangible. It is good fortune accumulated slowly but steadily, like the growth of a tree or the rising of the tide, which results in the forging of a rich and expansive state of life. We might not discern any change from day to day, but as the years pass, it will be clear that we've become happy, that we've grown as individuals. This is inconspicuous benefit.

When you chant Nam-myoho-renge-kyo, you will definitely gain the best result, regardless of whether that benefit is conspicuous or inconspicuous.

*That reminds me of the experience of the Kanagawa Joint Prefecture young men's high school division leader. It seems the turning point in his faith came when he was seventeen. He was working part time for a butcher when he severed four fingers on his left hand while operating a meat saw. In the ambulance on the way to the hospital, his mother sat by his side, urging him: "You must chant. Nam-myoho-renge-kyo is all we have now!" Surgeons worked on his hand for more than eight hours. Though they managed to reattach all four fingers, there was only a fifty-fifty chance that he would regain full use of his left hand.*

*For the first time in his life, he prayed to the Gohonzon with all his might. Upon his release from the hospital, all the members of his local Soka Gakkai district were waiting to greet him. Everyone had been chanting Nam-myoho-renge-kyo for him—all during the operation and throughout his stay in the hospital. At that time, he says, a fierce resolve welled up inside him to never part with the Gohonzon or turn his back on the warm and caring world of the Soka Gakkai. He eventually regained full use of his fingers. I think we can call his experience one of conspicuous benefit.*

## THE SUPPORT OF OUR FELLOW MEMBERS IS A TREASURE

No matter what happens, the important thing is to continue chanting. If you do so, you'll definitely become happy. Even if things don't work out the way you hoped or imagined, when you look back later, you'll understand on a much more profound level that it was the best possible result. This is tremendous inconspicuous benefit.

The true benefits of Nichiren Buddhism are of a lasting and inconspicuous nature that accrues in the depths of your life. Conspicuous benefit, for instance, might allow you to eat your fill today but leave you worrying about your next meal. As an example of inconspicuous benefit, on the other hand, you may have only a meager meal today, but you are steadily developing a life where you will never have to worry about having enough to eat. The latter is a far more attractive prospect, I think.

## LIFE ITSELF IS A SOURCE OF JOY

*Absolutely nothing is wasted in faith.*

The more we exert ourselves in faith, the greater the benefit we experience.

Of course, it's possible to get by in life without practicing Nichiren Buddhism. But sometimes we are confronted by karma over which we seem to have no control, or are buffeted about because of an inner weakness. What a tragic loss it would be if we could never change ourselves, if we could never exclaim confidently at the end of our days what a wonderful life we've led. That is precisely why a guiding philosophy in life is essential.

My mentor, President Toda, said: "For what reason have we been born? As the Lotus Sutra passage 'living beings enjoy themselves at ease' (LSOC, 272) states, we have been born to enjoy ourselves. How dull it would be, then, if we did not do so! When we believe in the Gohonzon with all our heart, we will savor a state of being in which life itself, and everything we do, is a source of joy."

President Toda used the term *absolute happiness* to describe the state of mind in which we can feel that life itself is a joy. If you persevere in faith, you will definitely come to experience this.

Our Buddhist practice boosts the power of our "engine," strengthening our life force so that we can always declare, "I'm ready for anything!" When our engine is weak, even a small slope will leave us gasping and struggling painfully as we attempt to surmount it.

*Obviously, there are many fine, upstanding people in the world who don't practice this Buddhism.*

That's very true. There are many people who demonstrate admirable integrity and character. It is a mistake to judge people merely on the basis of whether they practice Nichiren Buddhism. Since there are so many wonderful people who are nonmembers, it simply means that those of us who are members should strive to develop our humanity and character all the more.

I hope you will forge friendships with people of character and integrity and humbly seek to learn from their example.

Nonetheless, no matter how capable or in control people might appear on the outside, it's difficult to see what's inside their hearts. Often people may look happy, but underneath they may be hiding some personal agony or grappling with a serious problem. Or though they may seem happy now, there is no guarantee that they will always remain that way.

When you get right down to it, does material wealth assure happiness? Does fame? Does living in a big house? The answer is an emphatic "No." All the time, we see people embroiled in bitter battles over money; people plunged into misery when fame and popularity disappear; people ruining their lives when they let status or power go to their heads; and people living in large, luxurious homes where family members cannot stand one another and a cold and hostile atmosphere pervades.

Such things as money, fame and material possessions offer a fleeting satisfaction, something that can be called relative happiness. However, when we transform our lives internally, when we develop within ourselves a brilliant inner palace, then we can be said to have established absolute happiness. If we develop a state of mind as vast and resplendent as a magnificent palace, then nothing—no matter where we go or what we may encounter in life—can undermine or destroy our happiness.

The most fundamental issue all of us have to grapple with is death. Not even the greatest or smartest person on earth can solve the suffering of death inherent in the human condition. Only a correct practice of Nichiren Buddhism enables us to surmount the fundamental suffering of death and apprehend the eternity of life.

*Does our prayer while chanting reach the deceased?*

It does, indeed. Life is eternal. Suppose a person dies in pain and suffering. Even after death, that person's life may remain in a state of suffering. It might be likened to someone moaning due to a nightmare while sleeping.

If you chant Nam-myoho-renge-kyo with the deceased person in mind, you can remove the suffering from that person's life and impart ease and joy through the rejuvenating and illuminating power of Nam-myoho-renge-kyo. And since chanting is that powerful, there is no way that it cannot help move in the direction of happiness the lives of your parents and friends who are still with you.

Only Buddhism solves the fundamental sufferings of birth, aging, sickness and death inherent in the human condition. These sufferings have remained essentially unchanged throughout human history, plaguing us in our technologically advanced world today as much as they did the ancient Egyptians. One reason why people around the world are seeking Buddhism so earnestly is that it solves the question of life and death.

The wonderful thing about Nichiren Buddhism is that, through chanting Nam-myoho-renge-kyo, you can transform the four sufferings of birth, aging, sickness and death into four castle walls or ramparts that fortify the palace of your life. Though it might be difficult to appreciate at first, the "mud" of our suffering provides the building material from which we can erect a solid bulwark for our palace of happiness within. The deeper the mire of suffering, the more indomitable a palace we can establish.

Youth, above all, is a time for laying the foundation for a truly magnificent palace of life.

## Establishing a Solid Foundation

*Yes. There are many people who have made their days in the high school division the foundation for their future. The Hokkaido young women's high school division leader struggled with relationship problems in her second year of senior high school, something that forced her to chant Nam-myoho-renge-kyo very seriously. Before that, she had recited the sutra morning and evening only when she encountered a problem but hadn't really appreciated its value. As she pushed herself to chant Nam-myoho-renge-kyo, she came to learn through personal experience that when you change, others change.*

*So I think it's important for young people to learn the great benefit of chanting Nam-myoho-renge-kyo while they're still in high school.*

Chanting Nam-myoho-renge-kyo establishes a foundation of good fortune in young people's lives. If you establish a solid foundation now, there is no limit to the structure you can build upon it later. Many things contribute to building that foundation. Diligent application to one's studies helps, as does exercising to develop physical fitness and stamina.

But our inner state of life lies at the core of our mental and physical well-being. Buddhist practice is the only means by which we can strengthen, purify and develop our inner life.

We have to exercise our minds through study. We have to exercise our bodies through physical activity and sports. We also have to exercise our life-condition through chanting Nam-myoho-renge-kyo. When our inner condition of life changes, our minds and bodies also change. They will be refreshed and revitalized.

Chanting Nam-myoho-renge-kyo charges our batteries. If we take care to charge our batteries regularly, then we'll always be full of energy and vitality. If we fail to keep our batteries charged, we won't have energy when we need it most and as a result may be defeated by our environment.

Those who saturate their lives with Nam-myoho-renge-kyo and learn to keep their batteries charged while they're young are building a foundation for lifelong happiness.

*The young men's high school division leader of the Shin'etsu area said that he didn't recite the sutra until his second year of high school. He was the captain of his school's boxing team. When he reached the national high school finals, he gained the conviction that anything could be achieved if one simply made the effort.*

*But in the winter of his second year in high school, he suffered a slipped disk and was told by the doctor that he could no longer box. He fell into a serious depression; the light had gone out of his world, and nothing seemed to matter to him anymore.*

*Then, a young men's division leader in his area started coming by to encourage him, telling him confidently: "Nothing is impossible with faith. Things will definitely turn around, you'll see." With this encouragement, the young man gradually applied himself to the practice of reciting the sutra morning and evening and chanting Nam-myoho-renge-kyo. He recovered from his slipped disk, and the following summer, again qualified for the national finals.*

*The encouragement of people close by can be a great source of strength for those who are suffering.*

*If I may change the subject slightly, a student was wondering whether it's necessary to kneel when we chant. She says that her legs grow sore and numb when she sits that way, and she cannot concentrate on chanting.*

It's perfectly all right to sit in a chair or, if you sit on the floor, to arrange your legs comfortably.

It's important to want to sit before the Gohonzon as though going to meet the original Buddha, Nichiren Daishonin, and that our daily practice of reciting the sutra morning and evening and chanting Nam-myoho-renge-kyo be enjoyable. Bearing these points in mind, what's most important is that you continue in your Buddhist practice throughout life. There's no need to be overly concerned with formality.

*A member asked about closing our eyes while chanting or reciting the sutra.*

It's best to keep your eyes open and to look at the Gohonzon. It's generally considered impolite not to look others in the eye when speaking to them. I think this is also true when we are facing and addressing the Gohonzon as we recite the sutra and chant Nam-myoho-renge-kyo.

Of course, if you do close your eyes occasionally, there's no need to worry. It's just that when we close our eyes, it can be more difficult to commune strongly with the Gohonzon.

This, of course, does not apply to people who are blind or sight impaired, who need simply chant or recite the sutra to the Gohonzon within their hearts.

*What is the meaning of the prayer we offer to the functions in life and the environment that serve to protect us (*shoten zenjin*), as part of our practice of reciting the sutra in the morning?*

*Shoten zenjin*, literally, benevolent gods or deities, refer to the functions of the universe that work to protect those who exert themselves in the faith and practice of the Mystic Law. We could say that such benevolent functions take the Mystic Law as their food or nourishment. When they can "dine" on the Mystic Law, their spirits and energy increase. So our prayers of appreciation toward them are said to imbue them with the "flavor of the Law." When we offer Nam-myoho-renge-kyo in reverence, the Buddhist gods respond to us in reverence. That is, the protective functions of the universe and the protective functions in our own lives mesh and begin to act in harmony.

Then, when we recite the sutra and chant Nam-myoho-renge-kyo, the Buddhist gods throughout the universe join us in greeting the Gohonzon. The Buddhist gods—protective functions—are thus set in motion toward the realization of our prayers.

## PRACTICE FOR ONESELF AND OTHERS

*Would you please explain the prayer beads?*

It is customary to place the prayer beads around the middle fingers of both hands—the three tufts on the right hand and the two tufts on the left—twisting the loop so that it crosses over between our two hands. The prayer beads are said to be fashioned after the human body: The three tufts on the right are our head and both arms; the crossing over of the loop indicates our navel; the two tufts on the left are our two legs.

Each set of prayer beads comprises 108 beads, representing the 108 earthly desires, the sources of suffering. The four smaller beads in the loop stand for the four bodhisattvas who are the leaders of the Bodhisattvas of the Earth in the Lotus Sutra.

*That would be bodhisattvas Superior Practices, Boundless Practices, Pure Practices and Firmly Established Practices.*

Yes. Profound meaning is attached to each of these four bodhisattvas, but I won't go into detail now. Suffice it to say that the true identity of Bodhisattva Superior Practices is Nichiren Daishonin. The four bodhisattvas represent the power to work eternally for the happiness of all humanity.

The prayer beads therefore symbolize that, through chanting to the Gohonzon, we can transform all problems and suffering into fuel to propel us toward happiness.

Moreover, our joined palms represent the fusion of reality and wisdom—the fusion of our lives with the Mystic Law—while the meeting of the five fingers of both hands represent the "mutual possession of the Ten Worlds." The mutual possession of the Ten Worlds means that none of the Ten Worlds—that is, hell, hunger, animality, anger, humanity, heaven, voice-hearers (learning), cause-awakened ones (realization), bodhisattvas and Buddhahood—are separate from one another. This is precisely why the power of the world of Buddhahood is manifested in the other nine worlds of our daily lives.

We should remember, however, that such things as prayer beads, Buddhist altars, incense and the like form part of the ritual aspect of faith. Such formalities are subject to change depending on the era or place, and in most cases, change is acceptable.

The substance of our faith is what matters most.

Also, the dual nature of our practice—for ourselves and for others—will never change. Practice for ourselves constitutes chanting Nam-myoho-renge-kyo and carrying out the practice of reciting the sutra with faith in the Gohonzon, while practice for others constitutes teaching others about the Mystic Law.

*What does the term* Gohonzon *mean?*

The literal meaning of *honzon* is object of devotion. *Go* is an honorific. Even people who declare that they are not religious will surely have something that they value or esteem most highly. Whatever people cherish most dearly—that is their object of fundamental respect, or object of devotion. Though they might claim otherwise, there are those for whom money is an object of devotion. For others, it might be social status. Some people make their boyfriend or girlfriend, or their family, their object of devotion. For some, knowledge is the altar at which they worship. And certainly there are people who venerate some deity or some concept of heaven or truth.

What you make the object of your greatest veneration will have a profound influence on your life. Nichiren Buddhism takes as its object of fundamental respect the life of the Buddha—the eternal essence of life at one with the universe. That object of veneration is not something abstract or out of reach, because it is life itself. Nichiren Daishonin writes: "Never seek this Gohonzon outside yourself. The Gohonzon exists only within the mortal flesh of us ordinary people who embrace the Lotus Sutra and chant Nam-myoho-renge-kyo" (WND-1, 832).

The eternal life of the universe exists within each of us. The Gohonzon resides within each of us. Nichiren Buddhism is a philosophy of utmost respect for human beings and for life. Nichiren Daishonin embodied the essence of his own life in the form of the Gohonzon to make it possible for us to summon forth the Gohonzon within our lives.

In a sense, there is no simpler Buddhist practice than reciting the sutra and chanting Nam-myoho-renge-kyo. We do not have to undertake strange austerities as in some esoteric Buddhist traditions. In the case of a machine, for example, the more sophisticated the technology, the greater the ease of operation and use. Similarly, because Nichiren Buddhism is such a highly developed and powerful teaching, it enables us to tap the life-state of Buddhahood through the simplest form of practice.

On the other hand, since we carry out Buddhist practice in the midst of our busy daily lives, it is easy for us to overlook or neglect it. In that respect, there is perhaps no more difficult practice when it comes to continuing. Nonetheless, if we challenge ourselves to keep up a little each day, before we realize it, we will have built a path to happiness in the depths of our lives; we will have established a solid embankment that will prevent our ever being swept in the direction of unhappiness.

# *16*

# WHY DO WE HAVE AN ORGANIZATION?

*Let's talk about the role and function of the Soka Gakkai organization. Someone asked me: "Why do we have an organization? Is there anything wrong with people just doing their best in Buddhist practice individually?" Another commented, "I don't like group activities, so I'm uneasy with the word* organization.*"*

*Many members have expressed joy at being a part of such a compassionate group as the Soka Gakkai.*

*At a meeting commemorating May 5, Soka Gakkai Successors Day, you shared with us President Toda's statement that "the Soka Gakkai is more important than my life" (*The Human Revolution, *p. 1787). We were all very moved by those words, and many of us renewed our determination to cherish and protect this great organization.*

*Most high school division members have been in the Soka Gakkai ever since they can remember. Each person's attitude about the organization varies depending on personal experience and circumstances.*

The word *organization* probably conjures certain images for some people, but the fact is, everything in this world involves some sort of organization. The human body itself is made up of more than sixty trillion cells, all working in concert. That's an amazingly efficient organization. And this vast number of cells is not just clustered together at random. Each cell has its own distinct role to fulfill. Some form muscles, others form nerves, and still others, blood. The body works as a whole because all these cells carry out their unique functions in harmony with others.

*It's truly an example of unity.*

Yes. Coordination is very important. Everything involves closely coordinated organization. This is true not only of human beings. All life functions in an organized way. From the tiniest plankton to the largest whales, all life forms on our planet are "organisms"—organized entities. Even the molecules that make up these organisms themselves are organized structures of atoms. Our planet, too, is one great organization where all manner of sentient and insentient beings—animals, plants and natural resources—exist to form a coherent whole.

*From that perspective, the universe is also an organization.*

Yes. That's true. The earth is part of the organization known as the solar system, which is itself part of the galaxy known as the Milky Way, a still larger system comprising some two hundred billion stars like our own sun. When several galaxies join together, they form galaxy clusters, or superclusters. The universe is a collection of vast numbers of such clusters. If we were to send a letter to a being on another planet, our return address would have to be appended to read something like the following:

Planet Earth
The Solar System
Orion Arm, The Milky Way
Local Galaxy Group, Local Supercluster
The Universe

It's the same with human society, as well. Countries, cities, towns, villages, businesses and schools—all are organizations. This is because close teamwork and interaction are necessary for them to function most effectively.

It is the same with sports. A soccer team is an organization. And even for individual sports like tennis, judo or fencing, practicing and competing with others—in a club, for instance—can be helpful in polishing one's skill and becoming a winner. Working closely with trainers, nutritionists and others can also be indispensable to success.

Everything is an organization.

When a couple unites to create a happy family, they are quite naturally forming an organization.

Then there is the invisible organizational framework that we find exists within our local communities, where communication has become a vital key in maintaining good relations with friends and neighbors.

You are in some way connected to everything around you—to society, school, your family and so on. Everyone is part of some kind of organization. No one in today's world, except perhaps a hermit living on a remote mountain somewhere, is exempt.

It is only natural, therefore, when we seek to achieve a great objective or to develop ourselves so that we can make great accomplishments, that some sort of organization is essential.

The Soka Gakkai is an organization working to realize the great objective of kosen-rufu—of achieving peace and happiness for all humanity based on the principles and philosophy of Nichiren Buddhism. Such an objective cannot be accomplished through the efforts of one person alone. It becomes possible only when people in various spheres of society come together, organize themselves into a cohesive force and work to achieve that goal.

Nichiren Daishonin designated six senior priests, and Shakyamuni had ten major disciples. These, too, may be regarded as organizations. Both Nichiren and Shakyamuni formed a network, or organization, through which they endeavored to spread the teachings of Buddhism as they raised and protected their followers.

## THE ORGANIZATION IS A MEANS, THE PURPOSE IS PEOPLE'S HAPPINESS

*So organizations exist for a purpose.*

Exactly. But it's important to note that there are both good and bad organizations. An organization that inflicts suffering on people and leads them down a path of destruction is nothing but evil. The war machines of militarist Japan and Nazi Germany during World War II are cases in point. In contrast, an organization that seeks to improve relations among people around the world, to work for a more positive, constructive direction for humanity, is a worthy and honorable organization. The SGI is such an organization.

*The world of the Soka Gakkai is one where people warmly encourage one another. A high school division member in Saitama related her efforts to support and encourage a fellow member who had stopped going to school. At first, the girl she wished to help refused to see her when she visited, so she began to write letters about school, about her interests and hobbies, and also about faith and practice. She kept writing, and a year later, the member finally responded with a letter, stating that although she wasn't attending school, she continued to chant every day. She also requested that the young woman continue her correspondence. With tears in her eyes, this young woman told me of the deep joy she felt knowing that her sincere concern had gotten through. Moved by her fellow member's spirit to challenge and not be defeated by her problems, she became all the more determined to continue growing and improving herself.*

That's wonderful. The organization of the Soka Gakkai emerged naturally from that spirit—the spirit to somehow encourage another person, to want to see others become happy. The Soka Gakkai didn't appear first and then become filled with people. People began forging bonds with one another, and then those ties of friendship spread, naturally giving birth to the Soka Gakkai organization. For that reason, we must be aware that the organization exists for people. People don't exist for the organization. Please never forget this point.

I hope you will give your lives to being the staunchest friends and supporters of those suffering or in distress. And I hope you will cherish the Soka Gakkai, an organization of and for the people—that you will revere it, support it and work for its development. This is my heartfelt request of all of you.

*The young women's high school division leader for the Chubu region shared her gratitude for the Soka Gakkai. She said: "Through my activities in the*

*Soka Gakkai, I can challenge my weaknesses. I feel tremendous appreciation to the organization for the simple fact that I've grown from a person who was overwhelmed by her problems into a person who is genuinely concerned about the welfare of her friends and chants for their happiness."*

*The young men's high school division leader of Fukui Prefecture [close to Kobe and Osaka, originally Hyogo and Osaka prefectures] helped truck in relief supplies after the Great Hanshin Earthquake that struck Kobe, Osaka and the island of Awaji in January 1995. In response to the disaster, many youth division members worked tirelessly through the night, distributing to earthquake victims the numerous donated supplies, such as blankets and hand-warmers, that had been delivered to Soka Gakkai community centers in Kobe and Osaka from throughout Japan. That episode deeply impressed upon him the unmatched strength of the Soka Gakkai organization, a body of ordinary people united in a common cause.*

Because those young people were united in their desire to do anything they could to help, they could make a powerful contribution. Our organization exists to mobilize such human goodness—people's desire to help and benefit others—and use it to create great value. You might say the Soka Gakkai is a body or organism that took form and came to life specifically to bring together the basic goodness of people's hearts, to further develop that goodness and strengthen it. Without the organization, there would be no cohesion or order to our efforts.

An organization dedicated to good enhances people's capacity to work for good and promotes unlimited growth and self-improvement. It does not hinder people's progress or lead them astray. It supports people's self-development, putting them on a sure course to happiness and personal growth. And it is for this purpose that our organization exists.

In that respect, the organization is a means. The end, meanwhile, is for people to become happy.

*Millions of people in Japan and throughout the world unhesitatingly state that because of the Soka Gakkai, they have found a way to become genuinely happy.*

The Soka Gakkai is a wondrous organization. There is without doubt no other realm as pure, genuine, warm and beautiful. Being young, you may be unaware of society's harsh and ugly side, and so may not fully appreciate just how great this organization really is. But let me assure you, there is none other like it.

For almost as long as our organization has existed, our members, including many of your own mothers and fathers who are practicing, have been ridiculed and insulted by arrogant people as they have worked with incredible patience and fortitude to build this great castle of the people.

There are people who criticize and attack our organization. But are they the ones who will teach others how to achieve absolute happiness? No, they are not. Those who recognized this encouraged one another to become happy and came together to help those who were suffering. And the result is the Soka Gakkai. This is a fact most solemn and sublime. The organization is the crystallization of genuine democracy, handmade by the people, for the people. It is the only body carrying out the widespread propagation of Nichiren Buddhism, which places the highest value on the dignity of the human being. It is the sun of hope for all humanity. That is why President Toda declared that the Soka Gakkai organization was more precious than his life. I feel exactly the same way.

## Individuals Grow Amid Human Relationships

*Some people have the impression that joining an organization means giving up their freedom or losing their self-identity, but the Soka Gakkai isn't like that at all.*

Organizations that deprive people of their freedom and identity definitely do exist. They exploit people to achieve their own objectives. This is a negative aspect that organizations can have.

However, though you may dislike organizations, is remaining alone really a sign of freedom? Can you guarantee that you won't lose sight of yourself anyway? That's hard to say. Genuine freedom does not mean living selfishly and doing just as you please; it is traveling the correct path in life.

The earth, for example, revolves around the sun. If it were to stray from its orbit even in the slightest, it would spell disaster. A spacecraft, if it assumes the correct course, can traverse the vast cosmos and reach its destination. This is the meaning of true freedom.

*If we depart from the proper orbit, we could wind up "lost in space."*

That's true. Sports, too, have their own set of rules. There's a certain way of doing things. Does freedom mean breaking these rules to suit your own convenience? I don't think so. Genuine freedom means making full use of your strength and skill while following the rules of the game. To live without a goal or purpose, doing whatever you please whenever you please, makes for a reckless and self-destructive life.

Our organization is one of great human diversity. This acts as a stimulus for our personal growth. In many sports, it's hard to assess your real ability if you train or practice only by yourself. We develop and grow through contact with many other people. In Japan, the mountain potatoes known as *taro* are rough and dirty when harvested, but when placed together in a basin of running water and rolled against one another, the skin is peeled away, leaving them shining clean and ready for cooking. It's probably inappropriate to compare people to potatoes, but my point is that the only way for us to hone and polish our character is through our interactions with others.

Being on your own without having to see or think about others may seem very comfortable and hassle-free, but you'll find yourself locked in a world that is terribly small and limited. By avoiding belonging to any group or organization, you deprive yourself of contact with many people and, in the end, you are left wondering about the meaning of your existence.

A society without any organization whatsoever would be chaotic and disordered; there would be mob rule, with everyone just doing as they pleased, regardless of the consequences. It would be like a ship sailing out to sea without a compass—either it will lose its way or end up wrecked.

In the realm of Buddhist practice, I urge each of you to find at least one trusted senior in faith with whom you feel comfortable discussing anything. President Toda gave the same advice.

*The young women's high school division leader of the Shikoku region told me how she was nervous and afraid when she moved to Tokyo to begin her first year at a university. Her young women's division leader at that time, despite her own demanding schedule, visited her frequently. She said that she could talk about anything with this person and said that encounters with such seniors in faith are one of life's great treasures.*

Developing personal relationships with people you can trust is important. Though we use the term *organization*, it is actually a collection of bonds among individuals. And this is the reason that the Soka Gakkai has cherished and supported each member unstintingly and continues to do so. To forget this would lead to an organization that constrains and oppresses people.

## "Many in Body, One in Mind" Describes an Ideal Organization

*Some people insist that they don't need the organization to keep up their practice of Buddhism. They say they can do it on their own.*

In reality, it's not so easy to do. And even if one could continue to practice Buddhism alone, it would amount to a self-centered practice, consisting of prayer and little action. Even if one were doing well practicing alone, for instance, what about others? How could that person truly help others?

Nichiren Daishonin taught his followers to proceed in the spirit of many in body, one in mind. This was his clear guidance. True practitioners of Nichiren Buddhism are those who act in exact accord with his teachings.

In modern terms, many in body, one in mind means an organization. Many in body means that each person is different—that people differ in their appearances, standing in society, circumstances and individual missions. But as for their hearts—their hearts should be one; each person should be one in mind, united in faith.

On the other hand, there is the condition described as many in body, many in mind, in which there is no unity of purpose. In addition, the concept of one in body, one in mind means that people are coerced into uniformity and made to think, look and act alike. This is akin to fascism, where people have no freedom; it ultimately only leads to a condition of one in body, many in mind, where people give the appearance of being united and committed to the same goal on the surface but in reality don't go along with that goal in their hearts.

*The best kind of organization, then, is made up of members who are diverse in every way but are united in purpose toward achieving a shared lofty objective—in other words, an organization that exemplifies the spirit of many in body, one in mind.*

Yes. Many in body means to allow each individual to give full play to his or her unique potential and individuality. One in mind means that everyone works together based on faith, sharing the same goal and purpose. This is true unity.

One can liken many in body, one in mind to a bamboo grove: Each bamboo stalk sprouts up independently, yet underground their roots are firmly intertwined. The world of faith is the same. Because we share the same "roots," because we share a common spirit and purpose, each one of us can grow limitlessly, reaching for the sky in our personal development and achievements. True unity is achieved when each person has the strength to stand alone—the conviction and fortitude to advance, even if you are the only one. Mutual dependency is not the answer.

## CHANTING IS LIKE THE EARTH'S ROTATION

The earth rotates on its axis while revolving around the sun. This allows sunlight to bathe the entire planet, causing life to flourish. We, too, engage in a sort of axial rotation when we practice for ourselves by reciting the sutra and chanting Nam-myoho-renge-kyo. Our connection and interaction with others and with society, then, constitutes our orbital revolution, like that of the earth around the sun. The earth's axial rotation and its revolution around the sun are interrelated. This is a universal law.

The function of our organization is similarly to enable us to support and encourage one another so that we each maintain the "axial rotation" of our personal practice and our broader "orbital revolution" of working with and for others, thus never veering from the proper orbit in life.

*It's sad to think that in our wonderful organization there are still people, including leaders, who stop practicing.*

I hope all of you will surpass those seniors in our movement who have turned cowardly, lost their faith and betrayed the trust of members. Other people are other people; you are you. The important thing is for you to grow into a fine person yourself, never letting yourself be influenced by those who would turn their backs on their fellow members.

Even in Nichiren Daishonin's time, numerous followers abandoned their faith, and after his death, too, many priests practicing under Nikko Shonin, his direct successor, also abandoned Nichiren's teachings. Even those who were revered by lay believers as venerable priests discarded their faith.

In the Soka Gakkai, as well, most of the leaders were quick to give up their faith when President Makiguchi was imprisoned for speaking out against Japanese militarism during World War II. And even during President Toda's day, there were many members who simply quit their practice because they were worried about the negative reputation the Soka Gakkai was gaining due to its broad and rapid development.

Those who persevere in their Buddhist practice throughout their lives are true followers of Nichiren Daishonin. Those who embrace the Gohonzon and never abandon their practice, no matter what difficulties lie ahead, are Nichiren's genuine disciples. This perfectly describes the Soka Gakkai members.

Compared to people in the past, people today have grown self-centered, irresponsible and undisciplined. To maintain a steadfast commitment to Buddhist practice in this directionless age is truly noble.

There are some who gave up their practice, influenced by the barrage of abuse and criticism hurled at our organization. But Nichiren Daishonin declared that our faith mustn't be like fire, flaring up one moment and burning out the next, but rather it should be like flowing water, moving forward unceasingly (see WND-1, 899). What's important is having faith strong enough to continue chanting Nam-myoho-renge-kyo and advancing toward kosen-rufu no matter what our environment, our circumstances or the conditions of society.

*One student said that she was extremely disappointed when she met certain senior leaders who were very arrogant and full of self-importance.*

President Toda fiercely scolded arrogant leaders and those who tried to use the Soka Gakkai for personal gain or gratification. He said that leaders should think of themselves as the members' servants and that haughty leaders ought to be expelled from the organization.

Leaders are there to serve the members. It is their job to work for the members' happiness. Leaders who forget this responsibility have already lost the vital spark of faith and are spiraling downward toward abandoning their practice altogether.

The Soka Gakkai is not about vertical or hierarchical relationships between leaders and members. A leader is merely one who takes responsibility and plays a pivotal role in keeping things working harmoniously.

Leadership positions in the organization are, after all, just made-up titles. Faith is what is crucial. No matter what leadership position one may occupy, if one loses faith, there will be no benefit. It is the same as quitting one's practice altogether. Leaders who lack faith are simply taking advantage of the Soka Gakkai and the sincere faith of the members. Nichiren Daishonin would surely condemn such people.

*What would you say to someone who asks if it's necessary to attend meetings that are clearly being held out of formality, as opposed to meetings that have real substance and value?*

I feel sorry for all those who attend meetings that lack substance or are led by a complacent or overbearing central figure. The responsibility for that, of course, rests on the shoulders of those involved in the planning and preparation of the meeting.

However, it's important to remember that everything is up to you. If you are determined to absorb everything you can, you will most likely learn something from any meeting you attend. If you were to make the effort to attend a meeting but return home without having gained a thing, that would be your loss.

In addition, once you've been involved in planning a meeting yourself, you learn that, while it's easy to criticize, it's a challenge to hold an inspiring meeting. Most important is that, if you feel the organization or the meetings you're attending are boring and unproductive, you make efforts yourself to change things. The organization is a means, not an end; it is not perfect.

In the early years of my practice, I wasn't happy with the Soka Gakkai organization. Back then, we lacked the element of culture, and I just couldn't bring myself to like the organization as it was. Sensing this, President Toda said to me: "If that's how you feel, then why don't you create an organization that you truly like? Work hard and devote yourself earnestly to building the ideal organization through your own effort!"

*That's so inspiring!*

*I can sense President Toda's great broad-mindedness in encouraging you that way. It is so impressive to see how you immediately set about putting his suggestion into practice.*

*Since this Buddhism teaches the importance of having a stand-alone spirit, I guess we should each do our best to try to change things for the better.*

## Buddhism Accords With Common Sense

This also applies to your stance in organizations such as your school or family. As a member of the organization known as school, you need to be committed to making it a better place. As a member of the organization that is your family, you need to make efforts to create the best possible environment. That spirit is vital. It is also common sense, and

Buddhism accords with common sense. The correct way to practice Nichiren Buddhism is to have the attitude that "I will be the driving force for change!"

Our organization dedicated to kosen-rufu was created so that we could deepen our understanding of Nichiren's teachings and also share it with others.

*There are many students who say that they would like to tell their close friends about their Buddhist practice but aren't sure how they should go about it.*

Just do what comes naturally. Religious freedom belongs to everyone, and no one can prevent us from talking about faith with others if we want to.

We have to keep in mind, however, that there is an appropriate time for everything. If you sat down to a formal dinner, for example, and were immediately served the main course, you might be a little surprised, since it's usually customary to serve an appetizer or salad first. When you visit someone's home, you don't just barge into the house; you wait until the host opens the door and invites you in.

Similarly, if you wish to talk with someone about Buddhism, there is a proper way to go about it. To friends, you might say something like: "I practice Buddhism. It's a profound philosophy that teaches us many important things, such as the nature of life and the universe. Through Buddhism, you can come to understand things that are not taught in school, things that are more fundamental and profound. It is a philosophy that has deep value and significance for our lives. Would you like to talk about this life philosophy of Buddhism sometime? Or would you like to read about it?" Even if they say they're not interested, through you they have made a connection to this Buddhism and will surely come across it again. We should use the same natural approach when encouraging our fellow members.

There's no need to be impatient. Faith is a lifelong process, spanning the three existences of past, present and future. What's important is to make plenty of friends and work at solidifying those relationships. Introducing others to Buddhism and striving for kosen-rufu are extensions of the spirit of friendship that wishes to see those we care about become happy.

*Some students say that they're apprehensive about sharing Buddhism with others, because they don't want their present condition or circumstances to give a negative impression of the Soka Gakkai. They want to wait until they've fixed up their lives or become shining models of faith.*

It's up to the individual. Just as these students seem to recognize, it's important to show actual proof of faith in one's daily life. But that doesn't mean that you should pretend to be something that you're not. It's perfectly fine for you to speak about Buddhism from the heart, in your own words, in a very natural way, just as you are. The purpose of faith is not to make yourself look good in the eyes of others. To have compassion for others means sincerely praying and working for others' happiness, no matter how they may regard you. They may not appreciate your sincerity at the time, but if you are genuine in your efforts, at some point they are bound to recall the friend who once encouraged them or who helped them through a difficult time. Surely this is a most worthy way to live.

*Some students have said that they are so busy with their studies and extra-curricular activities that they don't have time to participate in Soka Gakkai high school division activities.*

*There are also some students who are busy with part-time jobs to pay for their school tuition.*

All of these things are important. The challenge is to work hard and try to do the best you can in each of them. If everything were easy, there would be no challenge. The greater the challenge, the greater our exhilaration and sense of accomplishment when we succeed. By striving to do our best, we can become winners; we can become people of great substance. When plants are exposed to strong winds, their roots grow deeper. Everything works this way. Without challenges, we would grow lazy and decadent; our lives would be empty and barren. And emptiness means unhappiness.

# FOR STUDENTS: FAITH IS THE FOUNDATION; STUDYING, THE PRIORITY

*Some students believe that because their school studies should be their main priority at this time in their lives, it isn't necessary to exert themselves in Buddhist practice or activities. But I don't think that's true, is it?*

What is important—study or faith? The answer is both. They are important in different ways. Faith is our very foundation, our roots. From the roots grow a trunk, branches, leaves and flowers—these represent the various activities of human life. For all of you, the members of the high school division, your studies are your trunk—your first priority. Everything else—the branches and so on—comes next.

Faith is the engine that powers our growth throughout life. But without making concrete efforts to advance, that engine won't work. For students, advancement means studying. Even if you chant and engage in faith-related activities, if you do not challenge yourself in your studies, you will be like a stalled car that is going nowhere. Simply put, for those of you who are students, faith is your foundation, and study is your priority.

*So, while basing our lives on faith, it's vital that we work hard in our studies.*

Yes. And what is the purpose of study? It's to enable us to gain practical ability and knowledge so that we can contribute to society and to the happiness and welfare of many people. What's the purpose of faith? It's so that each of us can become truly happy and enable others to do the same. Faith is the driving force that lets us apply what we gain from our studies to serving people genuinely.

Simply becoming university professors or lawyers does not automatically make people great or worthy of respect. The question is, what have they done since acquiring that position; how much have they helped others?

A great person is someone who encourages many people and helps them become happy. In this sense, those who are playing an active role in the Soka Gakkai for the realization of kosen-rufu are the most

251

honorable of all. Those of your parents who are devoting themselves to this cause are far more worthy of respect than any famous celebrity or political leader. The members of our organization have worked with a powerful resolve to help those they have some connection with become truly happy. I hope you will always remember this spirit of the Soka Gakkai.

Perhaps, when you were younger, your parents went off to do activities for kosen-rufu while you stayed at home, and you may have felt lonely. I'm sure your parents would have found it much more relaxing to stay at home with you. Instead, feeling it would be selfish to think only of their own family's happiness and comfort and ignore others' suffering, they were always out working tirelessly to spread Nichiren's teachings. A mature person is someone who can understand and appreciate this fact.

My dream is that all of you will enjoy a brilliant future, play leading roles in all fields of society and throughout the world and fully reveal your potential.

That said, however, if you only seek and gain status or fame, you will be no different from the leaders the world has seen until today. Therefore, it's crucial that you become leaders who possess the spirit to do whatever you can to serve the people. When our world is illuminated by vast constellations of such outstanding, humanistic leaders, the time of kosen-rufu will have arrived. That will be an ideal society. The only way to truly develop this spirit is through faith—by perfecting yourselves and honing your character within the organization of the Soka Gakkai.

# 17

## WEAVING THE FABRIC OF PEACE

*You have shared guidance and advice on different aspects of daily life in a thorough, all-encompassing way. I know that the principles you have imparted will serve as a foundation to support all the high school division members throughout their lives. Thank you very much.*

*Today, we'll discuss with you the most important topics of human revolution and kosen-rufu.*

*Your preface to* The Human Revolution *contains the famous line "A great human revolution in just a single individual will help achieve a change in the destiny of a nation and further, will enable a change in the destiny of all humankind" (p. viii). I see this as not only the main theme of the novel but a description of your life, President Ikeda.*

*Human revolution—transforming or revolutionizing our lives at the most fundamental level—holds the key to realizing change in all spheres. Nonetheless, some members remain unclear as to just what human revolution means.*

Human revolution is not something extraordinary or divorced from our daily lives. Here are some practical examples.

Let's say there's a young boy who spends all his time playing and never studies. Then, one day, he decides to try to improve his future chances, and he begins to take his studies seriously. That is his human revolution.

Or perhaps a woman only seeks happiness for her family on a superficial level. She's satisfied with her life until, one day, she asks herself: "What if our present happiness doesn't last? Maybe I should look for more solid, enduring happiness."

She begins practicing Nichiren Buddhism and, basing her life on this philosophy, starts working for her family's absolute happiness. That is her human revolution.

Or perhaps a father thinks only of his small world—himself, his family and his friends. Then, one day, he decides to step out of these narrow confines just a little to extend a helping hand to the ill or suffering, giving earnest thought to how he can help them find happiness. As a result, he starts participating in SGI activities for that purpose. That is his human revolution.

In other words, human revolution is expanding your view beyond your restricted, ordinary, everyday world and striving for and dedicating yourself to achieving something more noble, more profound, more all-embracing.

*Could we say it means striving, even just a little, to become a stronger person?*

Yes. That spirit of "even just a little" is important. Will you take a step forward, or will you be content to stay where you are now? Everything in life is determined by that.

*The Kyushu young women's high school division leader shared the following experience with me recently. A member going to music school was having trouble getting along with others, including her mother, and started skipping classes. She began chanting Nam-myoho-renge-kyo about her problems and soon started attending school regularly again. Her friends said that even her piano playing improved. And she began to get along better with her mother. This experience led her to have more appreciation.*

*This young women's leader said that what makes her happiest is that because of this practice, she's become a person who prays for others' happiness.*

*While we hear many such inspiring stories, some members feel the challenge of human revolution is beyond them. They're convinced that their lives can never change. They describe themselves as weak-willed—always making resolutions just to break them almost as quickly as they are made.*

There's nothing wrong with that. If we were all perfect from the start, we wouldn't need to do human revolution!

In fact, those who at first may be completely overwhelmed by their environment or constantly defeated by their weaknesses, but who then undergo a dramatic transformation as a result of solid Buddhist practice, can be wonderful inspiration for others.

The times we experience the most intense suffering, unbearable agony and seemingly insurmountable deadlock are actually brilliant opportunities for us to carry out human revolution.

If you're the type whose resolve tends to melt away easily, if you find it difficult to stick to your goals, then just renew your determination each time you find yourself slipping. You will achieve your human revolution without fail if you keep struggling valiantly, pressing forward despite setbacks and disappointments, always thinking: "This time I'll make it! This time I will succeed!"

*I see.*

Life is complicated. We are defined by all sorts of factors—personality, habits, karma, family background. It is difficult to free ourselves from these, as they are all intertwined and linked.

Many spend their days running around busily, absorbed with trivial worries and shallow concerns. It's quite common for people never to get beyond the six lower paths of life—hell, hunger, animality, anger, humanity and heaven—and in that condition, to find that their lives have gone by in a flash.

But when we resolve to break through those lower worlds and access the states of bodhisattvas and Buddhahood, showing greater compassion in our conduct and behavior, we undertake a revolution in our own actions—a human revolution.

Here's another example—university entrance examinations. Many of you may be feeling right now that that's all there is to life. And at the same time, you probably have friends who are experiencing problems. If, with the excuse that you must prepare for your exams, you ignore your friends' needs, you remain locked in the six paths. On the other hand, if you try to help and encourage them at this crucial point, realizing that you'll regret it if you don't, you are walking the path of a bodhisattva.

When such compassion spreads from the individual level to the family level, to the nation and then the world, an unprecedented non-violent revolution for peace is taking place.

## HUMAN REVOLUTION:
## AN IMPORTANT THEME FOR THE TIMES

*Our society is a perfect example of the six lower paths. It is a society domi-nated by hunger and animality.*

*Today there are so few role models of decent, admirable lives. The news is filled with government and business leaders involved in corrupt and under-handed dealings.*

*Simply making structural changes or reforms won't help, either. The bad guys will just find sneakier ways to get around the system and do even worse things.*

*There needs to be a fundamental change. People must change.*

There are all sorts of revolutions—political, economic, industrial, sci-entific, artistic and those in distribution and communications. And there are many others. Each has its significance and, often, necessity.

But no matter what one changes, the world will never get any better as long as the people—the guiding force and impetus behind all endeavors—remain selfish and lack compassion. In that respect, human revolution is the most fundamental of all revolutions and, at the same time, the most necessary.

Immediately after World War II, the president of Japan's prestigious University of Tokyo, Shigeru Nambara, stressed the need for a "human revolution." Aurelio Peccei, co-founder of the Club of Rome, also under-scored the need for a reformation, renaissance and revival of humanity. Thinkers the world over have arrived at the same conclusion.

*When you met with the Brazilian poet Amadeu Thiago de Mello in April 1997, he said, "I thought that there was no longer anything that would move me as a poet, but when I came upon your philosophy of human revolution, I was greatly moved—for the first time in decades."*

Human revolution is going to be an increasingly important subject of discussion in the years ahead. Human revolution is to lead people's attitudes toward life, society and peace in a new and positive direction.

I believe that human revolution will be an important theme in the twenty-first century.

*Is human revolution any different from the normal process of growth and development?*

Revolution means an overturning. It means a sudden and dramatic change.

Gradual change over the years as we grow and mature is part of life's natural process. But human revolution occurs when we transcend that normal pace of growth and undergo a rapid change for the better.

The process of human revolution is one of steady, marked improvement, enabling us to keep growing and developing throughout our lives, for all eternity. We will never hit a limit, a dead end, in our journey for self-perfection. Faith is the engine, the power source for our ongoing human revolution.

*I think that few people can accomplish human revolution with only intellectual stimulation—for example, by reading books about ethics and moral principles.*

An uncountable number of such books have been written, as well as books on self-help and self-improvement. If human revolution could be achieved simply by reading, if we could change our destiny through the power of words alone, it would be an easy matter indeed.

The SGI is in pursuit not of abstract intellectual doctrine but of a thorough, real human transformation—in which people change their fundamental attitudes and ways of thinking and focus their minds, actions and lives on the highest good. Essentially, this human revolution takes place when our lives are in the state of Buddhahood. When we fuse our lives with the enlightened life of Buddhahood, we can tap the power within to change ourselves fundamentally.

*Buddhahood, then, is that power deep within us that makes such self-transformation possible.*

*Let me share the experience of a member that was related to me by the Hokuriku young men's high school division leader. This member had three close friends with whom he spent a lot of time talking, reading comics and just hanging out. One day, during summer vacation, as they talked about the things they found wrong with society, the topic of destiny came up. They talked about their views on life for hours.*

*After that, one friend asked the member—who wasn't very active in the Soka Gakkai himself—to lend him one of your books, President Ikeda, to take home and read. They also all started reading the "Discussions on Youth" series together. In the process, the four friends, who had been the biggest goof-offs in their class, became the most serious, dedicated students.*

*I think that, in their heart of hearts, all people want to grow, to improve, to change. That's why even the smallest thing can become an impetus for growth.*

Human beings possess the unique capacity to aspire for self-improvement and personal growth. We can conceive changing the direction of life instead of merely following its flow.

When people speak of wanting to be a success, they generally mean gaining prestige in society. But doing human revolution is a more profound aspiration, for it involves changing and elevating our lives from within. The transformation achieved is everlasting and far, far more precious than prestige.

A human being is a human being. No one can become anything more than human.

For that reason, the most important thing is simply to become the best human beings we can. No matter how we adorn ourselves with the trappings of fame, rank, academic credentials, knowledge or wealth, if we are impoverished or bankrupt inside, our lives will be barren and empty.

What kind of people are we when all those externals have been stripped away? When we stand unadorned, except for our humanity?

Human revolution is the challenge to change our lives at their core.

Shakyamuni Buddha was born a royal prince, but he gave up everything. He cast off worldly titles and privileges to devote himself to religious practice, to seek the truth. He pursued his human revolution.

Nichiren Daishonin, who had no wealth or status—who proudly proclaimed his heritage as a member of the *chandala* class, the lowest stratum of society—also devoted himself selflessly to Buddhism.

## BECOME THE BEST HUMAN BEING

*Many of the rich, powerful and famous in society compare unfavorably to ordinary, hard-working people with their warmth and humanity.*

*All the average person wants is to live in peace and be happy. Yet we have seen time and again throughout history how leaders of nations, out of failure to pursue their human revolution, have plunged their fellow citizens into war and misery.*

We have had two world wars in the twentieth century. Millions upon millions have tasted the sufferings of hell. When we ponder why this happened, it becomes clear that humankind must change into a compassionate presence on this planet.

*The opening lines of* The Human Revolution—"*Nothing is more barbarous than war. Nothing is more cruel*" (p. 3)—*have profound significance.*

*And your sequel,* The New Human Revolution, *begins: "Nothing is more precious than peace. Nothing brings more happiness*" (vol. 1, p. 1).

Every August, I recall the day World War II ended. Japan surrendered on August 15, 1945. It was a sunny day, and I was staying with relatives in Nishimagome in Tokyo's Ota Ward. Our house had been razed by the authorities to create a barrier to block the spread of fires caused by air raids.

I had heard there would be an important radio broadcast at noon. I was expecting an announcement from the Imperial Headquarters, the nation's highest military council during the war, that Japan was going to launch an all-out attack on the United States. That was the general atmosphere at the time. That was what we had been taught to think.

Just before noon, I went to my grandmother's house in nearby Higashimagome. Everywhere was quiet and still. I listened to the emperor's address, but the reception was poor, and I couldn't make out what he was saying.

Neither my grandmother nor I had any idea whether Japan had won or lost. When I got back to Nishimagome, my younger brother came running to me in tears, crying, "We lost, we lost!" I thought the wartime hardships had finally driven him crazy.

We all stood about saying: "How could we have lost? It's impossible!" Not until evening did it finally begin to sink in that Japan had lost the war.

The city fell into a strange lethargy. People were worried what would happen when the Occupation forces arrived. Until supper, everyone sat about in a stupor.

But, at the same time, we began to realize that the sound of bomber raids, which had continued through the morning, could no longer be heard. They had completely stopped at noon. The skies were quiet.

A sense of relief seemed to spread.

That night, for the first time in months, we could turn on the lights in our homes as we pleased—we had been forced to live in semi-darkness during the air raids. "How bright!" I thought.

And I also thought what a good thing peace was. We were all relieved, yet no one dared to come right out and say: "I'm glad we lost. What a relief that the war's over!"

Many fine youth lost their lives in the war. My four elder brothers were sent to fight on the front.

*I am reminded of this passage from* The Human Revolution*: "Nothing is more pitiful than a nation being swept along by fools"* (p. 3).

My eldest brother died in Burma (now Myanmar). He was a fine young man of great integrity.

When we received the news, we couldn't believe it. About three years later, a young man who had served with him visited us and recounted how my brother had died. My brother had been hit by machine-gun fire from a low-flying aircraft and had fallen into a river during the drawn-out Battle of Imphal.

For a long time, I had difficulty picturing this. One day, many years later, I watched an in-depth television documentary on the Battle of Imphal. At last, I felt what it must have been like. And I was again made aware of what a senseless, tragic campaign it was.

During this disastrous battle, the Japanese army left a trail of its own soldiers' corpses in its path, which became known as the Skeleton Trail. It was a tragedy caused by leaders who made terrible misjudgments, were preoccupied with self-serving interests and forgot completely about the men who were carrying out their orders.

*Such dreadful things must never be allowed to happen again.*

Yet today, many warn of a resurgence of nationalism and authoritarianism in Japan. Everyone is beginning to forget the tragedy that took place just a half-century ago.

That's why the Soka Gakkai, which ardently calls out for peace, is so important. The initial reason I joined the Soka Gakkai was that I could completely trust Mr. Toda, because he had spent two years in prison during the war for opposing militarism. I didn't know anything about Buddhism. I believed in a person, in Mr. Toda. And following the path of the oneness of mentor and disciple with Mr. Toda became the path of my human revolution.

*And that has been the path of kosen-rufu itself, hasn't it?*

The determination to accomplish kosen-rufu adds momentum to the determination to accomplish your human revolution. Human revolution is like a planet's rotation on its axis, while kosen-rufu is like the planet's revolution around the sun.

Rotation and revolution are the foundation of all motion in the universe. If heavenly bodies did not move in this manner, it would be counter to the laws of the universe.

# KOSEN-RUFU: A PROCESS, AN ETERNAL FLOW

*Some people don't clearly understand what kosen-rufu implies. One member asked whether it means converting everyone on earth to Nichiren Buddhism.*

Kosen-rufu is the spread of the Mystic Law from one person to another. It is also its spread from ten thousand to fifty thousand. Yet, kosen-rufu is not about numbers. It is a process, an eternal flow.

Kosen-rufu will not end at some fixed point in time. We won't sit down one day and say, "Well, now kosen-rufu is finished." Not only would that spell our spiritual death, we'd lose all motivation to do human revolution.

Kosen-rufu is unending. Although we try to describe it by defining certain conditions, in reality, kosen-rufu has no set form.

*I guess the same can be said about our personal revolution, our human revolution—that it is a process, too.*

Yes. When a seriously ill person recovers, that is great human revolution. When a mean person becomes kind, that is human revolution. When people who treat their parents poorly begin to respect and love them, that is human revolution.

Human revolution cannot be pinned down to one specific thing. It is any action that leads to positive change or improvement in the inner realm of our lives. Like kosen-rufu, it is an ongoing process. What's important to ask ourselves is whether we are on the path of continuous personal growth.

*What is the literal meaning of kosen-rufu?*

*Kosen* means to widely declare. "Widely" implies speaking out to the world, to an ever-greater number and ever-broader spectrum of people.

"Declare" means to proclaim one's ideals, principles and philosophy. The *ru* of *rufu* means a current like that of a great river. And *fu* means to spread out like a roll of cloth.

The teaching of the Mystic Law has nothing to do with appearance, form or pride. It flows out freely—to all humanity the world over. Like a cloth unfolding, it spreads out and covers all. So *rufu* means to flow freely, to reach all.

Just like a cloth, kosen-rufu is woven from vertical and horizontal threads. The vertical threads represent the passing of Nichiren's teaching from mentor to disciple, parent to child, senior to junior. The horizontal threads represent the impartial spread of this teaching, transcending national borders, social classes and all other distinctions.

Simply put, kosen-rufu is the movement to communicate the ultimate way to happiness. To communicate the highest principle of peace to people of all classes and nations through the correct philosophy and teaching of Nichiren Daishonin.

*It is natural to want to tell others how great something is that we believe in. This is not limited to our Buddhist practice.*

That's right. Vendors or salespeople, for example, believe that their products—whether they be televisions, fast food or fresh vegetables—are the best and try to have as many people as possible know about and buy them. This is an example, in a sense, of the widespread propagation of one's beliefs.

School administrators believe their educational institution employs the best methods and produces the highest quality students. They want to have as many people as possible know this. Their activities to promote their schools are the widespread propagation of their beliefs.

Christianity carried out its own widespread propagation in the past. So did Islam, Hinduism and Communism. While we already know what happened when those religions were spread, we don't yet know the result of widely propagating Nichiren Buddhism. We are now carrying out this grand experiment and creating history as we go.

*That's wonderful. The work of kosen-rufu is really the most exciting drama.*

But unless each of us is certain of our beliefs and proud that we practice the highest Buddhist teaching, we cannot properly carry out kosen-rufu.

In all walks of life, there are and always will be corrupt, unscrupulous people. They find it impossible to remain for long in such a sincere, earnest movement. This was true of all who betrayed our organization in the past. Anyone who tries to join the kosen-rufu movement with a deceptive, scheming or malicious intent will soon be exposed.

*It seems clear, then, that kosen-rufu cannot be achieved unless we each strive to carry out human revolution in our own lives.*

You can also think of your human revolution as undertaking kosen-rufu in the microcosm of your own world. When many individuals pursue their human revolution, they can advance the kosen-rufu of society as a whole. In other words, kosen-rufu is advanced in direct proportion to the strides we make in our human revolution.

At the same time, when we abandon selfish interests and devote ourselves to kosen-rufu, a movement to lead others to happiness, our human revolution will progress. That is how closely the two are related.

It is wrong to isolate ourselves. Those who unite with caring, supportive seniors in faith, seniors who are sincerely devoted to kosen-rufu, grow by leaps and bounds and make great strides in their human revolution.

## PHILOSOPHY, IDEALS, DISTINGUISH US AS HUMAN

*Some ask why, if Nichiren Buddhism is such a superior teaching, everyone doesn't jump at the chance to practice it, and why those who practice are criticized.*

It isn't practiced readily by all precisely because it is true and right. Being kind to one's parents is right, but how easy is that? Studying is the right thing to do, but how many do it seriously? The same is true of Buddhism.

That human beings possess philosophy and ideals distinguishes us from other animals. All people ask, at least once in their lives, why they were born in this world. But animals don't ask themselves that question.

Another of our distinguishing features is our human yearning for principles that allow us to live honorably, peacefully, happily. It's also human nature that when we see a starving child on television, we want to do something to help. That is a natural instinct.

We cannot live alone, isolated from others. In Japanese, "human being" (Jpn *ningen*) is written with two Chinese characters that, when combined, mean "between people." It is through our interactions with others that we polish our lives and grow.

Therefore, it's only natural that, with as many people as possible, we share and promote understanding of the philosophy, the ideal, that we believe is most correct and valid. It is our right and our duty.

It's the nature of animals to gather food just for themselves. If we were to keep the means we have found for attaining happiness to ourselves, not sharing it with others, we would have succumbed to the states of animality and hunger. The wish to share the truth with others, to share the means for achieving happiness, is the hallmark of philosophy, of education, of culture and of Buddhism.

*That's what kosen-rufu is all about, isn't it? Widely sharing Nichiren Buddhism is a wonderful crystallization and expression of our humanity.*

Yes. It's not being stingy or closed. Kosen-rufu means sharing with our fellow human beings through heart-to-heart dialogue and friendship, and striving with them to find the way to become better, happier people. That alliance of individuals working for the happiness of all constitutes kosen-rufu.

*I feel, President Ikeda, that I have gained a deeper understanding of your efforts to engage in dialogue with people the world over and to forge an international alliance for peace.*

*On August 24 last year [1997], you celebrated your fiftieth anniversary of practicing Nichiren Buddhism. Fifty years ago, kosen-rufu must have seemed a fantastic dream. But today, because of your incredible efforts, Nichiren Buddhism has spread to 128 countries and territories [currently 192].*

I have only tried to keep my vow to walk the path of human revolution that my mentor, Josei Toda, taught me. Now I have fulfilled that vow to the letter. I have won. That's what's important—to win over ourselves. That is human revolution. That is kosen-rufu.

I am not concerned with the immediate future. I am not afraid of persecution or criticism. I am thinking about one hundred and two hundred years from now. My actions today are based on the future ten millennia hence.

From ancient times, it has been said that posterity judges teachers by their disciples. I have been the object of every conceivable groundless attack and insult, but I don't care in the least. Buddhism teaches that this is unavoidable.

I know, deep in my heart, that the evaluation of my true worth, of my success or failure, will be based on the activities, contributions and achievements my disciples will make in their local communities, countries and the world. There are many, many graduates of the high school division playing active roles in society all around the world. I find this enormously encouraging. It makes me very, very happy.

I have no regrets. I believe that I have done my best as a Buddhist and a leader.

My legacy will always be remembered. Why? Because I know that my disciples are achieving great things and making an important mark on our world. That means that my life has been victorious. I can claim a proud, glorious victory in my efforts.

I hope, pray and trust that you, my young friends, and many others behind you will follow me on this triumphant path into the future.

That is my only wish.

# PART FIVE

# THE QUESTIONS
## *of Youth*

# *18*

## WHAT IS FREEDOM?

*President Ikeda, thank you for making time to hold this second series of "Discussions on Youth." We appreciate how busy you are, and we're deeply grateful. We know that all of the members are eagerly looking forward to the start of this new series. We are determined to use this opportunity to grow and to learn as much as we can.*

On the contrary, please allow me to thank *you*. Let's embark together on a journey of heart-to-heart exchange. I am always delighted to do anything I can to bring joy to you, the young men and women who are the future leaders of our movement. Would you happen to know, incidentally, the origins of the Japanese word *seishun*, meaning *youth*? It is written with two Chinese characters, meaning "green" and "spring" respectively. In ancient China, the color green was identified with spring. Red, meanwhile, was associated with summer, white with autumn, and black with winter.

These colors aptly capture the different moods of the four seasons. In terms of our own lives, the time of infancy and childhood might be likened to winter, the season when all things are at rest and plants store energy beneath the earth's surface for the coming of spring. When the time is ripe, and spring finally arrives, all life stirs with the impulse to sprout, to bloom. In English, the word *spring* also has the meaning of a coiled spring, full of bounce and impetus. In Japanese, too, the word *haru* (spring) connotes energy welling up from inside.

According to the ancient Chinese view of the universe, the green spring is associated with the direction *east*—in other words, the direction from which the sun rises. (The direction of the red summer is south, the white autumn west and the black winter north.)

The green springtime of life—our youth—is meant to be lived with our faces turned toward the sun. As the season of growth, youth is both a time of great joy and great suffering. It is filled with all kinds of problems and worries. But it's important not to run away from them. The key is to keep seeking the sun, to keep moving in the direction of the sunlight, as we challenge the pain and agony that are part of youth and growing up. Please never give in to defeat. For a seed to sprout, it must exert tremendous effort to break out of its hard outer covering. To break through to the blue sky above, that sprout must then valiantly push its way up through a thick layer of soil.

The hardships you come across now will all contribute to your growth. Problems are part and parcel of the growing process. Therefore, the important thing is to keep pressing forward, no matter how tough or painful the going may get. Youth is the spirit of persistence—to keep making effort to grow and become more capable despite all obstacles. Those who continue striving for improvement remain youthful no matter what their age. Conversely, those who fail to do so, even if young in years, will be old and weak in spirit.

## True Freedom Is Not Freedom From Responsibility or Effort

*I see what you're saying. The theme for today's discussion is freedom. When asked about how much freedom they have, many high school students say they sometimes feel as if they have no freedom at all. Many complain that school rules about dress and other matters are too restrictive. They say they don't like attending schools with such strict rules.*

*Others have remarked that they don't like their parents being so nosy. When they get a phone call at home, for example, their parents may ask them whom it is from. When they leave the house in the evening, their parents may continuously try to contact them, even though they've told them where they're going. Some students comment, "They say it's because they love us, but they really go overboard sometimes!"*

*Still others complain that they have no time for themselves or the things they want to do. They are busy with their studies and extracurricular activities during the day and then have to attend private classes in the evening to prepare for college entrance exams.*

They certainly have a long list of grievances!

I understand what they're saying, though, and I think they're right. No one likes to be controlled by others, and it's only natural to wish that we could do what we want without people bothering us all the time. I'm sure there are students who dream of what freedom they would enjoy if there were no rules, and if they had plenty of money and time and no parents nagging them. But that is a very shallow view of life, a very superficial perspective of human society.

There are wealthy people who seem free of all constraints, because they can travel around the world and buy whatever they want without having to work. But appearances can be deceptive. While their lives may seem enviably unfettered, many suffer feelings of emptiness. The freedom they enjoy is only superficial, and they feel boxed in and restricted.

An American businessman and his wife told me something very interesting. They remarked that they knew some of the richest people in the world, but they had seen many whose lives were really very sad: widows who felt hollow and empty after their husbands died, people who had lost all sense of purpose, and those who, having reached their goal of financial wealth, were suddenly confronted with their true selves and felt sad and lonely.

Real freedom ultimately hinges on what you decide to dedicate yourself to with all your heart. It doesn't mean simply to amuse oneself. It isn't spending money like water, nor is it having all the free time in the world. It isn't taking long vacations. Doing only as you please is not freedom; it is nothing more than self-indulgence. True freedom lies in the ongoing challenge to develop yourself, to achieve your chosen goal. This path is paved with the glittering gold of freedom.

*It's true that we tend to think of leisure as freedom, but the two are quite different.*

Actually, only because you enjoy great freedom can you study and attend school, recite the sutra morning and evening or participate in high school division activities. Regarding these things as unpleasant chores that keep you from doing what you want is a terribly misguided way of looking at life.

Do you look at going to school as a right or something that you're being forced to do? Do you see school as liberating or stifling? It all depends on your personal philosophy, on your wisdom. If you're passive, you'll feel trapped and unhappy in even the freest of environments. But if you take an active approach and challenge your circumstances, you will be free, no matter how confining your situation may actually be. As Nichiren Daishonin writes: "The characters of this sutra are all without exception living Buddhas of perfect enlightenment. But because we have the eyes of ordinary people, we see them as characters. For instance, hungry spirits perceive the Ganges River as fire, human beings perceive it as water, and heavenly beings perceive it as amrita.[1] Though the water is the same, it appears differently according to one's karmic reward from the past" (WND-1, 486).

Children who are suffering from serious illnesses or living in wartorn countries cannot go to school even when they want to. On the other hand, many children in more fortunate circumstances who do have the opportunity to attend school don't appreciate how free they really are. Being able to go to school is in fact a sign of the most incredible freedom. It's a mistake not to realize that.

*We are actually very fortunate to be able to attend school, aren't we?*

Yes. In the United States, there was a young man with a disabling and painful form of bone cancer known as multiple myeloma. In the last two years of his life, with his entire body encased in a cast because of multiple bone fractures, he visited local high schools in his wheelchair to talk about the terrible effects of drug abuse. He would say to the students: "You want to destroy your body with nicotine or alcohol or heroin? You want to smash it up in cars? You're depressed and want to throw it off the Golden Gate Bridge? Then give me your body! Let me have it! I want it! I'll take it! I want to live!"[2] His words deeply moved his audience. And during the war in the former Yugoslavia, children talked about their dreams. "I had many dreams, but the war robbed me of all of them," one said, and another, "Our dream is to live an ordinary life with our friends, to be able to go to school."[3]

Recently, in the African country of Rwanda there was a bitter and cruel civil war (1990–94). In one particular family, the children lost both parents; only they and their grandmother survived. Somebody had to work to support the others. Ultimately, one of the older boys dropped out of school to care for the rest. He was so sad that he couldn't continue school that he often cried all through the night. Today, his other siblings who are still in school share their lessons with him when he comes home from work in the evening.[4]

## AN EXPANSIVE STATE OF LIFE

*Compared to children in these and many other countries, Japanese high school students have a great deal of free choice.*

Exactly. But if that were the whole story, we'd have to conclude that everything depends completely on our environment. That's not the case. The human condition and life aren't so simple. In Buddhism, true freedom can be correlated to one's life-condition. Someone with an expansive life-condition is free even if confined to the most restrictive prison on earth.

Argentine human rights activist and Nobel Peace Prize winner Adolfo Pérez Esquivel once told me that prison taught him to have a conscious appreciation of freedom.

Natalia Sats, the late president of the Moscow State Children's Musical Theater, fought against oppression. She turned her prison cell into a place of learning, and encouraged her fellow prisoners to share with one another their unique knowledge. One could lecture on chemistry, another could teach medicine. Mrs. Sats, herself a singer and entertainer, sang songs and recited poetry by Aleksandr Pushkin, striving to inspire courage and hope in everyone.

The same was true of the Japanese educator Yoshida Shoin[5] (1830–59; Japanese scholar, teacher and writer whose students later played key roles in the Meiji Restoration). When he was arrested and incarcerated for opposing the policies of the military government, he presented lectures to the other prisoners, raising their spirits. In the end, even his jailers came to hear him speak.

And we can see the same spirit in the first and second presidents of the Soka Gakkai, Tsunesaburo Makiguchi and Josei Toda. Championing the causes of freedom of religion and peace, neither leader would give in to the forces of oppression, even if it meant imprisonment. Each possessed a state of mind of complete freedom, expressed in Nichiren Daishonin's words: "Even if it seems that, because I was born in the ruler's domain, I follow him in my actions, I will never follow him in my heart" (WND-1, 579).

*Those who refuse to be defeated by circumstances, no matter how harsh, are truly free.*

Yes. I'm sure you know the story of Helen Keller (1880–1968). At the age of eighteen months, she lost her sight and hearing. Her deafness also made it difficult for her to speak. But by working together with her teacher, Anne Sullivan, she gradually learned to read, write and speak, and eventually graduated from Radcliffe College in Cambridge, Massachusetts.

Surely no one could have been as restricted as she was—unable to speak, hear or see. Hers was a world of darkness and silence. But she drove the darkness out of her heart. At nine, she finally spoke her first sentence: "It is warm." She never forgot the astonishment and joy she experienced at that moment. She had succeeded at last in breaking out of the prison of silence that confined her.

As a result of unimaginable hard work, she went on to travel the globe to lecture and offer encouragement to people with disabilities. She came to Japan several times. She brought courage to the entire world. She refused to be beaten. She always turned her face to the sun, seeking the bright light of hope.

Being only human, however, she at times had felt forlorn and disheartened by the long hours she had to spend studying, having her textbooks painstakingly spelled out by Ms. Sullivan drawing each letter on the palm of her hand, while other students were singing and dancing and enjoying themselves. She wrote: "I slip back many times, I fall, I stand still, I run against the edge of hidden obstacles, I lose my temper and find it again and keep it better. I trudge on, I gain a little, I feel encouraged, I get more eager and climb higher and begin to see the widening horizon. Every struggle is a victory."[6]

*"Every struggle is a victory." Those are very moving words.*

She also wrote, "In the wonderland of Mind I should be as free as another."[7] This was Helen Keller's declaration of victory. She reached the summit of freedom, liberating herself through her own arduous struggle.

## HAVING STRENGTH AND CAPABILITY IS FREEDOM

*She lived her life with incredible strength and courage.*
    *One of our readers has a question: "I want to do my best, but the combination of school, family responsibilities and high school division activities wears me out. What should I do?"*

You need to develop strength. The stronger you are, the freer you will be. Someone without a lot of stamina may have a very difficult time climbing even a small, thousand-foot mountain. And a person who is sick might not be able to manage it at all. But a strong, healthy person can do it easily with zest and enjoyment. That's why it's important to develop your strength. You must build a self strong enough that you can be active in school, in club activities and in your Soka Gakkai activities. If you possess strength and capability, you will have freedom.

The same is true of sports and music, too. To play your chosen sport or instrument with complete mastery and ease, you have to gain an adequate level of proficiency and skill; you have to be prepared to make some sacrifices to practice with all your might.

Recoiling from effort or just doing as you please is not freedom. It is simply irresponsible and self-absorbed.

*In Japan, some elements of the mass media often cite "freedom of expression" in justifying sensationalist and damaging reporting. But such journalism is irresponsible and violates the freedom and human rights of others.*

*When will they realize that freedom of expression does not mean freedom to lie?*

Freedom exists in self-restraint. In human society, there are rules and an order by which we live and work. There is rhyme and reason, direction and purpose.

This is evident in the natural world, too. The sun rises at dawn and sets at dusk. The stars shine at night. They each have their role. They each follow a certain rhythm and order. They do not appear at random or on a whim; so, in a sense, their activities are restricted.

As high school students, your daily rhythm right now is getting up each day, going to school and regularly participating in high school division activities. I feel it is an extremely important rhythm for you to maintain. If you neglect such efforts, if you fail to develop your potential and strength, you won't be able to enjoy true freedom.

There are all kinds of assets that can contribute to our sense of freedom—intellectual ability, good health, physical stamina, mental and emotional strength, the ability to take care of ourselves and support ourselves financially. But the greatest asset of all is our spiritual state, our state of mind.

## DARE TO TAKE ON TOUGH CHALLENGES

*In other words, running away from responsibilities is not freedom.*

You can run away, of course. That freedom exists. But it is a very small, petty freedom. It leads only to a life of great hardship, a life in which you are powerless, weak and completely frustrated. Alongside this small freedom, however, exists a much greater freedom. The well-known Japanese novelist Eiji Yoshikawa (1892–1962) writes, "Great character is forged through hardship." Only by polishing yourself through repeated difficulties can you build a self that sparkles as brightly as a gem. Once you have developed such a state of life, nothing will faze you. You will be free. You will be victorious.

Once you realize this truth, even hardships become enjoyable. Daring to take on tough challenges—that in itself is immense freedom.

The sea and its waves make it possible for ships to sail from one place to another. Air resistance produces the lift that makes it possible for planes to fly through the sky. Hunger makes food delicious.

Freedom is a relative thing. It is impossible to have absolutely everything go our way all the time. In fact, if it weren't for the various restrictions and obstacles life presents to us, we probably wouldn't appreciate what it is to be free. After all, planes cannot fly in a vacuum; they need air resistance to stay aloft. On the flip side, if we didn't seek freedom, we wouldn't know what it means not to be free.

You may run away from hard work and effort, declaring yourself a free spirit, but you cannot run away from yourself—from your weaknesses, personality and destiny. It is like trying to run from your shadow. It is even more impossible to escape from the sufferings of birth, aging, sickness and death inherent in the human condition. The more you try to avoid hardships, the more doggedly they pursue you, like so many relentless hounds nipping at your heels. That's why there is no other way than to turn and face your troubles head-on.

Life is a battle to win ultimate and unlimited freedom. Faith in Buddhism allows us to use our karma and the sufferings of birth, aging, sickness and death as springboards to happiness. The purpose of faith is to forge that kind of self. Faith enables us to attain a state of unsurpassed freedom.

*I have a friend who is a specialist in her field and is fluent in English. She has many friends and is actively involved in Soka Gakkai activities. Now, she's even cutting back on her sleep to study for a state examination. I was deeply impressed when she said to me, "The toughest times are the happiest times."*

That's a very nice way of putting it. Freedom and lack of freedom are two sides of the same coin. The busiest people may seem to have the most constraints and demands on their time, but they often actually enjoy the most freedom.

Freedom cannot be measured in terms of time—the amount of "free time" we have has nothing to do with the amount of "freedom" we have. It's what we do with our time that counts. Two people with the exact same amount of free time will use it differently: One might savor it, while the other might complain, finding it either burdensome or too short. Similarly, you can spend the same hour watching television, the time passing by in a flash without anything to show for it, or studying, feeling a satisfying sense of achievement when you finish. That one hour can be a turning point in your life. Freedom is determined by your values, by what you place importance on in life.

When the great Russian writer Fyodor Dostoyevsky (1821–81) was a young man, he was arrested for participating in revolutionary activities and sentenced to death by firing squad. He was taken to the execution site, where he saw his fellow prisoners tied to posts and rifles aimed at them. He thought he would be killed momentarily, but he was given a last-minute reprieve.

Later, Dostoyevsky described this episode in one of his novels. The character being sentenced to death realizes that he has only five minutes to live and suddenly perceives those five minutes as a great treasure. He thinks: "What if I had not had to die! What if I could return to life—oh, what an eternity! And all that would be mine! I should turn every minute into an age, I should lose nothing, I should count every minute separately and waste none!"[8]

Dostoyevsky's experience was an extreme one, but it reveals a universal truth: Whether we have five minutes, five years or fifty years to live, we should cherish and value each moment.

When all is said and done, freedom is determined by our values—it depends on our mental outlook, our state of life. There are certainly cases in which we may actually have great liberty but fail to appreciate it and instead feel trapped and confined; whereas others in precisely the same situation may experience tremendous freedom. And two people may use the same freedom in entirely different ways: One may use it to create wonderful value, while the other may fritter it away without a care, producing nothing of lasting value or significance. There are also people who brandish the word *freedom* but actually undermine and destroy it.

Freedom includes value and nonvalue. In the end, those who can exercise self-control are truly free. The wise are free; the foolish are not.

*Going back to the subject of school rules, I agree that some guidelines or regulations are necessary, but at the same time, I feel that some schools do go overboard. The rules get so picky and detailed that it's hard to believe they serve any real purpose.*

It's true that no one likes to be unnecessarily restricted. There was an American educator named William Smith Clark (1826–86), who taught at the Sapporo Agricultural College (now a part of Hokkaido University) in the latter part of last century. He is remembered in Japan for his famous words "Boys, be ambitious!"

When the administrators of the men's college where he was teaching were about to institute a long list of rules, he declared: "You will not raise people with those rules. At this school, all we need is one rule: 'Be gentlemen!' That says everything."[9] Dr. Clark explained that a gentleman strictly observes the rules, not because he is bound by them, but because he always acts in accord with the dictates of his conscience.[10]

I agree. And no matter what circumstances we find ourselves in, our hearts can be free; we don't have to let our spirits be shackled or confined. We need to have the strength to soar on inner wings of hope and freedom and never be defeated by anything.

## SQUARELY FACE THE TASKS BEFORE YOU

*Some of our readers say that their parents don't understand their dreams for the future. They say that it's their future, and they should be able to decide what they will do with it.*

279

This is a matter that can only be assessed case by case. There are situations in which parents, because they have more experience and a better understanding of society, can see things more clearly. It is often wise for the inexperienced to seek advice and guidance from those who are more experienced, in order to choose the surest and most productive direction. That is an especially strong tendency in Eastern thought. And in most cases, doing what one's parents say works out very well. But there is also sometimes a danger that parents—perhaps because their thinking is a little too old-fashioned or because their love for their children makes them overly controlling—may, without winning their children's understanding or support, end up forcing them in a direction that causes resentment and rebellion.

Things change with the times, so I think the best course is ultimately to make your own goals and take responsibility for achieving them. It is important that you expend your own sweat and effort in choosing the path you will follow—one you feel is right for you and will not cause you regret—and then pursue it with all you've got.

I say this because life is long. You are the ones who have to live your lives, fight your battles and win your victories. Your parents won't always be there. I think the best way for both children and parents to be happy is for parents to support their children in the path they have chosen.

It is also up to you to prove to your parents and those around you that you are responsible and know where you're going. If you find your chosen path blocked by their opposition, you have to convince them of your determination and commitment, and let them see how earnestly you are grappling with the challenges in front of you. Those who try to avoid dealing with problems and challenges today will try to avoid them in the future as well. If that is the case, you will not convince anyone that you are serious or responsible.

*University entrance exams in Japan are fiercely competitive. Each university has a limited number of places, and everyone is vying to get in. If you win a place, you have pushed someone else out of one. One of our members has asked whether freedom includes succeeding at the expense of others.*

I think the answer to that question would have to be yes. Life is a struggle. We live in a harsh world. Freedom is not gained by being idle or passive. Whether we like it or not, ours is a competitive world.

All people are of course essentially equal; all deserve equal opportunities for freedom and happiness. This is the spirit of the United Nations Charter and the Universal Declaration of Human Rights, and also the spirit of Buddhism. But people are not robots. Everyone's thinking, personality, character and karma are different. Therefore, succeeding or getting ahead at the expense of others remains, unfortunately, a persistent aspect of human karma.

That's where our laws, our governments and our educational systems come into play. It's sad to say, however, that we haven't done enough in these areas. Human society today is very far from the ideal. But the most fundamental way to approach that ideal is the SGI's movement of human revolution. We are promoting a way of life in which people pray for and create happiness in a world filled with contradictions.

Getting ahead at the expense of others is symptomatic of the state of animality. Human revolution means becoming a person who works for the happiness of both oneself and others. For that reason, we must strive to create a society supported by the human revolution of each individual. In one sense, none of us can attain true happiness unless all others are happy. Basing one's life and actions on this awareness is what Buddhism calls the way of life of the bodhisattva.

Similarly, we cannot enjoy true freedom unless all others are free. In our world today, far too many people are chained by poverty, oppression, fear and ignorance; far too many are robbed of their freedom by war and discrimination. One who stands up to fight for the freedom of such people is truly free. I hope each of you will become that sort of person.

It is therefore important that you squarely face and challenge the tasks that lie before you, and complete them successfully. Then, just as a tree grows, blossoms and bears fruit by sending down roots and extending its branches to the sky, you will naturally come to know greater and greater freedom. For that reason, may you always advance toward the sun of hope.

1. *Amrita:* A legendary liquid, regarded in ancient India as the beverage of the gods. In China, it was thought to rain down from heaven when the world became peaceful. *Amrita,* meaning "immortality," is said to remove one's sufferings and confer everlasting life.

2. Julius Segal, *Winning Life's Toughest Battles: Roots of Human Resilience* (New York: McGraw-Hill Book Company, 1986), p. 99.

3. Kyoko Gendatsu and Eiji Inagawa, *Ushinawareta shishunki* (Lost Adolescence: Messages from Sarajevo) (Tokyo: Michi Shobo Inc., 1994), pp. 239, 272–73.

4. *"Afurika sekido chokka kara"* (From Equatorial Africa), *Mainichi Shimbun,* Osaka Issue, July 19, 1997.

5. Yoshida Shoin (1830–59): Japanese scholar, teacher and writer of the later Edo period (1600–1868). He established a private school and gathered a group of young samurai who later played key roles in overthrowing the Tokugawa shogunate and carrying out the Meiji Restoration.

6. Helen Keller, *The Story of My Life* (New York: Signet Classic, 1988), p. 75.

7. Helen Keller, *The Story of My Life*, p. 73.

8. Fyodor Dostoyevsky, *The Idiot,* trans. David Magarshack (London: Penguin Books, 1955), p. 58.

9. Translated from Japanese. Masatake Oshima, *Kuraaku Sensei to sono deshitachi* (Dr. Clark and His Disciples) (Tokyo: Teikoku Kyoikukai Shuppanbu, 1937), p. 102.

10. Masatake Oshima, *Kuraaku Sensei to sono deshitachi*, p. 103.

# *19*

## WHAT IS INDIVIDUALITY?

*Today's theme is individuality. We asked our members, "What kind of person would you describe as having individuality?" and received a variety of answers, including: "a person who isn't afraid to dress or look different from others"; "an interesting person, someone who does the unusual or is daring"; "someone who knows how to be themselves, who isn't influenced by others"; and "it isn't a matter of their appearance but an air or quality they exude."*

*People have their own ideas about individuality, but I think most would agree that it is a good quality. It seems contradictory, then, that there is a tendency in Japanese society to pick on those who do not conform to the "norm." People who dress or look different or who don't own the "right" or "in" things are often treated as outsiders. Consequently, they become afraid to express their individuality. This, at least, seems to be the situation in Japan today.*

Individuality has been described as a unique treasure we each possess. Just as no two people look exactly the same, we all have our individual characteristics. We each have a treasure that belongs to us alone. We have a mission that only we can fulfill. Everyone has a unique character, a unique identity.

That individuality makes for a way of life and mission that are ours alone. It is something special and singularly our own; no one else can possess it. Part of our very being, it is something we exude naturally, without thinking about it.

Life is about expressing and developing that individuality as fully as possible—in other words, it is about self-realization. We also call this *human revolution*.

The fact that we have been born into this world means that we each have a unique purpose to fulfill. If we didn't, we would not have been born. Nothing in the universe is without value. Everything has meaning. Even plants that we spurn as weeds have a function. Each living thing has a unique identity, role and purpose—the cherry as a cherry, the plum as a plum, the peach as a peach, the damson as a damson.

*You're referring, of course, to the well-known Buddhist principle of cherry, plum, peach and damson (see OTT, 200), indicating the diverse and unique ways in which we manifest our innate potential.*

Yes. There's no point in a plum trying to be a cherry. The plum should bloom like a plum, revealing its unique potential to the fullest. Not only does doing so accord with reason, but it is the right path to happiness and fulfillment in life. Each of us has a distinct identity— that's what makes life interesting. How dull things would be if we were all alike!

*Yes. Human society is full of diversity. Some people are logical, others intuitive, while others tend to be scholarly, athletic, scientific or humanistic. There are eloquent people and quiet people, impatient people and easygoing people. There are those who are highly methodical and those who are very casual. Some are impulsive and others cautious, some bloom early and some late. Everyone has different talents and aptitudes, too.*

## Believe in Yourself and Work Hard

That's absolutely right. But there is also an important thing that we mustn't forget. True individuality never comes to full flower without hard work. Therefore, you're making a big mistake if you think that who you are right now represents all you are capable of being. Also, it's natural, especially in your teens, not to have a clear idea of who you are.

We are always changing. If you decide passively, "I'm a quiet type now, so I'll just go through life being quiet," then you won't fully realize your unique potential. On the other hand, you can challenge yourself to become someone who, though quiet and reserved by nature, will nevertheless say what needs to be said at the right moment, clearly and completely, someone who has the courage to speak out and stand up for the truth. Through such effort, you'll come to develop your own distinctive way of communicating that is refreshingly different from your more talkative peers. That is what is meant by individuality.

The same can be said about study. To decide from the outset that you're not good at studying, without having made any real effort to do so, is escapism.

Each of us is different, but we are all alike in that we possess tremendous potential. The truth is that you can do almost anything if you set your mind to it. Most important is that you never lose confidence in yourself and thereby limit your potential.

Generally speaking, one person is about as smart as the next. Your grades at school right now are not a measure of your full potential. They don't define you. No matter how tough things get, it's important to remember that if others can do it, so can you, and be determined to challenge the limits of your potential. You have to believe in yourself 100 percent. Constantly comparing yourself to others, swinging between feelings of inferiority and superiority, is a sad way to live.

Only those who are determined to give their all, to try their very best and make effort upon effort, sparkle with true individuality. Such people can also respect and appreciate others' individuality. They never try to sabotage others' success or pick on people because they're different.

*One of our readers writes: "I have many friends who excel at sports or studies and show lots of individuality. But I'm not particularly good at anything and think I'm really boring. Is individuality dependent on talent?*

Talent and individuality are two different things. Our individuality is an indivisible part of us that we nurture and develop throughout our lives. It encompasses our whole self, including our character and our way of life. It is refined as we struggle against the surging waves of difficulty in life and society. When we live true to ourselves, our individuality shines and grows stronger.

People who are good at sports or excel in school tend to get all the attention, while those who work hard but don't achieve spectacular results tend to go unnoticed. But in the course of their persistent efforts, their individuality, their special qualities, come to shine brilliantly.

Faith in the Mystic Law enables us to channel our individuality in the most positive direction. Those who possess the loftiest individuality are people who cast aside self-interest and dedicate themselves wholeheartedly to serving others. They are people who work for the happiness of their fellow human beings, the welfare of society and the propagation of the Mystic Law, indifferent to whether they are recognized for their efforts. The greatness of their character as individuals makes such actions possible.

True individuality is not a superficial, external phenomenon. It is not the mass media image of individuality, which is a shallow, ephemeral creation. Individuality, in the best sense, is synonymous with character, with human integrity. A person of genuine individuality is not self-centered but a well-rounded individual working for the benefit of humanity and the world.

## STANDING OUT FROM THE CROWD

*"Individuality" sometimes suggests eccentricity, someone who stands out from the crowd. Some of our readers said that the word reminds them of trendy people or those in show business. But, as you've just pointed out, that's a superficial definition of individuality.*

True individuality is not so superficial and artificial as merely *trying* to be different. Rather, it shines from the depths of your life as a result of discarding your attachment to shallow pretensions and devoting all your energies to achieving something of value.

As the German writer Johann Wolfgang von Goethe said: "Each one tries to make his own Self observable, and to exhibit it as much as possible to the world. This false tendency is shown everywhere... Everywhere there is the individual who wants to show himself off to advantage, nowhere one honest effort to make oneself subservient to the Whole."[1]

People who let themselves be controlled by appearances, popularity or fashion don't have a strong sense of self. They lack individuality in the truest sense of the word. Being obsessed with such things can make for an empty kind of individuality.

Appearances are deceiving; it's reality that counts. Individuality is not a matter of how you look but what you really are inside.

*Another reader writes: "In Japan, the media defines the image of high school girls as having dyed hair, wearing trendy loose socks and Ralph Lauren sweaters and carrying Hello Kitty mobile phones. They try to stereotype us, and I think that's wrong. I feel like we're being manipulated by the media."*

The influence of the commercial media is very powerful indeed. Fads are often engineered with profit in mind and then launched on the public. In that sense, sporting the latest fashions or must-have items is really the opposite of individuality.

Naturally, people should be free to wear what they wish. It's only normal for people to want to look nice and to be attractive. I'd like to stress, however, that youth has its own radiance: All of you are already beautiful without wearing a lot of makeup and faddish clothes.

During a visit to Japan, Natalia Sats, the founder of the Moscow State Children's Musical Theater, went out to do some shopping in a department store. When she came to the jewelry department, she turned to the Japanese interpreter accompanying her and said in jest: "You are still young. You are beautiful just as you are, without wearing such expensive things. But I am no longer young, and the beauty of youth has gone, so I have to compensate by wearing beautiful things!"

The point is, true individuality has nothing to do with how we dress or look. It is something we emanate from inside.

*Another of our readers has written to us: "I want to be free to express my creativity through music and fashion, and in the future, I'd like to work in one of those areas. But whenever I wear clothes that are a bit loud or unusual, my parents say, 'You're a Soka Gakkai member, so please dress more appropriately.' I appreciate their point of view, but I just cannot agree with them."*

There are various reasons why parents might react this way. Sometimes it could be because they lack understanding or are worried about what other people will think or are genuinely concerned for their child's best interests.

I can well imagine that you might feel your individuality is being suppressed if you are forced to do what others tell you. However, expressing your individuality and simply rebelling for rebellion's sake are two different things all together.

As part of a larger whole—be it a family or social group—it's important for us to have the spirit and wisdom to harmonize and get along with others. The ability to be flexible and to accommodate different views is itself a sign of a solid sense of self. We should neither be lazy, blindly following the crowd, nor self-centered, blindly rebelling against it. Rather, we should seek balance and harmony. Being able to demonstrate such wisdom shows a strong self-identity.

We mustn't allow ourselves to become self-absorbed and insensitive to those around us. No one is an island. We live surrounded by our family, our friends and the rest of the world. We are all connected. The key is to display our individuality within that web of relationships.

True individuality is not self-centered. It is a way of life, a way of being, that leads us and others in a positive direction in the most natural of ways.

## RESPECTING THE INDIVIDUALITY OF OTHERS, WHILE DEVELOPING OUR OWN

*Some people care a great deal about keeping up with the latest fads and fashions, and others don't. The problem is that there is the tendency for people to be singled out for criticism and attack if they are different from the rest. Several of our readers have commented that there is strong peer pressure to conform. If you don't dress like everyone else or hold the same opinions as everyone else, you end up as the target of general disapproval.*

This is a deep-rooted problem in our society. For better or for worse, Japanese people have traditionally placed great value on uniformity. This sets us worlds apart from Western culture. The Japanese viewpoint on individuality and the individual is completely different. This national character of suppressing individuality has greatly hindered Japan's progress.

In such an environment, people's actions are curtailed as if they were prisoners, the purpose being to deprive them of their individuality. It is a truly tragic abuse of human rights. In truth, if we respect and treasure the individuality of others while at the same time working to develop our own individuality, we can realize valuable progress for both ourselves and others.

To judge people by their appearances is an insult to humanity. It is the exact opposite of the spirit of treasuring individuality.

Rosa Parks, one of the pioneers of the American civil rights movement, is an esteemed friend of mine. She is very gentle and kind, but she has amazing inner strength and determination. Mrs. Parks said: "[My mother] taught me not to judge people by the amount of money they had or the kind of house they lived in or the clothes they wore. People should be judged, she told me, by the respect they have for themselves and others."[2]

*A leader of the Soka Gakkai's future division—collectively comprising the elementary, junior high and high school divisions—remarked to me: "Nowadays when students improve their grades, their classmates aren't happy for them. The atmosphere of competition is fierce, especially among students preparing to take university entrance examinations.*

*That's why at our meetings we always try to introduce members by pointing out some area of special interest or ability they possess. For example, we introduce a member who knows a lot about flowers as 'our flower expert' and a member who loves books as 'our book wizard,' and get someone who loves music to talk about the latest hit CD. We try to focus as much as possible on their individuality."*

*One of our members, who recently returned to Japan after having lived in the United Kingdom since he was a small child, said, "If I behave the way I did in the United Kingdom at school here in Japan, I stick out like a sore thumb." He says that Japanese schools give lip service to providing education "that respects the student's individuality," but in reality, conformity rules, and everyone looks the same.*

*I think the tendency to dissolve one's individuality into a group, to seek strength in numbers, to follow the crowd, is a negative feature of Japanese society.*

The purpose of education is not to suppress individuality but to cultivate and develop it. The most fundamental principle of government, of science, of all cultural activity, is respect for people's individuality. That is what we mean by human rights.

The reality of Japan's educational system, however, is that it is bureaucratic and conformist, judging everything about a student based on grades alone and ranking them accordingly. Many students voice their dislike for the system and wish they could escape it. Some decide not to think about it and just try to concentrate on getting through the day without too much discomfort.

This is a serious problem for Japan. Qualities such as creativity and originality are nipped in the bud with tragic frequency, and a nation whose citizens lack those qualities will be left behind by the rest of the world. A lack of creativity and individuality also means a lack of character.

People are not all the same. The enforcement of conformity, an injustice that destroys individuality, ignores basic human rights. In its ultimate form, it is tyranny and fascism.

*Under such circumstances, many people lose their self-confidence, becoming servile, nihilistic or violent.*

All people want to realize their unique potential. When that natural desire is obstructed, people either become totally apathetic or destructive. It also sows the seeds for bullying and fascism.

That is why it is so important for you young people not to be defeated by your environment. You mustn't lose faith in yourself. Each of you has a mission in this lifetime that only you can fulfill. Each of you has a life that only you can live and from which you can create something of value. Whatever else you may doubt, I hope you will never doubt this.

Even should someone look upon you as a lost cause, you must never look upon yourself that way. Should others berate you as having no talent or ability, you mustn't succumb to the negative message of their words. Unperturbed by anyone's negativity, grit your teeth, keep believing in yourself, chant Nam-myoho-renge-kyo and face your challenges with all your might.

## The Courage To Be Our Own Person

*How can we gain confidence in ourselves? Many people say that they have a hard time being themselves, that they don't know how.*

Chanting Nam-myoho-renge-kyo is key. Just as a mother bird warms her egg until it hatches, chanting Nam-myoho-renge-kyo enables the "egg of potential" that is you to develop and emerge. The inside of an egg is nothing but liquid. Looking at it, we can see no trace of a bird. But when the egg is warmed by the mother bird, slowly from this liquid forms a beak, eyes and wings, until a fine bird emerges that eventually can soar high into the sky.

*I think it's true that in our teens we are still like eggs, and most of us have no idea what we will hatch into.*

The same can be said of our individuality. When we're young, we don't fully understand what the term means, and that's perfectly normal. In fact, many young people who make bold statements about their individuality are often just copying others—"borrowing" someone else's image.

Goethe said that young people are like fountains. A fountain does not spout water from a source all its own, like a spring, but spouts water recirculated and fed to it. Similarly, taking in the ideas and fashions around them, youth can fall under the illusion that those borrowed ideas are their own, that these things somehow constitute their individuality.

*We have to take time to develop ourselves, to establish our identity and realize our potential.*

It was Nichiren Daishonin who said that chanting Nam-myoho-renge-kyo is like a mother bird that warms and eventually hatches the egg of potential (see WND-1, 1030).

When we speak of a Buddha, of someone attaining Buddhahood, we mean a person who has developed his or her individuality to the highest level possible, someone who has realized his or her fullest potential and undergone human revolution.

Chanting Nam-myoho-renge-kyo can also be compared to flowers——cherry, plum, peach and damson (see OTT, 200)—turning their faces to the sun or spreading their roots in the life-giving earth.

As for self-confidence—self-confidence comes from hard work and effort. You're deluding yourself if you think you can have self-confidence without it. Only those who strive to challenge a goal and work toward it at their own pace and in their own way; only those who keep trying, no matter how many times they may fail, can develop unshakable confidence in themselves. Self-confidence is synonymous with an invincible will. You cannot be said to have true self-confidence if your opinion of yourself seesaws from high to low every time you compare yourself to others. A life spent judging yourself in terms of others will only end in frustration and deadlock.

*The key, I guess, is learning to be true to ourselves. It takes a lot of courage to be ourselves, doesn't it?*

Youth is a time for self-discovery. The Japanese novelist Natsume Soseki (1867–1916), as a young man, set out on a journey in search of himself. Interested in English literature, he went to study in London. There, he experienced such culture shock that he developed a strong inferiority complex and even experienced a nervous breakdown. After a long period of inner turmoil and self-reflection, he finally arrived at an answer to the question that had plagued him: "What is literature?" He realized that the only solution to his troubles was to come up with a definition of literature through his own efforts. Because he had been focused primarily on the opinions of others, he had come to an impasse. He decided from then on to listen to his own voice and be his own person.

Later, Soseki addressed the following to young people: "'Here is the path I am meant to follow! I have found it at last!' When you can exclaim this from the very depths of your being, your heart will know peace for the first time. And with that cry, a hardy self-confidence will show itself."[3]

You are young. Show independence of mind, take up a challenge, any kind of challenge, and throw yourself into it with all your energy.

*In the journey of self-discovery, I think it is also important to listen to the opinions of others, because it can sometimes be difficult to see ourselves clearly.*

That's true. There are certainly instances when you think you are one way, while the people around you think you are just the opposite. Other people can often see things about you that you cannot. It's just like not being able to see your face without a mirror: The people around you can serve as a mirror to let you see yourself. Your friends or your parents may at times see you more clearly than you do.

The comments of people close to you can help you focus your individuality in a positive direction. The education, guidance, advice, warnings and even rebukes that you receive can all be used constructively to steer you along the right path. On the other hand, refusing to listen to others' advice, doing only what you want, cannot be described as individuality. That's just being stubborn, and it doesn't benefit anyone.

Even famous people are sometimes taken to task by members of their family. I'm sure that at home your fathers are sometimes scolded by your mothers! No matter how influential or important someone may be, they too have to heed warnings, advice and recommendations as they carry out their work.

When people point out your faults, remember that it's just part of the process of forging your individuality. Refusing to listen to advice is foolish.

Rebelling when someone says something to you and making things unpleasant for everyone is to no one's advantage. It's important to be wise. Having people point out your shortcomings and help you weed out your bad habits at the root is, in the long run, a great help to you. If the roots of those bad habits remain, they will gradually affect your life more and more adversely, moving you in a harmful, destructive direction.

*In other words, individuality does not exist apart from society and other people.*

True individuality is realizing oneself fully within the structures of society, while working on behalf of others. We establish our own value as individuals within society, using the practical wisdom we possess.

Therefore, observing society's rules is also an indispensable part of letting our individuality shine. In society, actions that violate the agreed-upon rules make one an outcast, depriving one of the very venues in which to exercise individuality. If, for example, you break your school rules out of sheer willfulness now, it is likely that you will continue such behavior and have problems fitting into society when you graduate from school or as you grow older.

People who are secure, who have a strong self-identity, are always willing to listen to the opinions of others. They have the strength and capacity to do so. By comparison, those who refuse to listen to others tend to be rather weak.

## THE IMPORTANCE OF GOOD ROLE MODELS, GOOD BOOKS AND GOOD FRIENDS

*One reader writes: "When I try to bring forth my individuality, I always end up imitating someone else I look up to, or some ideal. Is that all right?"*

It's impossible to nurture our individuality without learning from others, just as it's difficult to run a race without nourishing our bodies with food.

Learning, it is widely accepted, begins with imitation. Children learn how to live and behave by observing and imitating their parents. The same can be seen in the animal kingdom. All great men and women, all excellent people, all people of action, have developed their outstanding individuality by learning from and emulating others. That's one reason for reading the biographies of exceptional people. You will learn much from them. On the other hand, reading books that carry base and negative messages will only lead you to unhappiness.

Nichiren Daishonin cites the passage from the Nirvana Sutra: "Bodhisattvas, have no fear of mad elephants. What you should fear are evil friends!... Even if you are killed by a mad elephant, you will not fall into the three evil paths. But if you are killed by an evil friend, you are certain to fall into them" (WND-1, 11).

Positive stimuli contribute to the positive development of your individuality. While shaped by such things as education, family environment and your own efforts, your individuality and its development ultimately depend on your awareness. It's important to read good books and have good friends.

Youth is the time when you're still unsure about the best way to proceed—uncertain about which direction is beneficial and which is not. By acquainting yourself with the lives and achievements of courageous and admirable individuals, you will gradually get an idea of the direction you would like to follow. You will begin to understand who you are.

In any event, it is important to remember that your worth as a person is not based on your profession. It is not based on wealth, fame or academic credentials. What counts is how hard you have striven in your chosen path, how much good you have accomplished, how earnestly you have devoted your energies to it. It is your spirit of dedication, your sincerity, that determines your true worth. For that reason, your individuality constitutes the basis for leading a life of dignity and meaning as a human being.

When you spend all your money, it's gone. Material things break, and they cannot enrich you in any real, lasting sense. But the more you cultivate your innate individuality, the richer it becomes; the more you use and give expression to it, the richer it becomes. It never diminishes or disappears. Each of you possesses this wonderful treasure. Life is the struggle to make that precious treasure shine.

Your success or failure in life is not decided just by your time in high school. To win true victory in life requires that you keep polishing the unequaled jewel of your unique potential as you make your way through life, bringing it to shine with supreme brilliance.

1. Johann Peter Eckermann, *Words of Goethe: Being The Conversations of Johann Wolfgang von Goethe* (New York: Classic Publishing Company, 1933), p. 114.

2. Rosa Parks with Gregory J. Reed, *Quiet Strength: The Faith, the Hope, and the Heart of a Woman Who Changed a Nation* (Grand Rapids, Michigan: Zondervan Publishing House, 1994), p. 47.

3. Translation from Japanese. Natsume Soseki, *Watashi no kojinshugi* (My Individualism) (Tokyo: Kodansha, 1997), p. 139.

# 20

## WHAT IS THE POWER OF PRAYER?

Let's continue our discussion. I'll try to answer any and all questions that you have.

*Thank you. Today's theme is how prayers are answered. First of all, can we pray for anything that we want?*

You can pray for anything that you believe may contribute to your happiness or to that of others. For instance, you can chant Nam-myoho-renge-kyo with a prayer to improve yourself or to become a certain kind of person. Yes, you can basically pray for anything that you wish. But I wouldn't advise praying for negative things. Praying for something that will harm your progress toward happiness or that of others will only bring about a negative effect in your life. That's because doing so runs counter to the fundamental rhythm of life. The key to having our prayers answered is to be in this rhythm, the rhythm of the universe.

*Previously we discussed the meaning of reciting the sutra every morning and evening and chanting Nam-myoho-renge-kyo. After reading those installments, many high school division members started to challenge themselves to recite the sutra and chant Nam-myoho-renge-kyo. We asked some of them what changes they have experienced since they began chanting regularly.*

*One student said: "In my second semester, I was having problems with my friends. I chanted to the Gohonzon to change myself for the better, and I gradually could express my feelings more openly and honestly. I could see the good points of those friends I hadn't been getting along with. I'm very happy with the way things turned out through chanting."*

*Another student said: "When I chant, it's as if I'm a completely different person. I feel that I can take on any challenge and do anything I set my mind to. I really like the changes I see in myself."*

*"I was being bullied," said another student, "and I knew that I couldn't take it much longer, so I chanted very strongly to change something in my life. Not long after, I made a new friend with whom I get along well and can talk to about anything."*

*There were other responses, too. Some students expressed doubt that chanting to the Gohonzon could really be effective, or that it was really possible for them to become stronger and more confident. Still others said that, though they prayed with all their might and made sincere efforts, their prayers weren't answered.*

*Are all our prayers really fulfilled when we chant to the Gohonzon?*

Yes, they definitely are. It is said that when one chants to the Gohonzon, "no prayer goes unanswered." Every prayer will be answered without fail. Nichiren Daishonin writes: "Though one might point at the earth and miss it, though one might bind up the sky, though the tides might cease to ebb and flow and the sun rise in the west, it could never come about that the prayers of the practitioner of the Lotus Sutra would go unanswered" (WND-1, 345). Our prayers are answered with an even greater certainty than the sun rising in the east every morning. This accords with the Law of the universe.

The crucial thing is whether we are really practitioners of the Lotus Sutra, of Nam-myoho-renge-kyo—whether we are really putting the teachings of Nichiren Buddhism into practice.

Second Soka Gakkai president Josei Toda used to say: "Obviously, when you strike a bell, you're going to get a vastly different sound depending on whether you use a toothpick, a chopstick or a bell striker. The bell is the same, but if you hit it powerfully, it rings loudly. If you hit it weakly, it rings softly."

"The same is true of the Gohonzon," he said. "The benefit we receive depends entirely on the power of our faith and practice."

*That example is very clear.*

As the expressions *the power of faith* and *the power of practice* indicate, belief has power. The greater your conviction that your prayers will be answered—the stronger your faith—the more powerfully the Gohonzon, the Mystic Law, responds to your prayers.

The power of practice encompasses the strength of your chanting of Nam-myoho-renge-kyo and the energy with which you work for kosen-rufu—for the happiness of all people and the prosperity of society. The stronger the power of your practice for yourself and others, the more you can tap the power of the Buddha and the power of the Law inherent in the Gohonzon and in your life.

Although we say that prayers are answered, in Nichiren Buddhism, the fulfillment of our prayers is nothing supernatural. It's not about some transcendent being like a Buddha or god in a distant realm taking pity on us to grant our wishes.

Just as there are physical laws such as those governing electricity—laws that human beings in their ingenuity have learned to harness and put to practical use—Buddhism delves into and uncovers the Law of life and the universe. Just as the electric light was invented based on the laws of electricity, Nichiren inscribed the Gohonzon based on the supreme Law that Buddhism reveals.

Mr. Toda used to describe the Gohonzon this way: "This certainly doesn't do it full justice, but the Gohonzon can be likened to a happiness-manufacturing machine." The Gohonzon is the ultimate crystallization of human wisdom and the Buddha wisdom. That's why the power of the Buddha and the Law emerge in exact accord with the power of your faith and practice. If the power of your faith and practice equal a force of one hundred, then they will bring forth the power of the Buddha and the Law to the degree of one hundred. And if it is a force of ten thousand, then it will elicit that degree of corresponding power.

*So, just as we can enjoy the illumination of an electric light without fully understanding the laws of electricity, by turning on the switch of chanting Nam-myoho-renge-kyo, we tap the power of the Mystic Law and fulfill our prayers—without having to master the vast body of Buddhist doctrine, often described as a treasury of eighty thousand teachings.*

Of course, it is beneficial to study the Buddhist teachings. The more we study, the more it reinforces our understanding and deepens our appreciation of the excellence and profundity of Buddhism—which in turn serves to strengthen our faith and conviction. The fundamental purpose of Buddhist study is to fortify our powers of faith and practice.

## THE SOURCE OF ALL CHANGE

*We tend to think of prayer as something special, beyond the realm of ordinary concerns. But in fact, it is a normal, everyday thing, isn't it? It's the fruit of human wisdom, actually.*

As far as we know, only human beings pray. And we have done so from ancient times. People have prayed to the sun, to fire, to the mountains. Our species has long pressed its hands together in prayer to Nature, asking it for safety and happiness. Prayer is an expression of our reverence for the universe, our awe toward forces greater than ourselves. Prayer transcends the logical, the rational and the scientific. It comes from an intuitive recognition of the link, the relation, the correspondence between the individual and the universe. Pressing one's hands together in prayer is one of the noblest of human acts.

Prayer is instinctual to human beings. When we're in trouble, for instance, we instinctively wish to be helped or protected.

*Yes, I'm sure that we've all experienced that when we've been in a difficult situation. It's not something we can explain logically; it's just part of being human.*

I think that this instinct naturally evolved to take the form of prayer. People the world over have no doubt experienced this, in every culture since time immemorial. They felt this way though they possessed no theories or detailed, logical explanations to support those feelings.

They may not even have been fully convinced that their prayers would always be answered. Nevertheless, it is believed that religion gradually emerged from such prayer.

*So prayer didn't come from religion—religion developed from prayer!*

All people, even those who say that they have no religion, hold deeply cherished wishes and aspirations. We all pray for something in the depths of our hearts. Prayer in Nichiren Buddhism is a means, based on the Law of the universe, for closing the gap between those wishes and reality.

*There are so many religions and so many different objects of devotion.*

In Japanese, an object of religious worship or devotion is called *honzon*, literally meaning an object of fundamental respect. There are all kinds of objects of devotion. In some religions, even animals such as horses or snakes serve that function. However, Nichiren says, "All of these schools are misled concerning the true object of devotion" (WND-1, 258).

*Could you explain the significance of the object of fundamental respect in Nichiren Buddhism?*

The *hon* of *honzon* connotes the basis of life and the universe. And *zon* connotes veneration and reverence for that basis.

If you embrace something that is not the genuine basis of the universe as an object of fundamental respect, your life will become imbalanced; it will go off track. For instance, there are people who regard money, the media, technology or high academic status as their objects of supreme respect.

In Nichiren Buddhism, the fundamental Law of the universe is venerated as the object of fundamental respect. This Law is also the essence of our lives.

This might be a little difficult to understand, but when we pray to the object of fundamental respect, the Gohonzon, the Buddhist principle of the fusion of reality and wisdom is at work. The objective reality of the Gohonzon and the wisdom of our minds are fused at the deepest level. Prayer, in other words, constitutes a fusion of the ultimate Law of the universe and our minds.

You can think of this as the gears of a machine meshing. When a small gear locks its cogs with those of a large gear, it can display a tremendous force. In the same way, when we synchronize the microcosm of our lives with the macrocosm of universal life, we can tap unlimited power and overcome any problem. All Buddhist gods, Buddhas and bodhisattvas throughout the ten directions—that is, all the protective forces of the universe—will be activated so that we can realize our prayers.

*So prayer is what allows those gears to mesh?*

That's right. Nam-myoho-renge-kyo is the sound of the great rhythm of the universe, the power source of all cosmic activity. It is also the heart and essence of the universe itself.

The Mystic Law is the source of all change. That's why, when we chant the Mystic Law, Nam-myoho-renge-kyo, we activate the universal forces to support us. The rhythm of Nam-myoho-renge-kyo has been called the rhythm by which the universe moves. The power of chanting Nam-myoho-renge-kyo to activate the universe's protective functions appeared in a movie [*Innerspace*] a while ago, I believe.

*Yes, it was* Innerspace, *a story about traveling inside the microcosm of the human body. At one point, the protagonist chants Nam-myoho-renge-kyo to break through a crisis.*

*One student writes that she doesn't know how to pray and asks about the proper way of chanting.*

Basically, just be yourself when you chant. That's the most important thing. Revere the Gohonzon as the fundamental basis of your life, reach out to it in your heart and take your problems to it—do this naturally, as a child reaches for its mother. When you're suffering or when you're sad, there's no need to put on a good face or pretend that everything's all right. Just chant exactly as you are, directly giving expression to the feelings in your heart.

Nichiren writes, "What is called faith is nothing unusual" (WND-1, 1036). And he urges, "Faith means putting one's trust in the Lotus Sutra...as parents refuse to abandon their children, or as a child refuses to leave its mother" (WND-1, 1036). In other words, all we need to do is trust the Gohonzon wholeheartedly, praying sincerely that our desires will be realized. Such prayer definitely will empower us.

There is nothing extraordinary about prayer—it is simply wishing for something with all our heart.

And our heart is what matters most. It is important to chant with deep faith, reverence and love for the Gohonzon in our heart.

## QUANTITY OR QUALITY?

*One student asks whether he has to chant for a certain number of hours before his prayer will be answered. Or can he chant intensely for a short time? In other words, which is more important, quantity or quality?*

The value—or, if you like, the quality—of a hundred dollar bill is more than a ten dollar bill. Naturally, most people would prefer a one hundred dollar bill, right? Similarly, in faith, sincere, strong prayers are important. Of course, having lots of one hundred dollar bills is even better! Likewise, in chanting Nam-myoho-renge-kyo to the Gohonzon, both quantity and quality count.

Everything you do in the realm of Buddhist faith and practice is for your own happiness. The main thing is that you feel deep satisfaction after chanting. There are no hard-and-fast rules about having to chant a certain number of hours. Setting chanting targets can be helpful, but when you're tired or sleepy and are just mumbling along in a half-conscious daze, it's better to stop and go to bed. After you've rested, you can chant with concentration and energy again. This is much more valuable. We should be alert and earnest when we pray, not nodding off.

As I said, most important is that our chanting be satisfying and refreshing, so that we can exclaim when we've finished, "Ah, that felt good!" By reinforcing that feeling day after day, our lives naturally move in the most positive direction.

*I have heard countless experiences from members of the power of chanting.*

Yes, and the SGI is strong precisely because its members have such personal experiences.

*One member writes wondering whether skipping the morning and evening sutra recitation and chanting of Nam-myoho-renge-kyo for one day will invalidate all his practice up to that time.*

Skipping the daily sutra recitation occasionally is certainly not going to erase all your previous efforts. There's no need to worry about that. If you're running late for school and don't have time, there's no need to be anxious about missing the morning sutra recitation. In such cases, for example, if your mothers are practicing and are chanting for you, their prayers will reach you and protect you. More important, as long as you have sincere faith in the Gohonzon, the fortune you have accumulated will stay with you.

You need not feel guilty if you miss the sutra recitation. Of course, I'm not saying that it's all right to neglect your Buddhist practice. If you fall into the mind-set that you don't have to do it, your heart will gradually grow estranged from prayer. Nevertheless, because faith exists in daily life, there's no need to take things to extremes, such as making yourself late for school because of the morning sutra recitation.

*Our attitude toward faith and the Gohonzon is most important, isn't it?*

Even if you are busy and don't always have time for your daily sutra recitation, it's important that you don't give up doing it altogether. If you do, the flame of your faith will go out. Please don't cast aside the morning and evening sutra recitation.

Prayer enriches the spirit and heightens our sense of conviction, so it is a definite plus for all of us.

*When we are pressed for time, which should we give priority to, reciting the sutra morning and evening or chanting Nam-myoho-renge-kyo?*

Those who don't have time or find it difficult to recite the sutra morning and evening should just chant Nam-myoho-renge-kyo. To use the allegory of a meal, Nam-myoho-renge-kyo can be likened to the main course and the morning and evening sutra recitation to the side dishes. Of course, having both is best. But chanting Nam-myoho-renge-kyo comes first. Please chant—even if you chant Nam-myoho-renge-kyo only once. Nichiren Daishonin states that chanting Nam-myoho-renge-kyo just once contains infinite benefit.

And if you can recite the sutra, along with chanting Nam-myoho-renge-kyo, then you will feel even greater satisfaction.

Of course, it goes without saying that reciting the sutra and chanting Nam-myoho-renge-kyo morning and evening is ideal.

*Some students wonder if they shouldn't devote any extra time they might have to studying instead of chanting.*

Those who are busy studying and feel that they don't have time to recite the morning and evening sutra should give priority to their studies and then chant when they have some spare time. You're in charge of how you chant Nam-myoho-renge-kyo. So you're free to make your own decisions about how and when you make time to chant.

Studying is one of the duties of a high school student. A student who studies hard and is active in extracurricular school activities may not have much spare time. That's why making time to chant despite a busy schedule is truly praiseworthy. When you chant, you create the cause for your success. Chanting Nam-myoho-renge-kyo is for your benefit. It strengthens your life force and sharpens your mind. It enables you to tap the vital inner strength to give full play to your talents and abilities. If you have a level of capacity or ability as you approach an exam that measures, say, ten, chanting will give you the life force to actually give full play to that measure of ability, rather than the seven or eight that might usually be your best effort under such circumstances.

*I guess it's hoping for too much to perform at a level of ten if your actual ability is only at five.*

Yes, it's misguided to think that simply chanting without making any serious attempt to study will improve your grades. The realization of your prayers begins with making concrete efforts toward their fulfillment. If you really believe that things will turn out the way that you have prayed—as long as you just continue all your efforts—then your mind is filled with the hope, optimism and confidence that all prayers will definitely be answered. At the same time, by chanting Nam-myoho-renge-kyo, you will see, as clearly as the morning sun illuminates the earth, what you must do to succeed in your studies and your life. Chanting Nam-myoho-renge-kyo will give you the energy to keep trying to achieve your goals.

Faith and prayer are the engines that fuel our efforts—we have to make our own efforts. Please never forget that.

*That's clear. Just chanting with an unopened book at our side isn't going to make us any smarter, no matter how earnest our prayers!*

## APPRECIATION GIVES RISE TO GOOD FORTUNE

You cannot expect to get paid a salary unless you work. Similarly, our prayers are answered only to the extent that we exert ourselves to realize the Buddha's wish for the happiness of all humanity. The Gohonzon has no obligation to answer our prayers. It hasn't asked us to chant to it. We request the privilege of praying to the Gohonzon. If we have such a sense of gratitude and appreciation, our prayers will be answered more quickly.

*A member asks a related question: "Why are some prayers unfulfilled? Do those unrealized prayers also contribute to our personal growth?"*

There are times when our prayers seem to take ages to be fulfilled, or when they remain unrealized despite the most impassioned chanting of Nam-myoho-renge-kyo. But the important thing to remember is to keep chanting until they *are* answered. Our continued chanting gives us the chance to take a good hard look at ourselves, leading to positive changes in our daily lives. It's like work—you get a job and go to work, but you don't get paid the first day. Or it's like gardening—you plant a sapling and water it every day, but it still takes a long time for it to grow into a tall tree.

*There's an old Japanese saying about time and patience: "Peaches and chestnuts take three years to bear fruit, and persimmons take eight."*

With regular watering each day, a sapling steadily grows into a solid, sturdy tree. By applying yourself diligently every day, you can progress steadily in your studies. All good things result from continual, repeated efforts.

*Buddhism is the law of life, so all its teachings accord with reason and universal principles, don't they?*

Yes. Just because we've prayed for something doesn't mean that we'll automatically get it. But even if your prayers are not immediately answered, if you keep chanting every day, then at some point in time, you'll be able to make a great adjustment in the course your life is on. Without exception, you will look back and say to yourself that things worked out for the best, that your prayer was ultimately answered.

*That's why it is so important to keep chanting every day, isn't it?*

Many factors are at work when it comes to our prayers being realized. But by chanting sincerely with those prayers at heart, we can correct our life's orbit and move in a more positive direction.

Our prayers have a far-reaching impact on our lives. Though you may chant to do well in your studies, the effect of your prayers will extend much further, rippling across the whole spectrum of your life.

When all is said and done, to want to sit in front of the Gohonzon and chant is very important. It is an expression of one's determination to improve oneself. That spirit is important. That spirit is proof of our humanity, an expression of our noble spirit to accomplish something with our lives.

*What is the right speed for reciting the morning and evening sutra and chanting Nam-myoho-renge-kyo?*

Our chanting should not be too fast or too slow. It should also not be too loud or too soft. And it should have a good, vigorous rhythm. The speed of the daily sutra recitation also depends on such things as a person's age or gender, or the time and place. Don't worry too much about the speed. Just recite the morning and evening sutra in the way that seems most natural and comfortable to you. One of my seniors once said that we should recite the sutra morning and evening with the rhythm of a galloping horse.

## CONCRETE PRAYERS ARE IMPORTANT

*One member says: "When I was little, I was told that we should look at the character* myo *on the Gohonzon when we chant. Why is that?"*

Looking at the Gohonzon is like gazing at the universe—like having a vast, commanding view of the entire cosmos. The Gohonzon is a representation of the driving force and essence of the universe. Therefore, whatever part we look at, we're looking at the entire universe. It doesn't really matter where we fix our gaze. Still, it is easier to chant if we focus on the center. I have also been told in the past by my seniors that *myo* represents the human head, and that I should look at it when I chant.

[In *The Record of the Orally Transmitted Teachings,* Nichiren states with regard to the five characters of Myoho-renge-kyo, "Our head corresponds to *myo,* our throat to *ho,* our chest to *ren,* our stomach to *ge,* and our legs to *kyo*" (OTT, 28).]

Just look at the part of the Gohonzon that you feel most comfortable focusing on. Nichiren merely states that we should sit up straight, quoting the sutra where it says, "sit upright and ponder the true aspect" (LSOC, 390); he doesn't tell us where we should fix our gaze when we chant. In his great compassion, Nichiren gave us the freedom to chant in the way best suited to us. With his immense understanding and insight, he took into account each individual's autonomy, personality and circumstances, encouraging each to approach faith with flexibility and freedom. It was the self-serving priests of later generations who, intent on shoring up their authority, forced rituals and practices not described in Nichiren's writings or the sutra on believers.

*What about people who say that they don't want to pray to a piece of printed paper, arguing that it couldn't possibly have the power to solve their problems?*

Our Gohonzon may be printed on paper, but it most certainly possesses inherent power. A ten-dollar bill is printed paper, as are graduation certificates and the letters of appointment for cabinet ministers. All important documents are printed, and they all have their respective powers.

The paper is physical matter, but the words written on it are Nichiren's spirit and essence. The original Buddha of the Latter Day of the Law, Nichiren Daishonin, inscribed his life in ink on the Gohonzon. [He wrote, "I, Nichiren, have inscribed my life in sumi ink, so believe in the Gohonzon with your whole heart" (WND-1, 412)].

The Buddhist principle of the "oneness of body and mind" teaches that the physical and spiritual are one. Life exists in their unity; the Gohonzon embodies the life of the Buddha. When we chant to the Gohonzon, we are not chanting to a piece of paper.

*Words have amazing power. Each letter of a signature, for instance, includes within it the character and fortune of the signer.*

Textbooks are also printed paper, but by reading the words on that paper, we acquire knowledge, make new discoveries and encounter new ideas.

Or let's take another example: Suppose that you come across a sign with the two words *Tokyo Station*. Those two words include all the many different functions of the station, including that it is the starting point of the bullet train and the gateway to the city of Tokyo. Of course, Tokyo Station would exist without the sign, without the words, and its many functions would also still exist. But the sign and the words help people get to Tokyo Station easily so they can take advantage of those many functions.

*The characters on the Gohonzon are a means by which we can communicate with the universe, aren't they?*

Another example: A cellular phone is of no use without base stations that transmit the radio waves from one point to another. In the same way, the Gohonzon is a base station from which we can communicate with the universe.

As I mentioned earlier, it is important that our prayers be specific and concrete. Being vague and unfocused when you chant is like shooting an arrow without looking at the target. When you chant, it should be with a strong, passionate resolve to make your prayer a reality. To have the attitude "If I chant, everything will be all right" is just wishful thinking. Earnest prayer—prayer infused with one's whole heart and being—cannot fail to reach the Gohonzon.

Another thing to remember is that, as the focus of your prayers expands to include not just your wishes but the happiness of your friends, your family, your classmates, your society and humanity as a whole, you will expand your horizons and your breadth as a human being.

When I became Soka Gakkai president at thirty-two, my first two prayers were for Japan to have a good harvest, so that there would be no hunger, and for there to be no major earthquakes. On another occasion, I prayed that I alone would bear the brunt of any major persecution we suffered for kosen-rufu. My prayers were answered when I was arrested by the authorities on trumped-up charges in the 1957 Osaka Incident.

*Your prayers are of such a noble dimension!*

There's no need for anyone to imitate me. Prayer is not such a simple thing as that. That said, it's important to remember that your prayers always reflect your state of life. In that respect, prayer is a solemn means to raise your life-condition.

And to get exactly the results that you're praying for, it is crucial to make determined, single-minded efforts toward that goal. That is the true way to apply faith in daily life.

Those of you who proceed along this path day after day, year after year, will without fail grow—like saplings into mighty trees—to become people of outstanding strength and character.

# PART SIX

## YOUTH

### *and the Future*

# 21

## WHAT IS A GOOD FRIEND?

*One of the biggest areas of difficulty for high school students is their relation-ships—especially with their friends.*

*Yes, many of our readers have asked if you could discuss friendship once again. [Please see chapter 3, "Friendship and Perspectives on Life," pp. 37–55.]*

*Of all the different relationships we have—with our teachers, our parents, our seniors and juniors, our supervisors at part-time jobs and so on—those with our friends are an especially big part of our lives.*

That's true. In Japanese, we write the word for human being, *ningen*, with two Chinese characters, the first meaning person (*nin*) and the second, between (*gen*). This expresses the idea that human beings only exist fully amid their relationships *between* one another. None of us can live alone. So relationships, and relationship problems of one sort or other, are an inevitable part of life.

Sometimes relationships with others get so bothersome that you may want to shout, "I wish I could live somewhere where there are no people!" But that's impossible, unless you become a hermit.

So, where does that leave us? Basically, you have to work at cultivating good relationships with others. You have to become a person who can develop such relationships. That's all there is to it.

Relationship problems are opportunities for you to grow and mature. Such problems can be character building, if you don't let them defeat you. That's why it's important not to isolate yourself. No one can exist apart from others. Remaining aloof from others only cultivates selfishness, and that accomplishes nothing.

*A high school student said: "I think human relationships have grown rather shallow. It's rare these days for people to sit down and really share their thoughts and feelings with another person. It seems like they don't really want to form deep bonds."*

It's up to each individual how to live life. That, however, doesn't change the fact that having close friends can be tremendously rewarding. There's a Mongolian proverb "A hundred friends are more precious than a hundred pieces of gold." People who have friends are rich. Quite often, the encouragement and influence of friends spur us toward self-improvement. We are inspired to lead fulfilling lives and to create a better world—to work together with our friends toward that goal.

Having good friends is like being equipped with a powerful auxiliary engine. When we encounter a steep hill or an obstacle, we can encourage one another and find the strength to keep pressing vigorously forward.

*Good friends are a real treasure. But there are also bad friends, who can exert a negative influence. Several students wrote about this kind of person, saying things like: "One of my friends has a side I really dislike. He is always bullying others and getting them to buy things for him."*

*"There is a student who is constantly borrowing money but never returns it. He orders his friends to tag along with him, and he won't take no for an answer. He couldn't care less about what others want. I don't think he's a real friend at all."*

Buddhism teaches that we should associate with good companions (see LSOC, 114), meaning that we should be careful to choose good people as our friends and role models. It also instructs that we should distance ourselves from bad company. Nichiren, referring to a Buddhist scripture, states that even a good person who associates with evil people will, in two or three cases out of ten, be tainted by that evil (see WND-1, 310). We should therefore have the attitude, he says, to rebuke wrong, to rebuke destructive behavior.

By pointing out to someone that their actions are inflicting suffering and hurt on others, we can urge them to move in a more positive direction. Our honesty, in fact, can open the way to forging deep bonds of genuine friendship with that person. In other words, it's quite possible for a "bad" friend to become a good friend.

There are also cases in which friendship starts out as a casual thing, perhaps with two people just sitting around talking. Then one day, something happens that inspires them both to try to achieve some goal. They then become good friends, who have a positive influence on each other.

*We asked the high school students what they thought made friends good or bad. Most of them described a good friend as someone they can talk with about anything, someone who understands them, someone who is there for them, whom they can consult when facing a serious problem. Bad friends, on the other hand, were described as selfish; as those who gossip maliciously about people behind their backs, tell lies, let people down, broadcast others' confidences and secrets, break promises or cruelly ignore people out of spite. All the latter traits have one thing in common: an utter disregard for others' feelings.*

## BE PEOPLE OF INTEGRITY

Character and integrity are very important. A spirit of mutual respect and trust is a vital basis for real friendship. That said, there naturally might be times when you have arguments and disagreements with your friends. But there should always be an underlying spirit of respect and consideration for one another, no matter how close you are. In friendship, you mustn't think only of yourself.

Bad friends cause people trouble and grief through delinquent behavior. Good friends, by contrast, warmly encourage others, give them hope and inspire them toward self-improvement.

*We are very fortunate if we have such good friends.*

Yes, and to have friends like that, the first thing you must do is become such a person yourself. For example, when you notice someone is worried about something, offer a kind word. You could say, for instance: "You don't look so happy. Is something wrong?" When you make a promise, always keep it, no matter what. If you try to be that kind of person, you'll soon come to find yourself surrounded by good friends.

*One student writes: "I have a hard time making friends. There was a time in the past when everyone used to gang up on me and bully me. I was really hurt by that treatment, and now I'm afraid of people."*

There's no need to worry or be overly anxious if you cannot immediately form the ideal friendships you wish for. Life is long, and you'll have many opportunities to make friends. Just be patient, and don't give up. When you are young, you go through many changes, and so do your peers. The most important thing is to forge a strong self. Find your dream—the one that's right for you—and work to make it come true.

Sometimes friendship just happens. Sometimes you have to seek it out. Sometimes it develops from sharing similar likes and dislikes. However it starts, friendship is friendship.

*Yes, our interests, our likes and dislikes, play a big role in friendship, don't they?*

To have likes and dislikes is a natural human trait. In some cases, they may prevent us from being friends with someone, or may even destroy a friendship. But what's important is to cultivate the kind of character that makes you a good friend to others. Such a person may lose a friendship, but eventually an even better friendship will blossom.

*I've seen that no matter how they may appear on the surface, most of the high school division members are essentially pure-hearted. And that's what makes them particularly sensitive to lies and deceit. If they find that a friend has deceived them—even just a little—they feel that they can no longer be friends with that person, because their trust has been destroyed.*

*Another student writes: "I can't help it, but I just don't like myself.*

*Everyone else seems better off than I am, and I feel jealous."*

Yes, you may feel that way sometimes. But you are all still young. Each of you is a work in progress, still developing. And that's perfectly normal. To still be growing, to still be improving, is a wonderful thing. Just continue to press on tenaciously to find your way forward—despite the suffering and pain that is part of youth and growing up. Indeed, that's the only way to grow.

No matter what happens, please don't arrogantly jump to the conclusion that "People are all the same!" It's not as simple as that. All people have their less than attractive sides, but they also have sides that are beautiful and noble. It all comes down to what you do, not what anyone else does. If someone should betray your trust, vow that you'll never do the same thing to anyone else. Be determined to keep your promises to others. Take an interest in others' problems as your own, and work to help them overcome them. This kind of strong resolve is important.

Mr. Toda always urged the youth to be people of integrity.

*I read about your meeting with Russian physicist Dr. Anatoli Logunov and his fourteen-year-old granddaughter Anna [April 2, 1998]. Anna asked you why it was that some people make great progress, while others don't. She wanted to know what it was that set them apart. You replied that environment was a crucial factor: Even if different people made the same amount of effort, what they achieved tended to vary depending on their environment. One environmental factor, you stressed, was having good friends who keep you moving in a positive direction.*

There are all kinds of environmental factors that foster growth and self-improvement. Compared to love relationships or parent–child relationships, relationships with friends have a more universal, broad-ranging influence. The relationship between mentor and disciple, of course, exists on a much more solemn, profound dimension. Our friendships, nevertheless, are a close, everyday part of us.

Having good friends is a great blessing. A relationship based on selfish motives or that is spoiled by unpleasantness over money cannot be considered a good friendship. Similarly, relationships with people who don't know right from wrong, who engage in delinquent, inhumane or anti-social behavior—relationships that most everyone will disapprove of—are clearly bad. A real friend will not demand money from you or encourage you to do things that are wrong or dangerous to your or others' well-being. That is just evil disguised as friendship. You must speak out against it and avoid getting involved in it.

Don't prolong an association with bad friends. I even think it's fine to sometimes run away from such company. Discuss your situation with someone you trust. Don't just fret silently over it by yourself.

## A LIFE WITHOUT FRIENDSHIP IS LIKE A WORLD WITHOUT SUNSHINE

*One student writes: "I like to be by myself. I really don't enjoy doing everything in a group. Is that all right?"*

Yes, of course. You're free to enjoy your own company, if you wish. Just being together with people does not constitute friendship. It's perfectly all right to make friends in your own way, with people you can share your thoughts and feelings with.

Please remember that friendship remains one of the most important foundations of life. There are many famous sayings about friendship from all around the world. The great Roman orator Cicero said: "Friendship is closer than kinship" and "A life without friendship is like a world without sunshine." Aristotle said, "A friend is another self."[1]

Character and integrity are indispensable for making friends. True friendship cares nothing for social status. You can only make real friends when you open and share your heart with others. A selfish, egotistical person cannot make true friends.

As you grow older, it becomes harder to develop friendships untainted by self-interest. That's why it's very important to make good friends while you're young. Your friends from elementary school, junior high school and high school are like fellow actors on the stage of life. You will never forget them.

The relationship between parent and child is lifelong, as the relationship between husband and wife is also meant to be. I think that friendship, too, should be a lifelong bond.

That said, perhaps we can distinguish among friendships, dividing them into three groups according to their depth.

*What would those be?*

Have you ever heard of the three levels of devotion to one's parents, or filial piety, in traditional Eastern philosophy?

*Yes, I think I have.*

The first level of devotion to your parents is obedience, doing whatever they tell you to. Now, this might please your parents, but it is completely passive on your part. The second level of devotion to your parents is to make a positive effort to serve them. This might include giving them a gift or doing something that delights them. The third level is to introduce them to what you know is right and beneficial for them—even if they oppose it.

*From our perspective, I guess, the third level would mean teaching parents who aren't Soka Gakkai members about Nichiren Buddhism. Even if they oppose it, it's the means by which they can achieve indestructible happiness, not only in this life but throughout eternity.*

*What are the three levels of friendship, then?*

I think we could call them the three levels of human relationships. In the first level of friendship, we see people forging bonds of mutual affection and empathy in the course of ordinary day-to-day activities. They seek to enjoy their lives together. It's friendship based on mutual enjoyment, on having a good time together.

The second level of friendship is a little more advanced. The friends have their own goals; they each have a clear vision of the kind of person they want to become, the kind of future they want to build, the kind of contribution they wish to make to humanity. So they encourage and support one another as they work to realize their dreams and make something of themselves in the world. This is a friendship of mutual encouragement.

*I see, friends don't just hang out together and have fun, but they encourage and support one another in achieving concrete goals. Many of our high school division members write about that kind of friendship: "We worked together and built an incredible display for our school festival." "Before every exam, we've been setting ourselves study goals and encouraging one another in our studies." "As members of the school's swimming team, we all challenged ourselves to swim six miles, and all of us did it! It was exhausting, but I know it's something I'm going to remember with great pride." "All of us became really close through working together on preparations for the high school division general meeting. I'm so glad the meeting was a success."*

*Another student writes: "They say studying for entrance exams is a lonely struggle. My feeling is that it's a battle where you have to win against yourself. Studying for the exams, I've come to realize how important friends are in staving off feelings of isolation and loneliness."*

*Another writes, "My friend and I are striving toward our dreams for the future, and we're both determined to give them our best shot."*

*Many, many students have recognized that they are not alone—that knowledge has given them the strength to overcome tough challenges. That's why I'm sure most of our readers can deeply appreciate this kind of friend-to-friend encouragement and support.*

*What is the third and highest level of friendship?*

The third level of friendship is the bond of comrades who share the same ideals, a friendship in which both would willingly give their lives for the other. This is the kind of friendship that exists in the realm of faith.

Many people who have achieved great things in history have had this kind of friendship.

*This reminds me of the Japanese expression meaning a sworn friend.*

You could call it that, but more specifically it refers to the friendship of comrades, that is, the friendship of people of like mind, people who dedicate their lives to realizing a common cause. This kind of friendship demands absolute trust. Such genuine comrades never betray one another, not even under the threat of death. They never betray themselves, their friends or their ideals.

There are many examples of this kind of friendship, but one wonderful depiction of it is the friendship of Rossi and Bruno in *The Eternal City* by Hall Caine. The story is set in Rome at the turn of this century. Italy is threatened by foreign powers, and its government is corrupt. The people are suffering greatly. The hero of the novel is a young revolutionary, David Rossi. His dear friend is Bruno Rocco.

They feel the pains of the people as their own, and they rise up, speak out and fight against oppression. The government strikes back, and Rossi is forced to flee into exile. But Bruno is arrested and imprisoned. He is tortured but refuses to succumb.

Then, the authorities try to deceive Bruno. They show him a letter allegedly written by Rossi, the contents of which suggest Rossi's betrayal of Bruno. It is, of course, a forgery. The prosecutor insinuates, "Your comrade, your master, the man you have followed and trusted, is false to you. He is a traitor to his friend, his country, and is false to you." But Bruno refuses to believe these demonic whisperings. Drowning out the lies of his captors, he shouts with all his might, "Long live David Rossi!" He dies calling out his friend's name, continuing to believe in his friend's integrity.[2]

Rossi, his comrade's spirit alive in his heart, eventually opens the way to the realization of their cherished ideal: an eternal city, where all people live together in happiness and peace.

Mr. Toda gave me a copy of *The Eternal City* when I was young. It is a book I will always remember. "Read this and then pass it on to a dozen or so of your good friends," Mr. Toda said. "When you've all finished reading it, let's get together and discuss it." He taught us a noble kind of friendship that would withstand the fiercest storm. He taught us to never betray our comrades, no matter what attacks and hardships we faced. He taught us to move forward with iron unity until the victorious day kosen-rufu is achieved and the happiness of all humanity assured.

# THE HEART MATTERS MOST

*That's friendship on a grand scale. It's humanity at its best, hearts burning with selfless commitment.*

Yes, our heart is what matters most. The human heart can be very weak, fickle and ignoble. But it can also be stronger than anything, unflinching, supremely noble.

The great writer Victor Hugo was forced into exile during his struggle with the dictator Napoleon III. He was exiled for nineteen years. But he was determined that, no matter what persecution he endured, he would stick to his ideals with a vibrant, resolute spirit. Likening Napoleon III to Sulla, an ancient Roman tyrant, Hugo writes in the poem "Ultima Verba" (My Last Word):

> *Even if only one thousand are left, I will hold my ground!*
> *If only one hundred survive, I will still cross swords with Sulla.[3]*
> *When only ten remain, let me be the tenth.*
> *When only one is left, that one will be me![4]*

People not afraid to stand alone for their beliefs gain the support of true, steadfast friends.

*Today, many people lack ideals and beliefs. Because of this, sincere, hardworking people get called show-offs, and those earnestly trying to achieve something of value are denounced as impostors.*

"We are all born under sentence of death,"[5] it has been said. All of us will die someday. None of us can avoid that fate. The question, then, becomes how we spend the limited time we have. That is what counts. Some people waste their lives worrying and fretting about trivial, inconsequential things. Some even take their own lives. Nothing could be sadder or more foolish. Suicide is terribly wrong.

If we are going to give our lives to something, surely it should be to a noble cause, the cause of eternal truth and justice.

If we keep up our efforts even when the going is tough, we will earn respect. Most important is to persevere on the path you have chosen, irrespective of how difficult things may become or how others around you may change. Those who can do this will emerge as champions and victors in life. They will win in the end. Such people also are true friends.

I have friends like that. I have them all around the world. Your mothers and fathers are among them. My very reason for living is for the sake of all those unforgettable comrades. The SGI is strong because of such bonds of genuine friendship. I want all of you to inherit this noble spirit of comrades working for a common cause.

*We talk lightly about friendship, but really, it's a profound thing.*

Friendship forms an important foundation for our humanity. It gives sustenance and impetus to the struggle for world peace and the betterment of society. By expanding our circle of friendship, we create the basis for a peaceful society.

*It would be wonderful if all people were friends.*

All people are equal. Human beings therefore seek to forge friendships and build an ideal world—an "eternal city," where all coexist in peace and harmony.

When expounding his teachings, Shakyamuni Buddha always addressed all living beings. I think the term *all living beings* incorporates this universal spirit of friendship—the spirit to treat every person and every living thing as equally precious and worthy of respect, the spirit to bring happiness to all.

While all people becoming friends is the ideal, we know that this, unfortunately, is not the case in the world today. That's why it's so important to forge friendships with as many people as we can. We must face the challenges of reality and make what changes we can, small as they may be. The accumulation of such efforts will gradually lead to lasting world peace.

*You, President Ikeda, have built bridges of the heart all around the world through promoting cultural and educational exchange as well as grassroots exchange among ordinary citizens. I feel that our own efforts are paltry in comparison.*

Even the most ambitious undertakings actually come down to one-on-one, person-to-person relationships accumulating over the years. I have friends all around the world because I have always valued each encounter and sincerely treasured each person. It's always one-on-one, always. Don't fall under the illusion that people who talk big and make flashy gestures are truly great.

A drop of rain from the sky, a drop of water from a river and a drop of water from the ocean are all just that: drops of water. The friends we make in our own small circle contribute to the spread of friendship around the world. Our individual circle of friendship is part of the global circle of friendship; these are one and the same. Making one true friend is a step toward creating world peace.

1. Aristotle, *The Nicomachean Ethics of Artistotle* (London: George Bell & Sons, 1895), p. 255.

2. Hall Caine, *The Eternal City* (New York: D. Appleton and Company, 1902), p. 293.

3. Sulla (138–78 BCE) was an ancient Roman tyrant to whom Hugo likens Napoleon III.

4. Translated from French. Victor Hugo, "Ultima Verba," *Les Châtiments* (Paris: Nelson Éditeurs, 1957), p. 362.

5. *Great Thoughts*, compiled by George Seldes (New York: Ballantine Books, 1995), p. 194.

# 22

---

## It Takes Courage

*We're all looking forward to hearing your thoughts on courage.*

Courage is very important. Whether we have courage has a crucial bearing on the direction our lives will take. People who have courage are happy.

*I think that everyone wants to have courage. The high school division members offer many examples of situations in which they wish they could bravely take the initiative. For instance, when they know that a friend is making a terrible mistake but don't say anything because they're afraid it will destroy their relationship. Or being too fainthearted to lend a helping hand when they see a disabled person in distress on the street. Or even something so simple as being afraid to ask questions in class or after school.*

*One student noticed that a classmate wasn't at school anymore. He wanted to phone him to find out if he was all right, but since they hung out in different groups, he just decided to let it go. When he later learned that the classmate had transferred to another school, he regretted not calling him when he had the chance.*

*These may seem like small things, but they cause the students a lot of heartache.*

Others might think these are rather trifling concerns, but to those actually facing such issues, they're very serious. Small things matter. What may look like a small act of courage is courage nevertheless. The important thing is to have the spirit to take a step forward.

As long as we're alive, we'll face all kinds of problems. But no matter what happens, we simply have to live with courage and press on, aiming always toward the future. No one can escape the realities of daily life. We have to deal with life and its problems. Young people have their problems, just as adults have theirs. Life and the world we live in are like a storm-tossed sea. We have to make our way through it, buffeted by all kinds of experiences. There is no other way. This is part of our inescapable destiny as human beings.

Everyone has their own hopes and dreams, their own way of life, their own ideals, joys, sufferings, pain and grief. No matter what happens, however, we have to get on with life. We have to keep moving, working toward realizing our ideals and dreams.

*That's so true. The loss of courage is the loss of everything.*

But no matter how wonderful our dreams, how noble our ideals or how high our hopes, ultimately we need courage to make them a reality. We can come up with the greatest ideas or plans in the world or be filled with boundless compassion for others, but it will all come to nothing unless we have the courage to put those intentions into action. Without action, it's as if our dreams and ideals never existed.

*I see what you're saying. We may possess magnificent treasures inside us, but if we don't have the courage to reveal them, it's just like keeping them locked up in a safe, hidden and unknown to others.*

That's why courage is the driving force or "engine" for our lives. Even studying and going to school require courage.

*If courage is the engine of our lives, it follows that those with great courage will be at an advantage.*

The courageous have the strength to persevere, calmly traversing life's ups and downs and advancing steadily toward the summit of their goals and dreams. Courage is a powerful asset. Those who lack courage stray from the correct path and succumb to apathy, negativity and destructiveness. They run away from hardship, seeking only a life of ease and comfort. Consequently, those who lack courage cannot devote themselves to the happiness of others nor can they improve themselves or achieve anything important or lasting. It's as if their engine is damaged.

*There's really nothing more important in life than courage, is there?*

The German poet Goethe (1749–1832) declared that the loss of such things as possessions and reputation is an insignificant concern. You can always set out to restore them. But the loss of courage is the loss of everything. [In a poem titled "Zahme Xenien VIII]," Goethe writes:

> *Possessions lost—little lost!*
> *Just reflect on yourself*
> *And acquire new ones.*
> *Honor lost—much lost!*
> *Just gain a good reputation*
> *And people will change their minds.*
> *Courage lost—all lost!*
> *It would have been better never to have been born.*[1]

If you summon your courage to challenge something, you'll never be left with regret. How sad it is to spend your life wishing, "If only I'd had a little more courage." Whatever the outcome may be, it is important to take a step forward on the path that you believe is right. There's no need to worry about what others may think. Be true to yourself. It's your life, after all.

## DON'T BLINDLY FOLLOW THE CROWD!

*I want to share a student's story. In the winter of her first year in high school, the group of friends she usually spent time with suddenly began to ignore her. She tried to talk to them about it, but they brushed her off. Even other classmates, who at first sympathized with her, began to turn on her. Malicious notes were passed to her in class. Friendless and alone, she was distraught, unable to fathom why no one liked or trusted her anymore.*

*She sought advice from one of her seniors in the high school division, who encouraged her: "Don't worry. This is a chance for you to grow. You have to beat this problem. Let's chant together and do our best!" The student decided to grit her teeth and keep going to school, but it was really hard for her to be there. And she finally told her parents that she wanted to quit school. Her mother said that she could stay home from school for one day but only on the condition that she chant for ten hours.*

I'm sure her mother was probably even more pained by and concerned about this terrible predicament than the daughter.

*Yes, I think so, too. When the student started chanting, she was feeling sorry for herself, thinking, "What did I do to deserve such suffering?" But as she kept chanting, a new feeling rose inside her—the confidence that she had the power to make wonderful friends. The next day she went back to school and put into action the challenge she had set for herself: greeting her classmates. She was extremely nervous when she opened the door to her classroom and said "Good morning," but she had faith that the day would come when they would respond. She persisted in her efforts.*

Yes, persevering on one's chosen path constitutes courage.

*At first, no one returned her greeting. But she kept it up. By the beginning of her second year in high school, some of her classmates were responding, and today, everyone in her class does.*

*In fact, she's now become a sort of adviser to both her classmates and student division members who are having human relations problems, and she's doing very well. She says that she's glad that she didn't give up and let her problem defeat her, and she's determined to become a bright source of courage and hope to others, just as her senior was to her when she was suffering.*

That's her declaration of victory. She really is to be congratulated. How happy her mother must be, too!

330

This student kept greeting her classmates. At first she was ignored, but she persevered. That's so admirable. Sometimes people laugh at brave acts in the beginning. They may see an act of courage as strange or peculiar. But later, they recognize it for what it was.

The German philosopher and poet Johann Friedrich von Schiller (1759–1805) said that those who are strong when they stand alone possess true courage. I have treasured those words since I was young.

It is wrong to blindly follow the crowd. Going along with something—without any real thought, just because everyone is doing it—and being quite content with not having to make any decisions yourself leads to mental laziness and apathy. And that's dangerous. This tendency is one of the greatest faults of the Japanese. If everyone says that war is good, everyone rushes to war without dissent or opposition, even if they know it's madness. No one has the courage to stand up and speak out, to rise up and say, "War is wrong!" We Japanese tend just to drift along with the flow, to hop on the bandwagon of superficially grand causes or fashionable trends.

But we mustn't be led astray. We must never give up our commitment to peace, our desire to learn and our love for humanity. Putting those ideals into practice and spreading them among others is an act of courage. It lies inside us. We have to summon courage from the depths of our lives.

Taking refuge in strength of numbers is not courage but cowardice. It's fascism, not democracy. In a democracy, all individuals have to recognize that they are society's protagonists—they play a leading role in society—and that as such they have a responsibility to fulfill. There's too much self-interest and selfishness in Japan. There's too much blind following, too much willingness to go along with the crowd.

Only when people have the courage to stand alone can they lead the world in the direction of peace and good. When such courageous individuals join forces in strong solidarity, they can change society. But it all starts with you. You have to be courageous. The rest follows from that.

## STANDING UP FOR WHAT IS RIGHT

*Talking about being brave enough to stand up for your beliefs reminds me of Rosa Parks.*

Mrs. Parks is a cherished friend and the mother of the civil rights movement in the United States. She is a courageous person and, at the same time, very gentle. She is mild-mannered but possesses a will of iron. [Rosa Parks died October 24, 2005.]

*I believe that Mrs. Parks visited the SGI-USA Headquarters in Los Angeles in May 1998. She even sat for a photograph with junior high and high school division members.*

I heard about that. Mrs. Parks has a great love for young people.

*A Japanese translation of her book* Dear Mrs. Parks: A Dialogue With Today's Youth[2] *has recently come out.*

*She said to the American members of the junior high and high school divisions: "I am very happy to be here today, surrounded by people of such beautiful spirit and such wonderful affection. I hope to continue to do everything I can for young people. They are our future. I know that if Dr. Ikeda were here with us, he would be just as pleased at this gathering of young people as I am, because he believes in freedom and love for all people."*

That was very kind of her to say. I, too, will do everything in my power for our young people, the leaders of the twenty-first century. Mrs. Parks has spent her life fighting against the discrimination and persecution of African Americans. She is indeed brave. Racial discrimination was terrible in the 1950s. In those days, Mrs. Parks lived in Montgomery, Alabama, where such discrimination was entrenched. "Colored" people were not allowed to sit with "white" people on the city buses. Even if they were seated in the colored section, the law required that they stand up and give their seats to white people when all the seats in the white section were filled.

*How horrible! Persecution and discrimination are absolutely wrong.*

Then, one fated day—December 1, 1955—Mrs. Parks got on a bus to ride home from work. She sat down in the colored section, and the driver told her to give up her seat to a white person. It was only expected that she'd comply, since she was an African American, and those were the rules. Everyone had up until then, including Mrs. Parks. But that day was different. She was tired of being intimidated. "No!" she said and refused to give up her seat. That one word went on to have a tremendous influence on the civil rights movement and the dismantling of institutionalized discrimination.

*What courage she had! I wonder where she found it?*

In the book you just mentioned, Mrs. Parks says: "I had no idea that history was being made. I was just tired of giving in. Somehow, I felt that what I did was right by standing up to that bus driver. I did not think about the consequences. I knew that I could have been lynched, manhandled, or beaten when the police came. I chose not to move, because I was right."[3]

*That's the crucial part: "Because I was right."*

Mrs. Parks found the courage to speak out because she believed that she was right. She wasn't trying to go down in history or to show off; she did not worry what others thought. She did what she did because she believed it was the right thing. That's courage. Courage is always identical to doing what is right, to justice. It comes from the wish to build a good and just society, to be a good human being.

If we are to do good, not only for ourselves but for humanity and the world, we need courage. This is the power that makes such actions possible—actions that may not call attention to themselves but that really shine with the brilliance of good.

Putting an end to schoolyard bullying is also an act of courage. So is enduring hardships and surviving tough circumstances. And so is trying to live a decent and honest life, day after day. By contrast, people

333

who are lazy and irresponsible or who have fallen into bad ways lack the courage to challenge themselves in daily life. In our families and among our friends, we should clearly state our opinions so that things will move in a positive direction. Our willingness to proceed in that direction and help others do so is a very admirable form of courage.

No matter what anyone may say, you should always do what is right. If you have the courage to do that, it's like having a magical weapon of unlimited power. In Buddhism, we call such a person a bodhisattva or a Buddha.

*Usually we associate courage with such things as taking part in some wild adventure, or performing a daredevil feat that no one else can.*

*There's also the idea that associates courage with being a good fighter. On television, in movies and in comics and video games, the hero is almost always someone who knocks out or kills his opponents. But that's just physical courage, brute courage. We're talking about something different here, aren't we?*

Yes, the courage that we're talking about is something very different from reckless bravado, which is always smug and self-centered. It gives no thought to others. It is high-handed, arrogant.

*Many politicians are like that.*

That kind of bravado may seem like courage, but it has no moral grounding. It's a wild, barbaric way to behave. It lacks the intelligence, the consideration for others and the spirit of cooperation that are essential to all human beings. It is completely alien to what human beings should strive for.

*Just leaping into the fray without thinking is another kind of foolhardy bravado. Of course, worrying so much about the consequences of your actions that you become a coward is also a mistake.*

We can find courage in many different areas of human endeavor. There is the courage to take part in an adventure and the courage that is needed to excel in sports, but this is only one aspect of courage. A more important kind of courage is that required to live a good life on a daily basis. For example, the courage to study hard or the courage to form and sustain good, solid friendships. This kind of courage we might even call perseverance, a virtue that sets our lives in a positive direction. This type of courage may not be showy, but it is really the most important.

*Courage isn't showy—I'm going to remember that.*

## COURAGE AND COMPASSION: TWO SIDES OF THE SAME COIN

The people in the spotlight, those who always seem to be doing big, flashy things, are not always courageous. And it goes without saying that slaughtering human beings through war, or using power and authority to intimidate or oppress people, are not acts of courage but of cowardice.

True courage means carrying out peaceful, just and beneficial activities. True courage is to live honestly and tenaciously. This kind of courage is priceless. It is steadfast courage, sound and healthy courage.

Those who steal, who oppress, who kill and maim, who threaten lives with weapons, who wage war are people who have no courage. People do such evil things because they are cowards. Cowardice is dangerous.

*When militarism raged in Japan, the Soka Gakkai's founding presidents Tsunesaburo Makiguchi and Josei Toda refused to follow the crowd. They stood up to the authorities for what they believed was right, bravely calling for a return to the road of peace and freedom. That must have taken tremendous courage.*

But at the time, they were denounced as traitors, thrown in prison and labeled cowards for opposing the war. It was an insane time. And I'm worried that we're seeing a trend toward the same insanity in Japan today.

*Today's mass media spread the most ridiculous lies, but are never made to answer for this. They violate people's human rights over and over, without shame or compunction. They brazenly sell their lies on street corners and advertise them everywhere. Our society has become abnormal. But living in the midst of this abnormality, people no longer notice just how abnormal it is.*

People who possess true courage aren't cowardly and base. They are honest and straightforward. That's why they are so frequently painted as villains or misunderstood. On the other hand, there are individuals who are great manipulators and become famous and popular through self-promotion and clever plotting. People see their fame and popularity and envy them. Many, unfortunately, are taken in completely.

But we shouldn't be swayed by praise or criticism. Those who do what they believe is right—even if they are misunderstood, scorned and persecuted—have a clear conscience and are true winners in life.

*Courage is a very down-to-earth thing, isn't it?*

It's a matter of perseverance. A mother's desire to raise her children into fine adults, no matter how hard she has to work to do it, is a noble form of courage. The other side of courage is compassion. They are two sides of the same coin—courage is the front side of the coin and compassion, the back. True courage is always backed by compassion. There is nothing evil or malicious behind it. If there is any malice or ill-intention, you can be sure it is not real courage. A mother's feelings for her children are the perfect example of courage and compassion.

By definition, courage must be backed up by justice and compassion. Mr. Toda used to say: "True compassion is very difficult for ordinary mortals. Emotions get in the way, or we just can't be bothered. Compassion is necessary, but it's hard for us to sustain it. We can, however, sustain courage. So though we know compassion is important, what we can actually do is be courageous."

In fact, if we act with courage, we find that our compassion for others grows deeper. Courage is the ultimate virtue for which we can strive.

*I want to introduce the experience of one of our high school division members from Shizuoka. At school, she was part of a closely knit group of seven students. As they spent more and more time together, they became increasingly aware of one another's strong and weak points. Gradually, all of them, except for her, began to gossip about any member who wasn't present at the time. She tried to persuade them to stop this, and the other six used that as an excuse to turn on her and pick on her.*

*In class, they would give her cold looks. They handed her letters filled with nasty remarks about her. Whenever they happened to touch her accidentally, they would scream, as if in horror, and run away. Every day was agony: With each indignity inflicted on her, she felt as if her heart were being torn out. Whenever she had free time, she'd hide in the girl's bathroom to avoid the humiliation that her six ex-friends were heaping on her.*

*Thinking how wonderful it would be to find someone she could trust and unburden herself to, she finally summoned the courage to tell her mother about her school problems. After her mother heard the whole story, she gave her daughter a copy of* Discussions on Youth. *The daughter read it very carefully, and as she did, she felt courage well up inside her. Once she realized that by chanting Nam-myoho-renge-kyo she could transform all her suffering into fuel for becoming happy, she decided to take positive action to change her situation.*

*She continued to pray: "I won't be defeated! I will become strong!" Gradually she gained more and more courage. Going to school wasn't a problem anymore. Before that, she had only gone because her mother drove her to and from school.*

*Eventually she made new friends. In the end, she even improved her relationship with the members of the original group who had ostracized her, and she gets along quite amicably with them today. She actually feels grateful to them, for they motivated her to become stronger and more independent.*

*The secret to getting others to change, she says, is to become a stronger person yourself. "I absolutely recommend that everyone chant Nam-myoho-renge-kyo. Those with problems will find answers, and those without will improve themselves," she says.*

Chanting Nam-myoho-renge-kyo is a powerful source of courage. It's the spark that starts the engine of courage. Chanting Nam-myoho-renge-kyo is an act of courage in itself.

Courage is the strength to live our lives the right way, to walk the right path. It can take many forms. For example, thinking what is the best way for your country and the world to achieve peace and then taking action to make that happen. That is the courage born of conviction. Or thinking what you can do to contribute to people's happiness and make society better, and then working constructively toward that goal. That is the courage of love for humanity. Thinking as a mother what you can do for your children, or as a schoolteacher for your students, or how you can help and support your friends—this is the unpretentious courage of daily life.

*Are you saying that there are different levels of courage?*

There may appear to be different levels, but they are alike in that all are courage. Great or small, courage is still courage, embodying the noble spirit to serve others. In contrast, looking out only for your own interests is cowardly and base.

*I've always thought that faith is the greatest courage.*

That's exactly right. There are courageous people in many fields, but the realm of religion has perhaps the most. Christian missionaries, in particular, have spread their religion no matter how harshly they were persecuted. Irrespective of religious belief, those who live and act in such a way are truly courageous.

Buddhism, too, is courage. Nichiren Daishonin declares, "Nichiren's disciples cannot accomplish anything if they are cowardly" (WND-1, 481). He continually stresses the importance of courage. For the sake of our faith, we must not let any persecution defeat us. That is courage. That is the noblest way of life. Those who follow it will be acknowledged by the heavens as true heroes. Not only will their names be remembered forever, but they will leave their distinctive mark on the history of humanity. They will inspire others to have courage and to become heroes, too.

Such individuals are great—they are bodhisattvas and Buddhas. Courageous are those who uphold correct faith and take action for the sake of their beliefs. They are heroes among heroes. Their hearts beat in accord with the fundamental rhythm of the universe. The sun shines wherever they are—illuminating their lives, their families, their classmates, their society, their country and their world.

Whatever you may have to challenge, I say to you, "Have the courage to take a step forward!"

1. Translated from German. Johann Wolfgang von Goethe, "Zahme Xenien [VIII]," *Goethe Gedichte: Samtliche Gedichte in Zeitlicher Folge* (Goethe Poems: Complete Poems in Chronological Order), ed. Heinz Nicolai (Frankfurt am Main: Insel Verlag, 1982), p. 1114–15.

2. Rosa Parks, *Roza Pakusu no seishun taiwa* (Dear Mrs. Parks: A Dialogue with Today's Youth), trans. Tomoko Takahashi (Tokyo: Ushio Shuppansha, 1998).

3. Rosa Parks with Gregory J. Reed, *Dear Mrs. Parks: A Dialogue with Today's Youth* (New York: Lee & Low Books, Inc., 1996), p. 42.

# 23

## WHY ARE THE GOOD DESPISED?

*Our topic this time is justice.*

*Many of the high school division members have requested that we ask you, President Ikeda, about the Osaka Incident, in which you were falsely accused of breaking the law and jailed.*

*You wrote about this incident in detail in the "Osaka" and "Trial" chapters of volume 11 of* The Human Revolution.[1]

I'll be happy to talk about it again for my young readers.

In those days, people looked down on the Soka Gakkai, regarding it as a gathering of the poor and the sick. Then, in 1956, three Soka Gakkai-backed candidates suddenly won seats in the upper house elections. This surprised the political establishment, which began to regard the Soka Gakkai as a threat.

Why did the Soka Gakkai decide to field candidates for public office? Our decision was based on Nichiren Daishonin's treatise "On Establishing the Correct Teaching for the Peace of the Land." Our aim, then, was to ensure the realization of a government based on a philosophy of peace, thereby bringing peace to our country and security and happiness to the people. Essentially, governments can create concrete policies only when they have an ideal or purpose as their basis. Without a solid philosophy, a government grows corrupt and becomes solely preoccupied with its vested interests.

The Osaka Incident was unmistakably the reaction of the political establishment to the Soka Gakkai's commitment to cleaning up the realm of politics and government. The authorities wanted, at all costs, to prevent the Soka Gakkai from establishing itself in the political arena.

*A high school division member who read* The Human Revolution *commented: "One scene that really stayed with me was when the prosecutors moved President Ikeda from the district prosecutor's office to a nearby annex, forcing him to walk the distance between the two buildings in handcuffs—in full view of the public. I can imagine how pained and upset the members who happened to see President Ikeda in that predicament must have been. And although no one could have been more frustrated and angry than President Ikeda himself, he still managed to convey a message of encouragement to those members as he passed near them. I found this so moving! I was also incredibly angered by the cruel and oppressive tactics employed by the authorities."*

*Another student writes, "I find it very strange that the authorities could get away with leveling charges against President Ikeda when they had no evidence of his guilt."*

Many innocent Soka Gakkai members were arrested, and their questioning by the prosecutor's office was also ruthless. The interrogators would grill the suspects from morning to night for days in a row. One of those questioned later said, "Although I knew I had done nothing wrong, after the relentless questioning, I began to wonder if perhaps I hadn't done something wrong after all..." The prosecutor's office abused its authority to terrorize with impunity defenseless, innocent people.

[One of the charged members later testified in court that the police detective questioning him brought unfair pressure to bear on him. The detective had played on the member's emotions, reminding him that his imprisonment would jeopardize his son's participation in a special school trip. If he confessed to the charges, on the other hand, the detective said, he would be released. "Don't you feel sorry for your son?" the detective chided. "Don't you have any compassion? Are you a heartless monster? If you continue to be so stubborn, we'll keep on at you until you come clean—we'll even take turns questioning you so that you won't be able to get a decent night's sleep."

During his testimony, with tears rolling down his cheeks, the man stated: "Even when I'm working, it's hard to make ends meet; if I had to stay in jail for who knows how long, my family would have starved. I felt as if my heart were being torn apart. I could not bear to tell a lie, because it would be like betraying the Gohonzon. But unless I cooperated with them, they wouldn't release me. Therefore, offering an apology in my heart to the Gohonzon, I lied and said, 'The chief of the General Staff told me to do it.'"][2]

Many weak, innocent people are falsely incriminated through underhanded tactics by the authorities. There have been many examples of this, and it may still be happening today.

*That's really terrible. All the Osaka members were furious. They cried: "What's going on? This is unbelievable! He hasn't done anything wrong— free Mr. Ikeda!" Several of them, concerned about your condition in prison, tried to visit you there and have various daily necessities passed on to you. Others were so worried that they stood in front of the prison for hours at a time. The Osaka organization's Brass Band played Soka Gakkai songs on the street nearby, hoping you would hear them inside.*

## "In Order To Protect My Mentor"

During my fourteen days in detention, Mr. Toda and all our Osaka members were very worried about me. To this day, I continue to chant for those fellow members who were imprisoned for alleged election law violations along with me.

When I was in jail, I was aware that conditions there were very different from the dark days during which Mr. Makiguchi and Mr. Toda, the first and second presidents of the Soka Gakkai, were imprisoned during World War II. I would have been embarrassed even to complain, considering what they went through. My confinement was just fourteen days. It certainly wasn't pleasant, but in the end, it was not that bad. The only time I was really distressed was when I heard that the police were thinking of arresting Mr. Toda or raiding the Soka Gakkai Headquarters.

I knew better than anyone else how poor Mr. Toda's health was at the time, and I knew that imprisonment might cost him his life. My only thoughts were that I must stop the police from getting to Mr. Toda or treading on the grounds of the Soka Gakkai Headquarters, our precious citadel of kosen-rufu.

*It was four-and-a-half years later, on January 25, 1962, that you were finally cleared of the false charges. The trial ran to eighty-four sessions, and you had to travel to Osaka many times and sit for long hours on the hard wooden seats of the courtroom. You also testified.*

*The sessions were held in the mornings but occasionally continued into the afternoon. For most people, I think that such tension and strain would be incredibly wearing and debilitating, but you managed to spend the evenings at meetings in Osaka, standing before members and encouraging them without showing the least sign that anything out of the ordinary was taking place. Those who knew what you were going through have said how tremendously moved they were by your indomitable spirit.*

At the end of the long trial, I was declared not guilty—a verdict that was only natural given my innocence of any wrongdoing. After the judge handed down his decision, the chief prosecutor came to me and said: "The verdict was just as I expected. It's only natural." As a prosecutor, that's something he probably shouldn't have admitted. It goes to show you just how terrible the power of authority can be.

*It's unbelievable that you were jailed, seeing how all you had ever done was work for the cause of good and justice. It's completely twisted.*

Yet that is how human society has been up until now. In "Civil Disobedience," the great thinker of the American Renaissance Henry David Thoreau (1817–62) says, "Under a government which imprisons any unjustly, the true place for a just man is also a prison."[3] Thoreau is saying that when a government is unjust, the very people who are labeled villains and put in jail are in fact the most just and decent people.

*In such a society, people who champion justice and truth are persecuted, while the corrupt and evil are praised and celebrated.*

I think that is frequently the case, and it is important for us to be aware of this and recognize it when it happens.

*I will never forget the heartless response of the Japanese government to the Great Hanshin Earthquake in 1995. What is government there for, if not to work for its citizens' well-being? Don't our political leaders have any conception of the value of people's lives, of their livelihoods?*

*We see the same thing in the case of HIV-infected blood products that were sold to hemophiliacs in Japan with government approval. Though government officials and the pharmaceutical companies knew that there was a high probability that people would contract AIDS from this blood and die, they continued to sell the contaminated products. Such behavior is impermissible. Only monsters could do such a thing.*

Authority is devilish by nature. The single aim of those who wield authoritarian power is to manipulate people to their own advantage and protect themselves. It's a topsy-turvy world: They treat anyone who opposes their aims or means as a criminal.

Buddhism teaches that the reason why evil people are protected and good people are despised is that the earth is ruled by the devil king of the sixth heaven. The dark spirit of the devil king of the sixth heaven arises in the hearts of those in power. Nichiren's life was also a series of harsh persecutions.

Buddhism is a struggle against devilish forces. With strong faith, we can resist and fight against all attacks and onslaughts. To win in this struggle is kosen-rufu. On our journey for kosen-rufu, we are destined to encounter many severe obstacles and negative forces.

# The Good Must Work Together

*Adults often say that they find today's youth scary, or that they don't under-*
*stand them. But I think that when you really look around the world, it's the*
*adults who are much scarier than the young people. In our world today, bad*
*people have free rein, and they do as they please—while people who are try-*
*ing to lead good, decent lives are often made to feel miserable.*

Your mission, my young friends, is to change that.

Seven hundred years ago, the three martyrs of Atsuhara—loyal followers of Nichiren who refused to recant their faith—were falsely accused of crimes and executed by priests hostile to Nichiren and in league with the political authorities of the day. Those attached to power are always envious and resentful of the good and just. It is an instinctive, primitive response on the part of those who wish to protect themselves and their own interests at all costs. Another thing is that corrupt people join forces with others of their kind easily and have not the slightest scruple in doing so.

Good people, on the other hand, don't form alliances so easily. The ideal we must aim for is a world in which good people can join hands and work together.

"I don't care what happens to anyone else, as long as I'm OK"—this is the kind of thinking that rationalizes the existence of nuclear weapons. It is an evil way of thinking. And that applies to both nations and individuals.

The crucial question is this: Are you going to ally yourself with evil or good? With wrong or right? Which road will you take in life?

Education, in its essence, should explore and teach how to live as a good human being. The same should be true of government and religion. Unfortunately, because this point is muddled and unclear, our world is now in chaos.

A certain philosopher said that we must champion truth, and our strength will be doubled." That's my lesson to all of you, too: Whatever persecutions you may face, my disciples, rise up for what is right! If you do, you will find that you have twice the strength that you thought you did.

*One of the biggest problems in Japan today, I think, is that people are embarrassed by such words as* good *and* justice. *They say that these words sound pretentious.*

To be generous, one could say that this is due to the purity of young people's ideals. The Japanese author Osamu Dazai (1909–48) wrote a novel called *Seigi to hohoemi* (Right and Laughter), which takes the form of the diary of its sixteen-year-old narrator, Susumu Serikawa, who wants to become an actor. He writes: "Perhaps I am a terrible hypocrite. I must be very, very careful. According to some theories, a person's character is formed between the ages of sixteen and twenty... But at the same time, I must not become too rigid and serious. 'Do the right thing with a smile!'—how I love those words! This is the first page in my diary."

Rather than doing the right thing with a frown on your face, it's best to do what is right in a relaxed and natural way.

*Some people say that doing the right thing just to look good is better at least than being bad. They assert that though you may simply be making a show of doing what's right at first, in the course of continued efforts, you will eventually end up really caring about what's right and working for good with genuine commitment.*

I want all of you to think about who created this atmosphere of ridiculing what is good and right. It was adults—adults who were doing bad things and wanted to keep on doing them.

Adults who have no personal morality may spout fine-sounding words, but their hearts are dark and corrupt. They have decided that justice and truth are lies, that there is always an ulterior, selfish motive behind them. That way they can feel better about themselves and their behavior. That way, they feel they don't have to change.

*Those are the kind of people who publish slanderous magazines, constantly violating the human rights of the people they report about.*

Nothing could be more foolish than allowing oneself to be influenced by such people into thinking that it's embarrassing to talk about what is good and right. You mustn't let slanderous adults take advantage of you.

It may seem easier to dismiss and ignore what's right and good, but if you do, you will never experience the true depth of life, true joy, fulfillment, self-improvement, value or happiness. Your life will be that of an animal's, driven solely by momentary desires. What a mindless way to live!

Just hold fast to what you believe is right and true. If you stumble, pick yourself up and keep going. By continually challenging yourself in this way, you will find that you are walking the road of the highest good.

*I have a question here from one of the members: "Why is it that the good and right are persecuted?"*

Precisely because one upholds what is right, one is persecuted. This is an important concern, past and present, relevant to all countries of the world. Until humanity as a whole has fundamentally transformed itself, this incomprehensible, illogical, yet very real situation will continue. We must face this dark reality. I hope each of you will think about this problem—about the actual examples of it you encounter.

Abraham Lincoln, president of the United States during the Civil War, abolished slavery and then was assassinated. Though, of course, it was right to work for the equality of African Americans, he was persecuted and killed for it.

Mahatma Gandhi of India rose up against colonial power that oppressed the Indian people. He opposed the high tax on salt, a daily necessity for even the poorest people, and was imprisoned on several occasions. Even though he always acted in the best interests of the people, he was, like Lincoln, assassinated.

Tsunesaburo Makiguchi and Josei Toda fought for what was right, opposing militarism because it caused the people terrible suffering, and yet they, too, were persecuted. Mr. Makiguchi died in prison.

History chronicles the stories of thousands of individuals who were persecuted for doing what was right. And there are countless people whose names have not been remembered but waged similar struggles.

# How Definitions of Right and Wrong Vary With the Times

*I think that in Japan, especially, people tend to attack anyone who is different or poses a threat to the status quo. "The nail that sticks out is pounded down," as the Japanese saying goes. This tendency is often used to serve the vested interests of the government and the media.*

Almost every famous person in Japan who has achieved something of value and has a modicum of integrity has endured some form of attack or persecution. It's the sly people who only care for themselves, who curry favor with the authorities, who get by unscathed. They don't make any waves.

The same is true in other countries, as well. It's a real tragedy that the media only focuses on the surface of events and doesn't bother to look into what's behind them—to consider their deeper implications.

*I think that neither the media nor people in general really make any serious effort to find out the truth.*
*In such situations, you begin to ask yourself just what justice is.*

Different ages have different standards of right and wrong, good and bad. The ruling powers of each age decide what most people of that era regard as right and wrong.

During World War II, for example, General Hideki Tojo was considered a hero in Japan. After the war, he was a criminal. During the war, General Douglas MacArthur was called a demon and the enemy in Japan, but after the war he was praised as a defender of justice.

Depending on who is in power, the same action may deem one either a saint or a villain. Thus the concept of justice and right is unclear and complicated.

*There are cases where terrible suffering and harm are inflicted on people in the name of right or good.*

That's true. During the war, it was regarded as right to go to war against others. This is frightening, when you think about it. That's why a firm sense of values that tells you what is truly right and wrong is so important.

The absolute minimum definition of what is right is that it benefits the welfare of others, society and humanity as a whole—that it contributes to happiness and peace. What constitutes wrong? Killing, stealing, lying, envy, framing the innocent, selfishness, destruction—in other words, thinking only of oneself or one's limited group.

*If we look at it that way, then what constitutes right and good is very clear.*

What is eternal, unchanging, right? That's the question we have to try to answer. The conclusion we reach is this: to live our lives in accord with the Mystic Law, the law of life as eternal as the universe itself, and to strive to realize universal respect for the dignity and sanctity of life. This is the eternal, highest right and good.

In other words, kosen-rufu is the highest right and the most just of causes.

*We have an incredible mission, don't we?*

That is why it is crucial that we succeed in our endeavors. Unfortunately, what is right does not always win. When it does not, that is a tragedy. Only when triumphant does right shine with its true colors.

Buddhism teaches the principle that life inherently possesses the functions of good and evil—that good and evil are essentially one. No matter how right a cause may be, if it is defeated by evil, it only ends up aiding evil and being counted as evil itself. Because right is defeated by evil, our world continues to suffer as it does.

We must put a stop to this. We must change the wheels that move the world and set them in motion toward fundamental change. We must do so on all levels: individual, family, group and nation.

The French Revolution (1789–99) was an uprising against the corrupt, absolute power of the monarchy. The French people put an end to the monarchy and established a republic of the people. The history books tell us that right won in this case, but if the people had not succeeded, their cause would probably not be described as just. There are many things you can say about what is right on the conceptual level, but in reality and practice, right is only proven when there is a decisive victory.

*My seniors are always telling me: "You mustn't be defeated! That's the invincible Kansai spirit!"*

Our organization in Kansai is strong because the members there burn with such spirit. That's why Kansai never loses. We must never lose in any struggle.

Countless anonymous, unseen struggles contribute to the cause of right in addition to the many that go down in history. There are struggles on all kinds of levels.

For example, your mother may have introduced Nichiren Daishonin's teachings to many others. Though unknown to others, these are admirable efforts for a great, right cause.

*What does doing right mean for high school division members?*

Well, in school, the right thing is to study. And the wrong is to prevent others from studying, or to engage in acts such as vandalizing school property. The purpose of school is study, so the right thing to do is direct your energies toward that end. To be selfish and, simply because you don't like to study, hinder other students or vandalize property is wrong and bad.

It is also wrong to witness evil or injustice and stand by in silence. In cases like that, good people should join forces to prevent bad acts such as bullying.

# There Is No Better
# Education Than Adversity

*When you look back on it, the Osaka Incident occurred because true democracy hadn't taken root in Japan. Maybe the political authorities couldn't believe that there could be an organization that just wanted to improve Japan, without any hidden agenda or self-interest. At the time, vote buying was rampant in Japanese elections among the established political parties, and it often went hand in hand with door-to-door campaigning. It was just the accepted convention of political life then.*

In fact, many say that door-to-door campaigning is a perfectly normal activity in a democracy. To go door-to-door and discuss politics with your fellow citizens is the most democratic behavior there can be. In the United Kingdom and the United States, door-to-door campaigning is regarded as a foundation of grassroots democracy.

But it is banned in Japan as a way of controlling people who would abuse door-to-door campaigning to try to buy votes. It goes without saying that vote-buying must never be condoned.

*Several high school division members have commented on this. One said: "The very least a democracy should do is protect people's human rights. It's indefensible for authorities in a democratic government—authorities whose very reason for existing is to defend those rights—to falsely incriminate innocent people. I cannot believe that the Osaka Incident could take place in a democracy. Such a thing could only happen in a dictatorship."*

*Another said, "Japan, even today, is a country without principles." And another said: "I thought that, now that the war was over, we were at peace, but recently I heard that people in our government are denying that the Nanking Massacre ever took place. I cannot believe it! It's fashionable in Japan today to show no interest in government or politics, to pretend it has nothing to do with you. But that's just a sham. We, the Japanese people, have to become more informed and intelligent."*

The reason that Japan's government does not improve is that people don't care enough and are not aware of their responsibilities. They are quick to vent their feelings, but their talk isn't accompanied by action. Things happen here that would cause riots, or very strong opposition, in other countries, but we have a long tradition of silently obeying the authorities. And so we don't act.

Japan has tossed aside the spirit of democracy that positions the people as sovereign. Most Japanese people enclose themselves in tiny, egocentric shells and lack the capacity to join forces and work for a great positive cause. A weak, self-serving national sentiment prevails. People criticize and complain, but they don't come together enough to change things. This is one of the greatest failings of the Japanese people.

*It's certainly true that plenty of people complain about our present situation, but they don't stand up and take action.*

The problems besetting Japan's democracy will not improve unless people make greater efforts to oppose government abuses of power and hold the authorities more strictly accountable for their actions.

Another problem is that we don't have any political leaders with strong principles and the courage and determination to carry those principles out. They're all puffed up with their own importance.

Elections represent an important way in which we, ordinary citizens, exercise our democratic right as sovereigns of the nation. We need a grassroots movement to make the Japanese people aware that they have the power to lead their own country.

Mr. Toda used to say: "I ask that you, the youth, keep a close watch on the affairs of government. You can't put the blame on anyone else [when the country is badly governed]. It's the responsibility of each citizen."

By the same token, trying to correct bad government by launching a coup or a violent revolution only results in chaos. It is essential that each citizen take action to move the nation in the right direction through democratic means.

Recent polls show that from 60 to 70 percent of Japanese citizens have no hope for the future. This is a terrible tragedy for Japan.

When the realm of politics deteriorates, it gives rise to an age in which corrupt people flourish and good people decline. We must not let that happen. To prevent that, we must each act—we must each do what we can in our immediate realm of influence.

We must never forget that the vast ocean begins with a single drop of water, and a journey of a thousand miles begins with a single step. The tallest mountain is made up of earth and stones; it is the accumulation of one grain of earth piled on top of another. And a peaceful society can only be built upon a solidly unified alliance of the people, upon a truly representative government that works for the welfare of all.

The people must produce political leaders from their own ranks who will live, work and die with, among and for the people.

*Roberto Baggio, the Italian soccer star, once told a group of high school division members: "We are together with a great mentor, President Ikeda. We are living in a wonderful age, when we can receive his guidance. I hope all of you will treasure this golden time and not waste it, as you do your very best."*

Mr. Baggio is a fine person. Four years ago in Milan [1994], I encouraged him to always fight his hardest up until the very last moment. And he has done just that. He has overcome daunting obstacles and is still fighting today. I am so happy for him. Don't ever let yourself be swayed from your fundamental beliefs.

*We have another question from one of the members: "Why are you, President Ikeda, so bravely able to challenge and overcome any difficulty? To tell the truth, I don't think I could do what you do. How can I become strong like you?"*

There is no education like adversity, as the saying goes.[4] The more persecutions and attacks a person endures and survives, the stronger and greater that person will become.

My own commitment is always to be with the people and for the people. Each day is a day of further personal growth and development, and I firmly believe these efforts lead directly to the growth and development of all other things.

I am not afraid of insult or criticism. I am not afraid when treacherous individuals appear. When you try to become a person who faces every situation fearlessly, you end up creating an indomitable self.

In life and in the various challenges we undertake, there will be times when we advance and times when we take a step backward. There will also be times when it's just best to rest. Life is full of changes. In the process of achieving your goals, it's natural to go through many changes.

Wisdom is important. Knowledge is important. We need the wisdom to correctly comprehend our relations with others and with society. Please develop sound insight. That is why it is so vital to cultivate the capacity to study and learn.

In the midst of such ceaseless change, there's one piece of advice that will never change: Regardless of the times or what other people say, don't let yourself be swayed from your fundamental beliefs. It's important to have conviction as firm and unmoving as Mount Fuji.

I want each of you to develop a self as unshakable as a majestic mountain, a self possessing courage, perseverance and ability.

1. SGI President Ikeda, then the Soka Gakkai's chief of the general staff, was unjustly accused of encouraging Soka Gakkai members to canvas door-to-door for votes—an activity that is illegal in Japan—and of directing them to buy votes during a 1957 upper house by-election in the Osaka electoral district. He was arrested in Osaka on July 3, 1957, on charges of violating the election laws and held in detention for two weeks of questioning.

By an astonishing coincidence, this was the same date that, twelve years earlier, second Soka Gakkai president Josei Toda was released from prison, where he had been placed for his opposition to Japan's militarism.

2. Daisaku Ikeda, *The Human Revolution* (Santa Monica, California: World Tribune Press, 2004), p. 1700.

3. Henry David Thoreau, "Civil Disobedience," *Walden and Civil Disobedience* (New York: Penguin Books, 1983), p. 398.

4. Benjamin Disraeli, *Endymion* (London: Longmans, Green, & Co., 1881), p. 273.

# 24

---

## WHY GO TO COLLEGE?

My entire focus now is on the twenty-first century—on how human beings can triumph in this century, on how we can make it a wonderful, positive age. That is my sole concern. And the starring roles in that century will be played by you—the high school division members, the members of the future division. It's all up to you. Your victory will be the victory of the twenty-first century and my victory as well.

*Thank you very much. As leaders of the high school division, we are striving to do our best, very much aware that our greatest mission is fostering the members of the high school division. The theme for today's discussion is college and future career paths.*

This is a most practical, important subject for high school students.

*Not only students who are in their senior year of high school but those in the other grades are concerned about what direction they should take after they graduate.*

*Some of them, unfortunately, seem to lack confidence in their ability to study and have given up before they even try to take the college entrance exams. Other students say that they are confused about what kind of school to attend. Their seniors have warned them that their level of education—be it high school, vocational school, two-year junior college or four-year university—will determine the kinds of jobs they can get, as well as their earning power and advancement in the workplace. For that reason, they've been told it would be better to go to a four-year university.*

You're absolutely free to choose your own path. It's your life. You yourself have to decide what's best for you. Certainly, there is some truth in those seniors' words, but the school you graduate from doesn't determine your entire life. Far more important is that you have the strength and depth of character to earnestly ponder the question "How should I live my life?" How much inner strength and depth you possess will determine how satisfying your life will be.

In the period of chaos after the war, Mr. Toda's company, where I worked, was on the verge of bankruptcy. One of my seniors said to me, "No matter what circumstances you may face, you have to live with the spirit 'Nothing ventured, nothing gained.'" That may seem rather simple advice, but it teaches us an important truth about life. If you have the courage to take a risk, then a way forward will definitely open.

Your future is not determined by the school you graduate from. It's determined by you and who you are as a human being.

Is one assured a happy life just because one graduates from a prestigious school? No, we know that's not true. And does graduating from a so-called second- or third-string school mean your life is a failure? Of course it doesn't. Many great people have completed only an elementary school education.

It all comes down to this: Those who succeed in the challenges they set for themselves are winners and lead happy lives. That is the key.

*Whatever path you choose to follow after graduating high school, you must never forget to challenge yourself.*

That's why it's such a pity to give up on taking college entrance exams just because you lack confidence in your grades or your ability to study. A spirit of challenge forges a person who can take on any challenge. And no matter what the result of your efforts, I hope that you have the sense of satisfaction from having tried.

The same applies when you take your place in the workforce as well.

# DIFFICULTIES IN FINANCING COLLEGE

*One student says that, because her family is not very well off, she wonders whether she shouldn't get a job right after high school to help her parents out.*

That is also something that each individual must decide. I know many people who have only a high school education and are now making wonderful contributions to society. Mr. Makiguchi, who was a great educator, used to tell his students that even if poverty prevented them from graduating from any level higher than elementary or junior high school, they should aim to become people who would one day manage or employ graduates from prestigious universities. Such people, even though they may not have a university degree, can be called excellent students of the "university of life."

To you, the high school division members, however, I have to say that I want you to study hard in your youth. As part of that study, or as an extension of it, I also hope you will go to college. Here in Japan, where there is peace, you can study in relative ease and comfort. Youth is the ideal time in your life to study. Without doubt, studying while you are young will prove an invaluable asset for your whole life.

When I was your age, Japan was at war. Even though I wanted to study, it wasn't possible to do so freely. The study of English was forbidden because it was regarded as an "enemy language." It was also difficult to study in the troubled times following the war. It was a hard period financially as well. Still, I wanted to study, so I went to night school. And I hungrily devoured whatever books I could get my hands on. Everything I learned then has stayed with me and been of use to me in life.

*Compared to your situation, worrying about whether we should join the workforce after high school or go to university or a two-year college is a real luxury!*

*What should students do when their parents don't have enough money to send them to college and urge them to get a job instead?*

I can understand the parents' feelings, certainly. If students in such a situation still want to go to college, though, they can always attend night school or take a correspondence course. The rest is a matter of effort. For example, they can work their way through college with part-time jobs to support themselves and pay for tuition.

There are many complex situations in life. Sometimes things don't work out as we'd like. The same is true in society. The important thing is to not be defeated by such setbacks.

Life is long. Things won't always go our way. Indeed, it's a fact of life that things often don't go the way we hope. That's why life is a struggle, and we suffer so much inside. How can we reach a personal summit of achievement we can be satisfied with? Life is all about that challenge.

Today, scholarships and student loan programs can provide support for financially disadvantaged students. If you make an effort, you may be able to take advantage of these for college study. Such programs are more advanced in other countries, and in many respects Japan lags behind. Japan needs to invest more in this area for the sake of the future.

*In Japan, scholarships offered by the government-sponsored Japan Scholarship Foundation, as well as those offered by local, regional and national government agencies, are available. Many major newspapers, too, have programs through which students can work their way through college by delivering newspapers. Soka University also has an independent scholarship program.*

A debt incurred to build the foundation of your future is nothing to be ashamed of. People in Japan tend to be very narrow-minded and regard taking out a loan as a sign of poverty. But that kind of thinking is extremely shortsighted. I hope that you won't fall into that trap and be too embarrassed to take out a loan or be afraid of the work required to pay it back. Those who have no desire to study are poor, while those filled with an enthusiasm for learning are rich.

*A high school division member received his high school diploma by studying at night school. He then got into a four-year university. He had started out at a regular, daytime high school, but he couldn't seem to find purpose in studying.*

*He also had some problems with other students. After a few months into his freshman year, he just stopped going to school.*

*One day, when he was really down on himself, he came across one of your speeches. There was a part where you said: "No doubt there will be times when you find yourself in a situation where you feel completely worthless or incompetent. Such times are in fact opportunities for you to bring forth new potential." Profoundly moved by these words and deeply regretting his attitude, he decided to go to night school, resolving to study harder than anyone else.*

*He worked at a gas station during the day and attended school in the evening. After class, he would go to baseball practice as a member of the school's team. But just before he was to take his university entrance examinations, he found himself in another slump.*

*On that occasion, too, he was inspired by some words of yours. You said: "I studied at night school. Like many others in those turbulent years following World War II, I had no money, so I had to work during the day to put myself through school in the evening. It was a painful struggle, but an experience of which I will always be proud" (see page 7). Reading this, he felt a renewed determination, and he studied as hard as he could. His grades improved dramatically, he took the qualifying examination, and he was admitted to the university of his choice.*

How admirable! He really is to be commended.

The founder of the Tokugawa shogunate, Tokugawa Ieyasu (1543–1616), once said, "Life is like traveling a long road with a heavy load on one's back. One should not rush." There is no life without suffering. There is no youth without suffering. Therefore, the only choice we have is to win over our suffering or be defeated by it. What gives us the courage to triumph in this struggle is faith and the warm support of our fellow members in the SGI organization.

## CHOOSING A PATH

*Other students complain that although they want to attend a technical or vocational college, their parents are insisting that they go to a four-year university.*

They're lucky to have such parents! But if you are intent on pursuing a specialized vocational field, then you should have the courage to go for it and try to attend a relevant appropriate vocational school. If you're going to pursue something, you may as well have the spirit and determination "I'm going to be number one in my field!"

*I think that vocational schools and four-year universities each has strong points.*

In today's society, the person with a specialty in a given vocational field may have an advantage in finding work. But I also think it is an important and wonderful thing for students to attend a four-year college, as many of their parents may wish, and pursue a more specialized field later. Attending a university and exposing yourself to a wide range of learning is a good way to refine and cultivate your intellect and develop yourself overall. Higher education is an important tool for building character, too. Extensive learning is something common to people of refinement and culture the world over. Such education provides the opportunity to rise to a high level of personal development.

Education can be likened to climbing a mountain. The higher you climb, the broader your field of vision becomes and the wider the world that unfolds before you. You begin to see things that you could not see before. The question of where to study—whether at a vocational school, a two-year college or a four-year university—is something that only you can decide based on many factors, including your family circumstances, academic ability and personal goals and ambitions. If you make the decision yourself, you'll have no regrets later. Of course, in deciding what to do, it is important to consult others—your parents, teachers, seniors and friends. But once you make your decision and put it into action, don't look back. You mustn't live a life filled with indecision and lingering regret.

Never forget that other people are other people, and you are you. You mustn't feel envious or jealous of others, thinking: "I wish I was like him" or "I wish I was like her." Please forge a solid, unwavering identity.

Success or failure in life is decided in the final chapter, not the opening page.

*A second-year high school student has written: "I just don't know right now what direction I want to take. Do I need to decide what I want to do in the future before entering university?"*

You can take plenty of time deciding what direction you want to take. There's no need to make up your mind right now. After you start university, study different subjects and are stimulated by new friends, you'll gradually get a clearer idea of the path you want to pursue. If you always concentrate fully on the challenges at hand, your mission will reveal itself to you naturally over the course of time.

*I want to share a story about one of my friends. She wanted to study engineering, and she did. She got as far as graduate school, and then she came across a certain book:* Chiteki shoga: Motsu kodomo e no kyoiku (Education for Mentally Disabled Children). *She was incredibly moved by the book and quit graduate school. She then decided to become a teacher and is now studying to do so.*

*I have another friend who graduated from a two-year college course and then trained as a nurse. She is now working in the nurse's office of a high school.*

*Like these two young women, many people have found what they really wanted to do in life through such things as a chance encounter with a book, the influence of friends or actual work experience.*

Yes, friends are a treasure. I remember that in 1972 I visited a dormitory at Cambridge University in the United Kingdom. It was an impromptu visit, and the two students in the room that I happened to stop by hastily did their best to straighten the room. I'll never forget what good friends they seemed to be. I'm sure that they encouraged each other, studied together and helped each other grow and develop. I felt sure that this dormitory must produce great people.

Dormitories fulfill an important function; living in a dormitory can be a lesson in life. Not a lesson where one studies alone in isolation and self-absorption, but a lesson where one learns how to forge ties of friendship and build lasting human relationships.

## EFFORT IS NECESSARY FOR SUCCESS

*Some students complain that, though they want to get into a certain university, they just don't have the scholastic ability.*

If there's a university you'd like to attend, then study hard enough to do it. You need to make an effort to succeed. Study many times harder than others do. Playing and dreaming won't get you what you want. You might think: "Ah, wouldn't it be wonderful if I could learn English overnight!" or "There must be some way to excel while having fun at the same time!" But it's never that easy.

Nothing great is achieved without serious effort. There is no easy road to learning. Be resolved to study so hard that you will surprise everyone. That tremendous effort will become a wonderful, noble, fulfilling memory, a proud medal of honor of the days of your youth.

*Some members seem to think that they can get by with a minimum of study because they are chanting.*

That is wrong. It is a big mistake to compare academic study and faith on the same level. Thinking that you don't need to study hard because you chant shows an incorrect attitude toward faith; it is the kind of misguided thinking we see in escapist religions. When it comes to study, the person who studies hardest succeeds. This accords with reason. Faith, in contrast, is what forges our spirit so that we can sustain that effort.

For instance, you can sit before a rice cooker and pray all you want, but unless you add some rice and turn it on, you won't have any rice to eat. Similarly, you can have all the faith in the world, but if you don't study, you'll never get anywhere academically. It's like a motor that is only idling and produces no forward motion.

*Faith is the engine that enables us to study many times harder than others.*

Mr. Toda often used to say, "You need to have the faith of one and work as hard as three if you're going to succeed in life." The opposite just goes against reason. It's just fanaticism. Nichiren Daishonin tells us quite firmly that faith that is not related to society diminishes the true greatness of Buddhism.

*[Nichiren Daishonin writes, "Regard your service to your lord as the practice of the Lotus Sutra" (WND-1, 905).]*

During your youth, study as hard as three people and have the faith of one—no, for this period in your life, to have the faith of even half a person is fine. Even if you cannot do the morning and evening recitation of the sutra right now, you can strive to challenge yourself gradually in faith and eventually develop a consistent, confident practice.

I want you, the high school division members, to be champions of the spirit of challenge.

*Many of our high school division members are seriously pondering what vocational school or university to attend after they graduate. One high school graduate, who is spending an additional year studying after failing the university entrance exams, says she feels lonely and isolated. In addition, she finds herself easily distracted from her studies. This is causing her a great deal of anxiety. She wonders if she should simply enroll in any university that accepts her.*

If you have the opportunity to attend a university, even if it's not your first choice, it may be wise to do it. Entering a top school doesn't guarantee that you'll become a top-class person. It is through your own efforts that you succeed. You must never forget this.

A university is just a means to an end, and you are that end. Your goal should be to become a fine human being and a winner in life. The ultimate success or failure of your life will be determined in your final years. Just because things don't go as you had hoped at the start doesn't mean that you won't be a winner in the end.

Remember, many who entered the "best" universities have ended up with unhappy lives—or worse, criminal lives.

*Many are saying that key areas of Japanese society—political, financial and economic—are now in a virtual state of collapse. The leaders of these spheres are almost all graduates of top universities.*

## THE DANGER OF KNOWLEDGE WITHOUT WISDOM

One of the causes of the chaos in society is the confusion of knowledge with wisdom. Knowing how to apply the knowledge we have acquired—this is where wisdom comes in. We can accumulate all the knowledge we like, but without wisdom to guide us, it produces nothing of value. Memorized information alone always remains on the level of the conceptual.

Wisdom, in contrast, operates on the level of real life. It is a source of power for living, for surviving and coping. It is wisdom that leads to our success and happiness. Knowledge alone cannot produce happiness. Many people don't understand this, and remain under the illusion that knowledge is all that matters.

*Some have put scientific knowledge, for example, to destructive uses.*

*And others have used business and economic knowledge only to enrich themselves at others' and society's expense.*

A society that values only knowledge and lacks wisdom is bound to reach a dead end. A certain philosopher has pointed this out as a fundamental failing of Japanese culture.

*The relationship between knowledge and wisdom is crucial, then.*

Knowledge gives rise to wisdom. If you like, knowledge is the pump; wisdom is the water that we get from the pump. If we cannot obtain water, the pump is useless. At the same time, without knowledge—without the pump—we won't be able to obtain water.

*Doesn't it seem that Japan's educational system is on the wrong track?*

As it stands now, students undergo highly competitive examinations to get into college but then graduate easily, without having to study much. This goes completely against reason! It is an example of the impasse we face as individuals, as a society and as a nation. Our national policies with respect to young people and our educational system are in a terrible state of disarray.

*Recently, the influential educational advisory body, the University Council under Japan's Ministry of Education, Culture, Sports, Science and Technology released an interim report, "The University in the Twenty-first Century and Educational Reform" (June, 1998). The Council offers several suggestions for reforming the present system that allows students to graduate from college without serious study. Among the proposals are preventing students from taking an excessive number of class credits each semester and then taking only the exams without attending the classes. Grades would be based not only on exams, but also on attendance and the successful completion of homework and term papers.*

*Some have criticized such suggestions as turning university into high school.*

*At the same time, the report suggests allowing students with excellent grades to graduate in three years instead of the usual four; allowing students to enroll from the fall semester, too, instead of only in the spring, as is now the case; and introducing one-year intensive graduate school courses.*

In terms of population, the number of young people in Japan is decreasing. It is estimated that by 2009, every high school graduate who wants to go to a university will be able to do so.

Needless to say, the present university entrance examination system is far from ideal. We must improve the entire educational system, including the university level. But no matter what changes we make to the system, they will be meaningless unless we change our basic philosophy.

It is important, I feel, that we help students develop a questioning mind, so that they will always ask themselves for what purpose a given thing is being done or pursued.

*When you see the elite students graduating from the top schools and becoming leaders in the government and bureaucracy, where all they seem to care about is fulfilling personal ambition, you cannot help but wonder what they think the purpose of their university education was.*

Some say that our universities are producing "knowledgeable barbarians." If universities produce people who look down on those who couldn't attend college, what good is it? In one sense, college exists precisely for those who cannot attend it. Those who are privileged to attend a university should spend their lives working for the sake of those who couldn't enjoy the privilege.

*The reason that tuition at national universities is less expensive than at private universities is that they are subsidized by our taxes. This is the first thing that university officials should say to new students at the entrance ceremonies: "You are able to attend this university because of the hard work of many, many others, who could not attend. Pursue your studies so that you may serve them in some way."*

*Unfortunately, the focus at most Japanese universities has not been serving the people but acquiring the authority to control and dominate them. It's completely backward.*

## SOKA UNIVERSITY: BASED ON THE SPIRIT OF MENTOR AND DISCIPLE

That is the reason I founded Soka University. I wanted to create a university truly committed to producing talented people who are dedicated to serving their fellow human beings.

Mr. Makiguchi once said to Mr. Toda: "In the future, we must found a school based on the theory of value-creating (*soka*) education that I have been formulating. If we cannot do it during my lifetime, you do it during yours. We will build a school system of value-creating education, starting with elementary school and continuing all the way through university." On another occasion, he said: "I really want to start a university. If we do that, we'll produce truly talented people."

Mr. Toda first spoke to me about founding Soka University in late autumn 1950, in the cafeteria of Nihon University in Tokyo. "Daisaku," he said, "let's build a university. A Soka University. For the sake of humanity's future, I must create a Soka University. But this may not be possible for me to achieve during my lifetime. If that's the case, I am counting on you, Daisaku. Let's make it the best university in the world" (see *The New Human Revolution*, vol. 15, p. 88).

Mr. Toda said this to me when his business had failed, and he was in the direst of financial straits. Despite this serious personal setback, his spirit remained undaunted. He burned with boundless hope for the future. In the midst of that desperate struggle, Mr. Toda entrusted me with the mission of establishing Soka University.

I resolved to realize, no matter what, this dream of my predecessors, Mr. Makiguchi and Mr. Toda. I established Soka University with the intent of making it the best university in the world, just as had been Mr. Toda's wish. I chose April 2, the anniversary of my mentor's death, as the university's founding date.

*Soka University is founded on the solemn spirit of the oneness of mentor and disciple.*

The name *Soka University* appears in Chinese characters on the school's main gate to the school, a reproduction of Mr. Makiguchi's calligraphy that he left in Mr. Toda's care. I, in turn, inherited this work of calligraphy from Mr. Toda and cared for it until we had it reproduced for the gate. Soka University truly reflects the spirit of both Mr. Makiguchi and Mr. Toda. It is also my very life.

On a bronze statue outside the main administrative building, I had the following words engraved: "For what purpose should one cultivate wisdom? May you always ask yourself this question!" I did this because I want all Soka University students to become individuals who serve the people, individuals who never forget the sufferings of the people.

There's the wonderful French expression *noblesse oblige*. It means "nobility has duties"—the higher one's position, the greater one's duty to others. This is a fundamental philosophy of leadership in Europe. It accords with the belief that those in positions of leadership have a duty to protect the people, to demonstrate superior courage and ability, to have self-discipline, integrity and selfless dedication.

*I have heard that, in the United Kingdom, a higher proportion of Oxford and Cambridge students died in World War I and World War II than those from other schools. They felt a strong sense of duty to defend their country and their comrades, so they always fought in the vanguard on the battlefield.*

I think that this same sense of responsibility should be found in all who receive a higher education—they have a duty to serve society.

*Soka University's correspondence course has also produced many talented individuals. I recently heard the story of a young man who had gone to a municipal high school in Tokyo's Nerima Ward. A member of the baseball team, he put all his energy into the game and little else. As a result, his grades were only average. It wasn't until the final baseball season when his high school career was over—that is, in the middle of the second term of his last year at school—that he finally began to study for the university entrance examinations.*

*He was highly motivated to pass the exams, so from that time on he studied very hard— up to five hours a day on weekdays with an additional ten hours in the library on Saturdays and Sundays. But he failed to get into any of the universities of his choice. "Right in the middle of the exam," he says, "I was suddenly overcome by a sense of pointlessness. I saw myself getting into a good school, enjoying myself and having a good time for four years, then getting a good job... But I didn't want that life!"*

*He began to think long and hard about the purpose of university study and the purpose of life itself. At that juncture, he encountered your writings, President Ikeda. The enthusiasm of high school division leaders also inspired him to find the profession to which he wanted to dedicate his life.*

*He enrolled in Soka University's Department of Correspondence Education. He says that when he attended a special on-campus session for correspondence students, he was inspired by the passion of his fellow students, who were of many different ages and professions.*

*A year later, he took an examination to change his status to a full-time student, and he passed. Having decided to become an attorney, he began to study for the national bar examination. He took the bar exam five times before he finally passed, and today he is busily, happily employed as an attorney.*

*"Through my experience," he says, "I came to truly understand these words from President Ikeda: 'Only labor and devotion to one's mission give life its worth.' It was my feeling of responsibility and mission to become a person who could make a contribution to society that kept me going until I finally succeeded. I intend to keep on moving forward, never forgetting to challenge myself!"*

## Happiness Is Found in Challenging Difficulties

*One of my seniors at work told me his story: Though he had quit high school once, he later got back on track and was eventually accepted into a prestigious university.*

*He related that in his first year of junior high school, he started playing the guitar. He joined a band and performed with them, and he never really wanted to go to high school. And though he ended up going to high school, all he really cared about was his band. In a class of one hundred eighty students, he usually ranked about one hundred sixty. He was also rebellious toward his teachers, and he dropped out of high school in the middle of repeating his sophomore year.*

*He worked a part-time job, but began to worry about his future. Then, a senior from the young men's division paid him a visit. "You're escaping reality," the senior told him. "Going to college isn't everything, but shouldn't you try to do something to challenge yourself?"*

*That young men's division leader had only completed junior high himself, but he worked hard to contribute to society. He kept visiting and encouraging the young man for an entire year.*

*Eventually, my colleague was roused to action, and he began to study hard and chant Nam-myoho-renge-kyo an hour every day. After a year, he passed the high school equivalency examination.*

*The next spring, he sat for the university entrance examinations and failed. He was extremely discouraged by the setback, but once again the young men's division member encouraged him, and after a year of studying and waiting, he took the exams again and was accepted by the college of his choice.*

*My colleague told me: "It all depends on your drive and will to succeed. I can never fully express my gratitude to my senior in the young men's division who helped me find and bring forth that drive and motivation."*

The SGI is a wonderful organization, isn't it? You must win in life, win over your weaknesses, win in society and win in exams. The important thing is first to be victorious, and then to gain the nourishment you need for your happiness.

Life is a win-or-lose struggle. Buddhism is about winning, too. Society is concerned with reputation, government with punishment and reward, and Buddhism with winning or losing.

The world, society in general, operates on the level of appraisal, or popularity—whether one is spoken well of or ill of by others. The nation rewards those it considers to do good and punishes those who do bad. Both society and government operate based on such relative values. But Buddhism is win or lose—there is no halfway.

What is life's purpose? To be a winner, to be happy.

What is happiness, then? At its essence, it is fulfillment—to wear the golden crown of your own deep, personal satisfaction.

What, then, is fulfillment? It is fighting against difficulties. Without problems, without challenges, there can be no fulfillment. And without fulfillment, there is no happiness.

There is no happiness without hardship; it simply cannot exist.

People tend to forget the process—the path—of battling hardships and search only for the end result—the destination—of happiness. Overcoming hardship and suffering is happiness replete with genuine fulfillment.

*This is a lesson that applies to us all, whether we decide to attend a university or not.*

Whatever path you choose, I want all of you to live, in a way that best suits you, positive, happy lives and to be able to say "I have won!"

# PART SEVEN

# THE ENERGY
## *of Youth*

# 25

## Life and Death Are One

We are finally approaching the countdown to the twenty-first century. This is your time. The future is in your hands. I hope you will make the twenty-first century wonderful.

Please make it a century in which the life of each individual is cherished and respected to the utmost.

A century without discrimination, without bullying, war or murder.

A century in which no child cries with hunger, in which no mothers or children take their own lives in despair.

A century without environmental destruction.

A century free of academic elitism, greed and materialism.

A century in which human rights are upheld as the most precious of treasures.

A century of true democracy, in which the people hold corrupt political leaders to account.

A century in which the people exercise sound judgment and pay no heed to misinformation spread in the media.

I hope you will make it a century in which each of your precious dreams comes true and your unique individuality blossoms to the fullest.

To realize these goals, it is vital that each of you achieve victory, that each of you grow into people of philosophy and compassion, into people who possess both real ability and the sincerity to understand others' hearts.

Your victory will be the victory of the twenty-first century. You are our only hope.

*We'll do our best to create a century of life.*

How we view life—the perspective we have on life, on death, on the human condition—is the basis for everything.

Japan today is in deep darkness. It has reached a deadlock, as has much of the rest of the world. What is the root cause of this?

It is a distorted understanding of the fundamental question of life and death. Society's leaders and the majority of people have avoided thinking about this most important of issues, brushing it aside in the pursuit of immediate wants and desires. And we are now seeing the consequences of this negligence. Therefore, if we do not turn our attention to the fundamental issue of life and death, nothing will ever really change. Now matter what superficial measures we may take, it will be comparable to trying to treat an illness with pain relievers without addressing the cause. Though our symptoms may temporarily ease, we are only deceiving our bodies, and we will not get better.

The British historian Dr. Arnold J. Toynbee (1889–1975) held that the cause of the world's misfortune is that leaders in all fields fail to ponder the basic question of death.

*Which means they do not really understand the true value of life, either.*

This is a major problem underlying environmental pollution as well. Look at the apathetic response to the terrible tragedy of industrial mercury poisoning known as Minamata disease[1] that occurred in Minamata, Japan, in the 1950s and 1960s. Neither the company responsible, nor the government bureaucracy, nor the politicians responded with an attitude that indicated valuing people's lives as the highest priority. All they offered was a cold-hearted, bureaucratic response that put the interests of big business first.

The consumption of fish contaminated with mercury from industrial waste discharged by the company into Minamata Bay caused healthy people to experience numbness in their extremities and rendered them unable to coordinate voluntary muscular movements. It devastated their nervous systems, causing some to go into convulsions and die. Children were born deaf, blind and with speech impediments. Innocent people were forced into a living hell.

Yet it took fifteen years from the time the first victims appeared, until 1968, for the Japanese government to finally recognize the disease as pollution-related. Why did they not act immediately? Why did no one make efforts to save these precious lives instead of wasting time coming up with all kinds of excuses and rationalizations?

Most, if not all, of the company officials, bureaucrats and government leaders involved had graduated from Japan's so-called top universities. But these people, representing Japan's best and brightest, lacked something crucial in terms of their humanity.

This frightening reality points to a fundamental flaw in Japan's educational system—the absence of humanism and a solid philosophy of life.

*I completely agree.*

# EACH IS BORN TO FULFILL A PRECIOUS MISSION

You are all still young, and most of you, I am sure, do not have a clear conception of death. That is only natural. But precisely because you are young, I want you to think seriously about such questions as "What is life?" "What happens when we die?" "Why are we born?" I want you to grow into adults who possess a firm philosophy of life and death. A philosopher has said that an awareness of death, of our own mortality, is what separates humankind from other animals.

*One of our high school division members in Tokyo had a close encounter with death as a member of his school's track and field team. In December of his freshman year, he was practicing landings for the high jump when he fell and hit his head. Dislocating and fracturing his cervical vertebrae, he was lucky that he did not die then and there. Six hours of surgery, which was successful in saving his life, he could no longer move his body without others' help.*

*The body he had once taken for granted now beyond his control, he sank into extreme self-pity.*

*Then, on January 2, he received a poem from you, President Ikeda:*

*Day after day I pray*
*For your health,*
*Because you possess a profound mission.*

*He was so deeply moved by these words that the courage to challenge his physical condition welled up from the depths of his being. He chanted Nam-myoho-renge-kyo and put great efforts into his physiotherapy sessions. He left the hospital on April 3, and today, he is back at school and even back on the track and field team.*

*He says: "I could have died, but I am fine now. I am very happy. My injury taught me anew the tremendous power of the Gohonzon. From this day on, as a high school division member, I intend to think carefully about my mission, which President Ikeda referred to in the poem he sent me, and carry it out without fail!"*

How admirable!

Every one of us has a mission, a mission we were born to fulfill. That is why, no matter what happens, we must press on in life through all things. The Japanese word for mission means to use one's life. For what purpose do we use our lives? For what purpose have we been born in this world, sent from the universe? Why have we been dispatched here?

Buddhism views the universe as one giant living entity. If we compare it to a vast ocean, each individual life is like a wave on that ocean. When the wave rises from the ocean's surface, that is life. When it merges back into the ocean, that is death. Life and death are one with the universe. The whole universe approves and cooperates in the birth of a single life. All of you have been sent here with the blessings and congratulations of the entire universe!

All life is equally precious. We cannot apply a hierarchy of value to life, making one living thing more worthy than another. Each life is unique and individual. Every person's life is as valuable as the universe—it is one with the life of the universe and just as important. Nichiren Daishonin declares, "Life is the foremost of all treasures" (WND-1, 1125). He also states: "The Buddha says that life is something that cannot be purchased even for the price of an entire major world system" (WND-1, 983) and "One day of life is more valuable than all the treasures of the major world system" (WND-1, 955).

That is why we must never take our own lives. That is why we must not resort to violence, why we must not hurt or bully others. No one has the right to harm the precious treasure that is life.

*One student writes that, when he was a victim of bullying, he questioned why he had to be born into such a painful world—why he had been born at all.*

Why have we been born? Youth is the time to search for the answer to this question. Youth is our "second birth." Our first is our physical birth, but it is during our youth that we are born as a person. That is why it is such a difficult period in life, why we have to go through so much. It is a struggle, like the struggle of a baby chick trying to break out of its shell.

The crucial thing is to never give up. As you struggle to find your way, please pray, think, study, talk with your friends and give your all to taking care of what is important now. If you challenge yourself without giving up, then your very own mission—the one that only you can fulfill—will reveal itself without fail.

*Yes. If the chick gives up halfway, it will never break out of the shell.*

## LIVING EACH PRECIOUS MOMENT OF LIFE

I hope you will not let your problems and struggles defeat you. Those beaten by their problems experience no fresh growth or "rebirth" as human beings. They end up living by instinct alone, like animals. And that is spiritual death.

You all know Mr. Mikhail Gorbachev, the former president of the Soviet Union, who is a friend of mine. Mr. Gorbachev is responsible for bringing an end to the Cold War. He is a true hero who had the sense to say, "This foolishness cannot go on!" Wanting to find a way that would bring happiness to all humanity, he took a decisive step toward change.

As the supreme leader of the Soviet Union, he was virtually all-powerful in his home country. He could easily have lived in comfort in the citadel of power. But he chose a different path—a dangerous, risky path. Attempts were made on his life, and he was betrayed and persecuted. But amid this, he refused to abandon his dream for a society that put people first.

When Mr. Gorbachev and his late wife, Raisa, visited our Kansai Soka Junior High School and Kansai Soka High School in November 1997, Mrs. Gorbachev addressed the students. "You will experience all kinds of hurts in life," she said. "Not all of them will heal. Nor can you always realize your dreams. But there is something that you can achieve. There is a dream that you can make a reality. Therefore, the person who triumphs in the end is the person who gets up after each fall and pushes onward. The ability to keep on fighting is a matter of the spirit. Spiritual death does not come to the person who is tired—it comes to the person who has stopped moving forward.

"You may think you are still young today, but before you know it, you will have reached maturity. That is life. Soon you will all have to take responsibility for your families, your nation and the entire planet.

"May your dreams come true! May wonderful things occur in your lives! May you all be happy!"

*What an encouraging message!*

The Gorbachevs experienced trials and hardships beyond description. "But we have survived," they said. "We have lived and we have fought." All of you are alive now—what an incredible thing that is! I hope you will not waste this wonderful treasure.

Speaking of Russia, I have talked to you before about how the great Russian writer Fyodor Dostoyevsky (1821–81) narrowly escaped being killed by a firing squad. While waiting for his turn with the executioners, he thought about how he would spend his final moments.

He knew that in five minutes he would be tied to a post and shot, thus disappearing from this world. He did not want to waste those five precious minutes—they were the last treasure he had. He had to use them carefully. He divided his remaining time into three parts. The first two minutes he would spend saying farewell to his comrades. The next two minutes he would devote to thinking to himself for the last time. His final minute he would take one last look around.[2]

At the same time, he decided that should he for some reason be spared, he would turn every minute into an age and never squander another second.

*What an intense experience that must have been!*

If you think about it, although we may not be destined to die five minutes from now, we are all, without exception, going to die at some point. Nothing is surer than this. It is 100 percent certain.

Victor Hugo once said, "We are all under sentence of death, but with a sort of indefinite reprieve."[3] Ideally, we should live every minute valuably, as if it were the last moment of our lives. Those who live aimlessly are left with a sense of emptiness at the end, but those who exert themselves fully throughout life will greet death peacefully.

Leonardo da Vinci says, "As a well-spent day brings happy sleep, so life well used brings happy death."[4] One aware that death could come at any time will live each day to the fullest. In a race, it is the goal that makes us run with all our might.

*Facing the reality of death brings meaning to life.*
*I guess if we did not die, our lives would become aimless and empty—just as we tend not to study unless we know there is an exam!*

That is true. A life without death might seem like a nice idea, but it would also mean that we would put everything off, thinking that even if we did not take care of things now, we could still do it in ten or twenty years. In fact, we would probably never do anything at all. We would all become completely decadent and lazy.

*I imagine that is what happens to people who spend their days living haphazardly, never giving serious thought to the reality of death.*

In the face of death, such things as wealth, status, honors and academic qualifications mean nothing. At that moment, all is ultimately decided by your life, unadorned of all external trappings. Are you fulfilled? Or is your life empty, weak and spiritless? That is why we need faith to forge and develop our lives.

*And we never know just when death will come. So we cannot afford to waste even a moment.*

No, we cannot. I have adopted the daily creed of "Make today worth one week!" I have not yet lived a hundred years, but I have striven to create several hundred years of value.

*If we live our lives earnestly and to the fullest each day, we will have no regrets.*

It is about having a sense of mission. Nothing is stronger.

José Rizal (1861–96), the hero of Philippine independence, gave his life for his mission. He was executed by firing squad, but in a letter to be opened after his death, he said, "I do not regret what I have done, and if now I had to commence again I would do the same as I have done, because it was my duty."[5]

*It would be wonderful if we could all end our lives feeling that if we had to do it all again, we would walk the same path.*

To live that way requires a firm view of life and death.

What happens to us when we die? What happens to our lives? Next time, let us look at the way Buddhism answers these questions.

*All of us, at one point or another in life, wonder why we are born, why we die and what happens after death. One of our high school division members said his uncle's death really set him thinking. When he saw his uncle's lifeless form, he said, he thought it looked like a wax figure. He could not quite grasp what death meant.*

*Another student writes: "When I have a lot of problems, I wonder why I am alive—what is the point of it all. I feel so lost sometimes, so sad and hopeless about life."*

*Yet another says: "When my grandfather died, I thought about life and death. I wondered why people die so easily, just like that. I also regretted that I had not done more for my grandfather while he was alive."*

## ISSUE OF LIFE AND DEATH IS FUNDAMENTAL

To ponder the question of death in this way is extremely valuable. It proves our humanity. Generally, as people grow older and their daily lives get caught up in busy routines, they tend gradually to stop thinking about such fundamental questions. But the question of life and death is very important—something we should think about deeply throughout our lives.

If we compare our existence to a tree, we can liken the question of life and death to the tree's roots. While it may seem like we have a whole variety of problems and issues to deal with, these are no more than the leaves and branches, which are all connected to the fundamental root issue of life and death.

*Some people take the attitude "I am still young. I do not need to think about such things now. It can wait until I am old and at death's door."*

Well, perhaps we can look at it the following way: Suppose a high school freshman wants to decide on her plans and goals for her freshman year. She cannot do that meaningfully without planning for the whole duration of her high school years.

*That makes sense.*

So she tries to plan her entire high school career. But now she finds that, unless she thinks about what she is going to do after graduation, she cannot plan her high school years wisely, either.

*Yes, unless you at least have a basic idea of what you want to do when you leave school—whether it be finding a job or going on to college—you cannot really decide how best to spend your time in high school.*

In the same way, one cannot meaningfully contemplate the question of how to live life without knowing what happens after life's "graduation"— in other words, after death.

*Yes, I see what you mean.*

It is very important, then, that you become young philosophers who deeply ponder this question of life and death.

If people let the belief that there is no life after death guide them, they can easily conclude that they can do whatever they like. And when they reach a deadlock, they may even think they can be done with it all by just putting an end to their lives.

*I agree. Going back to the example of high school, if there were nothing after graduation, most high school students surely would think it pointless to study hard.*

*People who believe there is nothing after death might still make some effort to live a pleasant, enjoyable life while they are here. But they probably would not work hard to perfect themselves or serve others.*

Of course, not everyone who thinks that death is the end lives recklessly. Not only are there social restrictions against living that way, but we human beings sense deep in our hearts that life is eternal and that there is a right way to live.

*Some who believe there is no life after death also assert that precisely because this is so, we have to make the best of the present, of this one and only lifetime. But not everyone thinks this way.*

In today's world, the materialist view that there is no life after death has become prevalent. I think that is why ethics and morality have degenerated into mere pretense. Dostoyevsky, in his great novel *The Brothers*

*Karamazov*, has the character Ivan observe to the effect: "Supposing there is no God, what then would be a crime? Wouldn't all things be lawful?" If we replace "God" with "life after death," the same question holds. We would have a world where anything goes, so long as you don't get caught.

*In fact, that seems to be the way the world is heading.*

    *Some say that if death were the end, then everything in life would be empty and meaningless.*

We are beings who search for meaning in life. As long as we have meaning, we can withstand any suffering. But without meaning, we could have everything we want and still remain empty, our spirit slowly dying.

    Just as adopting the larger perspective of your entire high school career gives meaning to your freshman year, broadening your perspective to include not only this lifetime but what happens after death enables you to grasp the meaning of your life. Without a perspective that transcends death, we cannot appreciate the true meaning of our lives. That is why an understanding of life and death is so important.

*Buddhism teaches that life is eternal. In our last discussion, you described the universe as a great living entity, like a vast ocean, and each individual life as a wave on that ocean.*

    *When the wave rises on the ocean's surface, that is life. And when it merges back into the ocean, that is death.*

    *But I am still a little unclear about what that "merging" means exactly.*

Mr. Toda once said that if you drop some ink into a pond, it will dissolve and disappear. That is what death is like. Later on, if you use some device to recapture the components of the dissolved ink and bring them together again, that is life, he said.

*Though an individual life merges back into the life of the universe, its identity does not disappear.*

That individual life does not cease to exist. When it encounters the right conditions, it will become manifest once again. But if you ask whether that life exists as a tangible thing after death, the answer is absolutely not. We cannot locate it here or there in the universe. It has become one with the universe as a whole. It is neither existence nor nonexistence. In Buddhism, we refer to this as the state of non-substantiality, or emptiness.

Let me use a metaphor. Today, radio waves crisscross the globe in vast number. Electromagnetic waves of all different frequencies are flying all around us right here and now—some for radio, some for television and some for other communications. Some originate locally and some in other countries. Though we may say those waves exist, we cannot see them or hear them, smell them or touch them. But if we have a radio, a television set or some other appropriate receiver, and we tune it to the right frequency, we can hear the sounds or see the images those waves carry.

*A television set becomes the necessary condition to make an invisible wave visible in the form of a video image.*

We could perhaps call this the wave's transition from death to life. This is just a metaphor, of course. In much the same way, though, individual lives merge into the universe upon death. Like radio waves, they do not crash into or obstruct one another. And, by the same token, they do not ride on someone's back or hold hands! Each becomes one with the universe, yet retains its individuality.

## SPIRITUAL AND PHYSICAL ASPECTS ARE ONE

*Is that individuality different from the concept of a spirit or soul that is separate from the physical body?*

It is completely different. Buddhism teaches that a distinct spirit or entity such as a soul does not exist after death. In all life, mind and body—the spiritual and physical aspects—are one. Both in life and after death, an entity's physical energy and spiritual energy cannot be separated. They are one and indivisible.

The idea that the spirit can depart the body and fly about here and there after death is superstition. Life—in which the spiritual and physical energy are always one—merges into the great universal life, while preserving its individuality.

*When we die, the brain is destroyed, so how can there still be any spiritual energy? The reason that most people today think there is nothing after death is that they believe that the spirit or mind resides in the brain, and as such it cannot persist after the brain cells have died.*

That is an important point. I have gone into this question in detail on various occasions, and I hope you will study those discussions and writings, too. The crucial point is that the brain is the place, or physical vehicle, for the activity of the mind or spirit—it is not the mind or spirit itself.

For example, the great French philosopher Henri-Louis Bergson (1859–1941) compared the relationship between our brain and our consciousness to a hook and the clothes hung on it. When the hook is gone—that is, when the brain is dead—the clothes fall to the floor. In other words, mental activity becomes impossible. But the hook is not the clothes.

*Speaking of Bergson, I understand that the first time you were invited to a Soka Gakkai discussion meeting at the age of nineteen and heard that it was a gathering where people talked about "the philosophy of life," you asked, "Are you referring to Bergson?"*

Yes, that is right. Bergson was active during the late nineteenth century to the early twentieth century, a time when the metaphor of clothes and a hook would have been most fitting. Today it might be better to use the example of televised images and sound, and a television set, which is needed to make them appear.

In this scenario, memory and other mental activities are like the images and sound. They cannot appear without a television set, which we can liken to the brain. And just because your favorite actor or actress appears on television does not mean you will find a picture of him or her inside the television if you take it apart. In the same way, when the brain dies, mental or spiritual energy loses the vehicle for manifesting itself, but that does not mean that that energy itself has ceased to exist. Nor does the body's physical energy cease to exist when the body dies. It loses the vehicle for its activity and becomes latent, dormant.

*And the next time we are reborn, such latent energy becomes active again, doesn't it?*

Yes, the dormant energy is manifested and activated once more when the phase of life is entered again. However, strictly speaking, our lives are not "reborn"—they exist continuously. The identity of our lives does not change.

Our lives—in which body and mind are one—continue unchanged. The essence of life is not that of a soul that leaves the body and floats up into the sky or some specific place.

*I have heard of people who say they have seen a ghost or heard the voice of their dead grandmother. Are such experiences just dreams or illusions?*

No, those can be real experiences. But the person is not seeing a ghost. It may be that the wavelength of a person who is in the state of death resonates, for some reason, with the wavelength of the living person, and the person experiences something like a vision or the voice of the dead person. The realm of life is full of mysteries. You might think of it as similar to cases when for some reason you hear another conversation on your telephone line while you are talking to someone else.

*Yes, I sometimes find that happens when I use my cell phone.*

Mr. Toda used to say that such things as seeing ghosts or hearing voices happen when your life force is weak. Because you are weak, you are overpowered by others' signals, and you end up acting like a radio or television receiver for them. That is why you are the only one who hears or sees these things.

If your life force is strong, that will not happen. In fact, by chanting, you can send the waves of the state of Buddhahood to the other individual and help him or her find peace.

*There are some lives that do not merge peacefully into the life of the universe, then?*

Yes, some merge back into the universal life in dreadful pain and suffering. Some are terrified, as if a horrible monster were pursuing them. And some sleep restlessly as though being tormented by nightmares while sleeping.

*Can we help such individuals with our chanting?*

Yes, we can. The sound of our chanting reaches the lives of those who have entered the state of death. Of course, it also reaches those who are still alive. The power of Nam-myoho-renge-kyo can illuminate anywhere in the universe, even the farthest reaches of the state of hell, filling it with the warm light of hope, peace and comfort.

The words *Mystic Law* are composed of the characters *myo* and *ho*. *Myo*, meaning mystic, or wonderful, symbolizes death and *ho*, meaning law, symbolizes life. Together, as the Mystic Law, or *myoho*, they represent the "oneness of life and death," the two phases of our existence. Life and death may seem separate and independent of each other, but within that dynamic exists the identity of our life that is one and unchanging. It continues forever through alternating periods of life and death.

Nam-myoho-renge-kyo is the fundamental rhythm of that eternal life. Chanting Nam-myoho-renge-kyo has the power to help even those in the state of death.

# Transforming Our Basic Life-tendency

*What determines whether an individual suffers after death or is at peace? Do hell and Eagle Peak really exist?*

Yes, they do exist, but not in any one place. The state of hunger is not somewhere beyond Saturn, for instance, and Eagle Peak is not just the other side of the sun. I want you to study more about the Ten Worlds [hell, hunger, animality, anger, humanity, heaven, voice-hearers or learning, cause-awakened ones or realization, bodhisattvas and Buddhahood], but the important thing to remember is that, just as the Ten Worlds exist within each person, they exist in the universe, too.

Suppose a person has a basic tendency while alive to be in the state, or life-condition, of hell. After death, that person will merge into the universal state of hell. The state of hell exists in our lives, but we cannot say that it is any particular place within us. Just because you have a toothache, you cannot really say that the state of hell is in your tooth. Your whole being is in pain, and your whole being is in hell. In the same way, when a person whose basic life-tendency is the state of hell dies, the whole universe for that individual becomes hell.

*What do you mean by "basic life-tendency?"*

It is the core nature or inclination of your life, the "base" to which you always tend to return. Every day we are subject to many external causes and conditions that prompt a range of emotions and responses. We get angry, we laugh, we reflect. And our lives are always in a state of constant change. Nevertheless, everyone has a unique life-tendency. For instance, some people are angry by nature and quick to lose their temper. Some have a weak life force and become depressed easily. Others live in the state of bodhisattvas and always think of others first. Our basic life-tendency determines which of the Ten Worlds our lives will end up in after death.

*That sounds pretty frightening!*

After death, the external causes and conditions present in life are no longer there, so your life-tendency becomes your entire state of being. In life, even a person whose basic state is hell, who is always suffering and for whom life itself is painful, may experience moments of joy or pleasure. But after death, such a person experiences only the state of hell.

*That sure is a great motivation for doing our human revolution while we are alive!*

A person's basic life-tendency becomes clearest at the moment of death. A veteran nurse who has cared for the terminally ill and been with many of them in their final moments says: "It seems that at the end of life, your entire life flashes before your eyes, like a movie. Not your becoming president of the company or succeeding in business or things like that, but what kind of a life you lived: whom you loved and were kind to and how; in what ways you were callous or cruel; a sense of satisfaction at having lived according to your beliefs or a deep hurt at having betrayed them. All of what you were as a human being comes rushing at you. That is death."

*Hearing that really makes one stop and think.*

At that moment, not fame, money, knowledge nor status can help you. Nor can your friends or family. You must face the truth of your life alone. Death is truly strict—uncompromising.

And the self that exists at that moment of death is the one that will continue throughout the state of death and beyond into the next life. That is why Buddhism teaches that we must elevate our lives to the state of Buddhahood while we are alive. We must do our utmost to cultivate and enrich our lives as human beings. That is the purpose of Buddhist practice. Nothing is more important in life than achieving human revolution. And the younger you are, the easier it is to accomplish.

*We have more questions about life and death. One member writes: "My grandmother, whom I loved very much, has died. Will I ever be able to meet her again, after I die?"*

Nichiren Daishonin says that you can. And this is the gentle comfort he gave to a mother who had lost her child: "There is a way to meet [your deceased son] readily. With Shakyamuni Buddha as your guide, you can go to meet him in the pure land of Eagle Peak... [The Lotus Sutra teaches that] it could never happen that a woman who chants Nam-myoho-renge-kyo would fail to be reunited with her beloved child" (see WND-1, 1092).[6]

By saying that mother and child will "meet in the pure land of Eagle Peak," Nichiren is telling the bereaved mother that her deceased child has attained Buddhahood. And he assures her that since she, too, is destined to attain Buddhahood, she will be able to join her son in the same world of Buddhahood.

The word *meet*, we could say, is used here in the sense that when our lives after death fuse with the universal life, we can sense our unity or oneness with the lives of our deceased loved ones; or, in the sense that we can meet with our deceased loved ones again in the future, in some other Buddha land in the universe.

Recently, astronomers announced that there might be as many as 125 billion galaxies in the universe.[7]

*What an enormous number! Not 125 billion stars, but 125 billion galaxies. That's mind-boggling.*

But from the Buddhist perspective of the universe, even that is still far from large. An even vaster view of the universe is described in the "Life Span" chapter of the Lotus Sutra. The scale of the universe described in that chapter is so immense that we can really only take it as an attempt to express the infinite.

*Does that mean that the scientific view of the universe is beginning to approach the Buddhist view?*

Yes, I think we can say that. At any rate, the earth is certainly not the only planet on which life exists—there are a countless number of such planets in the universe.

Sometimes we may be reborn with our deceased loved ones in

the Buddha lands among those planets. Sometimes we may be reborn together on earth, or other planets on which kosen-rufu has not yet been accomplished, and there work together to help those who are suffering. The Lotus Sutra teaches that each of us can freely decide all these things.

Life is eternal. Though we say we have "lost" friends or loved ones when they die, we could just as well say that they have just gone somewhere far away where we cannot see them for awhile, as when a friend travels overseas.

*So it would also be possible for our member's deceased grandmother to be reborn here on earth, and for the two of them to meet again?*

Of course. But they probably won't recognize each other! The grandmother will be much younger. The granddaughter won't just be able to see her and say, "Hi, Grandma!"

## SUFFERING HELPS US UNDERSTAND OTHERS

When Mr. Toda was a young man, he lost one of his children. He once said: "When I was twenty-three, I lost my daughter, Yasuyo. I held my dead child in my arms all through the night. At the time, I had not yet taken faith in the Gohonzon, and I was so grief-stricken that I slept with her in my embrace.

"And so we parted, and now I am fifty-eight years old. When she died she was three, so if she were alive now, I imagine she would be a fine woman in the prime of her life. Have I or have I not met my deceased daughter again in this life? This is a matter of one's own perception through faith. I believe that I have met her. Whether one is united with a deceased relative in this life or the next is all a matter of one's perception through faith."

Mr. Toda shared this experience to encourage a member who had lost a young child. He was responding to the member's question, "Is it possible to reestablish a parent-child relationship with my deceased child again in this lifetime?"

After losing his daughter, Mr. Toda also lost his wife. He suffered enormous grief and heartache, but he said it was that very suffering which allowed him now to encourage and comfort others and, as a leader of many people, become the sort of person who understood others' feelings.

Everything that happens to us has a meaning. Though you may be sad and filled with pain to the point it seems unbearable, as long as you keep pressing forward, resolved to never give up or to never be defeated, you will come to see the meaning of that experience. That is the power of faith. It is also the essence of life.

*Yes, I understand.*

*Mr. Toda said it's "a matter of perception." By "perception," does he mean the personal feeling or awareness we have in the depths of our life?*

Yes. Life, when you get down to it, is a question of how you really feel inside. It is not a matter of theories or words. You can talk about joy and happiness all you like, but if inside you feel only sadness and despair, all your talk of happiness will be meaningless.

Likewise, though you may understand intellectually that life is eternal, such knowledge will be empty if you fail to make efforts to cause your life to shine with eternal brilliance. Only when you do so can you be said to have a real understanding of the eternity of life.

*You have explained to us that everything has a meaning, but what about people who die young in accidents or from illness? Is there a meaning to such deaths as well?*

We must give them meaning. The law of life and death is universal, applying across the cosmos. But it always manifests itself uniquely for each and every individual; the possibilities are endless. Life is tremendously complex, with many causes and conditions at work therein.

For instance, our lives are governed to a large extent by our karma, which is formed by our actions in past lifetimes. We are subject to the effects of immutable, or fixed, karma, which determines the basic path our lives will take, including how long we will live.

We are also subject to the effects of mutable, or unfixed, karma, the results of which we may or may not see in this lifetime. If we compare these two types of karma to sickness, immutable karma is like a serious or even fatal disease, while mutable karma is a slight illness, like a cold.

*Both are the results of our past actions, though, right?*

Yes, so we cannot blame anyone else for our problems. Everything we are is the result of our own actions. Some people fret about why they were born into a certain family, or why they weren't born more beautiful or more handsome, but everything is determined by their own past actions.

The word *karma* is Sanskrit for action. All of our actions—what we think, what we say and what we actually do—are engraved in our lives. When our actions are good, we will receive positive effects that make us happy. When our actions are bad, we will receive negative effects that make us unhappy. It all eventually comes back to us.

It is even quite likely sometimes that people who commit acts of terrible cruelty and inhumanity may not be reborn as human beings in their next lifetime.

*The law of cause and effect is very strict, isn't it?*

The good and bad energy engraved in one's life does not vanish at death. We carry it with us into our next lifetime. Perhaps you can think of this as being similar to the principle of the conservation of energy taught in physics.

But Nichiren Buddhism teaches us that we can change all such karma.

*Even immutable karma?*

Yes. In fact, we must change it. No matter what sufferings or hardships we may encounter, we have to live bravely and strongly, challenging them until we triumph. The person who wins in the end is a true victor in life.

Victory is not decided halfway through. If we win in the end, we can look back on everything that has occurred up to that moment and realize that it all had meaning. On the other hand, if we lose in the end, everything in our life will have been meaningless, no matter how smoothly things may have been going until then.

# WHAT MATTERS IS HOW WE LIVE OUR LIVES

*What about people who die of illness? Is that a sign of failure in life?*

No. A person who has strong and invincible faith to the very end has triumphed. There are many people who, in spite of being fatally ill and suffering greatly themselves, have prayed for kosen-rufu and the happiness of their fellow members and encouraged others right up to the very moment of death. Their lives and their bravery in the face of death have given courage and inspiration to countless others. Such people will be reborn quickly with a healthy body.

I knew a young girl who was found to have a brain tumor when she was eleven. She died at fourteen. But through it all, she was so cheerful that she even inspired the adults in the hospital. She shared her bright, positive spirit with everyone she met. No doubt her illness caused her terrible pain, but she continued to chant and to encourage others.

Toward the end, she said to one of her visitors: "As for me and my illness, whatever happens is fine. I've stopped praying for myself. There are so many others worse off than me. I pray with all my heart that they will take faith as soon as possible and find out for themselves just how wonderful the Gohonzon is."

To her parents she said: "What if this had happened to you, Dad? We'd be in terrible trouble! And it would be just as bad if it happened to you, Mom. And if it happened to my little brother, I'm sure he couldn't handle it. I'm glad that it happened to me instead of any of you... I'm sure this is the result of a promise I made before I was born. If those who know me learn something from my life, I will be happy."

I heard about this girl's struggle with illness, and I sent her roses. I also sent her a Japanese fan on which I had written the words *Light of Happiness*, as well as a photograph I had taken of a field of irises in bloom. I heard that she was overjoyed when she received them.

The words she left to those around her were "Faith means believing until the very end." And she demonstrated those words with her own life. There was a long, long line of friends and family at her funeral. In her brief fourteen-and-a-half years, she had told more than a thousand people of the greatness of the Mystic Law.

Her name was Akemi Yamada, and she was from Kashiwa City, Chiba Prefecture, Japan. [She died in October 1982.] She won. That is what I feel. Her entire life, and all her suffering, had meaning. Or rather, through her struggle, she gave meaning to her suffering.

Akemi said that her illness was the result of a promise she'd made before she was born. Buddhism teaches the concept of deliberately choosing our circumstances. This means to live based upon the view that we have boldly volunteered to be born into this world beset with suffering, so that we might demonstrate the power of Buddhism to others through our struggles and subsequent triumphs. This is the way of life of a bodhisattva.

If those with faith had every advantage from the start, people would never know the power of Buddhism. That is why we have chosen to be born amid troubled circumstances, to show others what it means to do human revolution.

It is like a play, a great drama.

*So there can be meaning to a person's death, even if that person dies in an accident or of an illness.*

All of us will die eventually. The crucial thing is how we have lived. It is important to live as long as we can, but length is not the measure of a good life. What matters most is what we have done with our lives. That is what determines whether it has been a good life.

The American journalist Dr. Norman Cousins (1915–90) said: "Death is not the greatest tragedy that befalls us in life. What is far more tragic is for an important part of oneself to die while one is still alive. There is no more terrifying tragedy than this. What is important is to accomplish something in life."[8]

Dr. Cousins was a great journalist and activist for peace. In his later years, he carried out pioneering work in the field of mind-body medicine, based on his conviction that the body and mind are one.

At any rate, the important thing is not whether our life is long or short. For us who practice Nichiren Buddhism, chanting Nam-myoho-renge-kyo—the eternal good medicine—while we are alive is itself the greatest happiness. And when we die, through our connection with Buddhism in this lifetime, we will return quickly to the grand stage of kosen-rufu. It is just as if we take a short nap to rest, and then wake up again. The same is true of those who die in accidents.

Of course, we mustn't lose our precious lives through carelessness. Thinking that we're safe from accidents just because we practice Buddhism is a kind of arrogance.

Our correct attitude in faith should be to take extra precautions against accidents and illness precisely because we are practicing Buddhism.

## REGARD EVERY DAY AS A TREASURE

*Suicide rates are high in Japanese society today.*

Yes, they are high all around the world. This is an unfortunate, heartbreaking reality. People who kill themselves feel as if they have no way out. They don't have the strength to fight, or anywhere to take refuge or find solace. But seeking escape in death does not end suffering. In fact, by destroying the treasure that is their own life, they commit a grave offense that only adds further to their misery.

Those who commit suicide feel trapped and drained of life force. But such feelings come from living essentially in opposition to the fundamental law of life, the Mystic Law. The entire universe flows in the rhythm of life and death. The largest star lives and dies, the smallest insect lives and dies. All phenomena move in the rhythm of life and death.

The foundation of all life and death is Nam-myoho-renge-kyo. That is why our life force grows weak if we act counter to the Mystic Law and grows strong if we practice the Mystic Law.

At any rate, suicide is always and absolutely wrong.

*I know a person who was depressed and had lost her reason for living because her child had died, but thanks to the encouragement and support of fellow Soka Gakkai members, she has been able to make a new start in life.*

We are a family of the Mystic Law. We are connected by the "wireless communication system" of the Mystic Law that transcends life and death. Our chanting always reaches our deceased loved ones. And, if they wish it, they can be reborn as family or friends or somewhere close by us.

Their surviving family members should be confident of this and strive to lead the happiest and most fulfilled lives. Their happiness is, in fact, eloquent testimony to their departed loved one's attainment of Buddhahood.

*So the important thing is how those left behind live the rest of their lives?*

That's right. Buddhism expounds the "oneness of life and death," and the oneness of parent and child. So if the living family members are happy, those who have died will move on a course to happiness, too. Similarly, if the family members who have died attain Buddhahood, they will be able—as part of the protective forces of the universe with which they have merged—to protect their living family members.

*We may not be able to comprehend directly what death is like, but we can get an idea from life.*

That's the idea. We may speak of life after death, but it cannot be scientifically proven. But if we practice Buddhism and receive clear actual proof of the validity of its teachings while we're alive, it makes sense for us to accept Buddhism's teachings about what happens after death as well.

*If the teachings of Buddhism weren't true, our members wouldn't see that proof demonstrated in their lives. But they certainly do.*

We all have put this practice to the test, and all of us have likewise obtained some form of actual proof that it works. That means that some kind of law or principle is at work.

The foundation of all Buddhist teachings is a view of life as eternal. If this foundation were wrong, we wouldn't have actual proof of Buddhism's effectiveness while we are alive.

*Many say, though, that it is impossible to prove the existence of life after death and that we can only know what death is like by dying.*

Well that's true—you *can* only know what death is like by dying. But what are you going to do if, after you die, you find out that Buddhism was right? It will be too late to change your life then!

*Yes, you'd miss your chance!*

*Even if, just supposing, there were no life after death, all your efforts to perfect yourself through Buddhist practice still wouldn't be wasted, because you'd end up a better person and leading a fulfilled life. Either way, you'd still come out ahead! If we think of this as a bet, it's the best bet going!*

Buddhism is absolutely not mistaken about life and death. Science is not almighty; there are many things it cannot prove. In particular, modern natural science excels at investigating things that can be observed or measured by instrumentation that extends the realm of the five senses, but it has no means for inquiring into what lies beyond that.

*Science has no means to investigate life after death.*

Therefore, the proper scientific attitude should be to withhold judgment about things that it has yet to understand. Both Goethe and Tolstoy said the same thing. So did Gandhi. Science has no authority to declare whether life exists after death or not.

*To declare without proof that life after death does not exist is arrogant.*

Yes, it is a tremendous error. No other age has been so intent on refusing to face the fact of death and so ardent in pursuing worldly desires as this age of science, the twentieth century. Yet, it is no coincidence, I believe, that this century that has forgotten death has been the century of megadeath that has seen two world wars and a nuclear arms race carrying the threat of global annihilation. We cannot possibly hope to find a basis for respect for the sanctity of life in a view of life and death that maintains that there is no life after death and that human beings are nothing but aggregations of matter.

That is why I want you, the youth, to study and spread the philosophy of the sanctity of life around the world so as to make the twenty-first century a century of peace. Study the correct view of life and death, base your actions on it, and regard each and every day as a precious, irreplaceable treasure. Fill your life with hundreds of years' worth of value and lead an invincible existence, the legacy of which will shine on brightly for all time.

1. Minamata disease: A crippling disease of the central nervous system that affected thousands of people in and around Minamata, a city in southern Kumamoto Prefecture in Kyushu. The waters off Minamata were polluted by highly toxic industrial discharges from a local carbide plant owned by Chisso Corporation. The disease resulted from consumption of seafood contaminated with high concentrations of mercury. Deaths were caused and many children were also born with terrible birth defects for years afterward as a result.

2. See Fyodor Dostoyevsky, *The Idiot*, trans. David Magarshack (London: Penguin Books, 1955), p. 57.

3. From the *Great Thoughts*, compiled by George Seldes (New York: Ballantine Books, 1985), p. 194.

4. *The Notebooks of Leonardo da Vinci*, trans. Edward McCurdy (London: Jonathan Cape Ltd., 1938), vol. 1, p. 73.

5. Carlos Quirino, *The Great Malayan—The Biography of Rizal* (Manila: Philippine Education Company, 1940), p. 258.

6. This letter was written to the widowed mother of Nanjo Tokimitsu, the lay nun Ueno, on the occasion of the sudden death of her youngest son, Shichiro Goro.

7. In 1999, the American Astronomical Society announced this number, which was based on observations made by NASA's Hubble Space Telescope.

8. Daisaku Ikeda, *Watakushi no koyuroku* (Intimate Talks With Global Pioneers) (Tokyo: Yomiuri Shimbunsha, 1996), p. 20.

# POSTSCRIPT

I love young people. When I see a young person striving to accomplish something with energy and vitality, I feel hope for the future. Joy springs from the depths of my heart. On the contrary, when I see the dull eyes of someone who has lost the heartbeat of youth, I feel concerned and want to call out to that person.

To some, that may seem like meddling. After all, we live in a time when people tend to draw a line between their own affairs and those of others, and to refrain from crossing that line.

It is my belief that things can only change when we are willing to talk directly with others, that change begins only when there is dialogue.

I was born in 1928, and am of a generation far removed from those attending high school today. So many gaps may naturally separate our awareness and ways of thinking. Nevertheless, in these dialogues, I have presented my thoughts directly and without holding back.

Today crimes and other unfortunate incidents involving teens who have lost their way continue unabated. Whenever such events reach the news, debate ranges widely as commentators search for a culprit, for someone or something to blame. Most important, however, is that adults do all they can to convey their thoughts and insights to those of the younger generation, to communicate to them their experiences, successes, failures, reflections and convictions.

If they speak directly and honestly about these things, they can impart to young people the courage to overcome their suffering and worry. It is with this point in mind that I have conducted these *Discussions on Youth*. Today I am in the midst of conducting a series of dialogues directed toward middle school students titled "Dialogue of Hope."

Youth is a battlefield upon which suffering and hope contend. Which will win? Hope must prevail by all means! That is because, no matter how great your suffering may be, you were born to win. So long as you do not lose hope, dawn will definitely come. Within your heart is hidden an "invincible jeweled sword" that can cut through any trouble or worry.

In any event, I have said what I needed to say. From here, it is up to you to decide how you are going to live.

If even a single statement in this book strikes a chord in your heart, I will be happy.

**Daisaku Ikeda**
*August 24, 2000*

# APPENDIX A

## You Are the Hope of the World

**This installment features a discussion among SGI President Ikeda, SGI-USA youth division and high school division leaders. It appeared in the February 9, 2000, issue of *Koko Shimpo*, the biweekly newspaper of the Soka Gakkai high school division.**

*The high school division members in the United States have been very encouraged by the "Discussions on Youth" series. There are some specific issues that the youth of America want to ask you about.*

*These are universal issues faced by youth in America today. We are talking about juvenile crime and violence, relationships, and drugs and alcohol.*

*If not grappling with these issues themselves, our members are wondering how they can encourage others in such situations.*

The fact that you are seriously thinking about and trying to find a solution to your problems and those of your friends is in itself a sign that you are moving forward.

Of course, each person has a unique set of problems. And given that I cannot meet with you in person and hear the details of your individual situations, it may be difficult for me to fully appreciate what you're going through and offer satisfactory advice. In addition, what I say may not apply specifically to your particular problem. Nevertheless, in the hopes that it may be of some help in solving your problems, I will share my thoughts with you.

In any case, when it comes to getting specific advice on individual problems, please talk to someone close by whom you can trust.

I am ready to do anything for you, if it will lift your spirits even a bit. In fact, I wish I could fly to America right now and relieve you of your problems and encourage you. This is how I truly feel.

America is a land of freedom. But along with the sometimes dizzying freedom that can be found there, there is also a deep, impenetrable darkness. America is a microcosm of the world. This is where you live.

In a way, we could say that your problems represent the problems of all humanity. In that respect, your victory will open the way to victory for the youth of the entire world. It will also illuminate the path along which humanity must advance in the twenty-first century. You are the hope of America and the world!

## VIOLENCE IS AN ABSOLUTE EVIL

*Thank you, President Ikeda, for your high expectations.*

*Our members are struggling hard in situations that can be pretty tough. One problem in particular has been the upsurge in violence among youth. Because violence is rampant in their schools and communities, many young people have no hope and are living in fear.*

*I was shocked by the shooting that took place last April [1999] at Columbine High School in Colorado, in which thirteen students were killed by two classmates.*

*A student at another school complained that vandalism and violence is rampant on campus, and that there had even been a bomb threat. She said she found going to school very depressing.*

*Some members have said they have friends who are into violence, and that they are saddened when they see some of those people boasting about having beaten someone up.*

Nothing pains and saddens me more than to see young people—who possess such infinite potential for the future—physically harming and killing one another.

When I was around the same age as those who are in the high school division now, I lost my eldest brother in World War II. He was a kind, gentle person. Expressing his grave personal doubts about the validity of Japan's invasion of China, he told me: "Japan's behavior is abominable. What we are doing to the Chinese is unforgivable."

I will never forget how my mother took the news of his death. It was unbearably painful to look at her small back turned to us in silence, as she stifled her sobs. At that time, I vowed to fight to eliminate war and violence from the world.

Violence is an absolute evil. You lose if you resort to violence, regardless of the reason. You may think you have beaten your opponent, but ultimately you have lost. For when you harm another, you actually harm yourself. When it comes down to it, people who readily use violence and have no respect for others' lives have no respect for their own lives.

*The Columbine shooting ended with the two gunmen killing themselves. Following the tragic incident, President Clinton issued the following statement: "We must do more to reach out to our children and teach them to express their anger and resolve their conflicts with words, not weapons."* [1]

I agree. The essence of violence is cowardice. It is because they are cowardly that people rely on brute force. They lack the courage to pursue dialogue.

Nonviolence is an expression of real courage. It takes more courage to pursue the path of nonviolence than it does to use violence. Mahatma Gandhi stated: "Non-violence is not a cover for cowardice, but it is the supreme virtue of the brave... Cowardice is wholly inconsistent with non-violence... Non-violence presupposes ability to strike." [2] A willingness to engage in dialogue is a sign of a thinking person.

Of course, responsibility for the prevalence of violence in our world today falls on society's leaders—on adults, including politicians, educators and people in the mass media. But nothing will change by simply criticizing them. It is up to you, the youth, to stand up with the determination to create a different society from now on. The important thing is that you begin to take nonviolent action, starting in your immediate environment.

What do you do, for instance, when you see a friend heading down the wrong path? If you really care about that friend, then you should stand by him or her. I hope you will be a good friend who not only listens attentively to what your friends have to say, but who can come out and tell them when needed: "What you're doing is wrong" or "Don't throw away your life." In his writings, Nichiren Daishonin cites the famous words: "If one befriends another person but lacks the mercy to correct him, one is in fact his enemy" (WND-1, 287).

Of course, you'll have to use wisdom in getting your message across. There's no other way. And to find the wisdom, you have to chant earnestly for your friends, praying that they will change their ways and get back on track. When you chant Nam-myoho-renge-kyo, courage will rise within you, and wisdom will well forth, enabling you to think of different ways to encourage them.

More important, you will become a person who genuinely wishes for your friends' happiness. If you are truly sincere, your friends will one day understand your intentions. Even if they resent what you say and stop being friends with you for a time, your deep concern for their well-being will stay with them. Your sincerity will bear fruit some day, and your friends will realize that what you were saying was true.

## Violence Stems From the World of Animality

*I was asked by a student about what she could do to stop her friend from stealing. She knows a number of students who steal.*

*I also knew many students in high school who stole from others. They broke into people's cars and houses. Some of them did it simply to prove they had the guts to. They always urged me to join in. When I told them what they were doing was wrong, they just laughed at me.*

*One day in high school, I finally gave in to the pressure from a friend of mine, and we broke into a video game arcade after all the employees went home, hoping that we could play some games for free. Unfortunately, an employee returned to the store just as we were about to leave. We quickly hid behind one of the machines, afraid that he would find us. We stayed there for about fifteen minutes, but it felt like an hour. After he left, we made our escape.*

*When I got home, I chanted desperately that I wouldn't be arrested. I also chanted for the courage never to do such a stupid thing again and for my friend to quit doing such things. I then talked to him about it and urged him not to break the law anymore. I think he may have felt bad about pressuring me into going that night and nearly getting me into trouble. After that, he stopped breaking into places and even helped me persuade others to stop doing the same.*

*I am now a high school teacher, and based upon that experience, I always tell my students that efforts to encourage others are never wasted.*

*Friendship halves our suffering and doubles our joy.*

*I was once discouraged when I felt that I was being treated unfairly. At that time, a friend of mine encouraged me not to get sidetracked and reminded me of my goals. Supported by this friendship, I felt I could overcome my difficulty and achieve my dreams. Above all, my greatest source of strength was my resolve to live the way of mentor and disciple.*

*When I was going through a hard time once, a senior in faith sent me a postcard. All he wrote on it was "Keep fighting for your dream!" Those words filled me with fresh determination.*

Friendship is the most beautiful of human bonds. It is a relationship that transcends gain and loss. It is not something superficial, nor is it merely to feel sympathy or pity for another person. It is a relationship where, no matter what happens to the other person, you still care about him or her from the bottom of your heart. Friendship is a precious, irreplaceable human treasure.

I hope that you will forge such friendship with one person after another. It may seem like a small thing, but war and violence can be banished from the earth when a network of such friendship enfolds the world.

Of course, efforts to control violence by external measures such as the elimination of destructive weapons, the establishment of more adequate laws and the signing of treaties between nations are also important. But violence stems from the condition of animality that is inherent in life. Even if we eliminate all weapons from the face of the earth, violence will never disappear unless we successfully control the animality within us. That is why transforming ourselves from within is so important.

Nuclear weapons embody the ultimate form of violence. Back in 1957, my mentor, second Soka Gakkai president Josei Toda, called on us youth to fight against the use of nuclear weapons. He not only insisted that all such weapons of mass destruction must be abolished but taught us about the need to rip out the claws of the demonic nature inherent in human life.

Nichiren says: "Life is the foremost of all treasures. It is expounded that even the treasures of the entire major world system cannot equal the value of one's body and life. Even the treasures that fill the major world system are no substitute for life" (WND-1, 1125). Our lives are more precious than all the treasures in the universe. The sanctity of life is the basis of Buddhist philosophy. It is vital that more and more people in the world embrace this fundamental belief.

*Based on the ideals promoted by the SGI, the SGI-USA youth division has been carrying out the Victory Over Violence campaign, calling on the youth of America to put the following four-point pledge into action: "I will value my own life; I will respect all life; I will actively pursue dialogue; and I will inspire hope in others."*

*As we each become able to cherish our own lives, we will naturally value the lives of others around us as well. Many young people are supporting this campaign. A number of schools have requested that SGI-USA youth give lectures on nonviolence to their students.*

That's wonderful. In any event, the important thing is that you do something, that you start something. Nothing comes from nothing. Zero remains forever zero. But one step can lead to infinite growth. One can become two, three and even tens of thousands. There is a saying in the East that one is the mother of ten thousand (see WND-1, 131).

# VIOLENCE AGAINST WOMEN IS DESPICABLE

*We also must bring an end to sexual violence against women, which inflicts immeasurable pain and suffering on its victims.*

Nothing is more despicable than violence against women. It is absolutely unforgivable. I want all men to remember this.

Unfortunately, there is a general trend in society today that encourages sexual promiscuity and violence. Such a trend also exists in Japan. But the thing is not to fall victim to it. I hope men will be gentlemen at all times. They are a disgrace if they behave otherwise. It's also important that women exercise wisdom and caution, taking utmost care to protect themselves.

I can only imagine the incredible physical and mental agony that women who are victims of sexual assault must suffer. Though you may perhaps lose trust in others, or feel defiled and broken, please remember that no one can destroy who you are. No matter how badly you have been hurt, you remain as pure as fresh snow.

Buddhism teaches that the lotus flower grows in muddy water. What this means is that our supremely noble lives continue to shine even amid the harshest of life's realities, just like the pure white lotus flower that blooms unsoiled by the mud.

Having gone through what you have, there is pain and suffering in others' hearts that only you can notice. Having suffered what you have, there is true love and affection that only you can find. There are definitely people out there who need you. If you give up on yourself, it is only you who will lose.

Nothing, no matter what happens, can change your inherent worth. Please have courage. Please tell yourself that you are not going to let this ordeal defeat you.

Those who have suffered the most, those who have experienced the greatest sadness, have a right to become the happiest of all. What would the purpose of our Buddhist practice be if the most miserable could not become happy? The tears you shed cleanse your life and make it shine.

To live with this conviction and keep moving ever forward is the spirit of Buddhism. It is also the essence of life.

You may not want to tell someone else about your pain and anguish, but I strongly recommend that you consult with someone you can trust —even just one person—and whose confidentiality you can rely on. You should not suffer all by yourself.

Nichiren states, "Chanting Nam-myoho-renge-kyo is what is meant by entering the palace of oneself" (OTT, 209). The precious palace of life is nothing other than the life-state of the Buddha. Even an atomic bomb cannot destroy this inner palace. Please use life's painful experiences to open up this palace of happiness within your life.

*You're talking about the palace of Buddhahood, aren't you?*

Buddhahood is an inexhaustible wellspring of infinite potential. You can draw from it and draw from it, and it will never run dry.

Buddhism expounds the principle of "three thousand realms in a single moment of life." This principle holds that each life-moment is endowed with three thousand different functions, which influence not only our own lives but those of all around us; they also influence society, our natural environment and the earth. They encompass the entire universe.

Therefore, once you have decided to do something, the three thousand functions and your entire being start working to help you reach your goal. The entire universe also starts moving toward the fulfillment of your goal. If you pray, "This is how I want to be," and continue to work toward your dream, you will gradually realize the future you have envisaged.

An ascending life, where you keep striving to grow and improve, is what we mean by human revolution. Human revolution doesn't mean becoming something special or different from who you are; it simply means striving to improve yourself, no matter what challenges you face.

Your future self does not exist in some far-off place; it exists in the heart and mind of your present self. That is why you have to face and tackle the realities that confront you. Just wishing to be a certain way and not making any concrete efforts will get you nowhere.

*Faith enables us to turn our dreams into reality.*

What is true success in life? It is winning in the struggle with oneself. Those who hold fast to their beliefs, even though they may be persecuted or thrown in jail by unjust authorities, are victors in life—just as we see in the examples of first Soka Gakkai president Tsunesaburo Makiguchi and his disciple, Josei Toda, who were imprisoned for their opposition to Japanese militarism during World War II.

People who are successful in society are not necessarily the ultimate winners in life. Money, fame and position—none of these things last. Human worth cannot be judged by such superficial criteria.

There are many people who, though not rich or famous, are living their lives honestly and sincerely for the benefit of their families and society at large. Many of your mothers and fathers are such great ordinary people. I hope you will remember this.

## Unwanted Pregnancy Is a Tragedy

*I think that women need the wisdom to protect themselves in intimate relationships with men.*

*A member once asked me: "What can I do to help my friends? One recently got pregnant, while another isn't thinking about the fact that she could get pregnant by her boyfriend or catch a sexually transmitted disease." I grew up in an area where there are many teen pregnancies. When I was in junior high, I knew three girls who got pregnant. One of them was an excellent student with good grades. I wish these young women could have had access to proper sex education and someone they could talk to frankly about anything.*

*When I was in high school, two of my classmates also became pregnant. One had an abortion, a traumatic experience for her both physically and emotionally. The other girl gave birth to her baby, and she ended up quitting school. Young people tend to feel invincible, thinking that no matter what they do, things will be all right. But no one can escape the law of cause and effect.*

*I heard another account of a junior high school girl who gave birth. At first, everyone offered encouragement and fussed over her baby. But eventually they drifted away, because their parents feared that they might follow the same path. The girl who had the baby found herself all alone.*

*This kind of thing happens all the time. A member told me that her boyfriend wants to have sex with her and asked me what she should do.*

*I don't think love means doing whatever your partner wants. Love can easily make us blind. So I'm worried that some teenagers will become carried away by the passion of the moment and wind up deeply hurt.*

Your stories make my heart ache. Unwanted pregnancy is a tragedy.

In your teens, you become curious about many things. And it's only natural for you to develop an interest in sex. But if you just go wherever your curiosity takes you, you could end up having lifelong regrets. Not only do you risk being hurt physically and emotionally, but you may lose many of the opportunities of youth.

Your teens are a time to build the foundation of your life. Your body and mind are still flexible, and you can readily absorb all sorts of things. It is a time when you can acquire all kinds of learning and skills. If you so desire, you can open the road to any future you wish.

It would be a terrible pity if you were to cast aside this freedom. You would also be doing a great disservice to your parents and to all who have come before you, who made it possible for you to have the opportunities that you do today.

The American civil rights heroine Rosa Parks makes the observation: "Our school system in America makes it very easy to get an education. Even if the buildings are old and the textbooks worn, the opportunity to learn is there. There were people who fought and died, even before the modern civil rights movement began, so that all of you would have that opportunity. We must not let their struggle and sacrifice be in vain."[3] I totally agree with her.

So, bearing this in mind, if you start going out with someone, I hope you will have a relationship that is appropriate for your age. I hope you will strive for a relationship in which you both encourage and support each other in reaching your future goals and help each other grow and develop.

*Helping each other grow and develop is important, isn't it?*

I ask men to always treat women with respect and women to possess the resolute strength not to be swept away.

If your boyfriend truly loves and cares for you, he will not force you to do anything that you don't want to. Quite often, by firmly saying no, you can discover whether or not your partner's feelings are genuine.

As for the question about the young woman who found herself with an unwanted pregnancy, I think it's important that her friend stand by her in true friendship. Offering sympathy is easy, but sympathy only goes so far. It may make her feel better for a while, but it won't help her get back on her feet and rebuild her life. Remember that your friend is probably hurting badly and feeling lost. So, while being careful to respect her wishes, please continue to warmly support and encourage her.

*I think one of the reasons that teenagers become sexually active is that there is a general idea in society that premarital sex is a good way for couples to find out whether they are compatible before marriage, rather than discovering later that they aren't and ending up in divorce. Teens are also influenced by the pleasure-seeking culture in which they live and which is manufactured by self-serving adults.*

*Another factor is commercialism that operates on the belief that there is money to be made by exploiting people's baser urges. Even many adults are confused about where they should place the highest value.*

## ALCOHOL AND DRUGS ARE THE MOST DANGEROUS TRAP

*The fact that alcohol and drugs are a serious problem in American schools is also a reflection of the problems in adult society. Many students think drinking alcohol is cool. Many start drinking because all their friends do and end up becoming alcoholics.*

*When I was in high school, some of my classmates drank. He was a popular guy in class, always joking around and even making the teacher laugh. We all thought he was a really cool guy. Some time later, we stopped seeing him at school. After graduation, I found out that he had become an alcoholic.*

I can understand young people wanting to be adventurous and do something different from their everyday routine. But drinking and taking drugs are definitely not a "cool" adventure, nor are they the epitome of freedom. They are far from it. They in fact represent the greatest trap you can fall into and ultimately deprive you of freedom. Why? Because you become a prisoner of your impulses, emotions and desires. It is an animalistic way to live.

A Buddhist teaching urges, "Become the master of your mind rather than let your mind master you" (WND-1, 502). It encourages us to be the boss, exercising control over our minds, our thoughts and feelings—not to simply act on every impulse. People who blindly follow their desires may appear to enjoy freedom, but ultimately they lose their freedom altogether.

*When I was in college, I knew a guy who was a talented classical guitarist. When I first heard him play, I was deeply impressed. I remember thinking, "Wow, this guy is the same age as I am and so talented!" At that time, I was struggling, trying to figure out which direction I should pursue in life. In contrast, he seemed to shine with brilliance and promise.*

*I later found out that he had a drug problem. By the time graduation rolled around, he was not the same person. He had lost his drive and energy, as well as his dreams for the future. I, on the other hand, was on my way to graduate school, filled with a sense of purpose and determination. How our situations had changed in only a few short years! I can clearly say that drugs were his downfall. From that experience, I resolved to help others avoid the same tragedy.*

When you're under the influence of alcohol or drugs, it's like you're dancing in a dream. But when you wake from the dream, harsh reality awaits you. In addition, no matter how cool people who drink or take drugs may look, any strength or ability they show is not their own; it is the work of the alcohol or the drug.

In my opinion, the truly cool are those who continue to make steady efforts to fulfill their dreams, even if their dedication goes unnoticed and unrecognized by others. A person of self-control is free in the truest sense. It is therefore vital that you continue to challenge achieving your goals.

*Yes, I feel that one of the reasons for the upsurge in violence and other seri-*
*ous juvenile problems is that many young people don't have specific goals in*
*life. Or, if they do have goals, the goals tend to be extremely short-term and*
*mainly focused on gratifying immediate desires. Many young people make*
*no time to reflect on themselves or ask themselves questions such as "What do*
*I want to do before I reach twenty?" "What can I achieve?" or "How can I*
*contribute to society?" Because they have no long-term goals, their actions are*
*governed by their moment-to-moment emotions.*

## THOSE WITH A DREAM WILL NOT BE SWAYED

That is simply living on impulse and animal instinct. One thing that
sets humans apart from other animals is that we cherish dreams and
hopes for the future. If you have a big dream, it can prevent you from
being swayed by trivial things. Even if you should experience a temporary setback along the way and think you cannot go on, the important
thing is to keep moving forward without giving up.

What is failure in life? Making mistakes does not signal failure,
but giving up on yourself when you've made mistakes or are feeling
discouraged does. Not getting back on your feet when you've suffered a
setback or disappointment—that is failure. True victors are those who
get up again each time that they fall down.

I believe you all know Orlando Cepeda, who was a major league
baseball player. Last year [1999], in what was a great personal victory,
he was finally inducted to the Baseball Hall of Fame.

*Mr. Cepeda played professional baseball for seventeen years, mainly with the*
*San Francisco Giants. He gained fame as a great power hitter.* [4]
*Everybody thought he would easily make the Hall of Fame. But things*
*took a turn for the worse after he retired from baseball and was arrested on*
*drug-related charges.*
*You cannot gain entry into the Hall of Fame just by having a superb*
*baseball record. You must also possess an exemplary record off the field. When*
*Mr. Cepeda was arrested, he lost everything.*
*However, in 1982, when his life hit rock bottom, he encountered*

*Nichiren Buddhism. From that moment on, he began to challenge himself anew. He devoted himself not only to changing his own life but also to helping young people get back on the right track. His efforts and contributions to society were taken into consideration and, in what many have described as a miracle, he was finally inducted into the Hall of Fame last year [1999].*

*Mr. Cepeda sent a message to the youth division of Japan last year. He states: "Because of President Ikeda's guidance, I have always been able to live my life dedicated to the pursuit of a noble human goal. As I continued to break through my inner darkness, I learned to work not only for myself but also for others. Please devote yourself to SGI activities, study President Ikeda's guidance and chant Nam-myoho-renge-kyo. Your potential is limitless. Please don't give up, no matter what. As long as you embrace this faith, you can make the impossible possible. I have been telling myself the same thing. I had nothing when I first began to practice Nichiren Buddhism. Now I have gained so much. I have become a much broader person. I have won over myself. We are indeed most fortunate to have a mentor in life like President Ikeda."* [5]

When I met Mr. Cepeda, I was impressed by his strong faith and conviction.

Answers and solutions to the problems and sufferings of youth do not suddenly appear. But it's vital that you do not run away from your problems, and that you have the courage to continue facing them. Even though you may not find an answer to your problems right away, please continue to tackle them squarely.

By doing so, you will find some day that you already have the answer. Therefore, the important thing is your sense of mission and the causes you decide to champion.

When I met with Dr. Allen Sessoms, president of Queens College, The City University of New York, on January 18, he commented that American youth used to have clear causes to fight for, "enemies" to fight against. They had targets to focus on, such as the Vietnam War or bad government or racial discrimination. But today, he noted, the causes that youth should direct their energies toward are getting harder to identify.

As a result, the youth lack positive outlets for expressing their passion. In reality, there are many causes—quite large ones in fact—that they should take up, such as environmental degradation, overpopulation and poverty. But it is not easy for youth to recognize them as causes without good knowledge of them, Dr. Sessoms said.

All sorts of injustice and evil still exist in the world. It is the mission of youth to fight against them. Strong are those who have resolved to create a better world than the one in which they now live. Such a sense of mission elevates your life.

In 2001, the Orange County campus of Soka University of America will open. Its mottoes are: "Be philosophers of a renaissance of life," "Be world citizens in solidarity for peace" and "Be the pioneers of a global civilization."

I hope that young people will gather from all over the United States and the world to study on this campus, and that from this campus, they will set out into the world once more. I hope that many future Nobel laureates will appear from among their ranks. I also hope that those of you who may not be able to study at this school will somehow support those who do.

It is my hope that you, the youth of America, will appreciate the significance of having this university in your country—a university that will serve as a great center for peace in the new millennium.

Please remember that your fellow members in Japan and the entire world—and all the members of humanity—are waiting for you, the youth of America, who embrace the great philosophy of the Mystic Law.

Youth of the world! I call on you to take care of everything in the twenty-first century!

1. *National Catholic Reporter,* November 12, 1999 issue.

2. Mohandas K. Gandhi, *Gandhi on Non-violence: Selected Texts From Mohandas K. Gandhi's Non-violence in Peace and War,* ed. by Thomas Merton (New York: A New Directions Paperbook, 1965), p. 36.

3. Rosa Parks, with Gregory J. Reed, *Dear Mrs. Parks: A Dialogue with Today's Youth* (New York: Lee & Low Books, Inc., 1996), p. 52.

4. In 1958, Mr. Cepeda was named the Rookie of the Year. In 1967, he was voted the Most Valuable Player of the National League. He hit a total of 379 home runs during his playing career and was a seven-time All-Star. He was one of the most feared hitters in major league baseball in the 1960s.

5. Message sent to the Saitama Culture General Meeting on September 12, 1999.

# APPENDIX B

## YOUTH ARE STRUGGLING BETWEEN PROBLEMS AND HOPES

**On the afternoon of February 28, 2000, at the Hyogo Culture Center in Kobe, SGI President Ikeda, founder of the Soka school system, took commemorative photographs with students of the Kansai Soka Elementary School, the Kansai Soka Junior High School and the Kansai Soka High School, who would graduate in March 2000. On that occasion, he offered the students encouragement and fielded questions from several of the high school students.**

You have really worked hard during your time at school. Today, I want you to be completely at ease, as if in your own home. Please take off your jackets, sit comfortably and relax.

If any of you have a question you want to ask me, please feel free to do so. Just think of me as your dad.

## THE JOINT STRUGGLE OF MENTOR AND DISCIPLE

Does anyone have a question?

*I do. Thank you for taking a picture with us today. It was my wish to learn about the spirit of the shared struggle of mentor and disciple while I was in high school. With that in mind, I have spent a lot of time reading your essays and other writings. I know that I'm still young, but I am determined to try to match your spirit, even if only a little, and work for peace.*

Thank you! Actually, you don't have to worry too much about such things right now. When I speak sternly about the importance of disciples striving with the same spirit as their mentor, I am addressing adults. I am particularly strict toward those who, having gained important positions through the support and assistance of many people, forget their debt of gratitude, grow arrogant, betray their benefactors, and do bad things.

You have your whole life ahead of you. I want you to concentrate on studying now. Think about getting better grades on your examinations. That is your personal shared struggle of mentor and disciple at this time in your life.

Study hard, so that your parents will say with pleasure: "Your grades are improving. That's great. You've done well." That will make me the happiest of all.

Don't worry about reading my writings—spend that time reading your textbooks instead!

Have you decided where you're going to college yet?

*Soka University.*

Is that so? That's wonderful. Thank you for choosing the university that I founded!

You don't need to have a deep understanding of the joint struggle of mentor and disciple just yet. Let's talk about this some more when you're a university student.

Please be true to yourself. That's enough.

*Yes, I will. Thank you.*

All right, who's next? You don't have to stand up.

*President Ikeda, what is your dream?*

I'm so busy that I don't have time to think about dreams! I'm always thinking about the world.

Actually, dreams are the unique birthright of human beings. A life without dreams is gray and colorless. A person who has no dreams cannot accomplish anything great and often ends up as a loser.

Please have dreams! Have hopes and aspirations!

Effort is what determines whether or not your dreams come true. There are times, however, when social conditions are so bad that you cannot realize your dreams. Or there may be karmic elements, things you cannot see that still prevent you from achieving your goals.

Though not all your dreams may come true, I hope that you will still always live with some dream in your heart. This is what youth is all about. And having dreams is the sign of a person who will continue to grow throughout life. Any dream is fine. Please possess your own dream, one that matches your unique character.

My dream is to realize the dream of Mr. Toda. He is my mentor, a fact that will absolutely never change. The Buddhist Law is not a manmade thing, something that can be either proven or denied by reasoning alone. It is an absolute law, the unchanging law of the universe, something as inevitable as the rising of the sun and moon, the coming of day and night.

Nam-myoho-renge-kyo is the essence of that universal law. The entire universe moves in the rhythm of Nam-myoho-renge-kyo. My mentor and I are linked together by the rhythm of Nam-myoho-renge-kyo. And that is why I must realize his dream and ideals, why I must keep exerting myself.

Unless your dream is something that will truly contribute to your growth and self-improvement, it can end up simply being selfish and egoistic, an empty wish. A noble dream encompasses happiness, truth, altruism and peace. It is, in fact, in the pursuit of these goals—happiness, truth, altruism and peace—that we formulate dreams of genuine value and meaning.

*I understand.*

Take care of yourself. Students determine the worth of a school, not its teachers or public opinion. It all depends on the students. This was the profound insight of Mr. Makiguchi and Mr. Toda, who were both educators—and it is the conclusion of leading thinkers the world over. People may say, "That school follows such-and-such a system, so it's a great school," but that's not true.

*I throw the javelin on the track team. Thank you for your constant encouragement!*

No, thank you. Is your mother well?

*Yes. She has been delivering the* Seikyo Shimbun *[the Soka Gakkai's daily newspaper] for twenty years now.*

That's wonderful! Please thank her for me. Please be good to both your parents!

Does anyone else have a question?

*Yes. During my three years in high school, I was deeply impressed by the words "Difficulties and hopes coexist in our lives, and when you challenge yourself, new opportunities arise."[1] Do you have a quote or motto that is your favorite?*

I want to present you with these words now: "Win in your endeavors!" Please do not let yourself be defeated, giving in to despair and feelings of insecurity. Everything in life is a struggle. If you win, life is wonderful, and you feel great. If you lose, you feel awful.

Any goal is fine. The important thing is to strive toward it, triumphing in each challenge along the way.

Winning doesn't mean getting rich or becoming important. There are many rich and important people who succumb to negative influences and grow corrupt. Such people cannot be said to have won in life.

True victory is winning over your own mind. Others' opinions don't matter. Nor is there any need for you to compare yourself with others. A genuine victor in life is one who can declare: "I lived true to myself, and I have won! I am a spiritual victor!"

Please remember that.

## Learning About Life in a Dormitory

*I live in a dormitory. I am indebted to my dorm mom and dorm dad and many others for all they have done for me during my stay there. How do I convey my appreciation?*

I am also grateful to all who help run our school dormitories. Living in a dorm can be very educational; it can teach you important lessons that will stand you in good stead in the future.

How can you express your gratitude to those in the dorm who have taken care of you in so many ways? The only answer is with sincerity. Sincerity is the most important quality you can have. This is my personal belief. Nothing compares with sincerity.

Yesterday [February 27, 2000], I met with Rector Adolfo Torres of Argentina's Universidad Nacional del Nordeste. He is a fine human being. Leading world thinkers and first-rate people are always completely honest. They never try to trick or manipulate others. They have shining characters and rich humanity. All of their actions are marked by sincerity. Those who are sincere are the most worthy of respect.

Our society is rife with jealousy and envy. The sincere may be deceived and taken advantage of. They may be maligned. Or, when they try to explain the purity of their motives, no one may pay them any heed. But there is a saying—a little old-fashioned, I know—that "Sincerity is communicated to Heaven." This means that if you act with sincerity, your intent will reach the heavens, and you will have good results.

People who possess sincerity of conviction cannot be defeated. They will live without regrets.

Fun and games are ephemeral pleasures. And you cannot count on the opinions of others. It all comes down to you. You have to live with integrity and be honest with yourself.

Both Mr. Makiguchi and Mr. Toda, incidentally, acknowledged

the educational aspect of dormitory life. Almost all students in Japan's prewar high schools [corresponding to present-day universities] lived in dormitories. In dorms, you experience living with other students, forming strong bonds of friendship and going through the trials and tests of friendship along the way.

In some cases, experiencing dorm life in one's youth can be more educational than classroom education. Of course, the things you learn in the classroom are important, but in a dormitory you can get an education about people.

Both Oxford and Cambridge universities in England have student dorms. In fact, I once visited Cambridge University in England with my wife [in May 1972]. While there, I asked to see the dormitories. The people at Cambridge seemed a little surprised at my request, but they responded gladly. A professor guided us, and, when we entered the dormitory from the garden, we found two students hurriedly straightening their room for their unexpected visitors. They were fine young men. All of the students in the dormitory were talented people who would go on to be future leaders in their fields.

I also talked at some length with those who ran the dormitories about various aspects of the significance of dormitories in education.

I am of the opinion that if parents love their children, they will let them leave home and learn independence. Today in Japan, many children who are doted on by their parents and grow up in what seem to be very good families end up failing when they enter society. I think this is because they have been raised to be too dependent.

It may seem desirable to grow up at home, being spoiled and pampered by your parents. But in reality, it is not desirable. By contrast, a child that is "toughened up" a little by life in a dormitory tends to be strong and a success in society. That is why educational institutions that produce world leaders have them experience dormitory life.

Many of our Soka Junior and Soka High School students who live in dorms are wonderful students. Many people who have experienced dormitory life have gone on to be great men and women, shining and strong. In this regard, also, I have the highest respect for all those who run our dormitories. They are taking care of my "sons" and "daughters"—I am grateful to them.

ddressing the students, President Ikeda went on to say: "I applaud those of you who have been active in school club activities and team sports. You have helped build our schools' tradition. I know you really challenged yourselves, and I wholeheartedly praise these efforts of your youth." He then presented the members of the baseball team with a box of new baseballs.

President Ikeda also presented candy necklaces to students who had lost their mothers or fathers. The other students warmly applauded as he did so. Praising students who had studied diligently in spite of struggling with various hardships, the Soka schools' founder said: "I will solemnly pray again for the deceased parents of all our students. Some of you may have parents who are ill. I will pray for your parents' health and long life."

He told the students about the ceremony the previous day, in which he was awarded an honorary doctorate by Argentina's Universidad Nacional del Nordeste, saying that "a representative of the university proclaimed that the title of honorary doctorate is the jeweled crown of highest knowledge. I always regard any award I receive as the result of the activities of our Soka University and Soka schools graduates around the world. I hope that in the future, all of you will become fine scholars and leaders. That is my greatest personal dream."

## CHOOSE BOOKS OVER TELEVISION

As he rose to go, President Ikeda continued to encourage the students as long as time would permit.

To a student wearing glasses, he said: "Don't make your eyes any worse. If you cause lasting damage to your eyes, you will regret it later. Don't watch television too long. It will hurt your eyes. Spend that time reading instead."

To a student who had a long commute to school, President Ikeda said: "I know it's hard to travel so far to school, but everything in your life is part of your training and will make you stronger."

To all the students, he said: "Youth is a time when you worry and agonize over all kinds of problems. It is also a time when you can soar with energy and enthusiasm—a time to burn with hopes and dreams. Youth is a struggle between problems and hopes.

"You mustn't let your problems defeat you and ruin your life. Please don't make your parents and your family sad. Those who triumph over their problems and advance in the direction of hope lead wonderful lives.

"No one is free from problems. Everyone has them, to a greater or lesser degree. Having problems is a natural part of life. The important thing is not to let them defeat you. And do not forget to do what you have to do now—whether it is to study or earn a degree or certificate—so that you do not put yourself at a disadvantage in the future."

1. Chinese Tang-dynasty poet Wang Po (Wang Bo; 649–76).

# GLOSSARY

**benefit** (Jpn *kudoku*) In Buddhism, the increase in virtuous qualities and other gains one experiences in life as a result of Buddhist practice. Nichiren identifies the character *ku* with extinguishing evil and *doku* with bringing forth good. He also identifies benefit with the positive results of purifying one's mind and other faculties through the practice of chanting Nam-myoho-renge-kyo.

**bodhisattva** (Skt) A being who aspires to attain Buddhahood and carries out altruistic practices to achieve that goal. Compassion predominates in bodhisattvas, who postpone their own entry into nirvana in order to lead others toward enlightenment. In contemporary terms, it refers to a Buddhist practitioner who is sincerely devoted to working for the happiness and growth of both self and others.

**Bodhisattvas of the Earth** Those who chant and propagate Nam-myoho-renge-kyo. *Earth* indicates the enlightened nature of all people. The term describes the innumerable bodhisattvas who appear in the "Emerging from the Earth" chapter of the Lotus Sutra and are entrusted by Shakyamuni with the task of propagating the Law after his passing. In several of his writings, Nichiren Daishonin identifies his own role with that of their leader, Bodhisattva Superior Practices.

**Buddha**  One awakened to the eternal and ultimate truth that is the reality of all things, and who leads others to attain the same enlightenment. Nichiren Buddhism recognizes the potential of every person to become a Buddha.

**Buddhist gods**  Also known as heavenly gods and benevolent deities, a generic term for the Buddhist gods and deities that were traditionally revered in India, China and Japan. They became part of Buddhist thought as Buddhism flourished in those areas. Rather than primary objects of belief or devotion, Buddhism views them as functioning to support and protect the Buddha, the Law, or Buddhist teachings, and practitioners. They may be thought of as representing the natural functions in the environment and society that respond to the Buddha nature emerging in the lives of practitioners and function to support and protect them.

**cause and effect**  (1) Buddhism expounds the law of cause and effect that operates in life, ranging over past, present and future existences. This causality underlies the doctrine of karma. From this viewpoint, causes formed in the past are manifested as effects in the present. Causes formed in the present will be manifested as effects in the future. (2) From the viewpoint of Buddhist practice, cause represents the bodhisattva practice for attaining Buddhahood, and effect represents the benefit of Buddhahood. (3) From the viewpoint of Nichiren's teachings, cause and effect are simultaneous—inherent in each moment of life. The moment one chants Nam-myoho-renge-kyo, the cause for attaining Buddhahood, the wisdom and life-condition of Buddhahood, the effect, emerges in one's life.

**devil king of the sixth heaven**  The king of devils, who dwells in the highest of the six heavens of the world of desire. He works to obstruct Buddhist practice and delights in sapping the life force of other beings. Nichiren identifies this with the devilish nature that arises from the fundamental darkness or ignorance innate in life and causes those with power to persecute practitioners of the Lotus Sutra. Also called the heavenly devil.

**Eagle Peak** A small mountain located northeast of Rajagriha, the capital of Magadha in ancient India. Eagle Peak is known as a place frequented by Shakyamuni Buddha, where he is said to have expounded the Lotus Sutra and other teachings. It also symbolizes the Buddha land or the state of Buddhahood, as in the expression "the pure land of Eagle Peak."

**earthly desires are enlightenment** A Mahayana principle based on the view that earthly desires cannot exist independently on their own; therefore, one can attain enlightenment without eliminating earthly desire—they are one with and inseparable from enlightenment. While we cannot rid ourselves of earthly desires, we can use them as fuel to attain enlightenment.

**fusion of reality and wisdom** The fusion of the objective reality or truth and the subjective wisdom to realize that truth, which is the Buddha nature inherent within one's life. Since enlightenment, or Buddhahood, is the state in which one fully realizes the ultimate reality, the fusion of reality and wisdom means enlightenment.

**Gohonzon** (Jpn) *Go* means "worthy of honor" and *honzon* means "object of fundamental respect." The object of devotion in Nichiren Buddhism and the embodiment of the Mystic Law permeating all phenomena. It takes the form of a mandala inscribed on paper with characters representing the Mystic Law—Nam-myoho-renge-kyo—as well as the Ten Worlds, including Buddhahood. Nichiren Buddhism holds that all people possess the Buddha nature and can attain Buddhahood through faith in the Gohonzon.

**human revolution** A concept employed by the Soka Gakkai's second president, Josei Toda, to indicate self-reformation—the strengthening of one's life force and the establishment of Buddhahood—that is the goal of Buddhist practice.

**karma** The potentials arising from past and present actions that reside in the inner realm of life, which manifest themselves as various results in the present and future. Karma is said to be formed from mental, verbal and physical action, that is, thoughts, words and deeds.

**kosen-rufu** (Jpn) Literally, to "widely declare and spread [Buddhism]." Nichiren Daishonin identifies Nam-myoho-renge-kyo as the teaching to be widely declared and spread during the Latter Day. In the SGI, kosen-rufu is also understood to refer to the establishment of a peaceful and humane world built on the activities, contributions and example of those who practice this teaching.

**Latter Day of the Law** The last of the three periods following the death of Shakyamuni Buddha—the Former Day of the Law, the Middle Day of the Law, and the Latter Day of the Law. His teachings fall into confusion and completely lose their power to lead people to enlightenment in the Latter Day of the Law, which is said to last ten thousand years. From the perspective of the Lotus Sutra, the Latter Day of the Law is the time when the teaching it contains will be spread widely.

**Lotus Sutra** A scripture of Mahayana Buddhism, it teaches that all people can reveal their innate Buddhahood and that this supreme potential is eternal. The sutra also encourages its practitioners to spread the teaching of universal Buddhahood and help all people awaken to this truth. Reciting portions of the Lotus Sutra is part of SGI members' daily Buddhist practice.

**Tsunesaburo Makiguchi (1871–1944)** The founder and first president of the Soka Gakkai, originally called Soka Kyoiku Gakkai (Value-Creating Education Society). He was a forward-thinking educator, geographer and religious reformer who lived and worked during the tumultuous early decades of Japan's modern era. His opposition to Japan's militarism and ultra-nationalism led to his imprisonment and death during World War II. He is best known for two major works, *The Geography of Human Life* and *The System of Value-Creating Pedagogy*. His protégé and close disciple, Josei Toda, having been imprisoned along with Mr. Makiguchi, went on to lead the Soka Gakkai after the war to become Japan's largest lay Buddhist movement.

**many in body, one in mind**  A concept used to describe ideal unity. Nichiren Daishonin writes: "If the spirit of many in body but one in mind prevails among the people, they will achieve all their goals, whereas if one in body but different in mind, they can achieve nothing remarkable," (WND-1, 618). "Many in body" expresses the attributes of diversity and individuality while "one in mind" indicates the power of diverse people who share a noble ideal and goal.

**mutual possession of the Ten Worlds**  The principle that each of the Ten Worlds contains all the other nine as potential within itself. This is taken to mean that an individual's state of life can be changed, and that all beings of the nine worlds possess the potential for Buddhahood. See also *Ten Worlds.*

**Mystic Law**  The ultimate law of life and the universe. The law of Nam-myoho-renge-kyo. A translation of *myoho* of Myoho-renge-kyo, it is also rendered as the "Wonderful Law."

**Nam-myoho-renge-kyo**  The ultimate law of the true aspect of life permeating all phenomena in the universe. The invocation established by Nichiren Daishonin on April 28, 1253. Nichiren Daishonin teaches that this phrase encompasses all laws and teachings within itself, and that the benefit of chanting Nam-myoho-renge-kyo includes the benefit of conducting all virtuous practices. *Nam* means "devotion to"; *myoho* means "Mystic Law"; *renge* refers to the lotus flower, which simultaneously blooms and seeds, indicating the simultaneity of cause and effect; *kyo* means sutra, the teaching of a Buddha, and also indicates the power of the human voice to express the innate Buddha nature.

**Nichiren Buddhism**  The Mahayana Buddhist tradition that is based on the Lotus Sutra and urges chanting the phrase *Nam-myoho-renge-kyo* as a daily practice. On April 28, 1253, Nichiren declared that the Lotus Sutra is the highest teaching of Shakyamuni Buddha and that its essence, Nam-myoho-renge-kyo, is the very teaching in the Latter Day of the Law that enables all people to attain Buddhahood in this lifetime.

**Nichiren Daishonin**  The thirteenth-century Japanese Buddhist teacher and reformer who taught that all people have the potential for enlightenment. He identified the universal Law as Nam-myoho-renge-kyo and established the Gohonzon as the object of devotion for all people to attain Buddhahood. *Daishonin* is an honorific title that means "great sage."

**the oneness of body and mind**  The Buddhist principle of the oneness of body and mind teaches that the physical and spiritual are not distinct or separate but are one in essence.

**the oneness of life and environment**  The Buddhist principle that explains that the environment and all living beings within it must be regarded as inseparable, as a single, whole entity.

**the oneness of mentor and disciple**  This is a philosophical, as well as a practical, concept. Disciples reach the same state of Buddhahood as their mentor by practicing the teachings of the latter. In Nichiren Buddhism, this is the direct way to enlightenment, that is, to believe in the Gohonzon and practice according to the Daishonin's teachings. In addition, "oneness" expresses that the relationship between teacher and student, between mentor and disciple, must be based on the recognition that both possesses the same noble potential—the potential for Buddhahood—and strive together to accomplish the same vow.

**Osaka Incident**  The occasion when SGI President Ikeda, then Soka Gakkai youth division chief of staff, was arrested and wrongfully charged with election law violations in a House of Councilors by-election in Osaka in 1957. In January 1962, at the end of the court case that dragged on for almost five years, he was fully exonerated of all charges.

**powers of faith and practice**  Part of the four powers. The power of the Buddha, the power of the Law, the power of faith and the power of practice. In Nichiren's teachings, the four powers are known as the four powers of the Mystic Law, whose interactions enable one to have one's prayers answered and attain Buddhahood. The power of the Buddha is the Buddha's compassion in saving all people. The power of the Law indicates the boundless capacity of the Mystic Law to lead all people to enlightenment. The power of faith is to believe in the Gohonzon, the object of devotion that embodies the power of the Buddha and the power of the Law, and the power of practice is to chant Nam-myoho-renge-kyo oneself and teach others to do the same. To the extent that one brings forth one's powers of faith and practice, one can manifest the powers of the Buddha and the Law within one's own life.

**Shakyamuni** Also, Siddhartha Gautama, the founder of Buddhism. Born in India (present-day southern Nepal) about three thousand years ago, he renounced his princely status and set off in search of a resolution to the questions of birth, aging, sickness and death. Near the city of Gaya, he is said to have sat under a *bodhi* tree, entered meditation and attained enlightenment. In order to lead others to the same state of enlightenment, during the succeeding fifty years, he expounded numerous teachings, which were later compiled in the form of Buddhist sutras; the highest of which is the Lotus Sutra.

*shoten zenjin* Literally, benevolent gods or deities, refer to the functions of the universe that work to protect those who exert themselves in the faith and practice of the Mystic Law.

**Soka Gakkai** The largest lay Buddhist organization in Japan based on Nichiren's teachings. Founding president Tsunesaburo Makiguchi first used the term Soka Kyoiku Gakkai (Value-Creating Education Society) in 1930 when he published his book *The Theory of Value-Creating Pedagogy.* He asserted that the purpose of education should not be mere training for workers for Japan's growing industrial machine, but the development of the human ability to create "value" (i.e., gain, beauty and social good) in their daily lives. His close disciple, Josei Toda, determined to rebuild the Soka Gakkai after the end of World War II. Mr. Toda set about to develop its membership from less than 3,000 families when he assumed the presidency in 1951 to more than 750,000 before his death in 1958, thereby spreading the movement across Japan and throughout society. Soka Gakkai's philosophy is rooted in the concept of "human revolution," a process of inner transformation through Buddhist practice; a process that leads one to develop their character and to act not only for their personal fulfillment but also for the betterment of society.

**Soka Gakkai International** (SGI) A worldwide Buddhist association that promotes peace and individual happiness based on the teachings of the Nichiren school of Buddhism, with more than twelve million members in 192 countries and territories. Its headquarters is in Tokyo, Japan.

**ten factors of life** Ten factors common to all life in any of the Ten Worlds. They are listed in the "Expedient Means" (second) chapter of the Lotus Sutra, which reads: "The true aspect of all phenomena can only be understood and shared between Buddhas. This reality consists of the appearance, nature, entity, power, influence, internal cause, relation, latent effect, manifest effect and their consistency from beginning to end." Since the ten factors are common to all life and phenomena, there can be no fundamental distinction between a Buddha and an ordinary person. While the Ten Worlds express differences among phenomena, the ten factors describe the pattern of existence common to all phenomena. For example, both the state of hell and the state of Buddhahood, different as they are, have the ten factors in common.

**Ten Worlds** Ten conditions of life that a single entity of life manifests. Originally the Ten Worlds were viewed as distinct physical places, each with its own particular inhabitants. In light of the Lotus Sutra, they are interpreted as potential conditions of life inherent in each individual. The ten are: (1) hell, (2) hungry spirits (hunger), (3) animals (animality), (4) *asuras* (anger), (5) humanity (tranquility), (6) heaven (rapture), (7) voice-hearers (learning), (8) cause-awakened ones (realization), (9) bodhisattvas and (10) Buddhas (Buddhahood). Hell indicates a condition of intense misery, helplessness and futile rage; hunger, one of unquenchable craving; animality, a state governed by impulse and instinct; *asuras*, a condition of contentious ambition; humanity, the placid condition of people as they go about the activities of daily living; and heaven, the joy that arises from having a desire or wish fulfilled.

The first six worlds share the common trait of being largely dependent on one's circumstances and environment. The latter four are developed through an individual's initiative and effort. Voice-hearers, or learning, is the condition of those who seek enlightenment through hearing the "voice" of the Buddha or studying Buddhist teachings; cause-awakened ones, or realization, is the awakened state of those who arrive at the truth on their own by observing life and phenomena; bodhisattvas, the state of those who dedicate themselves to the enabling the enlightenment of others as well as themselves; Buddhas, or Buddhahood, the state of those who achieve supreme enlightenment and seek to lead all others to do so as well.

**three thousand realms in a single moment of life**   Also known as the principle of "a single moment of life comprising three thousand realms." "A single moment of life" *(ichinen)* is also translated as one mind, one thought, or one thought-moment. A philosophical system established by T'ien-t'ai (538–59) in his *Great Concentration and Insight* on the basis of the phrase *the true aspect of all phenomena* from the "Expedient Means" (second) chapter of the Lotus Sutra. The three thousand realms, or the entire phenomenal world, exist in a single moment of life. The number three thousand here comes from the following calculation: 10 (Ten Worlds) x 10 (Ten Worlds) x 10 (ten factors) x 3 (three realms of existence). Life at any moment manifests one of the Ten Worlds. Each of these worlds possesses the potential for all ten within itself, and this "mutual possession," or mutual inclusion, of the Ten Worlds is represented as $10^2$, or a hundred, possible worlds. Each of these hundred worlds possesses the ten factors, making one thousand factors or potentials, and these operate within each of the three realms of existence, thus making three thousand realms.

**Josei Toda (1900–58)**   An educator, and the second president of the Soka Gakkai whose life was dedicated to restoring and revitalizing the spirit of Buddhism in the present age. Imprisoned with his mentor, the Soka Gakkai's first president, Tsunesaburo Makiguchi, during World War II, Mr. Toda went on to develop the Soka Gakkai into one of Japan's most significant lay Buddhist associations as its second president, setting the stage for its growth into a dynamic worldwide grassroots movement. Based on the teachings of the thirteenth-century Buddhist reformer Nichiren, Mr. Toda developed a methodology of personal transformation called "human revolution" that has become the foundation underlying the Soka Gakkai International (SGI). Toward the end of his life, he advocated a vision of global citizenship and, in 1957, issued a historic declaration calling for the abolition of nuclear weapons, entrusting the task of realizing his vision to young people.

For more information, please visit our website at www.sgi-usa.org.

# INDEX

## A

Abueva, José, 157
academic study and faith, 7, 364–65
accidents, 398
action, 102, 407
adults, 402–03
adversaries, 43
adversity, 354–55
*The Ages of Gaia* (James Lovelock), 191
anger, 99, 112, 118
appearances, judging others by, 23,
    29–32, 45, 101, 109–11, 289
appreciation, 162–63, 221
Aristotle, 320
arrogance, 109, 118, 122, 164, 398
art and culture, 161–80
Athayde, Austregésilo de, 131
Atsuhara, three martyrs of, 346
authoritarianism, 168–69, 345

## B

Baggio, Roberto, 354
Balzac, Honoré de, 201
Battle of Imphal, 261
Beethoven, Ludwig van, 178
Bergson, Henri-Louis, 387
betrayal, 19–20, 41, 246, 264, 319
bodhisattva, 281, 334, 397
Bourdillon, Francis William, 133
*The Brothers Karamazov* (Fyodor
    Dostoyevsky), 384
Buddha, 292, 334
Buddhahood, 34, 81, 97, 130, 218,
    235, 257–58, 391
Buddhism, 8, 16, 26–27, 30, 81–82,
    96, 99, 103, 105, 109, 112, 121,
    130, 191, 214–15, 217, 225, 227–
    28, 235, 242, 259, 266, 292, 316,
    345, 372, 391, 395, 410–11, 415

Buddhist gods, 233

Buddhist meetings, 247–48

Buddhist practice, 5, 10, 14, 16, 25, 42–43, 53, 67, 69, 73, 97–98, 102, 172, 212–13, 215, 219–35, 291, 303–06, 338, 389

Buddhist study, 300

bullying, 122–24, 133, 290

Buraku Liberation League, 130

# C

Caine, Hall, 51, 323

Cambridge University, 424

Capa, Robert, 184

Carnegie, Andrew, 44

Carson, Rachel, 193–94

causes, 417–18

Cepeda, Orlando, 416–17

challenges, 11, 196, 220, 222, 250, 358, 363, 371–72

Chaplin, Charlie, x–xi

character, 28, 32, 34, 48, 64, 84, 108, 132, 290, 317–20, 362

Churchill, Winston, 26

Cicero, 320

Clark, William Smith, 22, 279

college, importance of going to, 357–72

"Columbian Gold Exhibition," 48

Columbus, Christopher, 152

compassion, 255–56, 336

Compendium of Eighteen Histories, 140

cooperation, 51

Corot, Jean Baptiste Camille, 179

The Count of Monte Cristo (Alexandre Dumas), 141

courage, 116, 327–39, 358, 406, 410

Cousins, Norman, 397–98

cowardice, 116, 331, 335, 338, 406

# D

Dante Alighieri, 61, 142

Dazai, Osamu, 45, 347

death, 229

deceased, praying for the, 14, 229–30, 389, 392–93, 399

democracy, 129, 331

Dempsey, Jack, 35–36

Deng, Yingchao, 62

determination, 20–24, 34, 43, 73 98, 104–05, 144, 255, 261

dialogue, 402

Dickens, Charles, 199

discrimination, 124–25, 127, 132

diversity, 96

The Divine Comedy (Dante Alighieri), 61, 142

Doppo, Kunikida, 184

dormitory life, 424

Dostoyevsky, Fyodor, 278, 380, 384

Dunhuang, 166

Dürer, Albrecht, 168

# E

earthly desires are enlightenment, 222
Edison, Thomas, 109
education, 96, 103, 290, 346, 362,
    364–65, 367–68
effort, 22–23, 25, 53, 202, 225, 310,
    411, 421
Einstein, Albert, 26
Emerson, Ralph Waldo, 142
*Émile* (Jean-Jacques Rousseau), 140
empathy, 12, 41, 114
emptiness. *See* non-substantiality
envy, 423
Esquivel, Adolfo Pérez, 81, 131
*Essays in Idleness* (Yoshida Kenko), 138
*The Eternal City* (Hall Caine), 51, 323
evil, 99–100, 350

# F

failure, 26, 416
faith, 103, 211, 214, 220–21, 225–28,
    247, 251, 257, 277, 345, 361, 382,
    394, 398
fascism, 331
fear, 169–70
foundation, 24
four sufferings, 230
freedom, 242–43, 271–79, 281, 415
friendship, 37–54, 65, 88, 129, 249,
    295, 315–26, 363, 408, 414–15

fulfillment, 372
future division, 3–4, 15, 75, 305–06,
    315, 318, 320, 327, 351, 357–59,
    364–65

# G

Gagarin, Yuri, 191
Gandhi, Mahatma, 26, 103–04, 158,
    348, 400, 406
Gaviria Trujillo, César, 48
global citizen, 83–93
globalization, 83, 89
goals, 21–24, 43, 74, 100–01, 255,
    415, 421–22
Goethe, Johann Wolfgang von, 102,
    150, 286, 291, 329, 400
Gogol, Nikolai, 141
Gohonzon, 218, 234–35, 299, 301–
    03, 307–09
good, 346–51, 353
Gorbachev, Mikhail, 379–80
Gorbachev, Raisa, 380
Gorky, Maxim, 79
grades, 6, 25, 126, 285
Great Hanshin Earthquake, 38–39
growth and talent, 64
Guillain, Robert, 159

## H

Handel, George Frederic, 178

happiness, 14–15, 27, 30, 64–65,
  79–80, 82, 96, 172, 228–29, 277,
  371–72, 410

*Hashire Merosu* (Run Melos!)

Hesse, Hermann, 199

history, 150–59

Hitler, Adolf, x–xi, 179

Homer, 199

hope, x, 22, 121, 403, 426

Hugo, Victor, 160, 205, 324, 381

humanism, 11–12, 52, 54, 85, 115,
  165, 171

human revolution, 177, 253–62, 265,
  281, 391, 409, 411

human rights, 121–33, 290


## I

illness, 396–98

*Imakagami* (The Mirror of the
  Present), 151

individuality, 172, 179, 285–96

injustice, 99–100

innovation, 177–78

integrity, 317, 319–20, 423

Ishikawa, Takuboku, 76


## J

jealousy, 54, 122, 423

"jeweled sword," 34–36


## K

karma, 225, 228, 394–95

Keller, Helen, 274

kindness, 34, 39–40, 99, 107–18, 151,
  164, 173, 324

King, Martin Luther, Jr., x

knowledge and wisdom, 366

kosen-rufu, 261–66, 345, 350


## L

language learning, 89–93

Lapu-Lapu (Filipino chief), 154

"La Vita Nuova" (The New Life)
  (poem), 61

leaders, 3, 6, 8, 12, 15, 118, 129, 140,
  150, 153, 211, 247, 261, 376

leadership positions, 247

*Le Monde* (newspaper), 159

learning, 144, 169, 184, 294, 360

Leonardo Da Vinci, 178, 381

*Les Misérables* (Victor Hugo), 205

Lincoln, Abraham, 348

life, 118, 360–61, 372, 409, 422

life and death, 376–79, 381–401

life force, 10, 97, 105, 175, 398

"Life Span" chapter (Lotus Sutra), 292

life-state, 273–75, 278–79, 310
life-tendency, 390–91
"Light" (poem), 133
listening, 293–94
literature, 195–207. *See also* reading
*The Little Prince* (Antoine de Saint-Exupéry), 62, 127
Lovelock, James, 191
*The Lower Depths* (Maxim Gorky) (play), 79
Luther, Martin, 214

# M

MacArthur, Douglas, 349
Magellan, 154
Makiguchi, Tsunesaburo, 76, 81, 88, 111–12, 115, 127–29, 145, 172, 180, 246, 274, 343, 348, 359, 368–69, 412, 422–23
Mandela, Nelson, 34–35
many in body, one in mind, 244–45
*Man'yoshu* (Collection of Ten Thousand Leaves), 199–200
Maruyama, Masao, 159
*Masukagami* (The Clear Mirror), 151
Maximilian I, Emperor, 168
media, 30, 63
Mello, Amadeu Thiago de, 185, 256
Melville, Herman, 199
mentor–disciple relationship, 27, 36, 54, 319, 420–21

Mikasa Elementary School, 111
Minamata disease, 376–77
mission, x, 8–10, 23–24, 27, 32, 65, 71, 121, 131, 144, 284, 291, 350, 363, 378–79, 382, 417–18
Mission for the Twenty-first Century Group, 15, 19
Mistral, Gabriela, 206
*Mizukagami* (The Water Mirror), 151
*Moby Dick* (Melville), 199
Mubarak, Hosni, 89
Muñoz de Gaviria, Ana Milena, 48
*Musashino* (The Musashi Plain), 184
Mystic Law, 217–18, 302, 389, 398–99, 421

# N

Nagayo, Yoshiro, 145
Nambara, Shigeru, 256
Napoleon I, 153
Napoleon III, 324
Natsume, Soseki, 171, 292–93
nature, 183–94
new age, 160, 176
Nichiren Daishonin, 41, 48, 74, 81, 100, 204, 214, 218, 239, 244, 247, 272, 274, 292, 295, 298, 301, 303, 309, 316, 338, 365, 379, 392, 407, 409, 411
Nichiren Shoshu priesthood, 186
Nichiren's writings, 204–05

Nikko Shonin, 246

non-substantiality, 386

nonviolence, 406

Norton, David, 79

nuclear weapons, 409

## O

*Odyssey* (Homer), 199

*Okagami* (The Great Mirror), 151

*Old Goriot* (Honoré de Balzac), 201

oneness of body and mind, 309

oneness of life and death, 389, 399

oneness of life and environment,
  183–84, 187

oneness of life and universe, 215–18

oneness of mentor and disciple, 261,
  369

organization, 238–44, 248–49, 252

Osaka Incident, 341–42, 352

## P

palms together, 234

Pande, B.N., 131

parent–child relationship, 12–14, 16,
  110, 114, 280, 321, 399

Parks, Rosa, 81, 132, 289, 332–33,
  413

Pascal, Blaise, 139

*Paul et Virginie* (Bernardin de Saint-
  Pierre), 199

Pauling, Linus, 27–29, 131

Peccei, Aurelio, 45, 256

Pérez, Adolfo, 273

personality, 95–103, 105

philosophy, meaning of, 87

*The Philosophy of Value* (Tsunesaburo
  Makiguchi), 76

prayer (s), 42, 212, 225–26, 298–311

prayer beads, 233–34

pregnancy, 414

propagation, 249–50

## R

reading, 137–45, 148, 196, 200–03,
  295, 425. *See also* literature

*The Record of the Orally Transmitted
  Teachings*, 308

*The Red and the Black* (Stendhal), 199

relationships, 59–70, 319, 321,
  413–14

religion, 170, 211–13

Rizal, José, 382

Rockefeller, John D., 68

Rodin, Auguste, 165, 179

Roentgen, Wilhelm, 26

Rolland, Romain, 24

*The Romance of the Three Kingdoms*
  (Luo Guanzhong), 141

Roosevelt, Eleanor, 101

Rousseau, Jean-Jacques, 140, 188

# S

Saint-Exupéry, Antoine de, 62
Saint-Pierre, Bernardin de, 199
Sats, Natalia, 273, 287
Schiller, Johann Friedrich von, 37, 331
science, 400
*Seigi to hohemi* (Right and Laughter) (Osamu Dazai), 347
self-confidence, 292
self-control, 97
self-identity, 66, 362
self-improvement, 46, 59, 65–66, 68, 70–72, 118, 202, 316
self-motivation. *See* willpower
*The Sense of Wonder* (Rachel Carson), 194
*Senzai wakashu* (Collection of a Thousand Years), 206
Sessoms, Allen, 417–18
sex, 413
sexual assault, 410
SGI, 15, 52, 83, 89, 128, 165, 240, 257, 281, 304, 325, 361, 372
SGI members, 44, 84–85, 361
Shakyamuni Buddha, 41, 115, 213, 239, 259
Shaw, George Bernard, 142
Shelley, Percy Bysshe, 121
*Siddhartha* (Hermann Hesse), 199
*Silent Spring* (Rachel Carson), 193
sincerity, 423

society, 81, 172, 372
Soka Gakkai, 15, 52, 129, 239–42, 244, 261
Soka Gakkai members, 246
Soka University, 368–70
Soka University of America, 418
Stendhal, 199
students, 251–52
study, 6, 8, 32, 63, 78–79, 126, 251, 420
substance abuse, 415
success, 26, 412
suffering, 5, 69, 100, 223, 277, 395, 397, 403, 410, 417, 426
Sugihara, Chiune, 86
suicide, 324, 398
Sullivan, Anne, 274

# T

*The Tale of Genji* (Murasaki Shikibu), 203
*The Tale of the Bamboo Cutter* (Japanese folktale), 200
*A Tale of Two Cities* (Charles Dickens), 199
talents, 73–74
*Taras Bulba* (Nikolai Gogol), 141
*A Teacher Called Takezawa* (Yoshiro Nagayo), 145
Ten Worlds, 36, 115, 125, 187, 265, 281, 390, 409

Thoreau, Henry David, 344

*The Three-Cornered World* (Natsume Soseki), 171

three thousand realms in a single moment of life, 411

"To the Clouds" poem, 206

Toda, Josei, x, 7, 20–21, 25, 27, 31, 34, 44, 74, 76–77, 87–88, 90, 96, 102, 110–11, 118, 128, 138, 140, 150–51, 173, 188, 200, 206, 218, 228, 242–43, 246–48, 261, 274, 298–99, 336, 343, 348, 353, 364, 368–69, 385, 388, 393–94, 409, 412, 421–23

"Toda University," xi, 90

Tokyo Fuji Art Museum, 48–49

Tojo, Hideki, 349

Tolstoy, Leo, 86, 400

*Tonko no kosai* (The Radiance of Dunhuang), 166–67

Torres, Adolfo, 423

Toynbee, Arnold J., 173, 200, 376

"Treasures of Japanese Art" (exhibition), 49

twenty-first century, xi, 118, 132, 187, 375, 401

**U**

"Ultima Verba" (My Last Word), 324

undefeated, 26

unity, 51, 264

Universidad Nacional del Nordeste, 423, 425

university study, 7–8

*Urashima Taro* (Japanese legend), 200

**V**

violence, 406, 408–11

victory, 16, 372, 396–97, 403, 422–23

viewpoint, 149

**W**

Wang, Gungwu, 153

war, 122, 187, 408; war experiences publications, 156–57

*War and Peace* (Leo Tolstoy), 198

Wasiqi, Abdul Baser 9

*Water Margin*, 140–41

Weizsäcker, Richard von, 156

willpower, 98

wisdom, 80, 355

work, 72–82

world peace, 82, 325–26

# Y

Yoshida, Kenko, 138
Yoshikawa, Eiji, 277
youth, x, 3–6, 19–37, 66–67, 160,
    230, 269–70, 292, 295, 359, 361,
    379, 401–03, 418, 425–26

# Z

"Zahme Xenien VIII" (poem), 329
Zátopek, Emil, 23
Zhou Enlai, 62, 130
Zweig, Stefan, 116